Financial
Engineering

Financial Engineering

A handbook for managing
the risk-reward relationship

Charles Errington

First published in the United Kingdom by
THE MACMILLAN PRESS LTD, 1993
Distributed by Macmillan Direct
Brunel Road, Houndmills,
Basingstoke, Hants RG21 2XS, England

Reprinted 1994

ISBN 0-333-59716-8

A catalogue record for this book
is available from The British Library.

While every care has been taken in compiling the
information contained in this publication, the publishers
and author accept no responsibility for any errors or
omissions.

Typeset and printed in Great Britain

Contents

Contents

Introduction

To the outside observer it may seem as if financial engineers perform some kind of alchemy. They are certainly involved in a process of transformation. There are even those at the leading edge, the arbitragers, who, albeit only for short periods, are able to turn base materials into gold. But there is really no magic involved in what they do, everything stems from the application of a few simple principles.

Foremost amongst these is the linked notion of risk–reward – the recognition that all financial instruments are ways of pricing the future, and that we require greater rewards the riskier that future becomes. Since many instruments have common risk characteristics, their rewards must be related. To the extent that it is possible to define an instrument's riskiness, we should be able to pinpoint its required reward amongst the spectrum of financial commodities.

All the financial engineering techniques described in this book address this issue of relative value. This necessitates a generic approach to evaluation and analysis, since it is only by establishing a common way of looking at all financial instruments that it is possible to establish these relationships.

But these relationships do not only exist on an intellectual level. The computerisation of financial markets has fostered the development of a huge range of instruments for risk transformation: futures, swaps and options being just a few of the chief examples. Their popularity has created a truly interdependent industry, with relative values between markets maintained in practice as well as in theory.

Today's financier needs to keep abreast of all the major markets, and the techniques developed by financial engineers, now so important to pricing, should be understood by all. The aim of this book, then, is three-fold. Firstly it seeks to present the generic analytical foundations common to all financial commodities, this is the approach in Chapters 1 to 5. The second objective is to examine in detail the characteristics of particular markets and instruments using these financial engineering techniques, Chapters 6 to 14 perform this task on a sector by sector basis. The different categories of instrument within each sector are introduced, then, in the following chapter, financial engineering techniques applicable to that sector are described that demonstrate pricing, repackaging, hedging and arbitrage opportunities.

Financial market interdependence offers the possibility of defining a risk–reward exposure with amazing sensitivity. The participant can choose when and in what conditions to take profits, and where losses. But this increased flexibility can cause confusion because of the sheer range of choices involved. Chapter 15 aims to provide a methodology for approaching management of the risk–reward relationship based around the idea that different strategies can be prioritised and that an optimal strategy can therefore be found. This does not mean, of course, that this is a way of achieving guaranteed profits, the no free lunch rule precludes that. Rather, it forces the user to ask the right questions, and matches the strategy to the answers given. It is a system of clarification.

But clarity is not to be underestimated as an objective. Financial market participants trade in information, the quality of the information is what defines their success. Hopefully, having studied the contents of this book, the reader will agree that the generic approach is not just one way – it is the only way – to understand what makes the financial markets tick.

1: Market Fundamentals

KEY CONCEPTS

Measuring Risk–Reward

The Chinese character meaning 'opportunity' is the same as the symbol that stands for 'crisis'. Perhaps, the Chinese were the first people to recognise this important truth: namely, that risk and reward are two sides of the same coin. They simply reflect our level of uncertainty about the future by defining the limits to it.

In financial communities, this idea assumes a particular significance. At the most basic level, what financial managers are attempting to do is anticipate the future. They use the linked notion of risk/reward to define the value of the various financial assets.

It is axiomatic that the projected yield which expresses the reward on an asset, is also the market's valuation of the risks associated with owning it. As these risks increase the reward required will be higher. In theory it is possible to plot a linear relationship between risk and reward. In a perfectly efficient market every financial asset falls somewhere along this line.

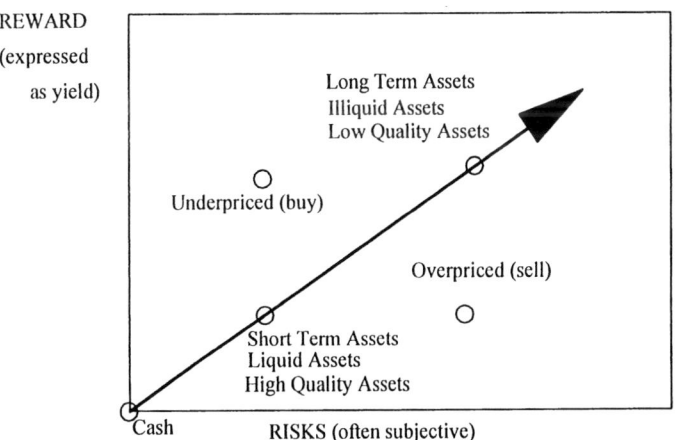

Figure 1.1 The risk–reward relationship

1

Financial market participants aim to outperform the market by selling those instruments that lie below the risk–reward indifference curve while buying those assets that offer a better than average risk-adjusted yield.

In practice of course, this is easier said than done. The projected yield of any given instrument (particularly for equity related assets) if it contains a capital gain component, will vary.

The risk side is even more subjective. Even if all possible risks could be taken into account, their relative importance is a question of judgement. Of course, event risks, by their very nature, cannot be discounted in advance. Nevertheless, the basic task of any financial manager is to maximise yield while minimising risk.

Distinguishing Characteristics of Financial Instruments

In markets for goods and services, subjective aspects cloud the issue of value equivalence, restricting their substitutability. As an instance: the relative value of two paintings is impossible to assess – it is a question of personal taste.

Financial instruments on the other hand, although they may include qualitative aspects (such as creditworthiness, or the reputation of a particular currency), can be expressed in purely numerical terms. This adds a layer of objectivity that makes them especially suitable for quantitative analysis.

The Bid–Ask Spread

As financial instruments are intangible, transaction costs are very low. The cost of dealing is expressed by the two-way price as quoted by market makers. Bid is the low price at which the market maker will buy the commodity; Ask or Offer, the higher price, is where he will sell.

The difference between them, the spread, is a valuable indicator. In very active markets, where there is lot of liquidity, the spread is extremely narrow. When trading conditions are thin, the spread will widen. The spread should be regarded as a cost of trading as it represents the amount that would be lost by a customer buying and selling the commodity in a stable market environment.

Generic Pricing

A generic approach to evaluation has gained ground in recent years that allows all transactions to be analysed using the same techniques. Whether looking at currencies, bonds, commodities or commercial transactions, everything can be valued in terms of its cashflows, dates and contingencies. Advocates of the generic approach point out that there are just two fundamental evaluation techniques which can be applied to every financial problem: *time value of money* measures reward and the *time value of uncertainty* accounts for risk.

Computerisation has triggered the widespread adoption of the generic approach. This has cemented the interdependence of the financial markets by providing a common framework for measuring value between instruments. The importance of relative value has been reinforced by the increasing importance of cross market instruments such as futures and swaps. It is not just risk managers and arbitragers – whose actions depend on the markets' interconnectedness – but all financial market participants who require a close understanding of them.

The Time Value of Money

No matter what their origin, all financial instruments with known cashflows occurring on specific dates in the future may be evaluated using the time value of money calculation. It is fortunate, therefore, that the basic calculation is relatively simple:

$$fv = pv \, (\, 1 + rt \,)$$

where
pv = amount at start of period (present value)
fv = amount at end of period (future value)
r = yield (expressed as per cent p.a.)
t = length of period (expressed in years)

This calculation gives us a measurement of yield that can be applied to any financial instrument with known future cashflows. The basic equation is also useful in two other forms:

$$pv \; = \; \frac{fv}{(1 + rt)}$$

gives the discounted equivalent of a future cashflow, while:

$$r \; = \; \left(\frac{fv - 1}{pv} \right) t^{-1}$$

provides the annual yield implied by the difference between two cashflows at the start and end of a given period.

How the cashflows are generated is unimportant. A pattern where the first cashflow is negative and the second positive implies lending, investing or buying an asset. The inverse pattern denotes borrowing, issuing paper or selling an asset.

3

Quotation Conventions

To discover the true yield for financial instruments, it is essential to focus on the raw cashflows and the actual period length. The issue is complicated by the fact that, for mainly historical reasons, the various categories of instrument are quoted according to market specific conventions.

For instance sterling interest rates are quoted in terms of a 365 day basis. (In this context the term, basis, refers to the standard number of days in the calendar year.) The period length (t) is determined by dividing the actual number of days in the period by the basis. A one year rate of 10 per cent would imply that a £1m deposit would repay £1,100,000 at maturity. By contrast, the US dollar and most other money markets assume a 360 day basis. So, a 10 per cent rate on a one year, $1m deposit pays $1,101,389 at maturity.

There are numerous other examples of market specific quotation conventions that can obscure true yield. The various quotation conventions are described in later sections that deal with specific instrument types. It is obviously vital that the valuation of financial instruments compares like with like. Care needs to be taken so that instruments are always analysed in terms of their cashflow implications.

The Time Value of Uncertainty

Volatility describes the extent of uncertainty. Formally defined, it measures the average oscillation in price over a given period. Its mathematical equivalent is standard deviation.

It is important to stress that the way volatility is used assumes nothing about the direction of the price movement. So a commodity with successive prices of 100:101:102:103:104 displays the same volatility characteristics as one with prices of 100:101:100:99:100.

Market participants use an annualised form of volatility to evaluate many contingent cashflows, particularly option related payment structures.

Using Probabilities to Value Uncertainty

Futures markets provide a mechanism for locking into purchases and sales of commodities, currencies and interest rates at a price fixed today for delivery on a specific date in the future. They provide a definite point of reference for traders and risk managers. The futures price, based on the current price and the relevant interest rate, reflects the market's consensus prediction, but it says nothing about the conflicting views that go to make it up. The variation in views about the right price is another important factor in determining price behaviour.

For instance, the futures price of a commodity is currently 100. This reflects average sentiment, but one would expect very different market conditions depending on the individual views that make it up. If these vary between expectations of 99 and 101, one would not expect much volatility without additional price sensitive events. If, on the other hand, the futures price is based on expectations varying between, say, 50 and 150, we could see quite considerable variations as the relative strengths of bullish and bearish sentiment altered.

The extent of disagreement on price is dictated by the amount of market uncertainty. By incorporating this information into their trading and hedging strategies, participants can develop a more accurate impression of the market environment.

The level of uncertainty will increase with time (we know more about tomorrow than we do about next year). In volatile price conditions, uncertainty is much greater. We can express the time value of uncertainty in a generalised form:

$$fv \quad = \quad \text{sum} \quad [fv_0.p(0) + fv_1.p(1) + ... + fv_n.p(n)]$$

where:-

fv = expected future value,

$fv_0...fv_n$ = fv in different market environments,

$p(0)...p(n)$ = probability of projected future environments.

The probability function p( ) is the subjective element in the price. The range and probability of projected future values depend on expected market volatility and the period length. Once an expected future value has been derived, its present value can easily be found by discounting the fv at the appropriate yield using the time value of money calculation.

This approach is particularly applicable for the pricing of financial options and is discussed further in the discussion on option pricing which follows.

Estimating Market Volatility

The market uses annualised volatility as its standard measure of uncertainty. But it is actually a contradiction in terms to talk about *measurement*: volatility is an expression of ignorance, as such it can never really be defined, it can only be guessed at.

Having said that, it is possible to arrive at an accurate picture of the level of volatility discounted by the market. This is done by analysing quoted option prices. The buyer of an option is taking out a form of price insurance by purchasing the right to buy (or sell) a particular commodity at a maximum (or minimum) price. She pays a premium, usually in advance, to the option writer. In volatile conditions the premium will be high, where there is more certainty it will be lower.

5

Looked at this way, it can be seen that the option premium expresses the value of uncertainty. With the aid of computers we can impute the volatility factor which relates to a given option premium.

Finding out the Future by Looking into the Past

A second source of inspiration when attempting to guess future volatility is the price database. By looking at the historical behaviour of a particular commodity it is often possible to get a general idea about the likely range of volatilities. Investigation into past price performance has its merits, particularly in establishing the likely range of future fluctuations. By looking at past volatilities, it is possible to get an idea of how far current volatilities are in line with past experience.

In applying historical analysis it is important to match the price behaviour being studied with the period for which volatility is being estimated. A history of three-month volatilities should be analysed to research the next three months. The periods studied should be carefully selected to correspond to the future. This can be particularly important in markets with seasonal characteristics.

The frequency of price data should relate to the trading requirement. A market maker will normally want to track every price change, some risk managers will prefer to look at daily or perhaps weekly price recordings. In general, the frequency of the price data should be consistent with the regularity with which a participant is likely to act in the market.

In the final analysis, empirical techniques can only ever give a rough indication about what may happen. They are useful, but only when employed by traders who understand the cyclical structure and event sensitivity of the market in which they are operating.

For example, many active markets swing between periods of relative stability and times of intense price activity. In a volatile environment, traders put a high price on certainty. It may be tempting to buy option protection, but this could prove a costly move. If volatility has been a feature over the past few months, the market may be about to switch to more stable conditions. In other words options are probably overpriced and option buyers will lose out.

Volatility and Market Asymmetry

The level of volatility is the critical input when pricing contingent cashflows. But no matter how much detailed research is conducted, volatility can only ever be guessed at. With most option pricing models, volatility is used to predict the statistically probable range of price outcomes using a normally distributed probability pattern. This implies an assumption that the variations in price sentiment are arranged symmetrically. In most circumstances this is clearly unrealistic: participants can, therefore, identify superior trading and hedging opportunities by using probability distributions which map uncertainty more precisely.

Although volatility may be an unsatisfactory measure in this respect, it has to be recognised that this is what drives option price behaviour. Just as the price reflects the consensus price, so implied volatilities, derived from option premiums, provide the framework for the level of uncertainty currently discounted in the market.

Pricing Methods

Contingent cashflows can only be evaluated by statistical methods. A number of such models exist for pricing options.

Several pricing models have been developed to allow dealers to value options according to their expected profit/loss; these are discussed more fully in the section on options below. Models vary in detail but all of them attempt to value options according to a weighted average of expected future cashflows.

Pricing models are only as good as their assumptions. Traditional models such as Black–Scholes and the binomial distribution imply that the chances of a price rise are approximately equivalent to the chances that the price will fall. More recent pricing techniques, such as the random walk model, allow directional assumptions to be included enabling bullish or bearish sentiment to be more accurately reflected.

However, none of these models should be seen as a black box. Ultimately, when to buy and when to write options is a subjective judgement based on forecasted prices. All pricing models should therefore be seen as an adjunct to, and not a replacement for, the dealer's view.

Opportunity Cost and Price Benchmarks

A key ingredient in the pricing of any financial instrument is its imputed opportunity cost. This is just another way of saying that instruments with similar characteristics are valued in terms of each other.

The focus on relative value is evidenced by the market's reliance on benchmarks for its evaluation. These provide common frameworks for looking at alternative strategies and allow market participants to traverse the markets in search of the highest yield for the lowest risk.

For example, all US dollar interest rates are linked to current T-bill, T-note and T-bond yields. Government securities provide market participants with a benchmark yield curve. The volume of the US Government's issuing programme ensures that there are actively traded securities for maturities out to 30 years. The fact that the US Government is also responsible for the supply of the dollar ensures that such bills, notes and bonds carry no risk of default. High market liquidity keeps trading costs low and allows the market to act as a sensitive barometer to trading sentiment. The negligible credit risk ensures that this sentiment is always governed by interest rate expectations.

The Risk Premium

The benchmark yield curve thus underpins all other dollar rates. In theory at least, all bond yields and deposit rates include a risk premium, the extent depending on the instrument's creditworthiness and market liquidity.

Take, for example, high yield non-investment grade bonds (better known as junk bonds). Junk bonds are speculative securities, formally defined as those issues rated at BBB (Standard & Poor's), Baa (Moody's) or worse by the credit rating agencies.

The implied yield payable on any security, a function of its price and the coupon it pays, is based on its rating and the prevailing benchmark yield for that maturity. The yields available to investors in junk bonds have always been significantly higher than those achievable by owners of Treasury bonds with similar maturities. The market perceives (rightly) that junk bonds are riskier investments than US Government securities, but the extent of this risk premium has varied according to the market's perception of the associated risks. In the mid-1980s junk bonds typically carried a risk premium of 1–2 per cent, encouraging an explosion in the number of leveraged takeovers. By the end of the decade, perceptions had changed radically and a risk premium of 5–6 per cent had become the norm.

This emphasises the most important aspect of risk premiums – they are not constant. Any trading strategy that does not take account of this simple fact contains hidden risks and may backfire seriously in the wrong circumstances. The trader who uses, say, T-bond futures, to protect a bond portfolio from rising interest rates, will only be covered to the extent that benchmark yields move in line with yields in the bond portfolio. If the risk premium were to increase, as might well happen with rising rates, where the flight to quality effect is likely to occur, the hedged portfolio would incur a loss. This is a form of basis risk, a subject covered in more detail in later chapters.

THE DYNAMICS OF PRICE BEHAVIOUR

Market Participants and their Motivations

Trading, hedging and arbitrage are the mechanisms underlying all market transactions. The distinctions are often blurred, however, as many transactions include elements of more than one activity.

For example, a forward foreign exchange dealer trades the interest differential between two currencies. However, foreign currency exposure is a side effect of trading forwards and foreign exchange swaps. The dealer may decide to lock out the currency risk with a foreign exchange hedge. So the same individual may be speculating on interest differentials and hedging currency risk.

It is nevertheless important to be able to distinguish between the motivations behind the various kinds of trading activity in order to understand what drives price behaviour. Broadly speaking, there are three kinds of market user, each of whom has a different attitude to the risk reward–relationship. Speculators are risk accepters; they are primarily interested in earning profits and there is no reward without some risk. For risk managers, the focus is on controlling exposure; they therefore seek to transfer the riskiest element of their positions. Arbitragers are concerned with relative risks and rewards; they seek to pinpoint and exploit mispriced risks in related markets.

The Speculative Motive

The speculative motive finds its expression in trading activity. For the trader, the aim of a purchase or sale of a financial commodity is to benefit from a price movement. Traders accept the market risk associated with transactions, and are exposed to price risk.

Professional traders are restricted in the amount of exposure they can run at once by a series of limits and controls designed to prevent financial institutions running unmanageable risks. These include stop-loss levels, limits on dealing with certain counterparties and countries, and maximum net positions both during a trading day and between days.

Speculation is also limited by the dealers themselves. Dealers will be expected to manage their books (the total of all their positions) in a prudent manner, not putting all their eggs in one basket. They may also take offsetting positions in linked markets to protect themselves against unacceptable risks.

The bulk of speculative activity is in the form of relatively short-term positions, often designed to benefit from cyclical movements. We might describe this as the surfboard school of trading: dealers going with the flow of price movements, changing direction with the waves of sentiment. But often the most significant speculative activity is what might be termed the tidal approach. By taking positions against the run of market sentiment, speculators stand to benefit from major price movements.

The litmus test of a speculator's position in either camp can be found by examining her attitude to event risk. For instance, when economic statistics are about to be published, does she trade to open a new position or is she closing out an existing one? Surfboard traders will tend to avoid event risk where they can, while the tidal types choose to embrace it.

Risk Managers

For there to be an effective market dynamic, the speculators must not only deal amongst themselves. This would be a nil sum game, ultimately unprofitable to all of the parties involved. Financial markets are accessed by consumers of the commodity and since their purpose is often risk reduction they have a different set of motivations to the speculating population.

The term risk manager has very wide application: since all financial markets are about the relationship between risk and reward, all participants, including the most aggressive speculator can, in some sense be described as such. In the context of this discussion, the definition needs to be limited to those whose primary purpose is risk reduction.

In this context, it is useful to draw a distinction between the hedger and the risk manager. Pure hedgers are concerned with transferring all their identifiable risks, they are not interested in any upside potential. Risk managers, on the other hand, place much more emphasis on classifying their exposure into acceptable and unacceptable portions. Only unacceptable risks are hedged, and risk managers will continually monitor their position as the environment changes.

To pinpoint the risk management stance it is often helpful to clarify the attitude to opportunity cost. Hedgers will be disinterested in this aspect, for risk managers, though it is a vital strategic tool. In the final chapter of this book I outline the ConTROL methodology which highlights the logic and procedures of the risk management process.

Arbitragers

The old maxim that 'there's no such thing as a perfect hedge' highlights one of the difficulties for risk managers. For arbitragers, however, this is the key that can unlock a (nearly) risk-free profit. There are numerous financial instruments which provide different mechanisms for achieving the same risk/reward profile. Many such technical links can be expressed mathematically. Arbitragers rely on such connections and seek out anomalous pricing. They make their profit by simultaneously buying an asset in a market where it is undervalued and selling its overvalued equivalent elsewhere. By holding mirrored positions until the anomaly is eliminated, when the positions are closed out they lock in the differential without being exposed to shifts in price levels. The arbitrage process is discussed in more detail in the following chapter.

The Market Gestalt

Financial markets come as close as we are ever likely to get to the economist's definition of the perfect market. Technology has stripped away many of the barriers to entry by new competitors. In essence, anyone who can afford to subscribe to Reuters and who has access to telecommunications and PC technology is able to participate.

The sheer scale of trading in the active markets renders them insensitive to the activities of individual institutions. Daily turnover in the FX market, for instance, is estimated at some $300–$400 bn, roughly the same as the total value of the reserves held by the world's major central banks. Not even the Bank of Japan has sufficient resources to dictate the value of the Yen if sentiment is pitted against it.

Objective Links Between Markets

Closely related markets have technical connections, with the possibility of arbitrage holding prices in harness. In such markets the relative prices move within a tightly defined range, the limits being determined by the arbitrage process. The price relationships between commodities traded for delivery on different dates (spot, forwards, futures) are delineated by the relevant interest rates; stock index instruments are related to the prices of their constituent stocks.

The inter-connectedness of such markets is continually increasing. Arbitragers rely for their activities on spotting technical links that are not properly reflected by relative prices, they seek to exploit anomalies. As an arbitrage relationship gets to be understood the anomaly disappears, and the pricing link firms up. In actively traded markets, where the arbitrage connections are well understood, the threat of arbitrage exerts even greater discipline on relative price levels than the supply and demand effects of the arbitrage process itself.

The efficiency of the short-dated FX swap market, for instance, precludes using the spot and cash markets to lock into a built-in profit. Forward points are themselves constructed according to the spot rate and the interest differential. This is just one example showing how anomalies are squeezed out of the pricing system when an arbitrage gains acceptance.

Subjective Links between Markets

The other main type of price relationship is indirect. Here the limits to price relationships are determined by market perceptions of relative risks and rewards, and these are liable to change with circumstances. As a result, although such prices will move broadly in line, basis behaviour is far less predictable.

Investors, traders and speculators may have differing levels of risk aversion but they are all seeking to achieve the same goal. They wish to maximise yield and minimise risk. Every financial instrument occupies a position on the risk–reward matrix. Those that fall below the indifference line are overpriced and should be sold. Those above it are priced too low and may be bought.

Ignoring regulatory restrictions for the moment, it is clear that, in a macro-economic sense, every financial instrument is a substitute for every other. When the market is in bullish mode funds will flow towards riskier/high yield assets, equity and the like. In a bearish environment the flight to quality effect is perceived: with lower yielding, more secure types of instruments in demand.

Strategic asset allocation is one highly visible manifestation of this effect. Strategic asset allocators focus not so much on individual securities, more on price behaviour in the major markets as a whole. They use computer assisted techniques to determine the most favourable cash/bond/equity combination for their portfolio at any given moment.

At the micro-economic level, the more similar the instruments being compared, the closer will be their price relationships. For instance, two bonds with similar payment terms, issued by borrowers of equivalent quality will have roughly equal risk premiums built into their prices. Any disparity will be met by bond switching activity, which, though not a pure mathematical arbitrage, has the same, equalising effect on prices.

Markets are Rational

There are two schools of thought as to the way prices behave in financial markets. The first group subscribes to the efficient markets hypothesis. Essentially, this states that, in the long run, prices will tend towards their equilibrium levels. Mispricing may occur, but this is equally likely to undervalue as to overvalue assets. An important subsidiary part of the argument identifies arbitrage as the balancing mechanism that irons out erroneous pricing between connected markets.

Proponents maintain that all known information about the future is already discounted in today's prices. The logic of their position leads them to maintain that the market cannot be consistently out-guessed, except by luck. Participants should therefore focus their efforts on matching their returns to the performance of a particular sector. This is the philosophy behind the recent trend towards indexation of fund performance.

Markets are Irrational

The other way of looking at discounted sentiment is to acknowledge what appears to be an empirical truth. In practice, markets rarely predict the future with much accuracy, they tend either to over- or to under-discount future prices. In other words, markets regularly get it wrong.

Contra market theorists point to the bandwagon effect as evidence of their viewpoint. In the early 1980s for instance, when the $/FF spot rate moved from saw world equity prices slashed by 30 per cent in a few days. What, they ask, was the new information that changed market sentiment so dramatically?

The answer, they suggest, is that although some new information came to light during these periods, there was certainly nothing that could explain such a radical change in price. What happened was that market participants adjusted the emphasis to attach to the existing base of information. Perceptions changed.

But does this not imply, they say, that prices were wrong in the first place? And if so, how do we know that the adjustment was appropriate, and the new price accurate?

In contrast to efficient markets advocates, who view all market participants as expressing rational expectations about the future to define an equilibrium price, the random walk school believes that there is no such thing as an attainable equilibrium. Instead, prices are driven by emotional and psychological factors and are continually oscillating above or below their theoretical levels.

Although they agree that markets are driven by news, they point out that, at any given moment, the market is focusing on particular sectors and specific lead indicators. Information is over-emphasised when it fits with the prevailing market view, and ignored when it runs counter to the current consensus.

Technology and the Transparent Market

The impact of technology has been to give all market participants instantaneous access to price-sensitive information, as well as the ability to act on it within

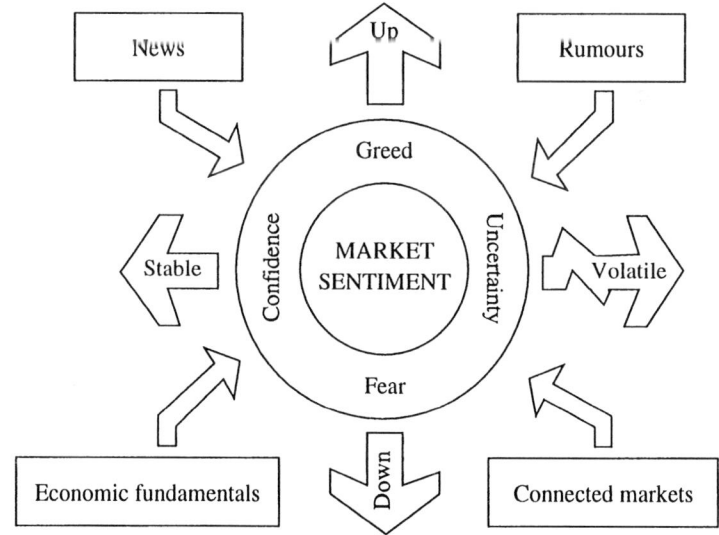

Figure 1.2 Emotions, expectations and events interact on price

seconds. In such circumstances the price effect of a news item is swift, and often unanimous. Unquestionably, this has increased the volatility as well as the interdependence of the financial markets.

Fortunately, technology has also allowed for the emergence of a range of instruments designed to manage such gyrations. Futures and options not only indicate market expectations for interest rates, currencies, equity and commodities, they also provide mechanisms for protecting value and insuring against volatility.

FINANCIAL INSTRUMENTS

Commodities offered for immediate (spot), forward and optional delivery form the basis of all financial transactions. These are the building blocks of any strategy. The risk manager uses forwards when he believes that prices will deteriorate, do nothing now (i.e. close out the exposure when it occurs via a spot transaction) if he is confident that prices will improve, and buy options if he is uncertain about what will happen.

With combinations of these three alternatives, it is possible to formulate trading strategies with an almost infinite variety of risk–reward profiles. The sheer variety of strategies available – bullish, bearish, pro- and contra-volatility, or custom built – makes the task of selecting the right strategy at the right moment all the more difficult. ConTROL, a practical methodology for carrying this out effectively, is explained in the final chapter of this book.

Spot Transactions

Spot Delivery
Typically, buyers and sellers of commodities, whether physical or financial, will be most active in the spot market. Spot delivery means that a trade done today will be carried out as soon as practicable.

The conventions for spot dates vary between markets. In many domestic cash markets, for instance, delivery can be made on the same, or the following business day. In the Euro currency cash and foreign exchange markets, however, immediate delivery is hampered by the existence of international time zones – Tokyo's day is over before New York's begins. In these markets the standard spot date is two business days (i.e. excluding weekends and public holidays) after the day the trade was conducted.

Other markets have established their own conventions. In the Eurobond market, for instance, spot delivery means that payment is made and the bond received one week after the day the deal was done.

Forward Transactions

Financial Forwards

In the forward markets participants can fix a price today at which they will buy or sell a financial instrument on the forward date. A forward is a contractual obligation where both parties must settle at the pre-agreed price, no matter what the spot price is on the settlement date.

Credit Risk Implications

Because forwards are agreements to conduct business in future they include an element of credit risk. The amount at risk, however, is not the total amount transacted. If an investor, who has agreed to buy $1m worth of US T-bills in three months' time at a price of 97, fails to honour his obligation, the seller does not receive his expected $970,000.

On the other hand, he still owns the T-bill. If interest rates have fallen he can now sell it to someone else for, say, 98. He will actually have benefited from the investor default, in the sense that he has realised an opportunity profit of $10,000. Of course had interest rates risen the price would be lower than 97 and he would have made a loss, but only to the extent that the price had changed.

The credit risk on a forward, then, is contingent on the price. Indeed, the amount at risk is the cost of closing out the resultant open position; in other words the price differential between the forward and the future spot price.

Of course, in practice, the investor mentioned above would not have defaulted, except perhaps for legal reasons, if the price had risen. In that scenario he could, simultaneously, have sold the T-bill on the open market and realise the $10,000 gain with no net capital outlay.

With forward transactions each counterparty has a price-contingent risk on the other. The forward purchaser of a commodity risks the seller defaulting if the spot price goes up, the seller is at risk to the buyer when the price falls.

Pricing Forward Transactions

Forward prices are often seen as having some sort of predictive power as to the future level of prices. Though there is an element of truth in this proposition it is misleading to look at them in this way. Forwards are determined by today's environment, they are derived by a combination of the current spot market and interest rates.

Any financial commodity may be traded for forward delivery so long as it is possible to borrow and lend to the date in question. The forward price is determined according to the cost of carrying a spot transaction forward. The process is described by the cash-and-carry arbitrage mechanism illustrated in the following chapter.

15

Forward Markets

For many financial commodities, forward transactions are commonplace. There are active forward markets for both currencies and interest rates. If the forward market exists already then prices are determined by supply and demand. But however a forward price is quoted it will always be close to its implied value. The spot price and interest rates are the technical basis for all forward prices in financial markets.

Futures Contracts

A future is a special category of forward transaction which is designed to be actively traded. It provides exactly the same type of forward pricing mechanism and has similar technical underpinnings.

Market Development

Futures have their origin in the commodities exchanges that have existed for raw materials for centuries. The first futures contracts were probably for rice, traded in Japan in the 17th century. Wheat and corn exchanges have existed in the UK and the US since the early 19th century.

For producers and consumers the problem was how to overcome price fluctuation. Planters of corn never knew what its value would be at harvest time. This depended on supply conditions, which were determined by factors outside their control, like weather conditions. Bakeries for their part needed a continuous supply of corn at a predictable price. They could obviously store grain, but this might involve them buying at too high a price if there was a bumper harvest the next year.

The exchange gave both types of participant the ability to buy and sell according to their future needs. Trading with them were speculators who took a different view of market movements and wished to take on the price risk.

Financial futures began in the early 1970s with the formation of the International Monetary Market (the IMM) as a subsidiary of the Chicago Mercantile Exchange. The first contracts traded were currency futures, and these were soon supplemented by contracts for trading interest rates, government bond yields and stock indices.

The Growth in Financial Futures

The past twenty years have seen a dramatic upsurge in the volume and variety of financial futures. The explosion in international trading, and violent price swings have made this inevitable.

When, for instance, a car manufacturer can achieve record sales in the USA but still return huge losses, because of a weakening dollar, it becomes imperative to find an effective mechanism for managing currency risk. Speculators also are more active when markets are volatile. Such conditions provide greater opportunities for profit.

The Logic of Standardisation

The major structural difference between futures and other forms of forward transaction is the standardised form in which they are traded. Forward transactions can be tailored to the precise requirements of the customer. Futures, on the other hand, are only available for specific grades, dates and amounts.

The rationale for such standardisation is that the contracts are easier to trade in this form. By focusing all the demand for a given commodity on a few, strategically selected delivery dates and grades the level of trading activity is greatly increased.

Futures hedgers sacrifice the precision of tailored forward contracts for the greatly enhanced liquidity that standardisation allows them. For this reason the futures markets tend to be accessed by active hedgers and other professionals, whereas forwards are used more often by occasional hedgers, who are less interested in trading their positions.

Delivery and Pricing

A futures contract is a purely notional instrument. It only comes into existence when a buyer and a seller agree on a price at which to trade. When this occurs the buyer is said to be long one contract, while the seller is said to be short one contract.

The owner of a long contract has an obligation to take delivery of a given grade and amount of the underlying commodity on a specific date in the future. The owner of a short contract has agreed to deliver the said commodity on the date in question.

The price of the underlying commodity is therefore a vital determinant in futures pricing. This is the case even though futures are rarely delivered in physical form. What normally happens is that, on or before the delivery date, holders of long futures close out their positions by selling to traders with short positions. The contract that was brought into existence by the initial transaction is eliminated and the participants realise a profit or loss equal to their price differential.

In order to maintain the integrity of futures pricing, there is an obligation on holders of open positions to make or take delivery of the underlying commodity. Having this as a possibility exerts a discipline on the futures market. For traders then know that the basis (the difference between cash and futures) will always then be zero on the delivery date. The threat of arbitrage activity between futures and the physical market as a result anchors the futures price to the price of its underlying commodity.

Eliminating Credit Risk

For futures to be traded effectively, every transaction in a particular contract must be identical to every other. If a futures trader has to consider the creditworthiness of his counterparty each time he trades, trading will be handicapped and price differences will open up, with the better rated institutions commanding finer terms.

It is, of course, in the interests of the exchanges to maximise liquidity, they earn a commission on every deal. Futures are therefore structured so as to remove credit risk considerations from the dealing process. This is done by the exchange acting as counterparty to both sides of every deal. It can do this because futures are traded in a closed market. Trades must be conducted on the exchange floor (or through the official screen based trading system) and can only be conducted by exchange members. Although the deal is struck and the price fixed directly between buyer and seller, the transaction is held as one long contract bought from the exchange and another short contract sold by it at the same price.

This ensures uniformity, but it also exposes the exchange to the risk of a default by one of its counterparties. Most exchanges hold large reserves against such a contingency, but the main way in which they protect themselves is by demanding a cash surety, known as margin and administering a system of regular position revaluations.

Margins and Marking to Market

Every time a trader opens a futures contract, whether long or short, he is obliged to place funds in a call account run by the exchange. The funds are returned to her when the contract is closed out again. While the futures position is in place funds are regularly transferred to or from this account according to the profitability of her position.

Many exchanges run a system of initial and variation margins. The initial margin is the minimum amount required when a contract is opened. The variation margin, sometimes slightly less, is the minimum amount needed to avoid an automatic default on an existing open position.

At the end of each day (sometimes more often), the last traded price for each futures contract is recorded and this becomes its marked-to-market value. If the price is higher than the previous day's close, owners of long contracts have their margin accounts credited by the exchange via a transfer of funds from short contract holders. Everybody's positions are then revalued at the new closing price. Traders are allowed to withdraw any surplus profits so long as the minimum margin amount is always maintained at the start of a trading session.

In other words unrealised profits and losses are taken during the life of the contract. This can pose difficult problems, especially for hedgers who do not have the infrastructure to administer the process efficiently.

There is a time value of money cost involved. Cash that is tied up in the form of margin cannot be invested elsewhere. Secondly, there may be significant administrative costs. Loss making futures positions may involve the owner in frequent margin calls, as the variation limit is breached by successive debits to their account.

The Underlying Instrument

In certain markets it may be difficult to deliver the underlying instrument as specified by the futures contract. Apart from the sheer impracticality of having to take delivery of, for instance, 40,000 lb of live cattle, the deliverable grade specified by a future is often an idealisation, not always attainable in the real world. This brings in the notion of futures contract equivalency.

Exchanges in such circumstances publish a list of deliverable instruments that approximate to the underlying instrument. Since their characteristics may differ from those of the specified grade, the amounts to be delivered are adjusted by a conversion factor so that their value is equivalent to the future.

For example a standard gold futures contract might be for 100 troy oz of 100 per cent pure gold. The exchange might permit delivery of 80 per cent pure gold instead using a conversion factor of 1.25 (100/80). This means that for every contract he is short at delivery the trader is permitted to make delivery of 125 troy oz of 80 per cent instead.

Index Futures and Cash Delivery
Stock index futures contracts give market participants the ability to hedge against, speculate on, and arbitrage with, equity positions. ECU futures offer similar opportunities for European currencies.

When both of these forms of contracts were introduced they presented the exchanges with a particular problem. At the time, neither existed in physical form, rather they were mathematical constructs.

In theory it was possible to specify delivery of each of the components in the quantity implied by its weighting in the overall index. In practice, the notion of requesting settlement of each of the 500 stocks in the S&P500 contracts was obviously a non-starter.

Index futures are therefore delivered in cash form. Holders of long and short positions simply mark their positions to market according to the index value when the contract closes down. The relevant amounts are transferred, positions closed out with the exchange and margin accounts repaid. The cash delivery procedure has worked well in such markets, and there is now a growing trend amongst exchanges to offer this mechanism on all of their contracts.

Ticks, Volumes, Open Interest
The tick value of a futures contract is the critical parameter in determining the cashflow implications of a given change in price. One tick is defined as the minimum allowable price movement for a given futures contract. Knowing the tick value allows the futures trader to monitor cash profits and losses via a simple calculation.

In the case of the silver contract shown below, prices are quoted in cents per troy oz. A tick is a tenth of a cent per troy oz. Since the contract is for 5000 troy oz the tick value is $5 ($0.001 × 5000). So, for instance, someone who owns 30 March long contracts at a price of 402.8 will revalue his position at 402.0 (settle price), a loss of 8 ticks. The exchange would then debit his margin account by $1200 (30 contracts × 8 ticks × $5).

Calculating the cash effect of a given futures price change is especially important for hedgers, when the future does not precisely correspond to the item being hedged. The hedger can use this to adjust the number of futures so that cash profits and losses are equivalent. This procedure is known as ratio hedging and is illustrated in Chapter 3.

Table 1.1 Silver (Commodity Exchange, New York)

5,000 troy oz; cents per troy oz Est vol 13,000; open interest +162				
Contract	*Open*	*High*	*Low*	*Settle*	*Open Interest*
MAR	404.0	405.0	401.0	402.0	60,277
MAY	409.0	410.0	406.1	407.3	14,222
JUL	414.0	415.0	411.5	412.4	8,052
SEP	419.0	419.0	416.4	417.8	2,749
DEC	430.0	430.0	425.0	425.5	4,011

Source: Wall Street Journal

Futures traders also monitor closely the amount of open interest. The open interest figure represents the total number of futures contracts outstanding. Because most futures are closed out before they reach delivery it also gives an indication of the level of potential liquidity available on that contract. The higher the figure the easier it should be to trade.

Notice, that in Table 1.1 the March futures contract displays easily the most trading activity. This is because it is the near-dated contract (i.e. the next to reach delivery). Futures traders of course are not as concerned with matching exposure dates as they are with minimising liquidity risk. As a result the most active contract will encourage additional participants to trade it.

The other relevant indicator is the estimated volume for the day. This indicates the total number of deals conducted including transactions that close out the contracts. It is therefore an indication of current liquidity. For all months, in the example above, 13,000 contracts were traded and the total number of futures outstanding rose by 162.

Trading in Futures Markets
Since futures traders operate in a closed, regulated market the quality of price information available to them is extremely high. Not just every deal, but every buy and sell price is continuously recorded by the exchange and displayed to all concerned.

As a result, traders can build up an accurate pattern of price movements and liquidity over time. This provides ideal conditions for advocates of charting techniques. Chartists (also known as technical analysts) ignore economic fundamentals, concentrating solely on the pattern of price behaviour. They seek to make profits by identifying recurrent themes while they are still developing.

Not all are convinced by the scientific authenticity of such techniques. However, in futures markets the quality of the price information encourages many participants to make use of charts in their trading decisions. The popularity of technical analysis makes it an important factor in futures pricing. With so many people trading on information about support levels and resistance areas, the predictions of the chartists become self-fulfilling.

Optional Transactions

Market Development
Options have existed for many years in a variety of markets. However, it was not until April 1973 with the creation of the Chicago Board Options Exchange (CBOE) that a traded market in financial options began to establish itself.

The first financial options were stock options and these increased in popularity throughout the 1970s as new exchanges opened in the USA, Canada and Europe (initially in Philadelphia, Montreal, Amsterdam and London). They were paralleled by the introduction of gold and silver option contracts on exchanges in London and New York.

The first currency options were traded in early 1982, interest rate options soon followed. In contrast to existing option markets the currency market-place generated much of its initial impetus from transaction related business between individual banks and corporates. Currency option contracts were introduced on exchanges at a later date when the market was more developed.

Main Characteristics
The holder of an option owns a voluntary right to buy or sell the underlying commodity at a prearranged price within a specified period. A premium is paid for this right, which provides a means of limiting price risk while still benefiting from favourable movements. This combination of limited risk and unlimited potential is the most important characteristic of an option.

There are two main types of option. A call option furnishes its owner with the right to purchase a commodity at a fixed price. A put option grants the buyer the right to sell the commodity at the prearranged price. If the market price of the commodity is below (above) the call (put) exercise price, there is no point in exercising the right, it is more efficient to buy (or sell) on the open market.

Calls and puts provide their owners with worst case protection. In this sense, they are analogous to insurance. The option may or may not be used, and it therefore provides the owner with an each-way bet on price movements. The premium paid for this right is normally in the form of an up-front fee.

An option may have any exercise price, but more valuable options will incur higher premiums. So, call options will tend to be more expensive the lower the exercise price, because fewer dollars are required to purchase the stated amount of the commodity. Put options, on the other hand, will have higher premiums as the exercise price increases. This is because more dollars are guaranteed from the sale of the specified commodity.

Different Option Types
The characteristics of individual options can vary widely according to their specifications. Listed below are some of the main areas where differences can occur.

The Underlying Instrument
The underlying instrument is normally a commodity for spot or forward delivery. Where the forward cash market is used the underlying instrument is generally the price prevailing on the option's expiry date.

Options on futures are also available at most exchanges to complement the futures contracts. Here, of course, the appropriate future is the underlying instrument for the option.

The Market-place
Exchange traded options are standardised contracts that can be actively traded. Contracts are available for specific amounts of a commodity with fixed delivery dates mirroring the futures; they are available with a limited number of exercise prices.

OTC (over the counter) options are tailored to the individual needs of customers giving more flexibility. However, the lack of any formal secondary market for many tailored options can pose liquidity problems. The buyer must also take account of a credit risk on the option writer.

Early Exercise
A European style option grants its owner the right to buy (or sell) the commodity at the exercise price on a specific date in the future. But some options contain a feature allowing them to be exercised at any time on or before expiry; these are known as American style options. The terms American style and European style were initially coined because of the different exercise features of options traded on the Philadelphia Stock Exchange and the European Options Exchange (in Amsterdam).

An American option may seem at first sight to be considerably more valuable than an equivalent, European one. Its characteristic of multiple opportunities for exercise would appear to offer much more flexibility, which ought to be reflected in the premium.

In practice, however, it is rarely beneficial to exercise before the expiry date. Exercising an option earns its owner the positive difference between the exercise price and the open market price, known as the intrinsic value.

There are other ways to realise the value of an option. The option holder can, for instance, sell his rights to someone else. By doing this he will normally earn some time value as well as the intrinsic value. These two elements of option value are discussed in more detail below.

There are specific circumstances where it is advantageous to exercise early, particularly for put options, and in some currency markets. But in general this is not an efficient way of realising an option's value. As a result the premiums quoted often roughly correspond for European and American style options.

The Exercise Price

The terms of most options specify that, when exercised, the buyer will earn any positive difference between the exercise price and the market. But this can expose him to unnecessary risks. For if the market suddenly moves on the expiry date, the expected worth of the contract might evaporate.

Asian style options are designed to protect the option buyer from such a situation. Their exercise value is calculated by comparing the exercise price with the average market rate of the underlying instrument during the life of the option. They are particularly useful for corporate treasurers who wish to protect against frequent, small market exposures.

A further refinement has been added by the introduction of look-back options. These allow the option buyer to select the best day's market price against which to exercise. These appear to offer the risk-averse hedger with the best of all possible worlds. However, though they can perform well in certain market conditions, they tend, in general, to be very expensive and should be viewed with some caution.

The Net Price

The net price represents the worst case price for the option holder. It is useful for buyers and writers of options to have an idea of the break-even points on puts and calls. These can be found by adjusting the exercise prices by the premiums paid or received to arrive at the net cashflows implied by the option position.

Intrinsic Value

The value of any given option is dependent on the relationship between its price and the prevailing open market rates. An in the money option has an exercise price that is advantageous relative to the market. An in the money call option is one whose exercise price allows the holder to buy the commodity more cheaply than in the open market. An in the money put means that the holder can sell the commodity at a higher price than that available in the open market.

When options are in the money they are said to have intrinsic value. The intrinsic value represents the potential profit from exercising the option at current rates and closing out the resultant positions in the open market. The price of an option on the expiry date is measured by its intrinsic value alone.

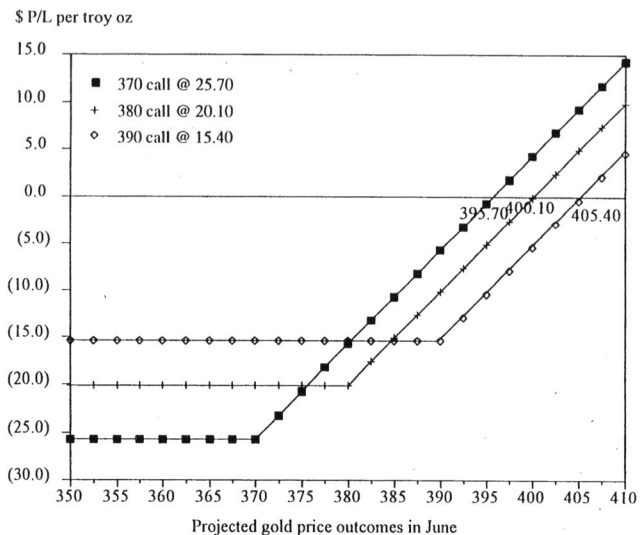

Figure 1.3 Net prices for gold call options

Options whose exercise price is the same as the current market rate are said to be at the money. An out of the money option is one whose exercise price is worse than the prevailing market rate.

It is important to differentiate between the various options and to analyse the relevant underlying instrument when measuring the amount of intrinsic value.

Extrinsic Value

The other component of the option premium is the extrinsic value (sometimes known as option or time value). This element of option premium reflects the likelihood of favourable movements in the commodity's price before the expiry date of the option, which may increase profit opportunities for option holders (or reduce losses).

One hundred per cent of the premium is composed of extrinsic value for all options that are at or out of the money. An at the money option has a 50/50 chance of being exercised. Therefore, just a small change in the price of the underlying instrument can have a large impact on the likelihood of exercise. Thus, the price sensitivity of the extrinsic value portion of premium is at its most pronounced when options are at the money. At the money option premiums are most sensitive to movements in the price of the underlying instrument when there is a short period to expiry.

The premium of an option that is out of the money will be less affected by the same price change, because the likelihood of exercise is not much altered.

The premium of an in the money option is strongly affected by a small movement in the price of the underlying instrument. However, most of this price change is caused by the adjustment in intrinsic value. As with out of the money options a unit change in price has a relatively small impact on the likelihood of exercise, so the effect on extrinsic value is limited.

Time Decay

All other things being equal, the greater the period until the expiry date, the more valuable the option. The value of the time factor will tend to decline gradually while there is still a long time until expiry. As the expiry date gets closer the pace at which value erodes accelerates. There is a cut-off about 45 days before expiry after which the declining time value becomes an important variable in the premium. This phenomenon is described as the time decay umbrella, because of the umbrella shape of the curve.

The length of the period until expiry and the stability or otherwise of the market price are both crucial when determining time value. Instability in the market price is measured by annualised volatility, as we saw earlier in this chapter.

The Concept of Fair Value

An option's premium reflects the market consensus about its expected future value, its so-called fair value. A number of advanced statistical models are employed in its calculation. These rely on computer based evaluation techniques, but we can get an idea of the pricing process by applying our generalised formula for pricing uncertainty to a European style option.

In the example below, the three-month forward price of a tonne of bricks is

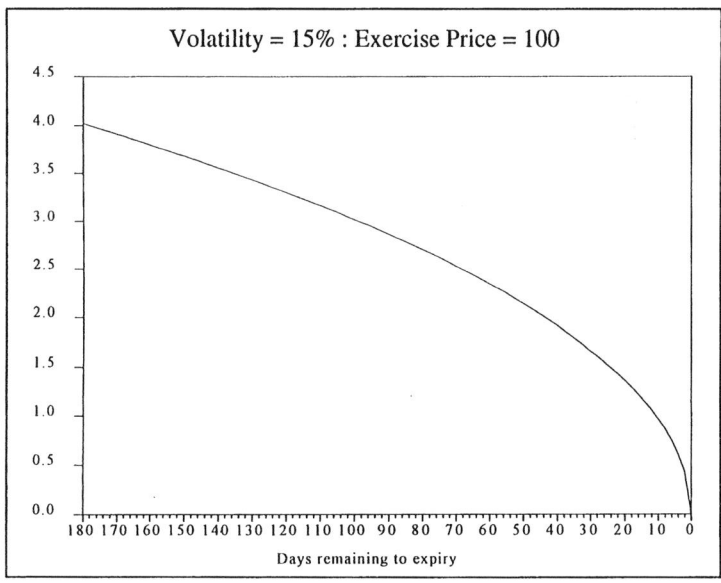

Figure 1.4 Time decay for an at the money option

currently trading at $100. The minimum price movement is $1 per tonne and the maximum change is +/– $2. In other words there are only five possible future prices for bricks: 98, 99, 100, 101 and 102.

A building contractor knows that it will require 1000 tonnes of bricks in three months' time. It has budgeted for a maximum cost of $101 per tonne. If it wished, the contractor could buy 1000 tonnes at the current forward price. However, this would preclude it from benefiting from any fall in prices. Another alternative is for the contractor to buy a call option.

Because it will have pay a premium to purchase the option, if it were to buy a call option with an exercise price of $101, the worst case cost (i.e. the net price) will be greater than its maximum budgeted outlay of $101,000. It may, however, be able to buy a call option with an exercise price of $100 or less.

The price of the call option depends on the market expectation of prices in three months. This is expressed by attaching a probability weighting to each possible outcome. If there is complete uncertainty, then every possible price will have the same likelihood:

Case 1: complete uncertainty about brick prices in three months

Price in 3 months	98	99	100	101	102
Likelihood	20%	20%	20%	20%	20%
Value of $100 call	0	0	0	1	2
Expected call value	0	0	0	0.2	0.4

The fair value for the $100 call will, in this case, be $0.60 in 3 months. To calculate the premium, which is paid in advance, we would need to establish the present value equivalent of $0.60. An environment where the 3 month interest rate is 10 per cent, gives a premium of $0.585 per tonne ($0.6 / (1 + 0.1 × 90 / 360)).

The illustration can be made more realistic by relaxing the uncertainty assumption. In practice, market participants will have a view as to which of the five possible price outcomes is most likely.

Case 2: limited uncertainty about brick prices in three months

Price in 3 months	98	99	100	101	102
Likelihood	10%	20%	40%	20%	10%
Value of $100 call	0	0	0	10	20
Expected call value	0	0	0	0.2	0.2

The fair value for the $100 call will, in this case, be $0.40 in three months. At 10 per cent, its present value equivalent is $0.39 per tonne.

From the cases shown, it can be seen that the option premium increases as uncertainty (i.e. volatility) increases. This effect should not be surprising: the option premium is, after all, the price of certainty.

Pricing Options

There are almost as many pricing models as there are participants in options markets. New refinements are constantly being introduced by the leading traders in an effort to earn extra profits from identifying pricing inefficiencies. As option pricing models get more sophisticated, there is a growing danger of the 'Black Box' syndrome ('I press a button and the computer shows the correct price').

However, high-flying mathematical concepts and sophisticated assumptions must not be allowed to obscure the fact that all such models are guessing the future. GIGO (garbage in, garbage out) applies: a pricing model is only as accurate as its assumptions.

In certain options market, currencies for example, the pricing tools are standardised. Dealers in such markets can quote the price in terms of annualised volatility using a modified version of the Black–Scholes model. This assists in the liquidity of markets by providing a single variable against which they can trade. Option premiums are governed by several factors: the price of the underlying asset, the risk-free interest rate, the exercise period, as well as volatility itself. Since several of these may be changing at the same time, monitoring option premiums can be complicated and would act as a barrier to trading.

The Black–Scholes Formula

Black and Scholes developed their formula to price options on stocks. Their approach was to use a log-normal distribution to describe the projected pattern of future price outcomes. Volatility is used, in the form of standard deviation, to alter the shape of the distribution. The price used to describe the mean outcome is the current forward price.

The model contains a number of unrealistic assumptions. It assumes that the direction of future price changes are as likely to be up as down. It takes no account of price jumps: the model relies on smooth variations in price. Despite such limitations, it has one great strength, its relative simplicity. As a result it is in widespread use in many financial markets as the core tool for pricing European style options.

Cox–Ross–Rubinstein

For all its merits, Black–Scholes is inappropriate for the valuation of American style options as it includes no provision for the possibility of early exercise. The binomial technique introduced by Cox, Ross and Rubinstein is designed to take account of such an outcome.

Taking the spot price of the commodity as the starting point, the model examines the effect of a two-way branching in price, depending on volatility. If the option is exercisable in the more favourable scenario, intrinsic value is calculated. The process is repeated a number of times to build an overall expected profit pattern.

The simplified example shown in Table 1.2 illustrates the process for a brick call with an exercise price of $100, when the spot price is $100, there are five future periods and volatility per period is one.

Table 1.2 The premium for an American option is
the sum of the present values of these expected amounts.

Period	t0	t1	t2	t3	t4	t5
Probability of exercise		25.0%	12.5%	6.25%	3.125%	1.5625%
						105
					104	
				103		103
			102		102	
		101		101		101
	100		100		100	
		99		99		99
			98		98	
				97		97
					96	
						95
Expected future values:	0.25	0.25	0.25	0.19	0.14	0.25

The way in which the probabilities are derived deserves extra explanation. Consider the situation of the option holder at time $t1$. According to the model, there is a 50 per cent chance that the spot price will now be $101 and a 50 per cent chance it will be $99. In the latter situation the option holder cannot earn intrinsic value by exercising, he will therefore retain the option until period $t2$.

If, however, the price is $101, $1 of intrinsic value is available through immediate exercise. The option holder will only exercise if he believes that the price will be lower at time t2. Within the framework of the model there is a 50 per cent chance of this occurring. There is therefore a 25 per cent chance (50% × 50%) of exercise on date $t1$.

The illustration understates some of the complexities captured by the model in the real world, especially the spot–forward price relationship, but it captures the essence of the technique.

Other Variations
Although they are both used successfully, neither of the models described above considers the way markets behave in practice. They assume that there is no directional bias to price movements, that price shifts are regular and that the current market price is the most likely price occurring in the future.

Such assumptions are clearly unduly restrictive. Their impact is often significant, particularly for options that are difficult to trade. Some participants have looked at other pricing approaches. Monte Carlo sequencing is a random walk process where large numbers of specific scenarios are simulated to build up an average expected profit. The limits to the process can be defined with much more flexibility: the user can, for instance, include maximum and minimum possible prices, and the smallest and largest adjustments allowed.

Others argue, with some justification, that the better approach is to understand the limitations of the basic models. These can then be used, with suitable modifications to the mean and volatility, to arrive at a judgement on future prices.

2: Cross-market Connections

ARBITRAGE AND PRICING LINKS

Opportunity Cost and Financial Market Interdependence

In the previous chapter we described how all financial commodities can be valued in terms of their basic risk–reward characteristics of cashflows, dates and likelihoods. Just two valuation principles, the time value of money and the time value of uncertainty, can be applied to any financial instrument. Even the most arcane of the latest computer pricing tools combines these two forms of valuation. We also saw how instruments with different risk–reward characteristics can be related by means of the capital asset pricing model and the notions of risk premium and benchmark values.

The intangibility of financial commodities makes them easy to trade and amenable to precision evaluation. Because the same techniques can be applied to the valuation of all financial commodities, analysts look at assets in terms of each other. Indeed, the global financial markets can be visualised as a vast network of interconnecting instruments mapping international sentiment regarding a sea of risk–reward possibilities. For these connections to be meaningful it must be possible for market participants to travel around the network, transforming their risk–reward profiles in the process.

Yield curves provide the ability to move an exposure through time; so known cashflows occurring on different dates can be valued in terms of each other. (This time relationship is best monitored using zero coupon yield curves, see Chapter 4.) Foreign exchange can transform a cashflow's currency exposure: swaps, FRAs, futures, options are just some of the other examples of instruments designed for risk transformation.

The network analogy is a useful one because it sets up an expectation that there will be numerous routes between any two points (i.e. risk–reward profiles). Now because financial instruments are actively tradeable, the cost of executing multiple transactions can be kept fairly low. This means that, rather than being forced to find the most direct path between two profiles (i.e. the route involving the fewest transactions), there are occasions when it is more cost effective to execute multiple transactions to achieve the same effect.

Consider the case of an investor who wishes to own a 10 per cent annual bond maturing in two years. Such a bond is available at cost of 100. He would therefore have to pay $100 today to own cashflows of $10 and $110 in one and two years. But he could also buy each cashflow separately via purchases of a 1 year and a 2 zero coupon bond. To own the same future cashflows using this method he needs to pay a total of $99.90, or a $10,000 saving per $m. Clearly he is unlikely to be deterred by the added complexity of doing two transactions instead of one when a small amount of extra effort will yield such a significant discount.

From this one example the reader might hypothesize that there are innumerable such opportunities because the different price pressures on subtly different instruments mean that their relative values are rarely likely to be equivalent. In practice, however, such price imbalances, known as anomalies, are likely to be temporary and relatively infrequent. If an anomaly is widely recognised supply and demand effects will tend to eliminate it. In the example shown, the two year bond's price would fall as traders sought to sell it; the zero coupon bonds' prices would rise because of the increase in demand. Any price advantage would soon be eroded. Once the relationship is generally understood, the pricing links between these related instruments are incorporated into their price behaviour.

The knowledge boundaries of financial markets are constantly expanding as new relationships are identified, exploited and then understood and assimilated.

By extending the network analogy a little further we can develop a conceptual model of the process. Imagine the market participants as drivers making their way through city traffic. The city addresses and streets become the network of instruments. Different drivers have varying levels of knowledge about the city's layout: some have good local knowledge, others stick to the main roads. As they struggle to reach their destinations their objective is to minimise travel time (i.e. maximise risk-adjusted yield). Some of the more enterprising drivers study the route in more detail and discover that at certain times they can travel faster via side streets, the so-called 'rat runs'. Inevitably these advantages are soon lost as other drivers spot the same alternatives and congestion erodes the time gain.

We might try to take the analogy further and speculate that with more drivers taking different routes and a better general understanding of the roads there ought to be a net benefit to the whole community. Average journey times should fall. The evidence for financial markets suggests that they become more efficient, but the comparative advantage available to more skilled participants is reduced. They have to find more and more ingenious paths to improve yields. This leads to an expanding financial universe with new categories of commodity and information being harnessed by traders. The securitisation of mortgages and car loans, the introduction of pollution control and insurance futures and options contracts are some recent illustrations of this effect.

The Arbitrage Process

Arbitrage aims to lock in profit and lock out market risk by taking advantage of anomalies between markets that have technical relationships. It is a self-contained transaction which relies on the assumption that these anomalies are temporary, encapsulated in the Efficient Markets Hypothesis.

Essentially, the arbitrager aims to construct a financial transaction where he simultaneously buys and sells the same financial 'parcel'. There are, as we have seen, a variety of ways in which this parcel can be assembled, the arbitrager seeks opportunities where it can be purchased at relatively low cost and sold at a higher price. The arbitrageable difference is an anomaly. Since both sides of the transaction are anchored to the same financial parcel, their values ought to be the same. The anomaly will eventually disappear, as the risk–reward characteristics of the parcel are realised.

The second part of the arbitrage process relies on this effect. The arbitrager sells his long position and buys back his short position at a later date when the anomaly has disappeared. Because of the mirrored nature of the arbitrage exposure, it does not matter whether the price of the underlying parcel has risen or fallen in the interim. Losses on one side of the position are matched by equivalent profits on the other.

Arbitrage can be seen as the flip side of hedging. Hedgers rely on a perfect price relationship between linked markets; arbitrage also relies on this in the long term but depends on imperfections in the price relationship at the outset. By taking equal and opposite positions in linked markets when an anomaly in the basis occurs, the arbitrager hopes to lock in the price differential without being exposed to market risk.

There are many different kinds of arbitrage, but all involve buying and selling nominally equivalent positions at the outset. Often these positions will be held until delivery/maturity, but the arbitrage may be realised earlier by undoing each position when the basis moves as expected.

Risks in Arbitrage

The riskiest part of any arbitrage is at the implementation stage. The more complex the structure, the greater the risk.

The locked-in profit on an arbitrage depends on numerous deals being done at current prices. If only a part of the arbitrage is in place and prices move it is possible to make a loss before the transaction has been completed.

For this reason arbitragers will attempt as far as possible to do all the legs of the transaction at the same time. They will be less likely to attempt arbitrage when markets are extremely volatile as they could be susceptible to price movements during implementation.

The other major risk component stems from the slightly different nature of the markets being accessed. It is inevitable that the two sides of any arbitrage will have slightly different characteristics. If they were identical in every respect there would be no possibility of an anomaly occurring.

To illustrate this, consider the case of an arbitrager who identifies an anomaly between a six month $/ECU forward price and the forward rates against the dollar for its constituent currencies. The ECU is an index of EC currencies, the contribution of each constituent currency being determined according to the relative GNPs of the economies concerned. The arbitrager buys ECUs six months forward and sells appropriate amounts of the various currencies. She then waits, confident that the anomaly will disappear. But instead, there is an EC finance meeting two weeks later at which the ECU is rebalanced, with different weightings being applied to the currency.

The relationship between the ECU and its currencies is fundamentally changed, and the arbitrage collapses. In other words there is always a risk that anomalies which seemed temporary may turn out to be permanent; the technical relationship may break down.

Does Arbitrage Perform a Useful Function?

Proponents of arbitrage point to the impact the process has on the efficiency of the financial markets. When an arbitrage opportunity is spotted it highlights a market imbalance.

Typically one market (A) is underpriced and the other (B) is overpriced. Arbitragers buy the commodity in market A and sell it in B. Demand increases in market A so the price goes up; more is supplied in market B so this price falls. This process continues until the price in market A is in line with market B.

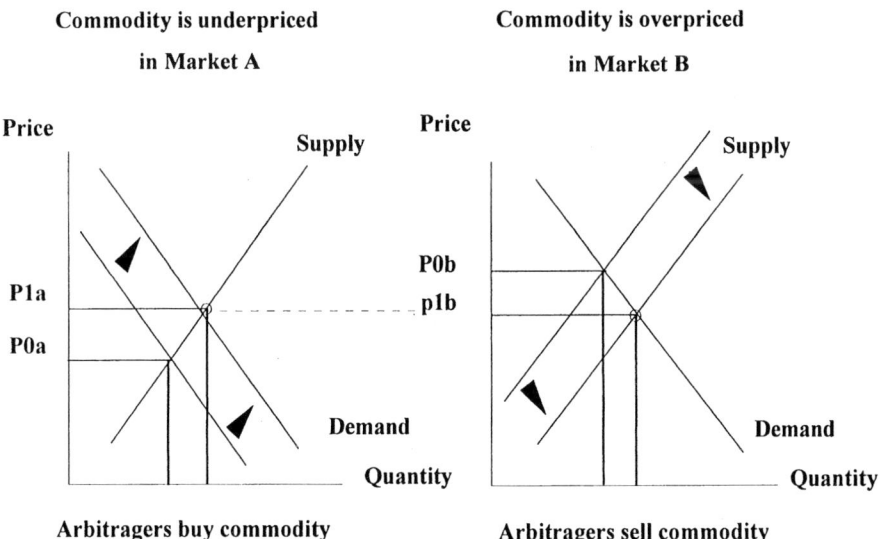

Figure 2.1 Arbitrage equalises supply and demand in related markets

Arbitragers say that they fulfil a vital role by correcting market imbalances, thus promoting a healthy and efficient market. It is also true that the potential for arbitrage activity deters some of the wilder price oscillations between markets and therefore encourages stability. However, there is evidence that, in practice, the short-term effects of arbitrage can sometimes send misleading signals to the market encouraging erratic price movements.

The problem is most likely to occur in markets where a significant proportion of participants are relatively unsophisticated. Arbitragers, by their actions are taking no view on price, but because holders of arbitrage positions are waiting to unwind their exposures when the anomaly disappears, there may be a significant amount of selling activity at particular stages in the market cycle. In such situations there is likely to be a significant price effect. Other investors following the market may notice this effect and misattribute it to a change in market sentiment. They could therefore be encouraged to sell their positions, precipitating further price falls.

This effect is insignificant in relatively stable market conditions. In a volatile market, however, there is a risk that short-term gyrations will increase and confidence will be damaged. The Brady Commission which reported on the causes of the Black Monday crash of 1987 identified arbitrage as one factor contributing to the severity of the sell-off. It recommended a system of circuit-breakers be introduced in the futures markets to ward off a recurrence.

Circuit-breakers are regulatory safety nets that cause certain futures markets to cease trading when volatility exceeds specified parameters. They are designed to prevent arbitrage taking place in unstable markets, but their value is questionable. Financial institutions resent the interference in the free market they represent. Many of them took large losses on their arbitrage activities in October 1987 and they argue that they have learnt their lesson and it is not in their interest to engage in arbitrage in volatile conditions. Besides, they reason it was the inflexible actions of portfolio insurers that triggered any domino effect. In retrospect it is also clear that the main contributory factor to the collapse of stock markets was sheer overvaluation. It is at least arguable that the wiping out of 30 per cent of stock values overnight represented only 5–10 per cent more than what was appropriate to the financial context. The real problem stemmed from the artificial boom of the 1980s and this should not be forgotten in any debate about systemic weaknesses.

Triple Witching Hour

Those that claim that arbitrage can have a destabilising effect on markets do have evidence to support their contention. On 31 October 1986 the Dow-Jones index sustained an 80 point fall in one day. The Halloween connotations were not lost on Wall Street traders and the triple witching hour was born.

Triple witching refers to key calendar dates in the trading cycle, when equities, index futures and options all reach delivery at the same time. On these dates the basis (the difference between the stock index and the value of its constituent equities, weighted by contribution) should approximate to zero.

The price movement in 1986 was attributed to large scale selling by program traders who were closing out massive equity positions in the futures and cash markets. This selling was the result of an earlier anomaly between the futures market and the equity market; it was a purely technical process. However, the resulting price moves rattled the market and pushed genuine investors into panic selling, sending equity prices into a nosedive.

Gold Cash-and-Carry: a Physical Arbitrage

One of the simplest forms of arbitrage is via the cash-and-carry operation (also known as basis trading). Cash-and-carry is widely understood as an arbitrage mechanism and profit opportunities are limited. By the same token it is the central pricing methodology for all forward markets. It is thus vital to understand the mechanism.

Like all arbitrage, cash-and-carry relies on the different ways that the same exposure can be constructed. This one takes advantage of the relationship between futures/forwards and their underlying instrument. The price relationship is described by the basis, which is the difference between the future and spot price of a commodity. There is also an implied value for the basis: instead of buying the future, a market participant might choose to borrow cash to buy gold at the spot price. The gold can be stored until the future delivery date when the borrowing is repaid. This transaction provides the participant with the same cashflow and exposure structure as would be achieved by buying the future.

If the actual basis moves outside the the implied basis range then an arbitrage opportunity occurs. The gold market example below explains how this might operate in practice. The illustration focuses on futures contracts deliverable in June 1991, five months after the 21 January spot value date.

To decide whether there is value in the basis we need to look at the five-month dollar interest rate. LIBOR is standing at 7 per cent. We can use the time value of money formula to establish whether it will be worthwhile to borrow until June to buy gold at the spot rate.

At 7 per cent, with a gold spot price of \$373.20, we would have to repay \$384.08 for every troy oz purchased, i.e. 373.20 (1 + 7% (150/360)). The June future is quoted at \$385.80. Since we know that in June, when the future becomes deliverable, both the actual basis and the implied basis will be zero it should be possible to achieve a locked in gain by a cash-and-carry operation, where the commodity purchase price is offset by selling the June future.

Per 1000 troy oz, the cashflows would be as follows:

In today's environment:

Value 21 January 1991
  –$3,732,000   Purchase 1000 troy oz gold
  +$3,732,000   Borrow at 5m US$ LIBOR of 7%
  –MARGIN×10   Sell 10 June 100 troy oz contracts @ 385-80

Value 20 June 1991
  –$3,840,800   Repay borrowing

In June (spot gold price: $400):
  +MARGIN×10   10 June contracts are delivered @ 400-00
  +$4,000,000   Sale of 1000 troy oz gold
  –$150,000   Realised loss on 10 June 100 troy oz contracts @ $400-00

The cash-and-carry operation nets $9200 in gross profit ($4m – 150,000 – $3,840,800).

Destabilising Factors

It is important to remember that other factors can unhinge what looks like a successful arbitrage operation. For instance, there is the fact that profits and losses are taken on futures as they occur. The interest cost of maintaining a minimum margin might exceed any arbitrage profits. We do not need to make wild assumptions to show how this can happen.

For instance, what would happen if the gold price rose swiftly just after the placing of the position? Clearly the arbitrager would realise losses on the short futures position, which would be reflected by successive margin calls.

Each short gold futures contract will be worth $100 less for every $1 rise in its price. So, if by the start of February, June futures had risen by $20 to $400, we would have already had to pay out $200,000 in extra margin ($20 × $100 × 10 contracts). Supposing, in addition, that the June futures price remains at this level until the delivery date, this amount will have to be financed until June. Assuming no increase in rates, the interest cost in June will be $5400 (i.e. 140 days interest on $200,000 at 7 per cent).

The net profit in this scenario declines to $3800 ($9200 – $5400). And this is just one of many potentially destabilising effects: if, for instance, over the same period interest rates had doubled to 14 per cent (admittedly unlikely, but not without precedent) the cash-and-carry profit would have been more than wiped out.

Limitations to Arbitrage in Physical Markets

For holders of gold bullion, which is a physical commodity, there is an additional expense of storing inventory. A typical monthly storage charge will approximate to around $7 per 100 troy oz so, for this cash-and-carry operation, the arbitrager will suffer an additional cost of $350 ($7 × 5 months × 10).

Gold, although physical, is sufficiently standard to be treated similarly to a financial commodity. But many commodities markets are much more idiosyncratic. It may be theoretically possible to perform a cash-and-carry arbitrage by buying live cattle and selling the equivalent futures, but the practical difficulties for a Wall Street firm in taking delivery of, say, 100,000 lb of live cattle means that some kinds of arbitrage are rarely if ever performed.

Futures prices in such markets tend often to be more closely related to future expectations than the level of interest rates. This may lead to the phenomenon of backwardation where futures are actually cheaper than the current spot prices. This occurred, for example, with oil prices during the Gulf War. Spot prices were kept high by the international tension, but futures prices were considerably lower as many oil companies saw the current price as historically high and sought to sell their future output at current levels.

Add to this, the illiquidity of many physical commodities, the cost in people, time, infrastructure, and it is not hard to see why technical anomalies can persist in commodities markets. In the highly liquid financial markets, physical storage is not an issue. As a result the integrity of the time value relationship is broadly maintained, anomalies are much smaller and more short-lived.

Reverse Cash-and-Carry and Physical Delivery

In order for spot and forward prices to be linked there must be a two way arbitrage threat. It must be possible both to buy and to sell futures against the underlying commodity. In this way there is both a maximum and minimum price implied by the technical relationship between spot and forward markets.

With physical commodities delivery must be made, it is not possible to sell a commodity without being able to deliver it. As a result the reverse cash-and-carry mechanism (i.e. selling a commodity and lending the proceeds until the future date) is only feasible if the arbitrager already owns the commodity.

With financial instruments there is normally no such restriction. They are intangible and transactions generally involve a transfer of rights and obligations together with a transfer of cashflows. The reverse cash-and-carry mechanism thus dictates the minimum price for a future relative to the spot price. Cash-and-carry and reverse cash-and-carry together thus establish a trading range for a future or forward transaction.

Cash-and-Carry in Spot and Forward Pricing

We have seen that the cash-and-carry mechanism dictates the implied forward price of a commodity according to its spot price and the time value of money.

Since it is possible to create an instrument with forward delivery characteristics synthetically, the threat of arbitrage is always present in forward markets. If the basis is too large futures are overpriced and they will be sold by arbitragers, if it is too small arbitragers will be buyers of futures. Dealers in futures therefore know in advance the minimum and maximum price for a given future and they will quote prices within this range.

Pricing a T-bill for Forward Delivery

In the example below we see how a six-month forward price for a three-month US T-bill can be derived using the cash-and-carry technique. By buying a nine-month T-bill at today's price using cash raised by borrowing for six months, the market maker ensures that she will, in six months own a three-month T-bill. The cost of the exercise depends on the amount of interest payable at the end of the borrowing period. She is therefore able to derive a break-even price at which she can sell a three month T-bill six months hence (in this case 97.76) without needing to know about future market conditions.

Spot value:
–$940,000	Buy $1m face value of nine-month T-bill @94
+$940,000	Borrow for 6 months @ 8%

In 6 months:
–$977,600	Repay $940,000 plus six months interest
+$977,600	Revenue from sale of three-month T-bill to client @97.76

In 9 months:
+$1,000,000	Gain redemption value of T-bill bought
–$1,000,000	Lose redemption value of T-bill sold

The three-month T-bill sold is of course the same security as the nine-month T-bill purchased: its maturity characteristics have changed with the passage of time.

In the above situation, the seller must negotiate a forward price of at least 97.76 if she is to break even on the deal. It should be evident from this illustration that the spot price and interest rates are setting the forward price. If the deal was struck at a price significantly different from this one there would be an arbitrageable opportunity.

Costing a Three-month Forward $ Sale versus DM

In the illustration below the implied forward rate charged by a market maker for selling $1m against a purchase of DM underpins the actual quoted price in the

$/DM forward market. In order to transact the deal without incurring price risk, the market maker must generate a $1m long position and a short DM position in three months. The cost to him of doing this determines the price he will charge. Cashflows shown are per $m on the forward date.

$/DM = 2.0000
three-month US$ interbank rate = 8 per cent
three-month DM interbank rate = 7 per cent

Spot value:
+$980,390	Buy $ @ $/DM 2.0000
–DM 1,960,780	Sell DM @ $/DM 2.0000
–$980,390	Lend $ @ 8 per cent for 3 months
+DM 1,960,780	Borrow DM @ 7 per cent for 3 months

In 3 months:
| +$1,000,000 | Receive $980,780 plus interest at 8 per cent |
| –DM1,995,090 | Repay DM1,960,780 plus interest at 7 per cent |

Notice how in this case, a swap is involved and the market maker both borrows and lends the relevant cash positions until the forward date. When establishing the price at which he is prepared to sell dollars against deutschmarks in three months, the market maker knows that he must receive at least DM 1,995,090 in exchange for $1m. His break-even forward FX rate would therefore be 1.9951. In practice, he would not need to create the forward in this way, he would use the FX swap market to offset the deal with his customer. This market is discussed in a later chapter, but it is the time value of money relationship between the two currencies, the interest differential, which anchors FX forward prices to the spot rate.

Put–Call Parity and Option Pricing

We have seen how the arbitrage process aims to identify anomalous pricing of equivalent risks in connected markets. The cash-and-carry mechanism uses the time value of money relationship to connect spot and forward markets. But options also provide tools for arbitragers, who can buy and sell them in combination to achieve locked-in profit.

The put–call parity argument provides the methodological foundation for such activity. Basically this states that call option and put option premiums must be related to the price of their underlying commodity. To see why this is so, consider the position of a trader who simultaneously buys a call option on bricks and writes a put option, both at an exercise price of 99. If, on the expiry date, the price of bricks is above 99, the put option expires worthless, the call option, however, may be exercised. If it is below 99 the option trader is forced to deliver

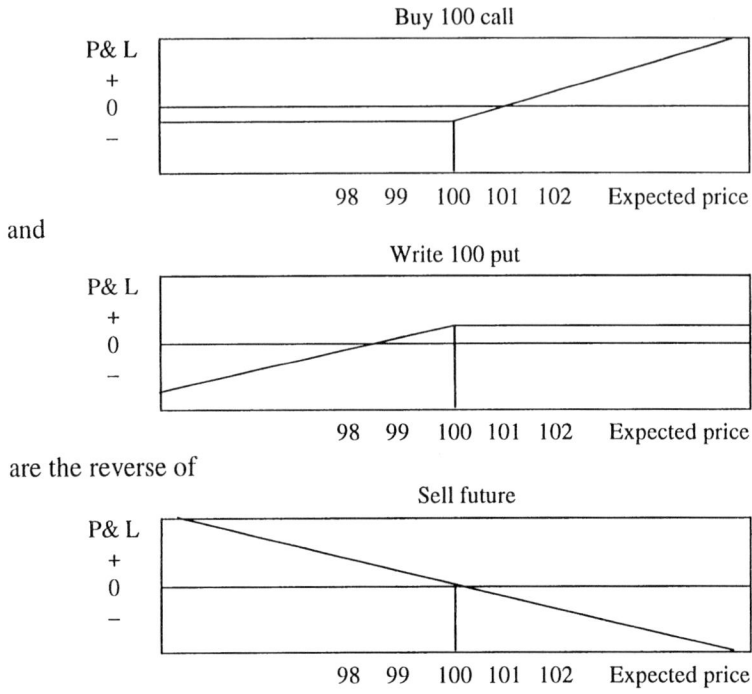

Figure 2.2 Put–call parity and the no free lunch rule

bricks at 99 and the call option is worthless. Supposing the brick futures contract for delivery on the expiry date is priced at 100. By selling a future the trader could be short of bricks at 100.

Since we know that there is no free lunch in financial markets, the net premium paid by the option trader must equate to 1. If it is less than this arbitragers will buy calls, write puts and sell futures to exploit the anomaly; if more they would write calls, buy puts and buy futures. The effect of such activity is to bring relative futures and option prices back into line.

Put–call parity is in fact widely understood and used as a pricing reference by options traders so direct arbitrages rarely occur. However, its importance as a risk transformation technique should not be underestimated, and there are sometimes indirect arbitrage opportunities. Indeed, option purists even argue that from a risk–reward point of view there are only two types of financial commodity – puts and calls – every type of asset can be expressed as some combination of these.

Program Trading: the Future of Arbitrage

Arbitrage opportunities take advantage of the fact that financial commodities can be built up out of their components. But we have seen that where the relationships are understood and assimilated, anomalies are extremely rare. This drives arbitragers towards transactions of increasing complexity. Index arbitrage is one example of this trend. For instance, the Standard & Poor's 500 index is a weighted basket of leading US stocks. S&P500 futures allow participants to trade US stock market risk. Theoretically, performing the cash-and-carry mechanism here would involve borrowing cash to buy the correct amount of each of the 500 stocks while simultaneously selling the future.

Even though the 500 stocks can be accurately tracked with a basket of 30–40 leading stocks, the large number of interlocking deals involved makes it difficult to spot opportunities, let alone execute transactions.

It is crucial to spot an anomaly early as the window of opportunity will disappear within a few days, hours or even minutes as supply and demand pressures bring the two markets back into line. For this reason, arbitragers use real-time software that can identify and execute orders automatically. This is only practical in markets where stocks are traded on computer.

In the future, though, it is likely that program trading techniques will become increasingly central to the workings of markets. Most investment banks are researching artificial intelligence techniques and many already have a variety of automated arbitrage systems in place.

Risk Arbitrage

The term has unfortunate connotations in the financial industry, perhaps because of the book, *Risk Arbitrage* written by Ivan Boesky before his downfall. Boesky's so-called technique was based on massive fraud and an insider trading network. It is not an arbitrage in the strict technical sense, but does share some characteristics in the sense that seeks to identify and exploit latent anomalies. The technique is intended to make profit from the under-valuation of companies, but is only appropriate when there is a lot of takeover activity.

In a nutshell, risk arbitragers buy into a company whose stock price values it at less than its break-up value. They simultaneously sell an identical amount of the stock of highly priced companies with similar sectoral characteristics. Barring accidents they are now relatively immune to economic shifts of mood. They then await a revaluation of the underperforming company, which will occur either because of an improvement in its fortunes or, and this is more likely, there is a takeover bid. In the last resort they always have the option of assembling their own buy-out syndicate and breaking up the company's assets.

There is one slight drawback to this otherwise solid plan, vividly demonstrated on Black Monday. The net asset value of a company, its break-up value, depends on how much people are willing to pay. If that changes, as it did in 1987, the 'arbitrage' falls apart. Risk arbitrage groups were some of the chief casualties of the crash, and the technique is now applied with caution.

BASIS BEHAVIOUR

What is the Basis?

The term basis has a variety of meanings in financial markets. In the context of this discussion, however, it expresses the relationship between an underlying exposure and a related financial instrument. Usually when practitioners use the term they are referring to the difference between the cash and the futures price of a particular commodity. Formally defined, it is equal to the positive difference between the cash price and the futures price. Accurate measurement of the basis and a clear impression of the way it moves through time are vital tools for speculators, hedgers and arbitragers alike.

Relationships between Cash and Futures

The owner of a long futures contract has an obligation to take delivery of a specified quality and quantity of the underlying commodity at a specific future date. Whenever a futures contract reaches its delivery date, it ceases to be a future and is converted into the underlying commodity.

In other words, at delivery the basis becomes zero. Practitioners are therefore able to predict the general trend in the basis for a given futures contract over time. Departures from this trend provide opportunities for trading, can improve hedging performance or produce arbitrageable anomalies.

Financial hedging strategies rely on the interconnectedness of markets and the basis articulates this relationship. Classical hedging strategies often assume that the basis remains constant. But the assumption that, for example, a 1 per cent increase in three-month $ LIBOR will be accompanied by a 100 tick fall in Eurodollar futures, though partly correct, is a dangerous over-simplification.

Widening and Narrowing Basis Patterns

Certain terms are useful when discussing basis relationships. When the cash market is weakening relative to futures, the basis is said to be widening. Basis traders will want to sell the physical commodity and buy futures – they seek to be short the basis. When the basis is narrowing (i.e. cash is strengthening relative to the futures price), traders are looking to be long the basis – they want to buy the commodity and sell futures.

The way that the basis works is perhaps best understood by looking at how it behaves in practice. Fundamental to basis behaviour is the concept of opportunity cost pricing.

This is to say that the relative costs of owning a physical commodity for a given period ought, in the long run, to equate to the cost of buying a future that is deliverable on the last day of that period. Otherwise, as we saw, arbitrage will occur, and the process will force the basis back to its equilibrium.

Widening and Narrowing Spread Patterns

One way to get a snapshot of the pressures on the basis is by analysing futures spreads. Spreads are similar but not identical to the basis. Whereas the basis describes the relationship between cash and futures, a spread relates different futures dates. In the exhibit below the spread between May91 and June91 contracts is –20 cents.

Figure 2.3 Brent Crude (International Petroleum Exchange)

1000 net barrels; $/barrel	
MAR	18.97
APR	18.70
MAY	18.30
JUN	18.10

Source: Wall Street Journal – 22 January 1991

The oil market on 21 January 1991 displayed an inverse spread pattern. On the date in question, a week after the start of the Gulf War, oil producers anticipated hostilities would be relatively short-lived and that prices would fall quickly as Middle Eastern supply sources were re-established. More importantly, spot oil prices were being forced higher by the supply constraints imposed by the conflict.

Oil producers therefore sold futures contracts to protect future revenues. This had the effect of driving futures prices down, leading to a price structure known as backwardation. In theory, it ought to be possible to realise a locked-in profit by selling the oil in the physical market against a matching purchase of futures. In practice, this physical arbitrage, known as reverse cash-and-carry, was prevented by the need for companies to maintain strategic stocks.

Other markets display positive spread characteristics. On the same day, for example, gold futures contracts are appreciating through time, displaying positive spread characteristics. The spread between Apr 91 and Jun91 contracts, for instance, is +320 ticks.

Figure 2.4 Gold (CMX)

100 troy oz.; cts/troy oz	
FEB	379.50
APR	382.60
JUN	385.80
AUG	389.00

Source: Wall Street Journal – 22 January 1991

Gold here is a carry market, i.e. the physical market trades at a discount to futures. Purchasing gold in the physical market against a sale of futures could provide a locked-in profit to the buyer so long as the cost of storage/financing is exceeded by the width of the basis.

The Basis in Financial Markets

In financial markets, the basis is closely linked to time value of money. The underlying commodity is easily arbitrageable, physical storage and handling costs do not cloud the picture. However, it would be a mistake to assume that the basis follows a predetermined pattern. Supply and demand factors in the cash and futures markets influence the basis in similar ways to commodities, and risk managers need to be aware of these.

Monitoring the Basis

Cash-and-carry and reverse cash-and-carry arbitrage opportunities define the limits to the basis relationship. If a financial instrument can be bought (or sold) in the cash market and its equivalent sold (or bought) in the form of futures for a locked-in profit, arbitrage will occur. The resulting market activity will affect the relative prices and tend to bring the basis back towards the level implied by the time value of money relationship.

Financial markets are highly price sensitive. The knowledge that arbitrage opportunities are available will often be enough to bring the basis back into line without them actually being exploited.

Even for those risk managers who do not want to monitor their hedges through time, the basis is an essential measurement to help decide when and how to put a hedge in place. For those prepared to invest time and energy in active management, improved performance is available through an understanding of basis behaviour.

Basis Trading

Basis traders use their knowledge of implied basis behaviour to determine their timing of purchases and sales of cash versus futures. They hold equal and opposite positions for short periods and trade actively. It is thus a dynamic form of arbitrage. By always buying futures and selling cash when the basis is narrow (i.e. futures are near their minimum implied level) and doing the reverse transaction whenever the basis is wide, they seek to earn arbitrage type profits.

Unlike the traditional arbitrager, the basis trader does not require the futures price to go outside its implied range. Instead she speculates that, in the long run it will tend towards its mid point and that over time this effect will more than compensate for the small risk in establishing each new position.

3: Risk Management

THE NATURE OF RISK

Risk in Financial Transactions

Every financial transaction involves risk. Market participants accept that a level of risk is inevitable; indeed, it is considered desirable, as without risk, profits would be impossible to achieve.

Risk is rarely eliminated, but it can be controlled. The main task, therefore, for the risk manager must be to balance and modify his exposures so as to avoid the adverse effects of negative conditions at minimum cost. In addition, he will hope to maximise his ability to benefit from a favourable environment.

He only has two basic strategies at his disposal: acceptance and transferral. However, very precise categories of risk can be addressed using options and futures.

Their use depends on having a clear understanding of the level and nature of the risks involved in any set of transactions. Clear identification and analysis make it possible to isolate and to formulate effective strategies for dealing with unacceptable exposures.

Hedgers who believe they are risk-averse will attempt to transfer all known price risks to other parties whenever possible. But as is explained below, risk managers who are prepared to take the time to isolate unacceptable risks, and only hedge these, will normally achieve superior hedging performance.

Sources of Risk

This book is primarily concerned with managing market related risks. Credit appraisal and assessment techniques should be applied in addition to the market methodologies described. Efficient dealing/execution facilities should be employed to minimise the risks associated with trading and settling deals. Having said this, it is often the case, particularly when dealing in marketable securities, that the same techniques that are used in managing price risks may also be employed in the management of all risk.

Default Risk
Default risk relates to the possibility that an agreed payment is not made in full and on time. The default risk of a transaction will increase the further into the

future is the projected payment, and the less reliable is the payer. There is a default risk only in transactions where payment is due in the future. In some cases the risk is minimal, effectively zero, and can be ignored. US government paper and most futures contracts fall into this category.

Default is often described as an all or nothing form of risk. In one sense, this is correct – a promised future cashflow is either paid or not paid on the due date. But for marketable securities this is an over-simplification. For, whenever default is at least a remote possibility, there is an impact on yield. The extent of this effect depends on the market perception of the likelihood of default. In other words, the price of a security will decrease as the credit perceptions about the issuer worsen.

Market Methods in Credit Risk Management

The LDC debt crisis in the early 1980s provides a useful illustration of how default risk may be managed as a form of price risk.

When the Mexican Government announced that, as from August 1982, it would reschedule all maturing government debt rather than honour its payment commitments, it sent a shockwave through financial markets. Mexico, as a major oil producer, had traditionally been regarded as one of the most credit-worthy of the sovereign borrowers. Its rescheduling announcement therefore cast a shadow over many forms of sovereign and government guaranteed debt.

With most of the world's leading banks heavily committed to the LDCs urgent action was needed to avoid an international credit crisis. After an initial round of stop-gap refinancing to defuse the emergency, the emphasis switched to the management of the banks' exposures. One of the ways in which this was addressed was by the secondary market trading of LDC debt.

LDC debt traders buy and sell government paper at a discount to par. The depth of this discount is mainly determined by the perceived likelihood of default. In other words, the default risk is articulated in the instrument's yield. Rather than being all or nothing the default risk impacts on price.

Although value impaired debt provides a dramatic illustration of the impact of changing credit perceptions on yield, in reality of course all financial instruments that are not credit risk free are, to a greater or lesser extent, sensitive to this price effect. Like all risks it helps to make up the risk premium component of yield.

Actual Risks for Investors

Market risk is simply the risk that the price will move in an adverse direction. This means different things to different market participants.

For a potential investor in a foreign currency at a fixed rate of interest an adverse price movement would be one which increases the cost of the potential investment. The price of a fixed interest asset will increase as interest rates fall. An asset paying 8 per cent interest will command a premium if current interest rates are at 6 per cent, as the extra 2 per cent gets built into the price. The domestic currency cost to the investor will rise as the foreign currency appreciates.

In general, investors wish to protect their minimum income and borrowers are anxious to contain their maximum cost of funding. For both potential lenders and borrowers there is an actual market risk. It is an actual risk because an adverse movement in interest or exchange rates will have a negative effect on profitability.

Opportunity Risks for Investors

The investor is not sensitive to falling interest rates or strengthening of the foreign currency after purchasing the 8 per cent asset. Similarly a borrower who has already fixed a rate of interest and exchange rate would no longer be concerned that interest rates are rising or the domestic currency is strengthening, because financing costs have been locked in at current rates.

It might be thought that there is no market risk once the rate has been set, but this is not the case. The market risk for the owner of a foreign currency fixed rate asset is that interest rates will go up, or its currency will weaken. This is because the owner is now a potential seller and will realise a capital loss if it attempts to sell it in a higher interest rate/weaker currency environment, so there is an actual risk if the asset is traded.

If interest rates do go up the investor may decide to hold the asset to maturity. This avoids him having to realise any loss. But for two years he will own an asset which pays 8 per cent in an environment where interest rates are higher, at say 10 per cent. In these circumstances the investor has suffered an opportunity loss of 2 per cent per annum. It is an opportunity loss because he could have adopted a different strategy that would have had positive implications for profitability.

The market risk for potential buyers (sellers) is that the price will increase (decrease). Market risk should be seen in terms of both actual negative cashflows and the loss of potential positive cashflows.

Managing Uncertain Exposures

Being able to manage known exposures depends on the accuracy of our forecasts of future price movements. However, there are often other areas of uncertainty with regard to the size and the timing of the exposure itself. Corporates, for example, may have unknown cashflows in the future that depend on seasonal fluctuations and other factors they cannot influence directly.

An exposure is extremely difficult to assess if we are not sure what cashflows will occur, perhaps because they are contingent on winning a contract. There are numerous instruments designed to aid in price risk management. If used properly, these allow us to limit market risks even when the timing and nature of an exposure are uncertain.

Trading Risk
Trading risk is an important aspect of the market risk of a transaction, whenever it is anticipated that the deal might have to be closed out in the future.

The bid–ask spread is the main indicator of the current level of market liquidity. It determines the cost of trading. A Eurobond trading at 100.00/100.10 may be bought and sold at a cost to the customer of 10 basis points, or $1 per $000 face value. The wider is the bid–ask spread, the less liquid the bond, and the higher the trading risk. Illiquid bonds therefore often trade at a risk premium to actively traded bonds with similar characteristics.

Basis Risk
Classical hedgers aim to eliminate price risk by the taking out of an equivalent balancing position, traditionally via futures or forward contracts, more recently using options. By this means they seek to fix the maximum cost (or minimum revenue) of a known future exposure. But we saw in the previous chapter that markets rarely mirror each other precisely; there is no such thing as the perfect hedge. Classical hedging programmes are rarely able to eliminate market risk altogether. Rather they transform the absolute price risk on the hedgeable item into the relative price risk between it and the hedge – the basis risk.

Variations in the basis can account for hedge underperformance. The attitude taken towards managing basis risk will depend on the outlook of the risk manager. In financial institutions and global corporate treasuries it is often actively managed. Basis variation may be seen as an opportunity for earning profits or eliciting superior hedge performance. In other institutions the infrastructure and attitudes required to manage basis risk are not always present. Such organisations view it as an unavoidable cost of hedging.

MANAGING RISK

The Process of Risk Transformation

At its most basic level a hedge involves taking an equal and opposite position to the one being hedged so that any loss on the original exposure is reflected by an equal profit on the hedge. It is identical in effect to the arbitrage process, although it is undertaken with the intention of eliminating risk rather than in order to earn profit. For example, matched funding (where a bank funds a loan or investment by raising finance for the equivalent period) can be seen as a fully hedged transaction as the bank's profit is independent of movements in interest rates.

A typical hedge takes advantage of the relationship between two different markets, often cash and futures. The basis and spreads describe this relationship.

Hedge opportunities exist because of the interconnections between various markets. Markets with the same technical underpinnings will tend to move in line with one another. By taking out the reverse position as a hedge, profit on the exposure is matched by loss on the hedge, and vice versa. In this way a hedge can be used to nullify absolute price risk.

Cross-hedging Techniques

It is not always possible to construct a hedge that precisely corresponds to the instrument being hedged. In such circumstances the risk manager may still be able to establish some price protection by use of a hedge instrument where some kind of technical relationship exists.

In the strict sense, many so-called hedging strategies are actually cross-hedges. Standard grades, quantities and delivery dates make it likely that a futures based strategy will actually be a cross-hedge. Whenever cross-hedging is used particular attention must be paid to monitoring basis variations.

A Physical Long Hedge

A chocolate drink manufacturing company estimates that it will need to buy 100 tonnes of cocoa every quarter during the coming year, The purchasing manager is concerned that the price of cocoa will increase and wishes to buy at prevailing prices. He has two main alternatives:

1. He can purchase 400 tonnes in the physical market.
2. He can buy the equivalent of 400 tonnes of cocoa in futures contracts.

Both courses of action contain risks and hidden costs. Option 1 for example will require him to pay for storing the cocoa until it is needed. He may become a forced seller should his company not meet its production targets. Payment in advance will act as a drain on cashflow. There is therefore a financing cost to be incurred (the cash could otherwise have earned interest until it was required).

The placing of a long hedge (by buying futures) is likely to be a simpler and less risky alternative. By buying forty 10 tonne cocoa contracts, the hedger is able to purchase the equivalent in advance without incurring physical storage costs.

The hedge itself is, of course, not completely without expense. The possibility remains that the hedger will need to sell some futures should he not require the full 400 tonnes, though the enhanced liquidity of futures contracts will normally allow him to do this at a better price than that available in the physical market.

Buying futures exposes the chocolate manufacturer to basis risk. On or before the dates on which cocoa is required, the futures must be sold. The hedger intends that any profit/loss on the futures will exactly offset the change in the price of the physical commodity. This requires movements in cocoa prices to be precisely reflected by adjustments in the futures markets.

But even if the basis were not to be affected by supply and demand factors, it will still change automatically with the process of time. In practice, other considerations will play an important role: the grade of cocoa, the precise quantity and the dates on which it is required will generally be different from those specified in the futures contract. All such differences will add to the company's basis risk.

The futures position must be financed via the maintenance of a margin account. The amount of capital required is less significant than the cost of acquiring cocoa for spot delivery, and with some exchanges it is possible to continue to earn interest on amounts lodged with them as surety. Nevertheless an indeterminate cost is incurred. A minimum amount of margin must be maintained for each open futures contract. As the prices for these are marked to market daily, holders of loss making contracts must transfer funds to position owners who have earned a profit. Successive margin calls on a non-performing futures position can impose significant administrative and time value of money costs on participants.

The hedger may still choose to purchase cocoa today – despite the extra cost, in financing, storage, delivery and insurance – if cocoa futures prices are too expensive. Remember too that the profile of the hedger will help to define the decision he takes. If the drink manufacturer has ample warehousing capacity the costs of storage might be seen as negligible. Another hedger without the same infrastructure might attach a significant cost to storage, thus reaching different conclusions about whether or not to buy futures.

Figure 3.1 Cocoa (Coffee, Sugar & Cocoa Exchange, New York)

10 tonnes; $ per tonne	
JUN	1260
SEP	1290
DEC	1338
MAR	1378

Source: Wall Street Journal

The chocolate manufacturer decides to buy 10 futures contracts each in June, September, December, and March the following year to correspond to its purchasing schedule. It is therefore locked-in (subject to basis variations) at an average cost of $1316.50 per tonne ((1260+1290+1338+1378)/4), a total price of $526,600. This of course assumes that all contracts are held until delivery and that when each contract becomes deliverable the company is able to buy 100 tonnes of cocoa in the physical market at the same price. The manufacturer has hedged against the risk of having to pay more than $1316.50, but, because there is no such thing as a risk-free reward, he has also eliminated the possibility of benefiting from lower cocoa prices.

A Financial Short Hedge

This same chocolate drink manufacturing company has a sterling denominated balance sheet. Its product is sold within the UK. In order to protect its profit margin, it will wish to hedge against the risk of a dollar appreciation against the pound. Supposing it believes it likely that the dollar will strengthen. As with the cocoa hedge there are again two main alternatives.

1. It can purchase $526,500 in the forward FX market against sales of sterling.
2. It can sell sterling futures contracts.

In theory there is a third alternative. The chocolate company could buy dollars/sell sterling in the spot FX market. At the same time it would lend dollars and borrow sterling until the June, September, December and March dates. The effect of these transactions is to lock into an implied FX rate for each of these future dates.

In practice, this route is likely to be much more expensive for the corporate, because so many deals are involved. Rather than take this long-winded alternative, corporate treasurers will access the forward FX market directly. But it is worth mentioning because it demonstrates that the technical underpinning for forward FX prices relies on the spot rate and the borrowing and lending rates for the two currencies. If they move away from this implied level, possibilities for arbitrage would open up.

The choice between futures and the forward market for the hedger depends on how much he is prepared to pay for protection. Futures offer, as a rule of thumb, 95 per cent price protection: the standardisation of contracts, in terms of grades, amounts and delivery dates, means that futures hedgers can never exactly match their exposures, but they are actively tradeable.

Hedgers using forwards can lock in the exact cost of their known future obligations, but the market exacts a premium from them for so doing. Typically, the futures equivalent trades on a far narrower bid–ask spread than its forward market equivalent. This adds to the cost of taking out a hedge, and also makes it more difficult to close out the position, should the situation change. This effect is exacerbated, the more non-standard are the financial transactions being sought by the hedger.

Figure 3.2 Sterling (International Monetary Market, Chicago)

£62,500; cents per pound	
JUN	1.9160
SEP	1.8890
DEC	1.8615
MAR	1.8345

Source: Wall Street Journal

Futures are quoted as shown in Figure 3.2. Assuming no basis variation, the chocolate manufacturer will have US dollar payment commitments in June, September, December and March of $126,000, $129,000, $133,800, and $137,800 respectively. To determine the correct number of futures to sell for each date, we need to convert these amounts to their sterling equivalent by dividing by the relevant futures price. The sterling amounts are £65,760 (@1.9160), £68,290 (@1.8890), £71,880 (@1.8615), and £75,120 (@1.8345) respectively.

Since one futures contract is equivalent to £62,500, the corporate can cover most of its dollar exposure via the sale of one contract for each date. So, even if the dates correspond precisely, the hedge is inexact.

The worked example below shows the cashflow implications of this strategy in two environments: scenario A assumes a weakening dollar with the rate in future rising to 2.0000; in B the assumption is that the dollar strengthens and the future £/$ rate is 1.8000.

In current environment:

> Value: January 22
> −MARGIN×4   Sell 4 sterling futures contracts @ 1.9160, 1.8890, 1.8615, 1.8345

Scenario A (spot £/$ @ 2.0000):
June

	+MARGIN×1	June contract is delivered @ 2.0000
	−$5,250	Realised p/l on June contract sold @ 1.9160
	−$126,000	Hedged purchase of 100 tonnes of cocoa
	+$126,000	Spot dollar purchase @ 2.0000
	−£63,000	Spot sterling sale @ 2.0000
add	−£2,625	Sterling equivalent of $5,250 (@ 2.0000)
equals	−£65,625	Effective cost of cocoa in sterling terms

September

	+MARGIN×1	September contract is delivered @ 2.0000
	−$6,938	Realised p/l on September contract sold @ 1.8890
	−$129,000	Hedged purchase of 100 tonnes of cocoa
	+$129,000	Spot dollar purchase @ 2.0000
	−£64,500	Spot sterling sale @ 2.0000
add	−£3,469	Sterling equivalent of $6,938 (@ 2.0000)
equals	−£67,969	Effective cost of cocoa in sterling terms

December

	+MARGIN×1	December contract is delivered @ 2.0000
	−$8,656	Realised p/l on December contract sold @ 1.8615

	–$133,800	Hedged purchase of 100 tonnes of cocoa
	+$133,800	Spot dollar purchase @ 2.0000
	–£66,900	Spot sterling sale @ 2.0000
add	–£4,328	Sterling equivalent of $8,656 (@ 2.0000)
equals	–£71,228	Effective cost of cocoa in sterling terms

March

	+MARGIN×1	March contract is delivered @ 2.0000
	–$6,938	Realised p/l on March contract sold @ 1.8345
	–$137,800	Hedged purchase of 100 tonnes of cocoa
	+$137,800	Spot dollar purchase @ 2.0000
	–£68,900	Spot sterling sale @ 2.0000
add	–£3,469	Sterling equivalent of $6,938 (@ 2.0000)
equals	–£72,369	Effective cost of cocoa in sterling terms

Scenario B (spot £/$ @ 1.8000):
June

	+$7,250	Realised p/l on June contract sold @ 1.9160
	–£70,000	Spot sterling sale against $126,000 @ 1.8000
add	+£4,028	Sterling equivalent of $7,250 (@ 1.8000)
equals	–£65,972	Effective cost of cocoa in sterling terms

September

	+$5,556	Realised p/l on September contract sold @ 1.8890
	–£71,667	Spot sterling sale against $129,000 @ 1.8000
add	+£3,087	Sterling equivalent of $5,556 (@ 1.8000)
equals	–£68,580	Effective cost of cocoa in sterling terms

December

	+$3,844	Realised p/l on December contract sold @ 1.8615
	–£74,333	Spot sterling sale against $133,800 @ 1.8000
add	+£2,135	Sterling equivalent of $3,844 (@ 1.8000)
equals	–£72,198	Effective cost of cocoa in sterling terms

March

	+$2,156	Realised p/l on March contract sold @ 1.8345
	–£76,556	Spot sterling sale against $137,800 @ 1.8000
add	+£1,198	Sterling equivalent of $2,156 (@ 1.8000)
equals	–£75,358	Effective cost of cocoa in sterling terms

With no financial hedge in place the total sterling cost of buying cocoa will depend on the future level of exchange rates. In scenario A above the total sterling cost will be £263,300 (63,000 + 64,500 + 66,900 + 68,900); while in scenario B the total will be £292,556 (70,000 + 71,667 + 74,333 + 76,556).

With the short sterling futures hedge in place the effect is significantly diminished. Hedge losses in scenario A and profits in scenario B offset the effect of currency volatility. The total cost is then £277,191 for A and £282,108 for B, a variation of less than £5,000.

So, a substantial proportion of the currency risk is factored out by a static, futures based hedging strategy. Of course, selling the precise amounts of sterling in the forward market would allow the hedger to eliminate completely the currency sensitivity of the transaction. In practice, many corporates, particularly if they plan not to modify the hedge during its life, will prefer to manage their currency risk by accessing the forward market.

A Ratio Hedge

In money markets it is rarely possible to hedge an exposure with a futures contract with an equivalent tenor. Futures are available for forward interest periods lasting 3 months, 5 years, 10 years or 20 years. The exposure being hedged will very often have an interest rate period that differs from these.

Such discrepancies expose the hedger to a significant basis risk. However, it is still possible to protect against adverse interest rate movements using the futures markets.

Consider the case of a bank which has issued a $100m floating rate note (FRN) paying coupons set according to six-month LIBOR with the next interest fixing date in June. It believes that interest rates are rising and therefore wishes to hedge its interest rate exposure in the futures markets. It decides to use the three-month Eurodollar contract which is deliverable in June. How does it determine the appropriate number of contracts to take out?

In the simplified example below, the costs of margin maintenance are ignored and the yield curve is assumed to remain flat. The ratio hedger wishes to immunise against the adverse effect of an increase in rates and will therefore seek to balance the cashflow effect on his hedge with that of his exposure.

The standard futures contract size is $1m and tick is equal to a 1 basis point change in interest rates; the tick value is therefore $25 ($1m × 0.01% × 90/360). The cost, in additional interest of a 1 basis point rise in interest rates, is $5,000 (i.e. $100m × 0.01% × 180/360). The ratio hedger will therefore sell 200 futures to achieve cashflow equivalence.

In February:
4m LIBOR: 8%
6m LIBOR: 8%

7m LIBOR: 8%
June future: 9200 (i.e. 100% minus 8.00%)

   –MARGIN × 200   Sell 200 June futures @ 9200

In June:
3m LIBOR: 9.5%
6m LIBOR: 9.5%
June future: 9050 (delivery price)

   +MARGIN×200   Buy back 200 June futures @ 9050
   +$750,000   Realised p/l on hedge ($25 × 200 ctcts × 150 ticks)
   –$4,750,000   Interest rate cost fixed for FRN (paid in December)

The bank's net interest rate cost, then, is $4m ($4.75m minus $0.75m), equivalent to a six-month rate of 8 per cent. However, the illustration above assumes a number of things. It looks at the effect of a parallel shift in a flat yield curve and this conceals the basis risk inherent in this hedging procedure.

In March, the implied June futures price is detemined by the four-month and seven-month interest rates. By the delivery date, however, the three-month rate has become the underlying instrument for calculating the price of the future. The price behaviour of the future will therefore be affected not just by three-month interest rates, but by other points on the yield curve depending on when the future is due to be delivered.

Secondly, the hedger is attempting to protect cashflows determined by six-month LIBOR with a three-month LIBOR based instrument. Such a ratio hedge will therefore perform properly only in conditions where the yield curve remains flat throughout the life of the hedge. In other words any interest rate changes must affect each maturity to the same extent.

Notwithstanding the basis risk, ratio hedging is in widespread use in both money and and bond markets, where it is seen as the most effective way of protecting against shifts in the yield curves.

The Delta Ratio

The number of futures contracts equivalent to à given exposure is described as the delta or hedge ratio. The delta ratio is a signed amount representing the number of contracts that must be bought or sold exactly to offset the change in value of the underlying exposure for a given, small change in prices.

It should be emphasised that the delta only applies to small price movements; significant price adjustments may alter the characteristics of the exposure. A delta neutral hedged exposure will therefore not necessarily be insensitive to changes in price, though this is the aim of delta hedging.

Delta has a special meaning in options markets. Here it indicates the change in the option premium when the market price of the underlying asset moves by one basis point. A by-product of the option pricing process, it is also used to immunise cashflows from small price movements. It measures the likelihood of option exercise in percentage terms. Option writers who are delta hedgers buy (sell) the underlying commodity in proportion to the amount of calls (puts) they have written. A writer of DM1m put might, for instance, decide to sell DM550,000 if its delta was currently 55 per cent.

What is Meant by Risk Management?

The term risk management has come into use partly for fashionable reasons, the techniques gaining widespread credibility in the wake of Black Monday. But it implies that the motive is risk reduction. This is generally the case, but not always. There is the danger that hedge strategies will underperform when they are directed solely at eliminating risk.

The yield (i.e. the projected reward) is in fact the price that the market is attaching to a given set of risks for the owner of an instrument. As soon as this is recognised it is quickly obvious that 'risk management' involves managing not just risk, but the risk–reward relationship.

The term has come to be applied to many different market participants. At one extreme, risk management relates to an essentially passive hedging activity: for example, the exporter who buys a currency option to protect against the decline in the value of his foreign revenues that would be caused by a strong domestic currency. At the other end of the spectrum, it is integral to the speculative activity: the currency trader, for instance, whose approach to risk management is to buy and sell frequently, relying on limits and trading rules to contain his risk within acceptable limits.

Different risk managers have different priorities. There is no point, for example, in devising a highly sophisticated programme requiring regular rebalancing if the hedging institution has neither the infrastructure nor the expertise successfully to put it into practice.

On the other hand, for the sophisticated institution, it may make little sense to manage exposures with the kind of totality that the occasional hedger might deem necessary. For it must be remembered that every time a risk is managed a potential reward is restricted.

Every risk management problem is different. It follows that the closer the risk manager's understanding of the issues involved the more effective will be his strategy for dealing with his unwanted exposures. It should already be apparent that, in order to derive the maximum benefits from any hedging programme, it is necessary to go further than the simplistic identification of a basic hedging relationship.

Any hedging programme needs to take account of a range of uncertainties: changing judgements, sensitivities, market conditions and underlying exposures. In the final chapter of this book, ConTROL is described as a methodology that enables the user to place a strategy in its proper context.

The Logic of Pre-emptive Hedging

The existence of financial options allows risk managers to choose between an almost infinite variety of strategies for fixing their worst case exposure. The relative performance of such strategies will depend on as yet unknown future price movements. Any hedge, therefore, involves opportunity risks (i.e. the possibility that a different strategy would perform better).

Even for hedgers who feel that they cannot second-guess the market, it is essential to be aware of how such strategies will perform if they are to make informed judgements about their exposure management.

A hedger who always uses the forward markets to fix the cost of raw materials in advance may believe that this is the most inexpensive hedge available to him. But this is not always the case; it will depend very much on how the price changes. Options are also available in exchange for an up-front fee, and these have the extra advantage of being non-binding. This means that whereas a forward purchaser will have to pay the agreed price even though the spot market is considerably lower, with an option there is no such compulsion.

In effect, this hedger is expressing the view that prices in future will exceed the current forward price. For if he really was uncertain about what would happen to the price, surely he would prefer to buy worst case protection with options so that he could benefit from any fall in price? Of course, it might be that the extra cost of buying option protection is prohibitive. But to ascertain their performance, the hedger will have to develop a market view.

The message is clear. Whether hedgers like it or not, selecting any hedging strategy implies a particular view of future price performance. Even if the hedger decides that the market knows best, it is far better to acknowledge this by making the view explicit. Only then can risk managers design cost-effective strategies.

In financial institutions (FIs) the risk–reward equation is implicitly recognised, but not always implemented in a thorough-going way. FIs make their profit by deploying financial resources so that revenues exceed the cost of capital. But the sheer complexity of many of the strategies that they employ to this end can make it difficult to analyse the precise effects of specific activities on the overall balance sheet. Asset-liability management is discussed in more detail in Chapter 6.

In companies, the main risk is the commercial one. So, for many corporate treasurers, management of financial resources is much more about risk reduction than yield enhancement. They are charged with minimising financing costs and protecting revenues. Their company's profit is generated by sales of its products and services. It is not surprising, then, that their attitude to risk management has traditionally been that it was just about buying cover against the worst case.

In recent years, though, the development of coordinated treasury functions, particularly for multinationals, has spurred the adoption of a more active approach to risk management by many corporations. Though a passive approach to hedging has its merits, and is still attractive for certain companies, there is no question that larger corporations derive improved performance from a more active approach.

4: Yield Curves

The Yield Curve

Yields for differing maturities are close substitutes for one another. Supply and demand determine the level of rates for each maturity. Their relative attractiveness depends on expectations about the timing and magnitude of future rate movements.

Take the example of an investor with a one year planning horizon. Her aim is to maximise earnings at the end of the year. Broadly speaking, she has two main alternatives: she can lock into today's one year rate or invest for a shorter period and reinvest capital and income at maturity.

If she expects interest rates to rise she will prefer to invest for the shorter period in the expectation of being able to reinvest at a higher rate in the future. On the other hand if she believes yields will fall during the year, she will wish to fix the rate for the entire year.

A borrower with similar expectations would, of course, do the opposite. So, when the prevailing market view is one of rising rates, short-term rates are forced down because investors out-number borrowers, while long-term rates go higher as the many borrowers who wish to fix a rate must deal with few investors.

Because such market pressures affect the shape of the yield curve, the decision process for our investor is no longer so simple. She may expect rates to rise, but if the market is also discounting this eventuality short-term rates will be lower than the one year rate. The resulting positively sloped yield curve means that, depending on the magnitude of the rise she expects, it may be preferable to lock into the one year rate. If the one month rate is 9 per cent and the one year rate is 11 per cent, the 2 per cent loss in the first month has to be recouped, so rates must average more than 11 per cent over the next 11 months. The investor's decision must be framed in terms of the market conditions and her action determined by how her own view relates to discounted sentiment. She therefore needs first to identify the market consensus.

The general shape of the yield curve contains a great deal of information about the consensus view regarding the speed and scale of future interest rate movements. Using time value of money analysis we can pinpoint the market's predicted yield curve for any date in the future. Not only can this be analysed, it can also be traded: there are numerous mechanisms for locking into future yields.

Figure 4.1 describes the mechanism for deriving a six-month forward T-bill discount rate. A 180 day T-bill is offered at a discount rate of 12.5 per cent (price

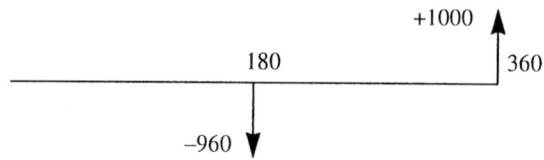

+1000

180   360

−960

Forward purchase of 180-day T-bill in 180 days
time at 8% discount rate (price =96.00)

Equivalent to:

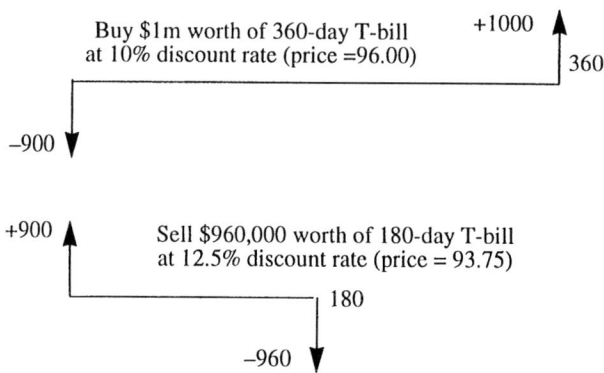

Buy $1m worth of 360-day T-bill   +1000
at 10% discount rate (price =96.00)
                                          360

−900

+900   Sell $960,000 worth of 180-day T-bill
              at 12.5% discount rate (price = 93.75)
                                          180

−960

Figure 4.1 Constructing a 180 T-bill price for forward delivery

= 93.75). A 360 day bill is also available at a discount rate of 10 per cent (price = 90.00). The dealer fixes the forward discount rate today. The $900,000 revenue from the sale of $960,000 worth of 180 day T-bills is used to purchase $1m face value of the 360 day paper. The net result is that the dealer has forward purchased a 180 day T-bill in six months' time at a discount rate of 8 per cent (effective price = 96.00).

It can be seen from Figure 4.1, the T-bill example shown above, that today's yield curve has embedded within it a whole series of future yield curves. In this case the 180 day and 360 day discount rates determine the implied 180 day discount rate for six months' time. A similar procedure can derive the 30, 60, 90, 120, 150 day discount rates for T-bills bought in six months.

Deciphering Expectations from Yield Curve Shape

Effective interest risk management is about anticipating as well as reacting to yield curve shifts. A close understanding of the yield curve is therefore fundamental. By analysing today's cash yield curve it is possible to see exactly when and by how much interest rates are expected to rise or fall in the future. Only when this is known can the practitioner hope to formulate a strategy that reflects his own view of future market conditions.

If the yield curve is flat the expectation is for no change in future interest rates. The more positive (i.e. the higher the long-term rates compared to the short-term) the curve, the swifter the expected rise in rates. Where there is an inverse curve, rates are expected to decline.

Interest rate futures can provide a good indication as to the course of three-month rates in the coming years. FRAs can often be used to look at particular future dates in more detail. But the cash markets provide the most comprehensive guide to market perceptions about the price of money in the coming months.

COMPOUND INTEREST

Compounding describes the process of adding interest to the existing base of capital to form an expanded capital amount on which interest will accrue in future. When valuing financial instruments with disparate maturities, the compounding frequency is a material element.

Albert Einstein once said that compound interest was mankind's greatest invention. A surprising remark coming from the century's most brilliant man, and no doubt it was made partly in jest. Nevertheless, it has to be admitted that there is something slightly miraculous about the exponential process. When one considers that, had his forbear, Isaac Newton, had the opportunity to place just one pound in a 5 per cent per annum compound interest deposit account 300 years ago, today's Newton Foundation would be worth well over £2 million, one can start to see what Einstein might have meant.

Comparing Yields With Different Frequencies.

It is intuitively obvious that receiving interest monthly is preferable to earning it annually. What is perhaps less easy to ascertain is the extent of the difference. If I lend someone $1000 at 12 per cent, even if I consider them to be completely trustworthy, I am bound to prefer receiving $30 every quarter to earning $120 at the end of the year. The key question is how many extra dollars and cents will be required to placate me at the end of the year for not having received interest in previous quarters.

This turns out to be a time value of money problem and the basic formula derived in Chapter 1 can be applied to it. In order to determine the annualised equivalent of a quarterly compounded rate we use the time value of money formula repetitively.

For the quarterly compounded rate to be equated to the annually compounded rate, interest received on each quarter must be reinvested to the end of the year rather than being paid out. The additional interest generated by this process represents the time value of money benefit for the quarterly rate versus the annual rate.

Since all interest is reinvested, the effect is to capitalise it, so that the principal amount at the start of each period is equivalent to capital plus interest at the end of the previous one. The time value of money formula expresses this mathematically:

PV_k = Present Value at the start of the kth compounding period
FV_k = Future Value at the end of the kth compounding period
t = Length of compounding period in years
r = Yield per period, expressed in % per annum

We know that

$$FV_k = PV_k(1+rt)$$

and

$$PV2 = FV1$$
$$PV3 = FV2$$
$$PV4 = FV3$$

so

$$FV1 = PV1(1 + rt)$$
$$FV2 = PV1(1 + rt)(1 + rt)$$
$$FV3 = PV1(1 + rt)(1 + rt).(1 + rt)$$
$$FV4 = PV1(1 + rt)^4$$

In our example, the 12 per cent p.a. rate is compounded quarterly, $t=0.25$ and $PV1=\$1000$. So:

$$FV4 = 1000 \times (1 + 0.12 \times 0.25)^4$$
$$FV4 = 1125.51$$

A 12 per cent quarterly rate is therefore equivalent to an annualised rate of 12.551 per cent. The 55 basis point difference implies a substantial time value of money premium for rates with a high compounding frequency.

The formula may be generalised as follows:

where

n = Number of compounding periods
FV_n = $PV1(1+rt)^n$

or

$$r = ((FV_n/PV1)^{(1/n)} - 1)/t$$

or

$$PV1 = \frac{FV_n}{(1+rt)^n}$$

Reinvestment Risk

Astute readers will have already recognised that yield comparisons between instruments with different frequencies depend on the unspoken assumption that all interest may be reinvested in the future at the current rate. This is unlikely to be what occurs in practice, nor indeed does it reflect the market's perception of future events (which are described by forward–forward yields).

There is in fact a procedure for eliminating reinvestment risks altogether by borrowing amounts that net off unwanted future income flows, but the technique is only suitable in specific situations. (See the section Decoding the Yield Curve for more on forward–forward deposits).

The assumption that today's rate will persist into the future gives market participants a benchmark for comparing yields with different payment profiles. It is widely used in both the money and the capital markets, but, when using it to make yield comparisons, it is as well to understand its implications. For instance, two five-year Eurobonds, paying coupons of 5 per cent and 15 per cent respectively, are priced so that they each offer the investor a 10 per cent annualised yield to maturity. The 5 per cent bond is offered at a price of 81.05, the 15 per cent bond costs 118.95.

Which of the two should the investor purchase to maximise his/her return at the end of five years? The 15 per cent bond has the greater reinvestment risk, as more income is received at the end of each year. The investor's decision will therefore depend on his view about the future course of interest rates over the next four years. If he believes rates will be higher than 10 per cent he will want to buy the 15 per cent bond so he can benefit from the extra income generated by reinvesting coupon proceeds. If he sees rates falling below 10 per cent he will wish to buy the 5 per cent bond, because it is less affected by reduced reinvestment income.

It should be self-evident that the reinvestment risk is greater the higher the coupon. The more that has to be reinvested the larger the amount at risk; zero coupon bonds, which have no interim payments, have no reinvestment risk at all.

Transforming the Compounding Frequency

Although the reinvestment assumption makes it an inexact science, it is nevertheless necessary to be able to convert rates quoted using one compounding frequency to another if we are to compare different financial instruments on an equal basis.

The arithmetic procedure for transforming compounding frequency is relatively straightforward. In the example below a quarterly rate of 8 per cent is transformed into its semi-annual equivalent.

The semi-annual rate assumes interest is paid every six months. Therefore, any interest that would have been paid out on the quarterly rate after the first three months is capitalised. In other words there are two quarterly compounding periods. The future value at the end of six months is therefore $(1 + 0.08/4)^2$, or 1.0404 per \$ invested.

The basic time value of money formula can now be applied to derive the semi-annual rate. This is, of course, 8.08 per cent, i.e. $(1.0404/1 - 1) \times 2$.

Exactly the same procedure may be applied in reverse to derive the quarterly equivalent of a semi-annual rate. There is a half of one six-monthly compounding period in each three-month period. The future value at the end of three months is therefore $(1 + 0.0808/2)^{0.5}$, or 1.02 per \$ invested. After annualising, this equates to a quarterly compounded rate of 8 per cent.

The procedure can be generalised as follows:

Rt_1 = Per annum rate with new compounding frequency
Rt_0 = Per annum rate with existing compounding frequency
t_1 = Length of new compounding period (as proportion of year)
t_0 = Length of existing period (as proportion of year)

$$Rt_1 = ((1 + Rt_0.t_0)^{(t_1/t_0)} - 1).(1/t_1)$$

Interbank interest rates describe the rates at which banks will borrow and lend among themselves for maturities out to two years. For periods maturing within one year, interest is paid at maturity. When the period is longer than one year, interest is paid annually and at maturity.

The headline interbank rates are therefore not entirely consistent with one another. The one month LIBOR describes deposits with a monthly compounding frequency, while one year LIBOR is annually compounded.

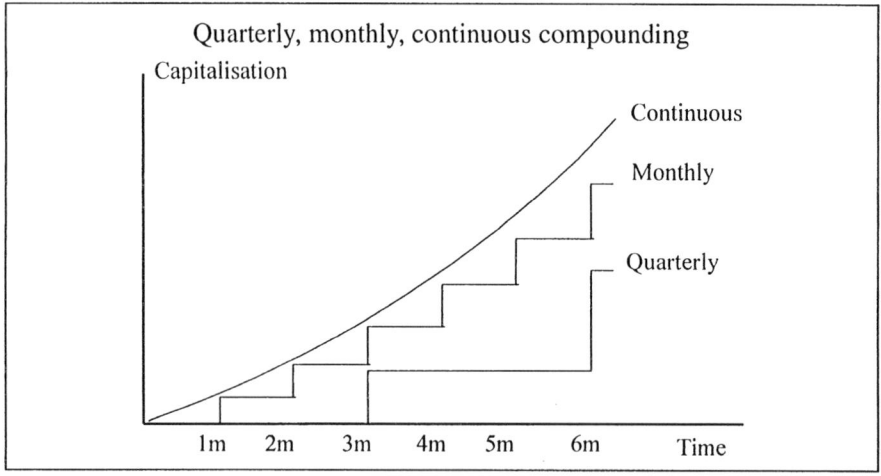

Figure 4.2 The compounding effect

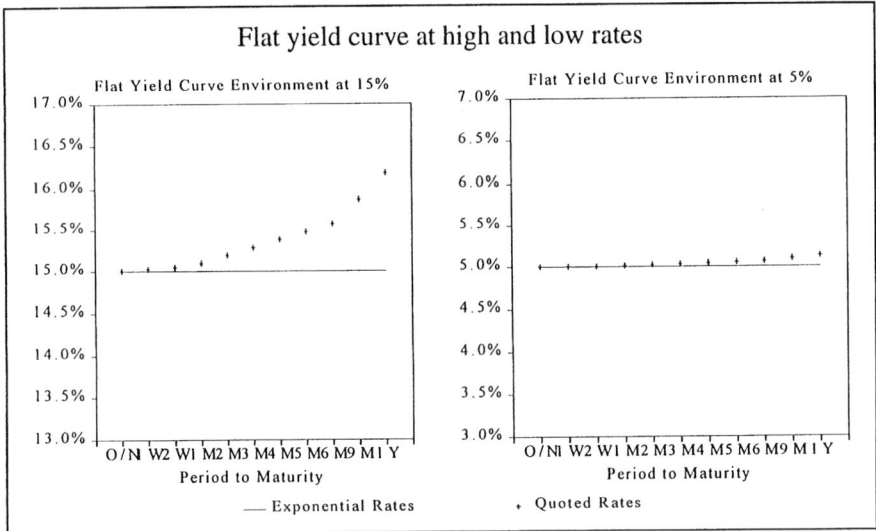

Figure 4.3 Exponential rates versus headline rates

The compounding effect is more pronounced the higher the overall level of rates, a one-month rate of 20 per cent, as compared to a one-year rate of 20 per cent is worth 161 basis points more when compounding is taken into account. At 5 per cent, the difference is just 11 bps. It is necessary to convert all rates to the same compounding frequency before attempting to draw conclusions about market expectations from yield curve shape alone.

Benchmarks for Yield Comparison

We have seen how, when comparing yields for rates with different frequencies, it is necessary to adjust the quoted rates so that all are expressed in consistent terms. Although any frequency may be used as a benchmark, in practice most market participants use either semi-annual or annual as the reference frequency.

One other benchmark, in widespread use in Australian money markets, is of particular importance to analysts. Continuous compounding is a valuable tool in the identification of arbitrage opportunities and in plotting basis relationships.

Continuous compounding assumes that all interest is capitalised immediately and is modelled using the exponent function, e. The exponential rate implies a stable rate of growth no matter what the period and is arguably the 'correct' method of comparing financial yields. The time value of money formulae for continuously compounded rates are as follows:

$$FV = PVe^{rt}$$
$$r = Ln(FV/PV)/t$$
$$PV = FV/e^{rt}$$

YIELD CURVE ANALYSIS

Decoding the Yield Curve

Today's yield curve contains within it the market consensus about future yield curve environments. Today's three-month and six-month interest rates, for instance, can be used to calculate an implicit three-month rate starting in three months' time. Indeed, since it is possible physically to lend (or borrow) on a forward–forward basis, the derived cash rate is realisable.

In practice, market participants seeking to borrow (or lend) at today's forward–forward rate will normally use interest rate futures or FRAs, and not access the cash markets until the forward date. Both FRAs and futures are more flexible and balance sheet efficient than physical borrowing and lending. However, the fact that a forward–forward rate can be generated in the cash markets does mean that there is a possible arbitrage opportunity between cash, futures and FRAs. As a result the forward–forward rate implied by cash underpins the prices for FRAs and interest rate futures by defining the implied basis range.

In Chapter 2 we saw how a forward price can be derived for the purchase of a three-month T-bill in six months' time. In the following example the time value of money is used to derive the yield curve in three months' time implied by today's rates. Mid-rates are used throughout so that the costs of dealing do not distort the expected future rates.

US dollar mid-rates quoted in London for, value 15 March

3 m	6.375	$t = 0.25$
6 m	6.500	$t = 0.5$
9 m	6.750	$t = 0.75$
1 y	6.875	$t = 1$

Implied yield curve for 13 June (90 days later)

For 3 m	Use 3 m and 6 m rates
For 6 m	Use 3 m and 9 m rates
For 9 m	Use 3 m and 1 y rates

The forward rate is generated by borrowing and lending the same amount until the start and end of the period. Capital and interest at the start of the forward period becomes the present value. This is compared with the amount at the end of the forward period, the future value, to derive the rate.

This can be expressed mathematically using time value of money:

Where:

t_F	$=$	Forward period
t	$=$	Period to start of forward period
t_E	$=$	Period to end of forward period

We know that

$$t_F = t_E - t_S$$

and

$$PVF = FVS$$

and

$$FVF = FVE$$

Since we know that:

$$r_F = (FVF/PVF - 1)/t_F$$

then, per $:

$$rF = \frac{((1 + r_E.t_E) - 1)/t_F}{(1 + r_S t_S)}$$

So, the implied yield curve in three months is as follows:

3 m = 6.52%
      i.e. $((1+0.065\times0.5)/(1+0.06375\times0.25) - 1) \times 4$
6 m = 6.83%
9 m = 6.93%

Having derived a future yield curve, in this case that implied for three months forward, the dealer is able to consider how far the market's prediction accords

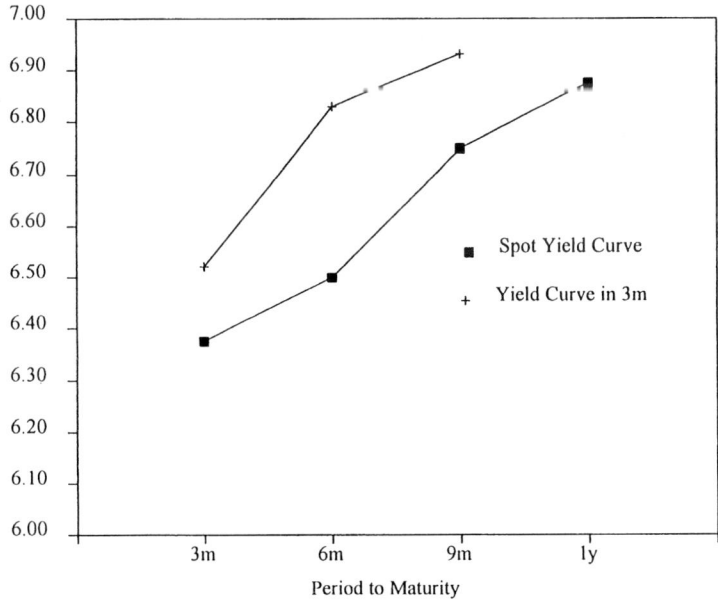

Figure 4.4 The spot yield curve and the implied 3-month forward yield curve

with his own view of future rates. He is then able to devise an appropriate strategy. If he believes the market has underdiscounted a rate increase he might seek to borrow at the forward rate; if he thinks it has overestimated it he may lock into the lending rate.

Deriving Zero Coupon Factors

We saw in Chapter 1 that, to find their present values, future payments and receipts are discounted at the appropriate interest rate. In this way it is possible to describe in time value of money terms the present day equivalent of any future cashflow. In the discussion on cash-and-carry the mobility of cashflows was demonstrated. By borrowing and lending activities, a net cash effect today can be moved to any future date or dates.

Yield curves are a convenient way of describing the time value relationship between different dates, allowing market participants to identify and quantify changes in sentiment. But the time value of money relationship can also be described in terms of the ratio relationships between dates.

A zero coupon factor is simply the amount of cash generated on the cashflow date by $1 (or equivalent) today. Zero coupon factors can be derived for all points on the yield curve using the basic time value of money calculation with the present value set to 1. For instance, the zero coupon factor equivalent to a six-month rate of 10 per cent is 1.05, for a one-year rate of 10 per cent it is 1.1. These factors are the future values of $1. Some market participants use a zero price factor; this is simply the reciprocal, 0.9091 in this case, and expresses the present value of $1 on the future dates.

We could borrow $1 for six months and lend it for a year. This would generate a payment of $1.05 followed by a receipt of $1.1, a 6m/12m forward loan. Using factors it becomes trivial to calculate the forward rate. We employ the basic time value of money equation:

$$r = \left(\frac{fv}{pv} - 1 \right) t^{-1}$$

so:

$$r = \left(\frac{1.1}{1.05} - 1 \right) \times 2$$

$$r = 9.52\ \%$$

Two sets of factors must be found, reflecting the bid and offer yield curves. The bid factors should be applied to outflows, since these are closed out by lending type activities. The offer factors relate to cash inflows on the future dates, which are netted off by borrowing techniques.

Once the factors have been derived the present value of any future cashflow can be found by dividing it by the relevant factor. Multiplying this figure by another factor makes it possible to make direct comparisons between cashflows occurring on different dates.

Finding Factors for Cashflows in more than One Year

Zero coupon factors for the first year will normally be based on interbank yields or T-bills. These are both benchmark yield curve for short-term money and are suitable because their relative lack of credit risk implies a minimal risk premium.

Beyond one year, government securities and interbank rates may still be used, but in either case coupons will also be paid before maturity. The zero coupon factor is defined as the future value of $1 on the date in question, but because there is an intervening coupon the future value is uncertain as part of it is subject to reinvestment risk.

One way out of this dilemma is to use Treasury strips prices. These are government bonds where each future cashflow is sold off separately. But some strips are relatively illiquid or subject to price variation for technical reasons. The main purpose of the zero coupon factor approach is to derive precise market information. For this reason most participants use coupon bearing government bonds, while some prefer to use interbank rates where available. There are no hard and fast rules about precisely which instruments contribute to the zero coupon factor yield curves. The thing to remember is that whatever instruments are chosen, be they cash, bonds, futures or a combination, it must be possible physically to perform the implied cashflow manipulations at the yields described.

If money market rates or bond yields are selected as the benchmark it is necessary to take account of interest paid before the final maturity. Money market instruments generally pay interest annually and the factor must reflect this.

By way of example, consider an eighteen-month bid rate of 10 per cent. This will repay £1.05 in eighteen months for every £1 invested (i.e. capital plus six months interest @ 10 per cent). However, the lender will also receive £0.1 in interest at the end of the first year. This receipt must be netted out before the zero coupon factor can be found. This is done by borrowing an amount at the one year rate such that the capital and interest repaid is equal to the interest receipt. If the one year offer rate is 10 per cent, we know that its factor will be 1.1. The amount that has to be borrowed is therefore £0.09091 (0.1/1.1). If this were to occur the net investment today would fall to £0.90909 (1 – 0.09091). So per £ invested the equivalent amount in eighteen months will be £1.155 (1.05/0.90909), and this is therefore the bid factor for that date. To find the other eighteen-month factor we transpose bids with offers in the above calculations.

The adjustment allows for the effect of stripping out intermediate cashflows. Positive cashflows are closed out by using the borrowing, i.e. the offer factors. To close out negative cashflows on intermediate dates, bid factors should be used.

The adjustment calculation is used repetitively for instruments with more than one interest date and in this way the zero coupon curve is built up. The general form of the procedure is described below:

Where:

FV_n = Cashflow occurring on factor date n per \$1
Cpn = Coupon rate
Price = Cost today of owning \$1 of bond (\$1 for interbank)
$t_1 .. t_k$ = Length of coupon period in years ending on date k
ZCF_k = Zero coupon factor for date k

$$ZCFn = \frac{FV_n}{Price - Cpn \times (ZCF_1.t_1 + ZCF_2.t_2 + \cdots + ZCF_{(n-1)}.t_{(n-1)})}$$

The formula will produce different result according to whether the zero coupon factor being sought is on the bid or the offer side of the yield curve. Offer side zero coupon factors are applied to the coupons to find a bid factor, bid factors are used to close out coupons if an offer factor is being identified.

Using Zero Coupon Factors in Yield Curve Mapping

Having derived bid and offer zero coupon factors, the results can be applied to the analysis of all cashflow based instruments. Using the factors as the benchmark provides for a much more rigorous approach to financial valuation. Analysts can use the factors to provide an arbitrageable cashflow map of future dates.

Central to the yield curve mapping approach that it is physically possible to generate cashflow amounts according to the ratios specified by the factors. So long as this is the case, yield curve mapping is a superior analytic tool for evaluation to other techniques in regular use. Bonds, for example, are generally priced according to a yield to maturity assumption. The price is in fact a present value derived according to an assumption of a single yield relating it to the stream of future cashflows. Similar quality bonds with roughly equal durations will tend to trade at similar yields to maturity. But supposing two such bonds have different cashflow characteristics: one has a 15 per cent annual coupon the other a 5 per cent coupon. We can find their present values by dividing each cashflow by the relevant factor. These implied prices would almost certainly be different from the actual prices quoted in the market.

There are several arbitrage opportunities here. We could identify an under-priced bond, buy it in the market and net off its future cashflows by borrowing against each of its cashflow dates. The bond can be held to maturity and the borrowing proceeds used to cover the cost of its purchase leaving us with a realised arbitrage profit. Alternatively we could use yield curve mapped pricing to identify opportunities for bond switching.

Yield curve mapping may also be used to enhance the accuracy of duration calculations. This technique is discussed in Chapter 12.

5: Currency Price Behaviour

FUNDAMENTAL DETERMINANTS OF CURRENCY VALUE

The Cyclical Nature of Currency Prices

Ever since the breakdown of the Bretton Woods agreement when the post-war fixed exchange rate environment collapsed, the value of currencies has been akin to that of any other commodity. In other words, supply and demand pressures now dictate whether one currency appreciates or depreciates against other currencies.

Predicting currency performance is notoriously difficult. In the world of foreign exchange intangible factors such as reputation, fashion and hype predominate. Economic fundamentals only impinge on value in the long-term, and, as Keynes once said 'in the long term we are all dead'. Currencies are notorious for the cyclical nature of their price behaviour – a market where the price can rise by 10 per cent then fall by 15 per cent (as the Deutschmark did against the dollar in just one day in July 1985) harbours substantial risks for the non-specialist.

It was currency market volatility during the 1980s that did more than anything else to persuade international corporations that they should adopt a more active role in the risk management of their financial exposures. When a major car exporter can return record quarterly losses at the same time as achieving record foreign sales, the need to manage currency risk becomes pressing.

Purchasing Power Parity

The theoretical underpinning of international currency values is the theory of purchasing power parity (PPP). PPP states that, in the long-term, currency rates will adjust to a level where consumers in the various domestic economies pay equivalent prices for the same goods. One light-hearted manifestation of this theory is the *Wall Street Journal*'s 'Big Mac Index'. The Big Mac Index is published on an occasional basis and measures the relative dollar-based cost of buying a MacDonald's hamburger around the world. PPP predicts that this should be the same, so countries where Big Macs are more expensive have over-valued currencies, while those where Big Macs are relatively cheap have under-valued currencies which are liable to increase in the future.

The Big Mac Index is, of course, an oversimplification of PPP. But it highlights one of the practical weaknesses of the theory. In order to measure accurately relative purchasing power, it is necessary to take account of differing perceptions of value around the globe. These may be because of infrastructural differences; consumers in an economy with free health-care will not place as much value on pharmaceutical products, a country with efficient public transport will not demand as many cars.

Differences in consumption patterns can arise for innumerable reasons: cultural and climatic variations, tax regimes and wealth distribution to name but a few. It is therefore extremely difficult to formulate a basis for measuring PPP values.

PPP and Inflation Differentials

Rather than rely on current patterns therefore, economic forecasters will look at inflation statistics as a measure of future currency price behaviour. According to PPP, the inflation differential between two economies will reflect their future relative price performance.

A high inflation economy will in future produce more expensive exports; future imports by contrast will become cheaper in terms of the domestic currency, assuming no change in the exchange rate. Since PPP assumes that foreign products are identical to the domestic ones in every respect other than price, the process is one of import substitution. The effect of this will be to open a balance-of-trade deficit in the high inflation economy as consumers buy more imports, and exports become harder to sell.

This balance-of-trade deficit implies a reduced demand for the domestic economy's currency by foreign importers as well as an increase in the supply of the currency because domestic importers will have to sell more of it in order to purchase more of the foreign currency to meet the increased demand for their imported products. The corollary of this is seen in the low inflation economy where increased exports and reduced imports lead to increased demand and reduced supply for that country's currency.

According to PPP, this supply–demand effect will make the exchange rate between the two economies self-adjusting. In other words, the high inflation economy's currency will depreciate against the low inflation currency by the relative inflation differential. Countries with a balance-of-payments deficit will see the value of their currencies declining against those with which they have a balance-of-payments surplus until the two have a neutral trade position.

Practical Limitations to PPP

Of course, this hardly ever seems to happen in practice. Countries like Japan and Germany can retain balance-of-trade surpluses for years on end. Perhaps more surprising, others (the USA for instance) can maintain balance-of-trade deficits for considerable periods without currency adjustments. Partly this has to do with issues like product quality and uniqueness, which limit the level of price sensitivity on internationally traded items. Eventually, trade imbalances will become unsustainable and currency price adjustments occur. However, the timing and scale of such adjustments owes more to international investor confidence than the technical workings of PPP.

The J-curve Effect

The other complicating factor is that even if there is an adjustment to the value of a currency, it is by no means certain that the trade position will move in the right direction. This is largely because of leads and lags in price responsiveness, the J-curve effect.

The extent to which foreign imports are reduced by a depreciating domestic currency is entirely dependent on changes in expenditure patterns. Experience has shown that it can take time for consumers to adjust their spending patterns after a fall in the domestic currency's international value. Domestic manufacturers cannot necessarily increase their production immediately to take advantage of any price differential. On the export side it is possible to reduce the foreign currency price of commodities quite quickly, but this will not necessarily encourage an instantaneous upsurge in foreign demand.

The result is that for perhaps a year to eighteen months after a currency's depreciation the balance-of-trade position may actually worsen before it starts to improve. The same occurs in reverse when a currency appreciates. For instance, Japan's vast trade surplus has not reduced despite the yen's rapid rise in the late 1980s. During the inverted J-curve period, the major exporters took advantage of the strengthening yen to invest in productive capacity overseas, and the manufacturing economy as a whole moved up-market to limit the price effect on its exporting capacity.

Hot Money Flows and the Capital Account

The idea that currency values should adjust to maintain balance-of-trade neutrality between nations according to inflation differentials is not supported by the evidence. In fact, perceptions play a much larger role in determining currency values than economic fundamentals.

Hot money flows are one expression of speculative interest in a currency. Essentially, these are short-term capital flows that are moved in and out of currencies in search of the highest reward and lowest risk. When one considers that only around 10 per cent of foreign exchange turnover is estimated to be related to trade, it is obvious that speculators have an important role to play in setting currency values.

Interest Rate Parity

Hot money flows introduce nominal interest rates into exchange rate price deter-
mination. Consider, for instance, a German investor looking to maximise his
returns over the next month. He is interested in the number of Deutschmarks he
will receive at the end of the period for a given amount invested. He can either
place his funds in a Deutschmark deposit account and earn the current interest
rate. Alternatively, he can use his Deutschmarks to buy a foreign currency, earn
that currency's interest rate over the next month and then sell the proceeds back
into Deutschmarks at the end of the period.

There is obviously extra risk involved in doing this, since he may realise a
capital loss at the end of the period if the foreign currency has depreciated
against the Deutschmark when he tries to sell it. The risk can be measured,
though, and is equivalent to the time-adjusted interest differential between the
two currencies. For instance, supposing the 30-day Italian interest rate is 3 per
cent higher than that for Deutschmarks, the investor's risk is that the Lire
declines by more than 0.25 per cent (3 per cent divided by 12) against the
Deutschmark over the next month.

The interest rate parity argument is used in conjunction with opportunity cost
pricing to determine forward FX rates. .

Table 5.1 shows some sample break-even future spot prices that define the
decision-making process for a US dollar based investor with $10m to invest for
90 days. Cashflows are shown in thousands.

Table 5.1

Currency/spot rate	Foreign currency equivalent	3m rate	Foreign currency proceeds	Break-even spot
US dollar/NA	−10,000	6.63%	+10,156	NA
Deutschmark/1.4760	−14,760	9.00%	+15,092	1.4860
Yen/130.46	−1,304,000	7.88%	+1,330,284	130.98
Australian dollar/1.2705	−12,705	11.25%	+13,062	1.2861

Break-even future spot rates are arrived at by calculating the conversion price
that will provide the investor with $10.156m after 90 days. The break-even
exchange rate against yen is therefore 130.98 (1,330,284 divided by 10,000). It
can be seen that the larger the interest differential the more the spot rate can
move before the investor starts to lose money. The Australian dollar can depreciate by 1.23 per cent (1.2861 divided by 1.2705) before it hits the break-even.
For the yen, however, where the interest differential is much smaller at 1.25 per
cent, the level of depreciation is just 0.4 per cent before the investor is worse off
than he would have been had he invested in US dollars.

Monetary Policy and the Exchange Rate

Since investors look at interest rates and currency strength when deciding in which currency they should place their funds, governments can affect the price of their currencies by changing domestic interest rates. By raising interest rates they encourage foreign investors to buy the currency and this pushes the exchange rate up. Lowering the interest rate relative to competing economies will have a depressive effect on the exchange rates.

It is vital to remember, though, that investors view a positive interest differential as a cushion against the capital losses they would suffer from a currency depreciation. If investors are convinced that a currency is overvalued, raising interest rates can have only a marginal effect on its value. Since the relative value of currencies can change by a large margin over very short periods, substantial interest differentials as well as other measures to improve economic performance may be required to have a meaningful effect on the exchange rate. The UK government learnt this lesson to its cost in 1992 when it attempted to halt a speculative surge against sterling by raising rates three times in one day, to no avail.

Nevertheless, in the short and medium term, relative interest rates will tend to have a more significant effect on exchange rates than PPP based analysis. Although PPP is important in the long term, its relevance to the level of the exchange rate is limited to the way in which it affects market expectations, rather than any direct relationship.

INSTITUTIONAL DETERMINANTS OF CURRENCY VALUE

Government Policy

In recent years there has been a sustained trend towards policies that promote the idea of 'sound money', but it has not always been so. In the post-war boom years it was accepted practice for governments to maintain large fiscal deficits in order to sustain and promote domestic growth. Both by increasing the supply of money to the markets, encouraging the expansion of private credit, and large scale issuing of government bonds, they are able to finance persistent trade deficits without necessarily having to contemplate a devaluation of the currency.

Foreign investors will sooner or later require higher yields to compensate them for holding the increased number of securities this will entail. A persistent trade deficit will therefore ultimately require interest rates to rise. This is precisely what happened in the early 1980s when President Mitterrand attempted to finance rapid growth in the French economy by a radical increase in sovereign debt. As French interest rates were forced up by the international investor community the French dash for growth soon ran out of steam and the government had to abandon its expansionist policies.

The French experience brought home a harsh fact of economic life. The interdependence of the global financial community has eroded the economic sovereignty of nations to the point where any government's room for manoeuvre is severely constrained. Not even the United States is immune: the price for the 1980s experiment with Reaganomics, where a huge budget deficit financed rapid growth, came down to earth with a bump in October 1987. The role of the dollar as the world's main reserve currency sustained the fiscal expansion for several years, but this only meant that when the end came it was that much more savage.

Central Bank Intervention

The world's major central banks have a significant role to play in setting the level of exchange rates. As controllers of the money supply and interest rates they can affect exchange rates indirectly. Some countries maintain exchange controls, but amongst the advanced economies it is generally agreed that the practice is anachronistic and it is dying out.

Central banks also play a role in setting exchange rates by intervening directly in the markets. Their effectiveness is limited, however, by the huge volumes of FX traded. According to some estimates the total global reserve base of the world's central banks is equivalent to little more than a day's turnover in foreign exchange.

The Coordinated Approach

It is no wonder then that central banks coordinate their FX intervention activities. They limit their role to smoothing out some of the more extreme cyclical variations in currency values. By coordinating their activities they improve their chances of affecting prices.

The main vehicle for this coordination, is the G7 Group (also the G3 Group, comprising the USA, Germany and Japan) of leading economies whose pronouncements are closely followed by FX dealers.

Timing and Credibility

For the central banks two qualities are of paramount importance if they are to intervene effectively: timing and credibility. As regards timing they monitor the markets closely in an attempt to avoid intervening to prevent or reverse a concerted move. Intervention in the face of a wave of speculation is liable to fail, so instead they attempt to set a market tone and limit their activities to times when the market is uncertain about the next price move.

Credibility is essential if the market is to move as central bankers hope. Any element of uncertainty, inconsistency or lack of purposefulness will be seized upon by speculators. Indeed there have been occasions when a badly coordinated attempt to support a currency has been taken as a sell signal and has had the opposite effect from that intended.

Financial Institutions

Commercial banks and investment banks are the main market makers for foreign exchange. Most activity is focused around the main money centres, Tokyo, London and New York. London, because of its central geographical location, is the most active centre of the three, accounting for some 40 per cent of daily turnover.

FX dealers quote two way prices in all the major currencies against the dollar. In addition, many banks make markets in the major cross rates (i.e. where neither currency is the US dollar). Typically they do not take on large speculative positions, aiming instead to make their profits by trading in and out of currencies on a regular basis.

Because of the sheer volume of FX transacted, the markets are acutely sensitive to information. Dealers keenly await the publication of economic statistics, buying or selling in response to how the figures measure up against market expectations. The price effect of any piece of news must always be viewed in the context of discounted sentiment. News is never good or bad in isolation: the dealing adage of 'buy the rumour, sell the event' is especially true in FX markets.

The Distortive Effect of Market Focus

At any given moment in the FX markets there will be a few currencies that are particularly actively traded. Speculative interest tends to focus on those currencies that are clearly over- or under-valued. The effect of this can be to overemphasise the price impact of these 'vogue' currencies while under-emphasising currencies that are not so much in fashion.

Similarly, there can be an element of post-justification in the market's response to news. News that confirms the prevailing view will be taken more seriously by markets, while news that contradicts the current consensus may be ignored, or dismissed as an aberration. It is vital therefore for currency managers to be acquainted with the current market tone, or context, if they are to predict the effect that any given news item will have on values.

By way of example,Table 5.2 lists some of the main economic statistics and illustrates their possible price effects in bullish and bearish market environments.

The example statistics in Table 5.2 show the importance of understanding the market context for any news item. What is most relevant is not the economist's definition of the impact of a statistic or news item, but how the market will respond. Participants must also beware of inaccuracies in published statistics. Trade figures, for instance, are arrived at by subtracting the total volume of imports from total exports. Relatively small reporting errors in these two very large figures can translate into large differences in the trade balance.

In January 1990, for instance, the UK reported a record trade deficit of £2.5 billion for December 1989. The government stated when it published the figures that they were subject to a margin of error of £2 billion! This highlights the fact that, especially when looking at trade numbers, a series of figures should be considered before arriving at a view as to the state of the economy. Despite this, there is normally an immediate psychological impact on price, particularly where the published number departs from the figure anticipated by the analysts.

Table 5.2 Lies, damned lies and statistics

Statistic (above expectations)	Bullish on currency	Bearish on currency
Inflation	Monetary policy will tighten Interest rates will rise *Buy signal*	Reduced competitiveness Balance-of-trade deficit *Sell signal*
GDP/Industrial Production	Strong economic performance *Buy signal*	Spectre of inflation *Sell signal*
Interest Rates	Inflation is under control *Buy signal*	Currency is weak *Sell signal*
Money Supply	Interest rates will have to rise *Buy signal*	Inflation will rise *Sell signal*
Trade Deficit	Offset by capital account Interest rates will rise *Buy signal*	Not sustainable Sell signal
Inventories	Economy slowing down Inflation will fall *Buy signal*	Manufacturers expect inflation Inflation will rise *Sell signal*

TECHNICAL DETERMINANTS OF CURRENCY VALUE

As we have already seen, psychological factors play a significant role in determining foreign exchange rates. For many traders these are considered so important that they ignore economic fundamentals altogether, preferring instead to concentrate on price pattern behaviour. Although it can be argued that this technical approach to predicting future prices is illogical it is used with success by many market participants and as such cannot be ignored.

Whether or not the study of recurring price patterns has a sound theoretical basis, the mere fact that it is widely used is enough to ensure that it has predictive power. If enough traders believe the price will move in a particular direction, their reasoning is immaterial. The fact that they all act on their assumptions will tend to confirm their prediction. If traders, in sufficient numbers, believe the dollar will strengthen, whether because of economics, technical analysis, astrology or the price of beetroot, their increased demand will itself push the price up.

The advent of screen based trading and digital data feeds has encouraged an explosion in price pattern analysis. The fact that each traded price can automatically be fed into a computer, means that price behaviour can be tracked with considerable accuracy. FX and futures markets, as the most liquid markets with very high quality information available in real time are particularly suitable for such techniques.

Momentum Modelling

Momentum modelling is one of the simplest and, arguably, the most effective form of analysis. It works from the assumption that price behaviour is cyclical and aims to measure the acceleration or deceleration in price changes. The idea is to spot the start of a new trend or the end of an existing one and it is particularly appropriate for market makers who aim to take regular, small profits from cyclical variations.

Moving averages are used to minimise the distortive effect of individual deals. The dealer compares a short-term moving average with a longer term one to try to determine when the market is overbought (i.e. the price will fall) or oversold (i.e. the price will rise).

The period length of the moving average will depend on the trader's requirements. A strategic position taker might compare a one-day average with a one-week average; many traders now look at much shorter periods: for instance the five minute average against the thirty minute average. Buy and sell signals are when the two averages cross over (known as cross-over points).

An illustration of the process, using two-day versus five-day averages for $/DM rates, is shown in Table 5.3 and Figure 5.1.

Table 5.3

Day	$/DM	Two-day average	Five-day average
1	1.4750	—	—
2	1.4760	1.4755	—
3	1.4766	1.4763	—
4	1.4768	1.4767	—
5	1.4774	1.4771	1.4764
6	1.4772	1.4773	1.4768
7	1.4770	1.4771	1.4770
8	1.4766	1.4768	1.4770
9	1.4766	1.4766	1.4770
10	1.4776	1.4772	1.4770

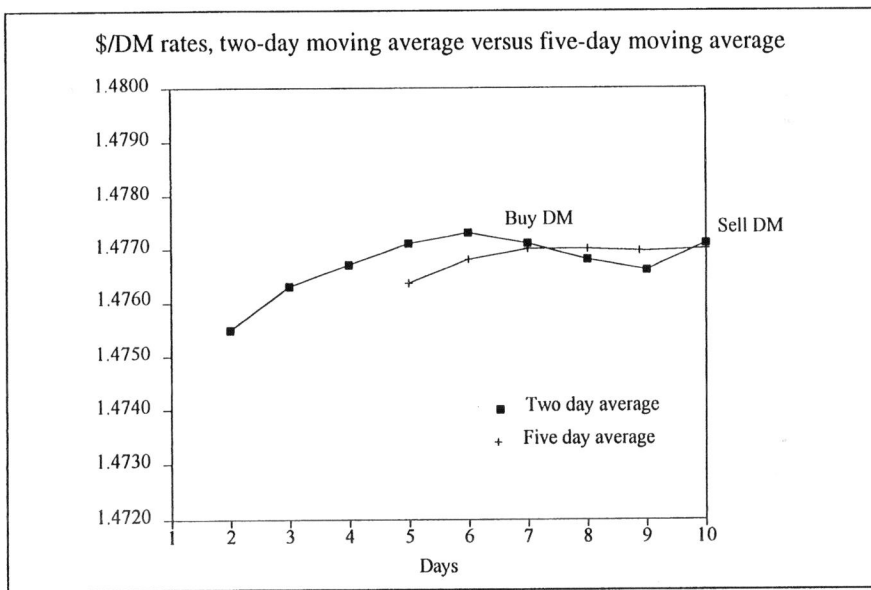

Figure 5.1 Momentum models chart cyclical behaviour

We can see that on day 8 the five-day moving average goes above the two-day. This indicates the start of a downward trend in the exchange rate (i.e. the DM is strengthening against the dollar) and suggests that the dealer should sell dollars and buy Deutschmarks. By day 10 the trend is reversing, as the five-day average moves below the two-day, and the dealer ought to sell Deutschmarks.

In the event this dealer has realised a ten pip loss on the two deals, which shows the risks of slavishly adhering to any system. He bought in DM1.4766 for every dollar he sold and had to pay out DM1.4776 to get that dollar back.

However, particularly if he monitors every single price fluctuation, adherents suggest that he should tend to make money in the long term.

Technical Analysis

The other method of monitoring price behaviour which has gained many followers is technical analysis, or charting. A complete explanation of the elements involved in this technique is beyond the scope of this book, suffice it to say that it has an important role in market psychology.

Chartists record every single traded price and predict trading channels within which they expect markets to trade. If any price goes outside of these limits (the lower limit is called a support level, and the upper one known as a resistance point), it is an indication that a new trading range has been established.

Chartists base their predictions on the idea that certain, identifiable price patterns recur, no matter what the commodity being traded. Example patterns might be flags, wedges and pennant formations, all of which are supposed to indicate that a previous price rise (or fall) will be followed by a subsequent price rise (or fall). Chartists speak an arcane language all their own; other recognised price formations include double tops and bottoms, head and shoulders, saucers and inverse saucers, V and W formations, descending tops and rising bottoms. For non-specialists, it is not essential to understand the minutiae of the charting process, but it is useful for them to be aware of the psychological implications of the technical analysts' predictions.

DETERMINANTS OF VALUE FOR INDIVIDUAL CURRENCIES

The US Dollar Sector

The dollar has a special place in international markets, and its value is determined by the health of the global markets as much as by the state of the American economy. Despite some decline in its popularity since October 1987 it is still the world's main reserve currency. It is widely used in international trade and often preferred by exporters to earning revenues in their own currency.

In recent years the US dollar has replaced gold as the main safe haven for investors' money. At times of international crisis or uncertainty demand for dollars will generally increase as investors liquidate their non-dollar assets in the flight to quality.

The Dollar's Role as a Reserve Currency

As a reserve currency, international investors hold the dollar as a store of value and this explains why the US economy was able to sustain a $200 billion trade deficit for several years in the 1980s. After Black Monday, the American Congress set stringent targets for the reduction of the US budget deficit, but at the time of writing the US remains easily the world's largest debtor nation.

The fact that many investors hold dollars for reasons that are unrelated to trade with the USA helps to underpin its value. One reason that the 1980s bull market was allowed to continue for so long was because investors recognised that it was in their own interests to continue to demand dollars. Japanese investors in particular held large dollar based portfolios and they recognised that a concerted attempt on their part to sell US dollars would result in their incurring huge losses.

The Dollar in Commodities Markets

International commodities are priced in dollars and this provides another reason for owning the currency. Economies that are major commodity exporters have an exposure to the US dollar and the value of their own currency is likely to be related to the strength or weakness of the US dollar.

Similarly, at the micro level commodities producers based outside the USA have a continuing exposure to the dollar. Since their costs of production are likely to be denominated in their domestic currency, while revenues are dollar based, as the dollar weakens their profit margins can be seriously affected. Indeed, almost every non-American manufacturer has some kind of exposure to the dollar: the domestic cost of energy and raw materials will be affected by variations in the dollar.

Dollar-related Economies

Recognising the influence of the dollar over their own economic performance, a number of economies have chosen to relate the value of their currencies to the value of the dollar.

Some countries, such as Canada, Hong Kong and Singapore have chosen to pursue a fixed exchange rate policy to minimise dollar volatility. In others central banks pursue an informal policy of smoothing out variations against the dollar via intervention in FX markets, interest rate manipulation and control of the money supply. The dollar's sway thus extends to many parts of the global financial community.

The European Monetary System

The European Monetary System (EMS) provides a fixed exchange rate regime via the Exchange Rate Mechanism (ERM) for subscribing EC member countries. The ERM was designed to encourage trade within Europe by promoting a stable exchange rate environment. In the 1990s its emphasis altered towards a system that would prepare the ground for a common currency. In 1992 systemic weaknesses in the system came to the fore. With the strong Deutschmark dictating currency relationships, interest rates in all other ERM currencies had to be maintained above German levels for the parities to be maintained. With the costs of German unification necessitating high German interest rates, other countries were locked into a recessionary cycle and were unable to reduce interest rates to encourage growth. This came in combination with a crisis of confidence in the future of Europe triggered by Denmark's rejection of the Maastricht Treaty and uncertainty about the outcome of a referendum in France. Sensing blood the markets sold the weaker currencies forcing several devaluations and the exit of sterling from the system in September 1992.

In 1993 the ERM's credibility was fatally undermined when pressure on the French franc forced member governments to introduce a new wide band of 15 per cent. In effect the fixed exchange rate system has, for the moment, been abandoned in all but name. At the time of writing, the collapse in the credibilty of the ERM mechanism has put its future in doubt as anything more than a *de facto* fixed rate regime between Germany and its satellite economies.

Practical Effects of the Exchange Rate Mechanism

The ERM's credibility is tied to the momentum for a European 'supra-nation'. In practice it has led to an increase in the importance of the Deutschmark in world markets and a wider role for the Bundesbank. As Europe's powerhouse economy, it sets the benchmark for subscribing European economies, whose domestic interest rates are determined by Deutschmark yields.

The process of adjustment to a low inflation, low interest rate economy can be extremely painful, involving as it does high unemployment and, possibly, recession. It remains to be seen whether the ERM can recover from its major shocks and whether it can accommodate the inclusion of some of the less developed European economies. One clear risk is that economic activity will be progressively transferred away from these and towards the German economy, so it may need to be bolstered by a much increased regional policy dimension. The key to the long-term success of the ERM rests in its ability to foster economic convergence amongst member nations. This has led to calls for a European central bank with responsibility for setting interest rates and control of Europe's money supply.

The Role of the ECU

As well as being the linchpin of the ERM, the ECU is the standard accounting unit for the European Community. The ECU began life as a synthetic basket of European currencies, but in recent years it has begun to develop into a major currency in its own right.

ECU exchange rates and interest rates are still related to its constituent currencies and the mathematical relationship is an arbitrageable one. However, major government issuing activity in both T-bill and Treasury bond form, notably by the UK, Italy and France, is encouraging ECU benchmarks to be determined directly rather than according to the level of its constituent currencies.

How Will the ECU Develop ?

Political momentum within the European Community and the logic of a single monetary authority for administering the ERM mechanism have created pressure for the ECU to be adopted as a single currency for the EC nations. The argument as to whether this should happen has by no means been won, but, among the converted, there are two main strands of thought.

What might be termed the institutional approach has been set out by the European Commission in its paper on monetary union. This envisages the formation of a European central bank which would oversee the replacement of European currencies by a single currency. It advocates target dates for this, and for the reduction in ERM bands to zero as a necessary precondition.

An evolutionary approach is proposed by the UK government. This calls for a 'hard ECU' to be introduced alongside the existing currencies. This ECU's key feature would be that it would not be allowed to devalue against any European currencies. Individual governments could, if they chose, convert some of their own currencies into ECUs by lodging funds with a European monetary authority, which would be responsible for setting ECU interest rates. By letting the ECU develop in parallel with existing currencies, so the argument goes, the inflationary implications of introducing a new currency could be avoided.

The UK government's argument, though it has technical merits, is not surprisingly given short shrift by its community partners. The UK has an opt-out on the common currency clause of the Maastricht Treaty and it is no longer a member of the ERM.

The Swiss Franc

The Swiss National Bank (SNB) has traditionally pursued a policy of allowing the Swiss franc to float freely against other currencies. Recently, however, the

SNB adopted an informal policy of shadowing the Deutschmark. In early 1991, it announced that the Swiss/Deutschmark cross rate would in future be the determining criterion for its FX intervention activities. As a result it is now viewed by market participants as a *de facto* member of the ERM.

The strength of the Swiss economy underpins the currency. Its strong manufacturing capability together with the large capital inflows that it enjoys because of the popularity of its private banking system allow it to maintain exchange rates above their PPP theoretical level and to keep interest rates low. However, it remains to be seen, following its announcement that, as from 1992, the anonymity of Swiss bank accounts were to be abolished, whether it can continue to attract substantial capital flows in the future.

The strong demand for the Swiss franc by foreign investors means that it displays many of the characteristics of a reserve currency. Although the state of the Swiss economy is the main determinant of its value, it is also linked to the health of the global economy. At times of high uncertainty, Swiss franc prices will often out-perform other currencies.

The Yen

The other major market sector is governed by the yen. The strength of the yen has been a feature of recent years and is related to Japan's status as the world's most important creditor nation. Demand for the yen is fuelled by the needs of importers and, as Japanese companies and its powerful investment institutions continue to extend their holdings of foreign assets, it is becoming much more important as an internationally traded currency.

Traditionally rapid GNP growth is seen as a bearish factor for the currency because of inflationary pressures. The Japanese economy has shown itself to be remarkably resilient and inflation, although increasing, remains low by international standards.

Problems for foreign companies in penetrating the Japanese economy are cited as one factor behind its being able to continue to deliver enormous trade surpluses, despite the appreciation of the currency. At least as important, however, has been the remarkable ability of Japanese manufacturers to continue to improve productivity, quality and productive flexibility, largely because of the widespread application of robotics and information technology.

Exotic Currencies

Currencies that are not actively traded internationally are known as exotics. These might include currencies such as the South African rand or Greek drachmas. Organisations with an exposure to exotics must also take account of the illiquidity penalty when assessing currency sensitivity. Deals are not always do-able, particularly if they are in any way non-standard. Every transaction will carry a heavy burden of cost, because of the width of the bid–offer spread in such markets.

6: Money Market Instruments

This section describes briefly the main types of interest bearing assets and liabilities. It also describes the quotation conventions for the various markets. Risk managers need to know precisely how much cash they will pay and receive, and on which future dates, if they are to make informed decisions. They must therefore understand the cashflow implications of the headline rates and prices as quoted on Reuters, Telerate, Bloomberg, etc.

T-bills

In many countries the most actively traded market is the Treasury bill market. Governments issue T-bills – short-term paper with specific maturities out to one year – on a regular basis, often weekly.

T-bills are usually issued at a discount to their face value and rates are quoted on a discount rate basis. The discount rate convention describes the amount of interest payable to the owner of an asset in advance. The mechanism for translating discount rates to their yield equivalents is described in Chapter 7. Apart from the UK, most markets use the actual/360 day convention when quoting rates. So, for instance, the 90-day US T-bill quoted at a discount rate of 8 per cent can be purchased at a price of 98.00 (90/360 × 8% × par).

Since the government is generally also the supplier of the currency its creditworthiness is not in doubt. Especially where the T-bill markets are actively traded, yields on T-bills will be lower than those available in any other market for the same currency and maturity. Recently a number of European governments have begun to issue ECU denominated T-bills. This is providing a benchmark yield curve for ECU short-term assets.

Interbank Deposits

Banks lend and borrow between themselves using the interbank markets. As the rates in these markets reflect their cost of finance they act as benchmark rates in other money markets. There are two main market segments: the domestic markets and the Euro markets.

Rates in the Euro markets will typically be a few basis points higher than the equivalent periods in domestic markets. This reflects the small, but perceptible, extra risk involved in holding funds offshore. The difference is greater where there is most regulation and most liquidity. US domestic rates will typically be quoted significantly below Eurodollar rates for example.

Interest rates in the Euro markets are widely referenced as a benchmark by other interest bearing assets. Some argue that it is not obvious why this should still be the case, but it came about because of the perception of banks as being the safest institutions with which to place money. It is certainly true that some very high quality assets pay floating rate interest below current interbank rates, sovereign debt for instance. But in the main, especially in Euro markets, all other floating rate borrowers pay a margin above the interbank rate.

When people talk about LIBid and LIBOR they are referring to the bid and offer rates quoted by banks in London, and this is probably the most widely used benchmark in the money markets. Sterling LIBOR is, of course, a domestic rate, while dollar LIBOR is a Euro market rate. Together with LIBOR there are a range of other reference rates: NYBOR (New York), SIBOR (Singapore), FIBOR (Frankfurt), PIBOR (Paris), HIBOR (Hong Kong) and TIBOR (Tokyo) are among the most common.

It is important to realise that LIBOR is not just one rate; individual banks quote different LIBORs depending on their funding needs. For this reason, instruments paying coupons according to LIBOR will normally specify exactly what this means. For example, the standard clause in a typical floating rate note prospectus defines six-month LIBOR at that quoted at 11 a.m. in London by six named banks, ignoring the highest and the lowest, and averaging the remaining four. The result is then rounded up to the nearest 1/16th per cent.

In active cash markets the bid–offer spread is usually 12.5 basis points. The main maturities are overnight, one week, two weeks, one to six months, nine months and twelve months. Rates are available on demand for broken dates, and for periods longer than one year on an *ad hoc* basis.

In most markets the convention for calculating interest is to divide the actual number of days by 360. In other words a six-month rate quoted at 10 per cent might pay 183/360 of 10 per cent of the principal amount at the end of the period. One exception to this rule is the sterling market which uses an annual basis of 365 days: a 10 per cent sterling six-month rate would, therefore, only pay 183/365 of 10 per cent at maturity. Interest on interbank deposits is normally payable at the end of each full year and at maturity.

Certificates of Deposit

Complementing interbank deposits are certificates of deposit (CDs). These are generally short-term securities that pay a fixed amount of capital and interest at maturity according to the interbank rates when they were issued. They are popular amongst banks as, unlike ordinary deposits, they can be easily traded. The price of a CD varies inversely with interest rates depending on its maturity characteristics.

A certificate of deposit is really just a securitised version of an interbank transaction with similar quotation conventions and maturity characteristics. The main difference is that when a deal is settled the two counterparties are not left with risks and obligations each to the other. Buying and selling CDs provides traders with more flexibility in raising and deploying funds. By buying a CD a trader is effectively supplying funds to its issuer. But because CDs are traded in a secondary market, this may take the form of a payment to an existing holder of an asset. Traders can also raise funds by selling CDs; this is equivalent to borrowing money until the CD's maturity date. On this date, the seller has lost his rights to the cashflow due, a net outflow. Traders can also access the repo markets using a CD, allowing them to borrow and lend for shorter periods than that described by the paper.

This contrasts with the bilateral nature of the interbank deposit markets. Since counterparties are lending and borrowing cash directly between themselves, they have to consider not just their interest risk requirements but also the credit risk implications. Although leading banks generally do not demand a premium from their peer borrowers, it is normal banking practice to set up a system of limits. If the borrowing bank has exceeded the lending bank's limit, they may be anxious, but unable, to deal in interbank deposits. The borrowing bank can still raise funds from the lender though by selling a CD issued by a third bank for whom the lending bank still has room on its books.

The CD market also provides the opportunity for the issuer to tailor the cashflow structure of its paper to investor demand, or some specific requirement of its own. CDs are simply promissory notes and any cashflow structure can be devised for them, although the less standardised they become, the less they are tradeable. Other types of CDs that have been popular at certain times include floating rate CDs (FRCDs) which have multiple interest payment dates based on relevant LIBORs and zero coupon CDs, which are compound interest instruments originally issued at a discount to par with more than a year until maturity.

Commercial Paper

First traded in the USA but now widely available in both Euro and domestic markets outside the States, commercial paper (CP) is a short-term security issued by a corporation or financial institution targeted at institutional investors.

It is similar to a large scale overdraft facility. The CP issuer launches, say a five-year, $500m programme. Once launched it provides very cheap, flexible funding. The CP issuer can now issue paper in response to investor demand with maturities between seven days and one year (270 days is the maximum in the

USA) up to a maximum of $500m. The paper is usually distributed via appointed dealers who earn a slim margin on the deals they transact. Although, as a security, it is in theory tradeable, most investors hold the paper until maturity.

Commercial paper, like T-bills, is priced at a discount to its par value at maturity. In the US, CP rates are quoted as discount rates, but in Euro markets they are generally quoted in terms of the yield equivalent. US dollar Euro CP is widely used by corporates in conjunction with the FX swap market to achieve cheap non-dollar funding for their activities. Euro CP rates are generally priced off the LIBOR yield curve, with the lowest rates being achieved by the highest rated institutions.

Medium Term Notes

The medium term note (MTN) market is growing rapidly and evolving fast. MTNs were originally conceived to serve a niche market, they were particularly suitable for institutions that have large scale, regular funding requirements. By setting up MTN programmes they could gain access to a flexible source of inexpensive capital. The MTN programme responds to investor demands for a series of cashflows on specific dates. The borrower issues paper with tailored payment streams. Like CP programmes they are generally distributed through appointed dealers. They are, in theory, tradeable, but most investors hold them until maturity.

MTNs are commonly used by investors for cash matching purposes. The investor is able to specify the precise cashflow structure for the MTN. Because of their irregular payment structures they can be difficult to trade, but cash matching investors are still prepared to sacrifice some yield because of the instrument's extreme flexibility.

Recently the structural advantages of MTNs have begun to be recognised by borrowers who have started to use the programmes as an alternative to the capital markets. There are now a number of MTNs with regular coupons, as well as floating rate MTNs and zero coupon issues. Because of their more standard structure, these kinds of structures have the same kind of liquidity characteristics as bonds, and are now used interchangeably by bond investors.

Links with the Capital Markets

As bonds approach their maturity date, they take on the characteristics of a money market instrument, becoming a short-term security. The yields for fixed rate bonds are quoted according to capital market conventions. Floating rate notes and variable rate notes are capital market instruments whose prices are set in the money markets, they are thus a close substitute for short-term securities. Bond structures and pricing are discussed in Chapter 10.

Repo Markets

The capital markets and money markets are also interrelated by the repo mechanism. A repo, short for repurchase agreement, is a mechanism whereby the owner of a bond can raise funds against a combined sale and repurchase of his bond. Repo rates closely mirror interbank rates and they allow securities houses to finance their activities relatively cheaply. This mechanism is particularly popular in markets where securities are well developed, the USA or the Japanese Gensaki markets for instance.

The mechanism works as follows. A securities house wishes to borrow money for a month at current money market rates. Its own creditworthiness would involve it in having to pay a significant margin over LIBOR. Instead it agrees with the lender (also known as the reverse repurchaser) to sell some bonds now and buy them back in a month at a price fixed today. This forward price for the bond is set according to the time value of money relationship for the repo period. The funds it receives today and pays back in a month's time are analogous to borrowing money, and the relationship between the two prices defines its cost of financing.

Since the lender owns a bond during the course of the loan, he is not concerned with the credit risk of the borrower. If the borrower is unable to buy the bond back, he can always sell it to someone else. As a result the creditworthiness of the bond rather than the borrower will determine the margin he requires. Since bonds used in repos are mainly government securities he can afford to lend money at LIBOR flat. There is one caveat here, and that is that the bond price if the repurchaser defaults may not completely cover the lost capital and income. Reverse repurchasers need to be careful to ensure that the securities they own will fully collateralise the lending.

FORWARD RATE AGREEMENTS

Definition

A forward rate agreement (FRA) is an agreement between two counterparties to exchange a fixed rate of interest with the LIBOR prevailing on the FRA's start date for the specified period. It is a swap, equivalent to two simultaneous cash transactions – each counterparty is, in effect, lending to and borrowing from the other the same capital amount over the same forward period.

Structure and Terminology

The payer of the fixed rate is said to be the FRA buyer; the fixed rate receiver (i.e. the LIBOR payer) is the seller of the FRA. The FRA buyer is borrowing at

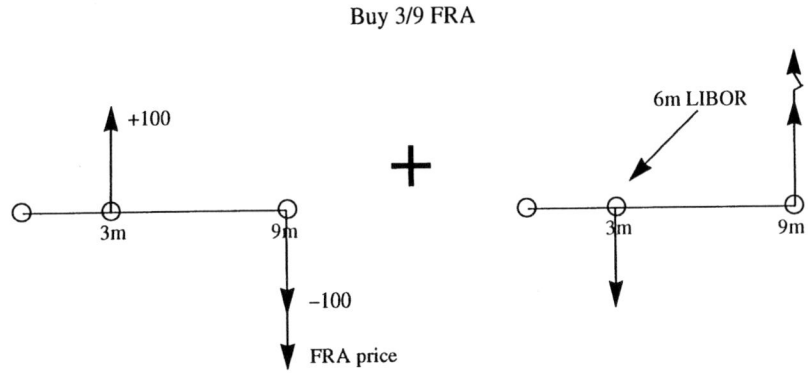

Figure 6.1 An FRA is two transactions in one

a fixed rate, while agreeing simultaneously to lend the same amount at the equivalent period's future LIBOR.

The FRA price is the fixed rate, the future LIBOR is known as the reference rate. Market makers quote two-way FRA prices on a spread of 5 to 20 basis points, depending on liquidity. FRAs are bought and sold in all the major currencies for periods ending within the next two years.

FRAs are over the counter (OTC) financial transactions and their terms are therefore individually negotiable. In theory, they are available in any size for any period and in any currency. In practice, the less standard the terms, the more illiquid and expensive the instruments become.

Individual FRAs are identified by their start and end dates. For instance the 3m/9m FRA in January describes the six-month period beginning in April and ending in October. Two months later, the same FRA would be described as the 1m/7m FRA.

Use in Interest Risk Management

The flexibility of the FRA is one of its key advantages. Corporates, especially, value the ability to match future periods and amounts exactly. As occasional users of financial markets, they are often less concerned about trading actively and are attracted by the opportunity to eliminate basis risk.

Amongst financial institutions FRAs are seen as a balance sheet efficient mechanism for transforming interest rate risk. As a result, in the major currencies, for the main periods, there is an active two-way market.

Hedgers are buying or selling an interest rate differential, rather than the principal amount. An FRA buyer is therefore betting that interest rates will rise, a seller, by contrast, believes that LIBOR will be lower than today's FRA price when the differential is fixed.

Pricing FRAs

As OTC instruments, FRAs are bought and sold by users of financial markets to manage the interest rate risk on their projected assets and liabilities. However, the flexibility of the FRA instrument has encouraged the growth of a significant interbank market. As such, pricing is determined to a large extent by supply and demand.

Having said this, the cashflows that make up the FRA instrument – it is essentially a fixed versus floating rate, single period, interest rate swap starting on some future date – are identical to the net cashflows that would be generated by the simultaneous lending and borrowing of equal amounts of capital over the same period, one side done at a fixed rate, and the other at LIBOR. Since banks, as market makers in money, are always able to lend at the LIBOR floating rates, it is clear that they would be able to replicate the cashflow effect of an FRA in this way.

Links with the Cash Market

There is therefore an arbitrageable relationship between any FRA and the underlying cash market. We have seen how any such relationship will cause prices in the related markets to move in line with each other, either because of the supply and demand effects of arbitrage, or, if any anomaly is not sufficiently large to trigger such activity, because the threat of a potential arbitrage exerts a discipline on market participants. Traders will hold FRA prices in line with the cash markets, because they know that if they do not, arbitragers will step in and they will lose money.

Because the relationship between the cash yield curve and the FRA market is a very direct one, arbitrage does not normally take place. Instead the cash market is seen as the technical price determinant for FRAs.

The Link with Interest Rate Futures

Because of the hedging relationship, although the cash markets provide the technical underpinning for FRA prices, in practice they relate more closely to current interest rate futures prices.

Prices in the interest rate futures market are also based on the cash yield curve. An interest rate futures contract is, after all, simply a standardised form of forward–forward deposit. Since the futures market is regularly accessed by professional money managers to hedge transactions and manage their interest rate risk, they best reflect the cost to them of buying and selling FRAs.

As all the major short-term interest rate futures contracts are for assets with a three-month tenor, whereas FRAs are available for a variety of period lengths, dealers using futures to price FRAs may need to make an adjustment to allow for any difference in compounding frequencies.

Delivery and Settlement

When counterparties trade in FRAs they are entering into an agreement to make or take delivery of the interest differential between the FRA price and the reference rate for a given nominal capital amount over the specified forward period. The effect of this is to enable potential lenders and borrowers to fix (or unfix) a rate in advance.

If the FRA transaction were to be simulated via the cash markets, the exchange of interest amounts would be made at the end of the forward period. In FRA markets, however, the practice is to settle the interest differential at the start of the FRA period. This is done to minimise the credit risk implications for the counterparty due to receive the differential.

Settlement at the start of the interest period implies a time value of money benefit to the receiver of the differential. The actual amount of cash involved is discounted to take account of this difference. The formula for settlement is as follows:

$$\text{Diffl} = \frac{\text{Notional amount} . (\text{FRA price} - \text{LIBOR}) \, t}{(1 + \text{LIBOR}t)}$$

where t = Length of FRA period expressed in years.

The LIBOR reference is chosen as the discounting factor on the grounds that this reflects the rate at which customers can borrow cash for the FRA period. However, the net receiver of the FRA would have to lend the differential amount to defer its receipt to the end of the period. Non-market makers can generally only lend at LIBid, which is usually 12.5 basis points less than LIBOR. So, there is perhaps some basis risk for FRA users seeking to hedge future LIBOR commitments.

To get an idea of the magnitude of this effect, consider the following, extreme situation: a customer buys a $1m 3m/15m FRA at 10 per cent. If, after three months LIBOR is less than 10 per cent, the FRA buyer will be a net payer. To defer the FRA payment for a year the buyer borrows the differential amount, at LIBOR. Since this is identical to the FRA discounting rate, the amount of interest to pay at the end of the period is exactly the same as would have been the case on a standard, forward–forward deposit.

But suppose that LIBOR after three months is 15 per cent. Here the interest differential would be +$50,000 if it were to be received at the end of the period.

95

In fact the FRA buyer receives $43,478.26 ($50,000 discounted for a year at 15 per cent). Should the FRA buyer wish to defer this receipt until the end of the interest period, he must invest this amount for a year at LIBid (currently 14.875 per cent). This will generate $49,945.65 in twelve months' time.

The example illustrates that the difference that this modification makes to the value of the FRA is, in practice, negligible. The shortfall of just $50.00 for a $1m FRA reduces the effective fixed rate by just 0.5 of a basis point, and this shows the effect at its most pronounced. The smaller the FRA interest differential, the less significant the effect: interest differentials will almost always be significantly less than 5 per cent, most FRA periods are shorter than one year.

Therefore, despite the fact that the interest differential is settled in advance, for analytic purposes it is sensible to analyse the impact of FRA transactions as if the full differential were paid at the end of the FRA period. This provides for consistency with other types of LIBOR related instrument.

Credit Risk Implications for FRAs

Unlike interest futures, which in some ways they closely resemble, FRAs normally reach delivery and are settled directly between the counterparties. Since no margin is payable in advance, there is a credit risk for each of the counterparties. Each is at risk to the other, not on the nominal amount, just on the interest differential.

The FRA price is unlikely to differ from the reference rate by more than a few percentage points. Many financial institutions use 5 per cent per annum as a maximum variation when calculating the credit risks on such transactions. An FI using this weighting that bought a $1m 3m/9m FRA would therefore assign a credit usage amount of $25,000 to their counterparty (5% × $1m × 0.5yrs).

The credit risk for an FRA is price-contingent. Only the net receiver of the interest differential has a risk of default. As a result, for any given period, the institution only has an overall credit risk on the net position with a counterparty. Banks, in particular, have used this argument to persuade the regulators that they should be allowed to net off FRA (and swap) positions for capital adequacy purposes.

Trading in FRAs

The two way nature of the FRA transaction means that each counterparty has both rights and obligations. As a result, an individual FRA cannot be traded in the same way as, say, a security.

Dealers in FRAs, therefore, rely on trading FRA positions to transform their interest risk. Some offer no-penalty incentives to their customers to encourage them to close out existing FRA transactions with them rather than do new business with some competitor. The no-penalty incentive allows a customer to close out an earlier FRA transaction at the current mid-price, rather than having to buy back at the offer price (or sell back at the bid).

In practice, the lack of tradeability of FRAs is not an undue restriction. FRA dealers will often use futures to hedge the interest rate risk on their trading book. They will trade FRA positions by reversing previous transactions, often with a different counterparty. As has been explained above, the credit risk on an FRA – price-contingent and on the interest differential amount only – is relatively insignificant. In interbank markets, therefore, credit risk is, for the most part, all but ignored by the trading community, and does not act as a brake on market activity.

Two distinct market segments have developed in the major currencies. FRAs on a yield curve of standard periods (1m, 2m, 3m, 6m, 9m, 12m, etc) are actively traded amongst treasury managers and other professionals. FRAs that have periods that correspond to futures contracts are likely to be especially actively traded. The other main market segment is between individual market makers and their customers, trading in non-standard periods and amounts to match particular interest exposures.

SHORT-TERM INTEREST RATE FUTURES

Definition

An interest rate futures contract is a standard agreement that provides the holder with an interest bearing asset on a specified date in the future. In common with other futures contracts the terms of the contract are standardised with respect to the size, credit quality and terms to enhance tradeability. Interest rate futures are offered on a variety of exchanges with delivery dates in March, June, September and December up to two years in the future. For popular contracts, such as the Eurodollar future traded on the International Monetary Market, other months are also available.

Pricing

Short-term interest rate futures are quoted on an index basis, as 100 minus the annual interest rate. A futures price of, say, 91.25 implies an interest rate of 8.75 per cent.

Table 6.1 Major contracts

Exchange	Commodity	Size	Tick/Value	Contract months
CBOT	30 day rate	$5m	0.01%/$41.67	1st 7mths +2 of Mar/ Jun/Sep/Dec
CME/IMM	1m LIBOR	$3m	0.01%/$25	1st 6mths
CME/IMM	90 day Eurodollar	$1m	0.01%/$25	1st mth, Mar/Jun/ Sep/Dec for 4yrs
CME/IMM	3m US T-bill	$1m	0.01%/$25	Mar/Jun/Sep/Dec
ME	3m Bkrs Accept.	C$1m	0.01%/$25	Mar/Jun/Sep/Dec
SFE	3m Bkrs Accept.	A$0.5m	0.01%/$12.50	1st 6mths Mar/Jun/ Sep/Dec
SFE	90 day Eurodollar	$1m	0.01%/$25	Mar/Jun/Sep/Dec
LIFFE	3m Sterling	£0.5m	0.01%/£12.50	Mar/Jun/Sep/Dec
LIFFE	90 day Eurodollar	$1m	0.01%/$25	Mar/Jun/Sep/Dec
LIFFE	90 day Euro DM	DM1m	0.01%/DM25	Mar/Jun/Sep/Dec
MATIF	3m PIBOR	FF5m	0.01%/FF125	Mar/Jun/Sep/Dec
MATIF	90 day Fr T-bill	FF5m	0.01%/FF125	Mar/Jun/Sep/Dec

CBOT	Chicago Board of Trade
CME/IMM	International Monetary Market (part of Chicago Mercantile Exchange)
ME	Montreal Exchange
SFE	Sydney Futures Exchange
LIFFE	London International Financial Futures Exchange
MATIF	Marché à Terme Financiers (Paris)

Hedging with Interest Rate Futures

Someone wishing to protect against a fall in interest rates will want to fix a lending rate in today's environment. The buyer of a future is purchasing the cash asset at today's rate. If interest rates do indeed fall, then the futures price will rise correspondingly. The owner of the future will then be able to sell it back at the higher price. This realised profit may be used to compensate the investor for the new, lower interest rate environment. In the same way, a potential borrower would protect against an interest rate rise by selling then buying back futures.

Mechanics of Trading

Unlike FRAs, interest rate futures are rarely delivered. Hedgers and risk managers buy and sell futures with the aim of realising a profit that, in cash terms, will offset any losses on their underlying exposure resulting from a change in the interest rate environment.

The standardised nature of futures contracts precludes risk managers from using them to immunise themselves completely against yield curve shifts. Instead, they are attracted by the high level of market liquidity. As a result, interest rate futures are more appropriate for the professional sector of the market, which prizes the ability to trade their positions more actively during the risk management period. Typical interest rate futures users are the treasury dealers in FIs and the global treasury management operations of sophisticated multinationals. They have both the expertise and the infrastructure required to deal successfully in the futures markets.

Margining and Hedging Costs

As with other futures markets, dealers in interest rate futures are required to lodge margin with the exchange every time that they open a new position. This margin amount is refundable when the contract is closed out, but, because the hedge may need to remain in place for several months, this can represent a significant cost of trading.

By way of illustration consider the case of the hedger who takes out 202 Eurodollar contracts at the IMM in January and holds the position open until June. The IMM may require an initial margin of $1500 per contract, so he is required to place $303,000 in a margin account for five months. Assuming for the moment that the futures price remains unchanged for the full five months, the fact that this capital is tied up could involve him in a loss of interest income. If the interest rate in January were 7 per cent he would sacrifice $8838 ($303,000 × 7% × 5 / 12).

The exchanges recognise that this expense may deter institutions from using futures, but they do require margins if they are to underwrite futures users' credit risk. Some exchanges offer reduced margins for offsetting futures positions because of the reduced overall risk. For instance, a futures trader who is long of one June contract and short of one September contract is exposed to relative price shifts rather than the absolute level of yields. Many exchanges offer reduced margins on time spread positions, such as this one, in recognition of their lower overall exposure.

Another important way in which futures users can minimise the margin interest cost is by lodging interest bearing securities rather than cash payments with the clearing house. A number of exchanges accept government securities such as T-bills, as well as cash, in settlement of margin account. Others are prepared to pay interest on margin accounts, but the rates offered tend to be much lower than those available elsewhere so there can still be a significant margin interest cost to futures users.

Variation Margin and Marking-to-Market

Buyers and sellers of futures contracts have their positions marked-to-market at the end of each trading session and this can impose significant administrative costs on futures hedgers. Margin is transferred from losers to gainers each time contracts are revalued.

For the owner of a loss-making position, this may require the transfer of extra funds into the margin account to ensure that the minimum margin is maintained (contract owners who do not meet the minimum margin requirement at the start of a new trading session are automatically held in default).

For the owner of a profitable futures position the extra funds in the margin account will involve a loss in interest unless they are transferred.

Futures administrators thus have a difficult juggling act if they are to minimise their trading costs. If they maintain the minimum margin requirement they will have to transfer funds in and out every day as the position is revalued, involving them in substantial administrative costs. On the other hand, if they decide to maintain more than the minimum requirement they will lose an unnecessarily large amount of interest.

This is one more reason why the futures market is favoured by professionals. For unless an institution is actively involved in trading futures it will be uneconomic for it to invest in the operational and systems support required to trade in futures cost-effectively.

The Cash–Futures Relationship

As with commodities, the basis relationship is delineated by the cash-and-carry relationship. In the discussion on FRAs above, we saw how market participants can build their own 'do-it-yourself' FRAs providing for an arbitrageable alternative if the FRA price moves outside of its technical restrictions.

Since interest futures, like FRAs, are also forward transactions of time deposits, they can be arbitraged in a similar way and are subject to the same technical pricing constraints. However, this arbitrage is balance sheet intensive, clumsy and price inefficient, so that in practice there is often a wide range within which futures can trade, particularly if they are not due for delivery in the near future. This is illustrated below where the implied basis range for a Eurodollar future is calculated using the cash markets.

Cash yield curve
9m   8.000 – 8.125
12m 8.125 – 8.250
Cash-and-carry operation
(lend \$1 for 12m @ 8.125%, borrow \$1 for 9m @ 8.125%, sell future)

Using the time value of money equation we can find the implied forward–forward rate for the three-month period commencing in nine months:

$$RFB = \left(\frac{(1 + 0.08125)}{(1 + 0.008125 \times 0.75)} - 1 \right) \times 4$$

$$RFB = 7.658\%$$

Where RFB = 9m/12m forward–forward bid rate
Reverse cash-and-carry operation
(borrow \$1 for 12m @ 8.25%, lend \$1 for 9m @ 8%, buy future)

Using the time value of money equation we can find the implied forward–forward rate for the three month period commencing in nine months:

$$RFO = \left(\frac{(1 + 0.0825)}{(1 + 0.08 \times 0.75)} - 1 \right) \times 4$$

$$RFO = 8.491\%$$

Where RFO = 9m/12m forward–forward offer rate

Arbitrage will occur if futures prices move outside of the implied interest rates for cash-and-carry operations. The price for the three-month contract deliverable in nine months should not fall below 91.51 (100.00 – 8.49%) or climb above 92.34 (100.00 – 7.66%).

The implied futures basis range is therefore 83 ticks according to cash. 9m/12m FRA prices are more likely to provide arbitrage opportunities because of their much narrower bid–offer spread. Although both are related to cash there is still considerable scope for price movements without a change in the underlying yield curve. In the case above, where the future reaches delivery in nine months, the basis risk is still relatively high. Futures can vary by more than eighty ticks without triggering arbitrage activity. Of course, as the future nears delivery, the convergence process will reduce the width of this band until, on the date itself, it has reached zero.

Sources of Basis Risk

There are therefore two main categories of basis risk for hedgers using the futures market. Firstly, there is the strong probability that the cash position being hedged is not exactly mirrored by the hedging instrument. Secondly, as we have seen, even where the future is being used to hedge an identical exposure, futures prices can fluctuate significantly without triggering the cash-and-carry operation.

Futures differ from the underlying exposure in one other important respect. The process of marking-to-market means that, in effect, the position is closed out on a daily basis and reopened at the new price. Rather than being paid or charged at the notional deposit's maturity date, profits and losses are taken as they occur. For this reason also the performance of a futures contract will be different to that of the underlying.

The TED Spread

A valuable indicator for money market risk managers is the so-called TED spread. This measures the difference in price between T-bill futures and Eurodollar futures for the same delivery dates. Typically a T-bill future will trade at a higher price than its equivalent Eurodollar contract. However, the width of the spread will vary according to the level of optimism or pessimism in the market. T-bill futures will trade at a higher premium to Eurodollar contracts when the market is more bearish.

Table 6.2 T-bill and Eurodollar futures prices at the IMM

Month	T-bill	Eurodollar	TED spread
Mar	9409	9282	127
June	9423	9293	130
Sep	9413	9285	128
Dec	9385	9256	129

Source: Wall Street Journal, 22 January 1991

In January 1991 T-bill futures were trading at an historically high premium to Eurodollar futures. This reflected the uncertainty that permeated financial markets at the start of the Gulf War. As a result there was significant demand for T-bills, pushing up futures prices. Although it does not undermine the validity of the TED spread, a point to bear in mind is that the 127 tick differential (March) does not reflect a difference in yields between the two contracts. T-bill futures are quoted on a discount rate basis, while Eurodollar futures prices reflect forward yields. A T-bill futures price of 9409, equates to a discount rate of 5.91 per cent. This translates to a 90-day yield equivalent of 6.00 per cent, so the yield differential is actually 118 basis points (the March Eurodollar prices three-month yields at 7.18 per cent).

OPTIONAL INSTRUMENTS

This section discusses the main forms of interest rate option available in money markets. IRGs options on futures are explained and their use in interest risk management is outlined.

Definition

An interest rate option is a contractual arrangement where the buyer owns the right but not the obligation to receive or pay a fixed rate of interest over a pre-arranged period. The seller, or writer, of the option guarantees this fixed rate in exchange for the payment of an up-front premium. There are two main types of contract: the option to receive a minimum fixed rate and the option to pay a maximum fixed rate.

Interest Rate Guarantees

In the money markets maximum and minimum interest rate guarantees (IRGs) are traded over the counter and complement the notional instruments available for managing interest risk. As OTC instruments their terms are individually negotiable between the counterparties but they are usually European style options, resembling options on FRAs. IRG calls, sometimes known as borrowers' options, may be used to guarantee a maximum interest rate. An IRG put, or lender's option, fixes a minimum interest rate for the period.

Premium Quotation
IRG premiums are quoted in terms of basis points per annum and paid in advance. A European style IRG call on six-month LIBOR, with an exercise date in three months' time, effectively furnishes its owner with the right to buy a three-month/nine-month FRA at the quoted strike rate. Suppose this IRG is available at a strike rate of 10 per cent and has a premium quoted at 20 basis points. The option buyer would therefore be required to pay a premium of $1,000 per $1m of protection against the six-month LIBOR prevailing in three months (i.e. $1m $\times$ 0.5 $\times$ 0.2%).

Net Rates for IRGs
Since the premium is quoted according to the period being covered by the option, an approximate indication of the worst case rate for a call can be found by adding the premium to the strike. A six-month 10 per cent IRG call with a 20 basis point premium would be said to have a net rate of 10.2 per cent. For IRG puts, the premium must be subtracted from the strike to arrive at the worst case rate. An 8 per cent IRG put, quoted at 25 basis points, guarantees its holder a net lending rate of 7.75 per cent.

However, there is also a time value of money factor to consider. The premium for puts and calls is payable in advance, so a financing cost needs to be incorporated if the net rate is truly to reflect the option buyer's worst case position. For IRGs on six-month LIBOR expiring in three months' time the relevant rate will be the cost of borrowing for nine months.

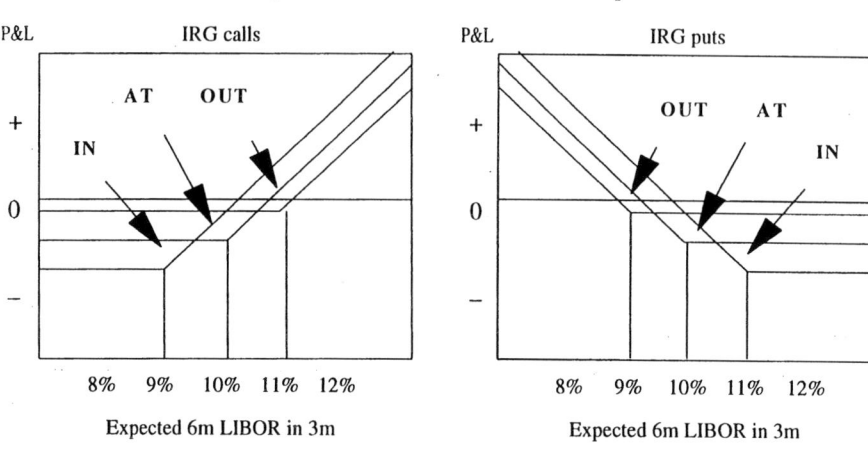

Figure 6.2 IRG calls and puts with in, at, out the money exercise rates

Suppose that nine-month LIBOR stands at 9 per cent. The net rate for the 10 per cent IRG call will be 10.214 per cent (i.e. 10% + 0.2% × (1+ 0.09 × 0.75)) while the 8 per cent IRG put will have a net rate of 7.733 per cent. The time value of money effect will, of course, be greater the longer the period to maturity of the underlying instrument and the greater the financing rate. Also, the more in the money is the IRG, because a larger premium has to be financed, the more significant the time value of money effect.

Settlement and Delivery
The writer of an IRG guarantees to pay the buyer at expiry any positive difference between the IRG strike and the reference rate (usually LIBOR for the relevant period). However, as LIBOR is usually paid at the end of the period, while options are settled at its start, an allowance is made for the fact the interest is paid in advance. The discounting formula is similar to that used for FRAs. For analytic purposes, though, it is sensible to view IRGs as if the full interest differential was paid at maturity, and this is the convention used in this workbook when considering their cashflow effect on risk management strategies.

Intrinsic Value for IRGs
We saw in Chapter 1 that an option's premium is a function of its intrinsic value and of extrinsic value. Options that are at the money have no intrinsic value, but considerable extrinsic value, the premiums for deep in the money options are almost entirely made up of intrinsic value, deep out of the money options have hardly any extrinsic value and no intrinsic value.

IRGs are European style options. The owner may not exercise until the expiry date when she will receive only intrinsic value. The underlying instrument for a 10 per cent IRG call on six-month LIBOR expiring in three months is, therefore, not today's six-month LIBOR rate, but the six-month LIBOR in three months' time. The 3m/9m FRA is the market's valuation of this future LIBOR rate. FRAs, therefore, are the underlying instrument for IRGs; their in, at or out of the money status is defined by their relationship with FRA prices.

Pricing IRGs

As European style options, IRGs can be priced successfully using the Black–Scholes method. The relevant forward price is the appropriate FRA price and any time value is determined by volatility estimates for interest rates. These define the future expected value for the IRG and the premium can then be found by discounting this amount at the borrowing rate to the FRA's maturity date.

American Style IRGs

An American style IRG provides its owner with the ability to exercise against the six-month LIBOR prevailing on any date up to its expiry date. Its intrinsic value can therefore be measured against today's six-month LIBOR. However, in certain yield curve environments this practice could result in American style IRGs having a lower premium than their European style equivalents. This would set up an arbitrageable opportunity between the two types of option. Arbitragers could buy cheap American style options, simultaneously sell European ones and exercise both at expiry to realise the difference in premiums as a risk-free profit.

Intrinsic value for an American style option is therefore calculated against the best LIBOR prevailing between today and its expiry date. The binomial pricing method, developed by Cox, Ross and Rubinstein, provides a statistical tool that values the benefit of this early exercise feature.

Options on Interest Rate Futures

Interest rate options are offered by almost every exchange where futures are traded. They take the form of call and put options on the underlying futures contract. A futures call gives its owner the right to buy the underlying contract, while a put provides for the right to sell the future.

Since the buyer of an interest rate futures contract is acquiring a notional instrument equivalent to a forward–forward loan, the futures call is a form of minimum interest rate guarantee, or floor. Similarly, the owner of a put on the future has the right to a maximum interest rate, it is therefore a type of cap.

Types of Futures Option

For each futures contract call and put options are available for strikes at regular intervals around the current futures price. Options on Eurodollar futures for instance have a strike price interval of 25 ticks. The contracts which are intro-duced depend on the price of the underlying future.

There are always at least six options available – those with strike prices closest to the underlying futures price. As the futures price changes, there must always be at least two options that are out of the money and two that are in the money. New options contracts may therefore be introduced by the exchange as the futures price moves. By the future's delivery date there can be more than six options being traded on it at the exchange.

Typically, options on futures are European style, i.e. they may only be exer-cised on the futures delivery date. Market participants can of course realise the value of their options positions before the delivery date by trading their posi-tions.

Table 6.3 shows premiums payable on puts and calls on the Eurodollar June contract at the IMM. On the date in question the June future is priced at 92.93.

Table 6.3 Options on Eurodollar futures
(International Monetary Market, Chicago)

$1 million; pts of 100%		
Strike price	*June calls*	*June puts*
92.25	0.73	0.07
92.50	0.53	0.12
92.75	0.36	0.18
93.00	0.23	0.30
93.25	0.13	0.45
93.50	0.07	0.64

Source: Wall Street Journal, 22 January 1991

Futures Option Pricing
As can be seen from Table 6.3 option premiums are quoted in ticks. This allows market participants to determine the net price (i.e. the worst case) by simply adding (or subtracting) the premium to (or from) the exercise price. A buyer of a 92.50 call would, for example, have a worst case cost of 93.03 (92.50 + 0.53), while the purchaser of a put at the same strike has a worst case selling price of 92.38 (92.50 – 0.12) for the June future. The value of a tick is the same as for the underlying future ($25 for Eurodollars), so traders are able to identify profits and losses quickly as premiums change.

Trading in Futures Options
As is the case with futures, exchange traded options are used mainly by market professionals. They form an essential component of any risk management strategy.

Traders and risk managers, by buying and selling options, can express a view on expected market volatility; just as they buy and sell futures according to their view on the direction of price movements.

Margining and Marking-to-Market

The mark-to-market mechanism for options is the same as for futures, with positions being revalued at the end of each trading session according to the last traded price. The amount of margin required by the exchange has to reflect the risk it is underwriting. Option buyers' risk is limited to the extent of the premium, whereas the risk for an option writer is, theoretically, limitless.

Margining mechanisms differ between exchanges. Some require option buyers to pay the entire premium into the margin account. Writers must maintain a margin related to the future that increases according to the likelihood of exercise. However, the system adopted by, amongst others, LIFFE is gaining acceptance. This assesses the risk on the net portfolio of the futures trader according to delta factors published each day by the exchange.

The risk numbers reflect the anticipated change in the value of the overall portfolio for a given change in the futures price. Margin requirements for both buyers and sellers are related to the underlying future by the risk number and change on a daily basis. A typical portfolio based margin maintenance system assesses the overall risk to the portfolio in a variety of market scenarios. The effect on the profitability trader's overall position is monitored for specific changes such as a 100 tick absolute fall in prices, a 1 per cent increase in volatility. The magnitude of the portfolio's worst case loss is used to define the basis.

7: Techniques for Treasury Traders

EVALUATING INTEREST EXPOSURES

Introduction

In this section we investigate a variety of pricing and hedging techniques used by treasury traders.Their uses differ and in many cases the cashflows are complicated, but they are all based on the same time value of money equation and the emphasis is always on identifying and valuing precise cashflow amounts on specific dates.

Discounts versus Yields

US T-bills are quoted according to their discount rates. This reflects the way they are marketed; T-bills are offered at a discount to their face value and the rate is therefore expressed as a time adjusted proportion of the future amount.

The discount rate will always be lower than the equivalent yield. The extent of this difference is governed by the period length and the interest rate level. It all comes back to the time value of money, for the discount rate describes how much interest would be payable in advance. As can be seen from the time lines in Figure 7.1, investors can structure transactions synthetically so that they receive income in advance. This is simply achieved by borrowing an amount, which at maturity nets off with the future income amount.

Figure 7.1 illustrates the equivalence of discount rates and yields. It also demonstrates how cashflows can in effect be 'moved' from one date to another by borrowing and lending activities.

Finding FRA Prices Implied by Today's Cash Markets.

3 m London Eurodollar	7.1250 – 7.2500
9 m London Eurodollar	7.3125 – 7.4375

In order to generate a 3m/9m FRA bid price for a customer using the cash markets, the dealer must calculate the cost of closing out the position at current rates. To do this he would have to lend to the market at the nine-month LIBid and borrow for three months at the market LIBOR. The FRA offer price would

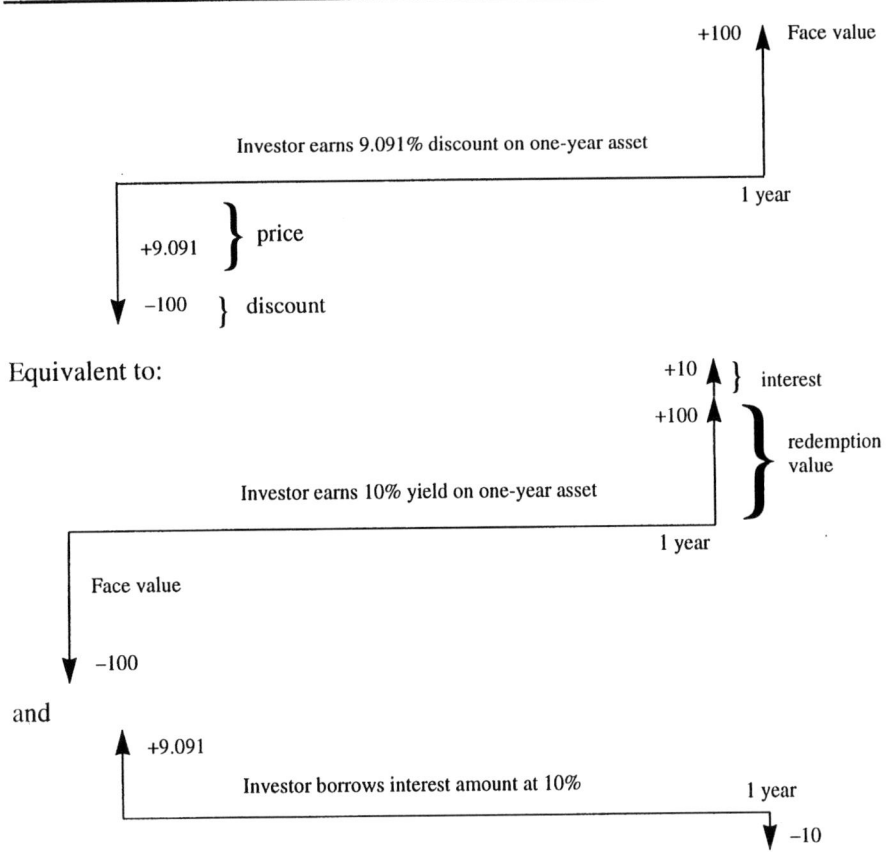

Figure 7.1 Discount rates have yield equivalents

be generated by borrowing from the market at its nine-month LIBOR and lending for three months at LIBid.

$$3\text{m/9m bid} = \left(\frac{(1 + 0.073125 \times 0.75)}{(1 + 0.0725 \times 0.25)} - 1 \right) \times 2$$

$$3\text{m/9m bid} = 7.21 \text{ per cent}$$

$$3\text{m/9m offer} = \left(\frac{(1 + 0.074375 \times 0.75)}{(1 + 0.07125 \times 0.25)} - 1 \right) \times 2$$

$$3\text{m/9m offer} = 7.46 \text{ per cent}$$

Notice that the bid–offer spread is relatively wide at 25 basis points. This reflects the high cost of generating FRA type positions in this way. The implied bid and offer rates represent the extremes within which FRAs will trade, but if there is an active interest rate futures or FRA market, the dealer will access these to close out the position, rather than the cash market.

Pricing FRAs with Interest Futures

The fact that futures are notional instruments and can be actively traded makes them natural hedging and pricing tools for FRA traders. However, as the period lengths of FRAs can vary, the rates implied by futures prices need to be adjusted to allow for the different compounding frequency.

Strips of futures are used to arrive at a benchmark price for a particular FRA. For example: in March, the 3m/9m FRA would be priced off the June and September futures contracts. Market practices vary as to how this is done.

The theoretically 'correct' method is to calculate the implied rate for a loan with all interest paid at maturity. The more common practice is to average the rates implied by the futures and then convert this rate to its semi-annually compounded equivalent. Both techniques are illustrated below:

Three-month Eurodollar futures
June contract	92.00	Equivalent rate: 8.00%
September contract	91.85	Equivalent rate: 8.15%
December contract	91.60	Equivalent rate: 8.40%

Theoretical approach (lend @ 8% for three months, lend capital and income @ 8.15% for three months)

$$R = ((1 + 0.08 \times 0.25) \times (1 + 0.0815 \times 0.25) - 1) \times 2$$
$$R = 8.1565\%$$

Hedging approach (average rates, transform compounding frequency to semi-annualised)

$$R = (1 + (0.08 + 0.0815)/2 \times 0.25)^2 - 1) \times 2$$
$$R = 8.1565(03)\%$$

The two approaches yield very similar results and either may be used to price FRAs. Arguably, for pricing very long periods when interest rates are high, the theoretical approach is the superior technique, but for most FRAs the hedging approach is the more practical method.

For FRAs whose interest periods do not coincide with futures dates the normal technique is to take a weighted average of the relevant futures periods. So, to calculate the benchmark price for a 5m/11m FRA in March (i.e. from July to February) the reference three-month rate is 8.208 per cent i.e. (1 mth x 8% + 3 mths x 8.15% + 2 mths × 8.40%) / 6. Its semi-annually compounded equivalent (8.293%) becomes the FRA bid price. The FRA offer price will be 5 to 20 basis points higher, depending on liquidity.

The following examples illustrate further how strips of futures may be used to derive FRA prices:

In January, the prices for three-month Eurodollar futures are as follows:

March	91.95	(8.05%)
June	92.00	(8.00%)
September	91.85	(8.15%)
December	91.60	(8.40%)

Strips of futures are used to find implied bid prices for the following FRAs:

(a) 3m/6m
The FRA period commencing in April and ending in July can be simulated by a weighted average of the relevant three-month rates.

$R3/6 \ = \ (8.05\% \times 2 + 8.00\% \times 1) / 3$
$R3/6 \ = \ 8.03\%$

(b) 3m/9m
The FRA period commencing in April and ending in October can be simulated by a weighted average of the relevant three-month rates, compounded up to its semi-annual equivalent.

$R3/9 = ((1 + (8.05\% \times 2 + 8.00\% \times 3 + 8.15\% \times 1) / 6 \times 0.25)^2 - 1) \times 2$
$R3/9 = 8.12\%$

(c) 3m/12m
The FRA period commencing in April and ending in January can be simulated by a weighted average of the relevant three-month rates, adjusted to its nine monthly compounded equivalent.

$R3/12 = ((1+(8.05\% \times 2+8.00\% \times 3+8.15\% \times 3+8.40\% \times 1)/9 \times 0.25)^3-1) \times 4/3$
$R3/12 = 8.27\%$

Incorporating Time Value of Money into IRG Net Rate Calculations

The time value of money effect of having to pay the premium in advance impacts on the worst case interest rate guaranteed by an option buyer. This effect is greatest for in the money options, when the maturity date is a long time in the future and interest rates are high. The following examples illustrate how the net rate calculation needs to be modified to take account of time value for IRG calls on six-month LIBOR:

(a) Interest rates are at 8 per cent, the option expires in three months and carries a premium of 15 basis points.

Net rate $= 10\% + 0.15 \times (1 + 0.08 \times 0.75)$

Net rate $= 10.159\%$

(b) Interest rates are at 8 per cent, the option expires in six months and carries a premium of 15 basis points.

Net rate $= 10\% + 0.15 \times (1 + 0.08)$

Net rate $= 10.162\%$

(c) Interest rates are at 12 per cent, the option expires in six months and carries a premium of 215 basis points.

Net rate $= 10\% + 2.15 \times (1 + 0.12)$

Net rate $= 12.408\%$

Remember that the net rate describes a worse rate with interest paid at the end of the period; the premium must therefore be financed beyond the expiry date to the maturity of the underlying instrument. Notice also that the time value of money effect for in the money IRGs can be significant, especially when interest rates are high and there is a lengthy period to the maturity date of the underlying asset. In (c) the net rate is 25.8 basis points higher than the 12.15 per cent implied by simply adding the premium to the strike. The same procedure is, of course, used for puts, with the future value of the premium being subtracted from the strike.

Intrinsic Values for European and American Style IRGs

The following illustrations use mid-rates in a variety of yield curve environments to calculate the intrinsic value for European and American style 8 per cent IRG calls on six-month LIBOR expiring in six months. The intrinsic values are then discounted to determine the equivalent payment in terms of premium.

European style IRGs intrinsic values are always calculated against the 6m/12m FRA price. American style IRG calls use the best (i.e. the highest) spot or forward rate for intrinsic value. The intrinsic values would not be realised until the relevant maturity date and the amounts must therefore be discounted using the appropriate rate to determine the impact on today's premium.

(a) 3m, 6m, 9m, 12m rates are all 9 per cent

$$\text{6m rate} = 9\%$$

$$\text{3m/9m FRA} = \left(\frac{(1 + 0.09 \times 0.75)}{(1 + 0.09 \times 0.25)} - 1 \right)$$

$$= 8.80\%$$

$$6m/12m \text{ FRA} = \left(\frac{(1 + 0.09)}{(1 + 0.09 \times 0.5)} - 1 \right) \times 2$$

$$= 8.61\%$$

For a European style IRG call:
Intrinsic value   = 0.61% (i.e. 6m/12m rate – 8%)
Premium equivalent = 56 basis points (i.e. discount @ 9% for 12 months)

For an American style IRG call:
Intrinsic value   = 1.00% (i.e. 6m rate – 8%)
Premium equivalent = 96 basis points (i.e. discount @ 9% for 6 months)

(b) 3m = 8%, 6m = 8.5%, 9m = 9%, 12m = 9.5%

  6m rate   = 8.50%

  3m/9m FRA = $\left(\dfrac{(1 + 0.09 \times 0.75) - 1}{(1 + 0.08 \times 0.25)} \right)$

      = 9.31%

$$6m/12m \text{ FRA} = \left(\frac{(1 + 0.095)}{(1 + 0.085 \times 0.5)} - 1 \right) \times 2$$

$$= 10.07\%$$

For a European and American style IRG call:
Intrinsic value   = 2.07% (i.e. 6m/12m rate – 8%)
Premium equivalent = 189 basis points (i.e. discount @ 9% for 12 months)

(c) 3m = 8%, 6m = 8.5%, 9m = 9%, 12m = 9.5%

  6m rate   = 8.5%

  3m/9m FRA = $\left(\dfrac{(1 + 0.09 \times 0.75) - 1}{(1 + 0.08 \times 0.25)} \right)$

      = 9.31%

$$6m/12m \text{ FRA} = \left(\frac{(1 + 0.085)}{(1 + 0.085 \times 0.5)} - 1 \right) \times 2$$

$$= 8.15\%$$

For a European style IRG call:
Intrinsic value   = 0.15% (i.e. 6m/12m rate – 8%)
Premium equivalent = 14 basis points (i.e. discount @ 8.5% for 12 months)

For an American style IRG call:
Intrinsic value   = 1.31% (i.e. 3m/9mm rate – 8%)
Premium equivalent = 123 basis points (i.e. discount @ 9% for 9 months)

The exercise illustrates how premiums for American and European style calls can vary significantly according to the shape of the yield curve and demonstrates the importance of looking at the correct underlying instrument when valuing IRGs. In (a) the yield curve is slightly inverse so today's LIBOR represents the best exercise alternative for American style options. In (b) where FRA prices are higher than spot rates, premiums for the two options will be similar. In (c) where the yield curve is kinked the 3m/9m FRA represents best value for American style options, and this is therefore the appropriate underlying instrument.

MANAGING INTEREST EXPOSURES

Hedging a Floating Rate Liability using FRAs

Interest rate exposures may be precisely hedged using FRAs, as they can be tailored to the exact amount and risk period required.

In January the issuer of $100m floating rate note paying six-month LIBOR plus 15 bps in June expects interest rates to rise.

January:
5m/11m FRA   7.65–7.75
Issuer buys $100m nominal of 5m/11m FRA at 7.75%

June:
6m Interbank   8.375–8.500
FRA differential   +0.75%
FRN coupon fixes at   8.65%

December:
–$4,325,000   Issuer pays FRN investor's interest at 8.65%
+$375,000   Issuer receives interest differential on FRA
                      ($100m × 0.75% × 0.5)
–$3,950,000   Net cost of funds (equivalent to 7.9%)
                      $3.95m/$100m × 2

By buying the FRA the issuer has managed to fix the interest cost at the FRA price (7.9 per cent is equivalent to 7.75 per cent plus 15 basis points). The net interest cost is fixed at this level. Since the FRA reference rate is also used to set the FRN coupon no matter what the interest environment, the net cost to the issuer will be 7.9 per cent.

Ratio Hedging

For hedgers and risk managers using interest futures the problem is more complicated. The number of futures bought or sold needs to be adjusted so that the cash profit (or loss) on the futures position is equal and opposite to the p&l on the hedged exposure. Interest rate futures are for standard period (usually three month) deposits. So, if the underlying exposure is for an interest period that is longer (or shorter) than the corresponding future, the notional contract value of the future must be adjusted upwards (or downwards). In addition, it may be necessary to make an allowance for the compounding effect when the hedging period is different from the period of the underlying position.

The objective is to construct a programme where the cashflow characteristics of the underlying exposure and the hedge mirror each other as closely as possible. The hedging strategy which follows illustrates the ratio hedging process as well as the importance of incorporating the compounding effect.

In January the issuer of $100m floating rate note paying six-month LIBOR plus 15bps in June expects interest rates to rise.

January:

Mar ED future	92.82
Jun ED future	92.93
Sep ED future	92.85
5m/11mFRA	7.15/7.20

Issuer sells 100 June contracts at 92.93
Issuer sells 102 September contracts at 92.85

June:

3m Interbank	8.250–8.375
6m Interbank	8.375–8.500
Jun ED future	91.75
Sep ED future	91.68

FRN coupon fixes at 8.65 per cent

Issuer buys 100 June contracts at 91.75
Realised profit: (100 contracts × 118 ticks × $25) $295,000

Issuer buys 102 September contracts at 91.67
Realised profit: (102 contracts × 117 ticks × $25) $292,500

December:

–$4,325,000	Issuer pays FRN investor's interest at 8.65 per cent
+$587,500	Realised profit on futures
–$3,737,500	Net cost of funds (equivalent to 7.475 per cent)
	$3.7375m/$100m × 2

In this case by selling futures the hedger has managed to fix the interest cost at 7.475 per cent. This compares with a locked-in rate that would be achievable via FRAs of 7.35 per cent (i.e. FRA price of 7.2 per cent plus 15 basis points). The difference illustrates the extra basis risk that futures hedgers take on when the delivery dates and maturities of the futures contracts do not exactly correspond to the interest risk being hedged.

Incorporating the Compounding Effect

Notice also that the hedger has sold a total of 202 $1m contracts to hedge $100m in interest risk. 100 contracts are sold to cover the period from June to September. The period from September to December is hedged via the sale of $102m worth of contracts. The extra two contracts are required because of the compounding effect. They reflect the fact that any interest received in September for the first three months of the risk period will need to be rolled forward to December.

The interest cost for the first three months is fixed at 7.07 per cent (by selling futures at 92.93). By September, $1.7675m in interest would have accrued ($100m × 7.07 per cent × 0.25yrs). The extra two $1m contracts therefore represent the nearest whole number of September futures required to roll this interest forward to December.

The example illustrates the importance of mirroring the interest risk being hedged as closely as possible to minimise basis risk. However, basis risk can never be eliminated by hedgers using futures to manage interest rate risk on cash positions. Futures market participants accept this limitation in exchange for enhanced tradeability. In designing hedging strategies they will, therefore, pay close attention to the liquidity of the contract months as well as trying to match the risk period. In the illustration above for instance, a risk manager might well sell 202 June futures if the June Eurodollar contract was being traded much more actively than the one for September delivery. In effect, he would be accepting some extra basis risk in order to reduce liquidity risk on the hedge.

Interest Rate Sensitivity for Long and Short Positions

For both corporations and financial institutions the interest risk management problem is, at root, about managing the relationship between assets and liabilities. Future payments must be financed as cheaply as possible, while maximising the current value of future cash inflows. Whether interest risk management techniques are being applied to a single cashflow, a coupon bearing security or the entire balance sheet, the problem remains the same.

Consider the situation of a risk manager who is anticipating the receipt of $1m in a year's time. We know that the present value of the future cashflow will depend on today's one year interest rate. If the risk manager wishes to realise its value now, he simply borrows an amount that with interest will be equivalent to $1m. So, at 10 per cent he would borrow $909,091. If interest rates were higher at, say 12 per cent, $1m in a year would be worth just $892,857 today.

The same applies in reverse to future short positions. A $1m payment in a year would cost $909,091 to lock out today by lending at 10 per cent for a year. In a 12 per cent environment it would cost just $892,857 in today's terms.

Risk managers are therefore sensitive to rising interest rates as far as their long positions (i.e. cash inflows) are concerned; they are at risk in a falling interest rate environment on the short portion of the book. In addition, the level of sensitivity is greater the further into the future the cashflows occur. The present value of a cashflow due in a few days' time will not alter dramatically even if interest rates change significantly. If the cashflow does not occur for several years, however, the effect on its present value will be considerable for even a small change in the relevant interest rates.

Measuring Interest Rate Sensitivity

The effect on profits of a given change in yield is inextricably related to the period until the cashflows occur. If the risk manager is concerned with a single cashflow, it is relatively simple to assess the sensitivity of its present value for a given change in yields.

More usually, though, risk managers are faced with a series of future cashflows, both payments and receipts. If they are to be able to establish an appropriate hedging strategy, they must identify the price sensitivity of the book as a whole. Further, since they are sensitive to a rise in interest rates on long positions and falling rates on their short positions, they will need to isolate these different types of risk separately.

Matched Funding

The best way to minimise the interest rate sensitivity of a portfolio is to maintain a set of mirrored positions. If all cash inflows are precisely offset by equivalent outflows then the loss on one side of the book from any change in yields will of course be mirrored by an equal profit on the other side.

For FIs, matched funding represents the least risky method of funding their lending activities. As market makers in money they can borrow at the bid rate and lend at the offer rate. They earn the spread between offer and bid (also known as the net interest margin) and have no exposure to changes in the yield curve.

In practice, of course, matched funding is not always possible. It is also distinctly unprofitable: the market is efficient and matched funders are unable to benefit from interest rate movements. Since market participants run unmatched positions they require a mechanism for comparing the effect on profits of owning assets and liabilities with disparate maturities.

Gap Analysis

Gapping is widely employed in assessing the interest rate sensitivity of the balance sheet as a whole. Basically the process involves analysing the cumulative net position across time periods. Cashflows are added together up to specific target dates. Typically, this might involve looking at snapshots of the net position daily for the next week, weekly out to one month, monthly out to one year and annually from then on.

Most market participants simply add future known cashflows together to arrive at the net, cumulative figure on each date, its gap. This can provide a useful snapshot of the overall complexion of interest sensitivity so that the risk manager knows, broadly speaking, for which yield curve maturities he will be most exposed to rising, and where he is sensitive to falling yields. But, because it ignores time value effects it presents a distorted picture.

The gap is an important first step in asset/liability management, but it is not well suited for more detailed analysis. The method's inaccuracies can be alleviated by using the present values of future, known cashflows when calculating gap values. This can be done very simply once the zero coupon factors have been calculated.

Selecting Gap Intervals

The gap idea can be made much more useful to risk managers who use interest rate futures and options on futures by relating gap intervals to futures delivery dates. By taking (present value based) gaps that coincide with these the risk manager can minimise basis risk. Arguably also it is better practice to 'clump' cashflows with the nearest future, rather than always roll positions forward.

So, the June gap, for instance, would comprise positions maturing between the start of May until the end of July. A positive gap of $12m would then indicate a futures hedge of selling 12 June contracts. Gapping can be used with duration based and yield curve analysis to inform risk management with an element of stochastic protection.

Building Uncertainty into a Futures Hedge

An FI decides to use three-month Eurodollar futures to hedge its portfolio. Its assets and liabilities each have a present value of $100m. The assets have a duration (their average period length, see Chapter 12) of two years. The liabilities have a duration of 0.5. Three-month Eurodollar futures have a duration of 0.25; each contract represents a $1m deposit.

When structuring a hedge the FI will be aware that every time an exposure is controlled a potential profit is lost. The total number of futures bought or sold will therefore depend on the FI's view on interest rate movements. If it is 100 per cent confident that interest rates are going higher, then it will only want to hedge the asset side of the portfolio. It would therefore sell 800 futures (i.e. 2.0 / 0.25 multiplied by $100m / $1m).

If, on the other hand, it is sure that interest rates will fall it will want to hedge just its short positions. Since these have a duration of 0.5 the correct number of futures to buy is 200.

These two strategies represent the polar extremes if the action is to be considered a hedging not a speculative operation. To immunise the net book against any movement in the yield curve, up or down, it would need to sell 600 futures (800 – 200).

By knowing the extremes as well as the neutral implied hedge the FI will probably sell slightly more (or less) futures according to how bearish (or bullish) its interest rate stance.

Exactly which Eurodollar futures contracts are used is a material factor in judging the performance of the hedge. If the yield curve changes shape then the futures will not necessarily offset the change in portfolio value, so from one standpoint the FI will try to select futures periods that correspond to the risk intervals on its portfolio. On the other hand, near-dated futures tend to be traded more actively so the FI might decide to take on extra basis risk to reduce its liquidity risk.

STRATEGIES FOR INTEREST RISK MANAGEMENT

This section introduces some sample interest risk management strategies. Eurodollar futures and options are used for expository simplicity, but the strategies shown apply equally to FRA and IRG combinations.

Table 7.1 Eurodollar (IMM) – September contracts

$1 million; pts of 100 per cent Future = 96.64		
Option Strikes	*Call*	*Put*
9625	0.44	0.05
9650	0.24	0.10
9675	0.09	0.20
9700	0.02	0.38
9725	0.01	0.62
9750	0.0004	0.86

Source: Wall Street Journal, 13 April 1993

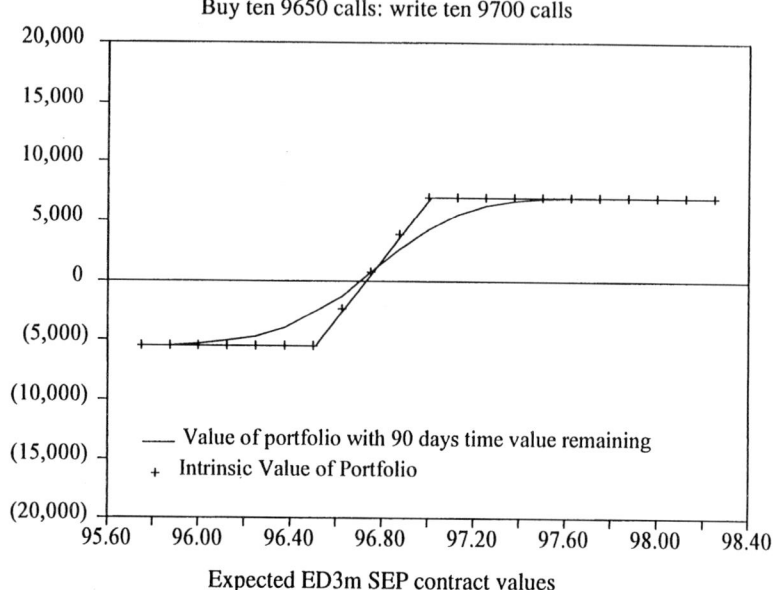

Figure 7.2 Bull spread strategy

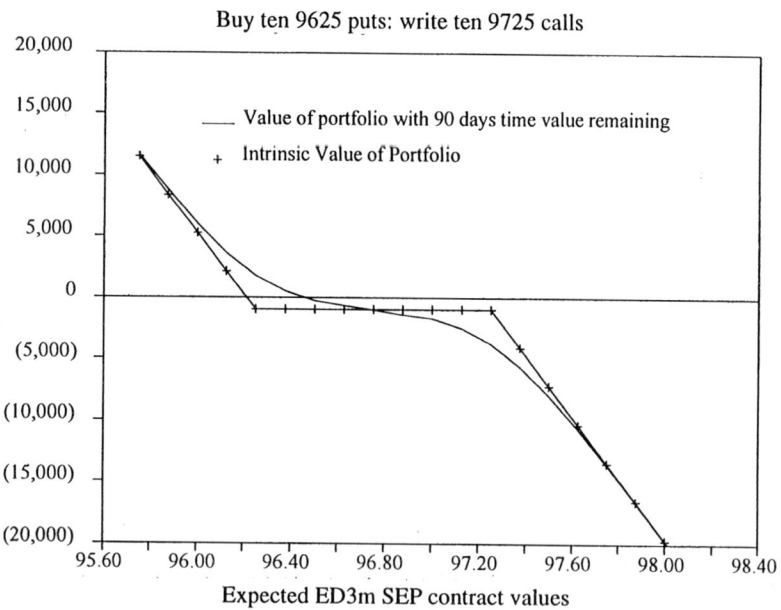

Figure 7.3 Short-range futures strategy

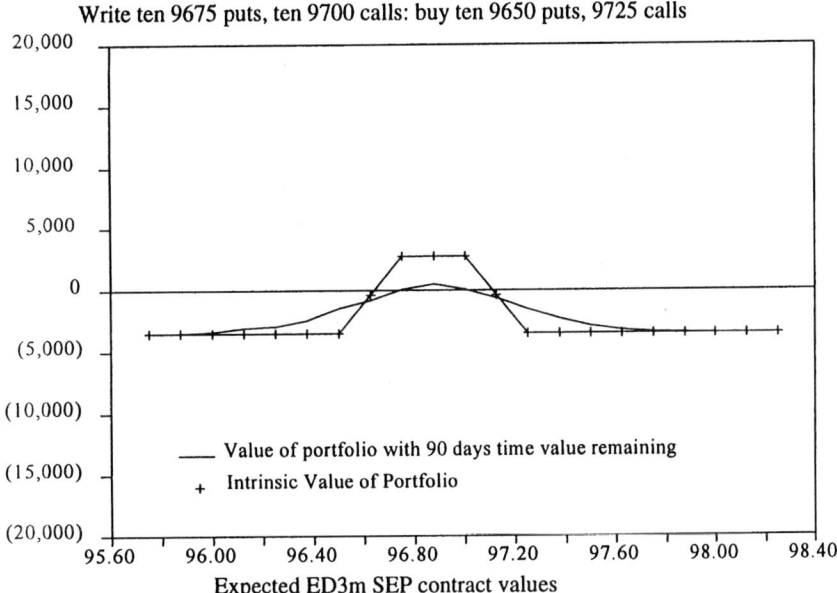

Figure 7.4 Contra-volatility strategy

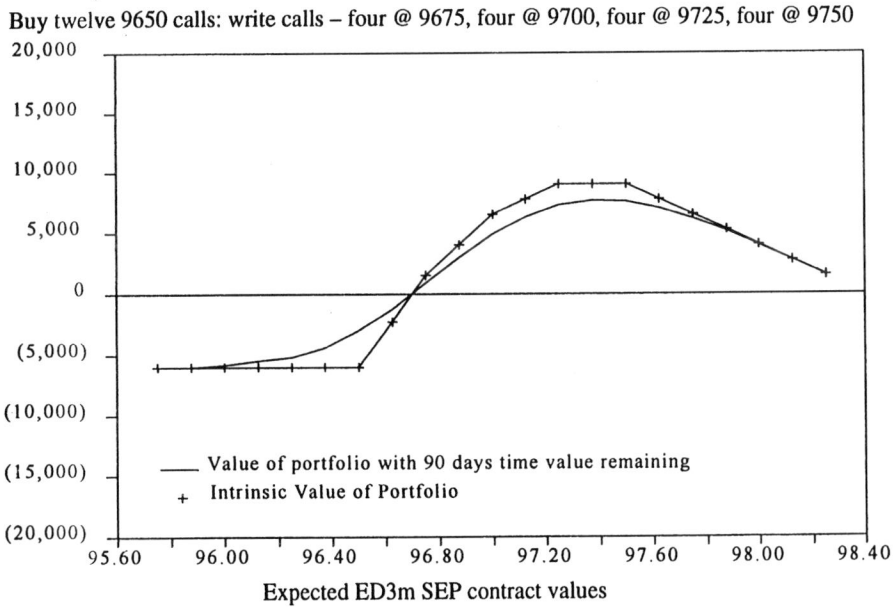

Figure 7.5 Bullish combination strategy

121

8: Foreign Exchange

SPOT MARKETS

This section describes briefly the market conventions in foreign exchange spot markets.

Spot Value

A spot deal is the standard transaction in FX markets. Counterparties enter into an agreement to exchange currencies two business days after the deal date (the spot date). So, a deal done on Wednesday would be executed on Friday; if Thursday was the deal date, spot value would be the following Monday.

FX transactions are settled according to the principle of *valeur compensée*. This means that an FX deal is a two-way transaction where both currencies must be settled at the same time. The practical implication of this rule (which is meant to limit credit risk for the counterparties) is that, because the spot date must be a business day in both financial centres, there are occasions when the spot date is three business days forward (for one centre).

Imagine for instance a US$/DM transaction agreed on Monday 2 July between a Frankfurt-based trader and one in New York. 4 July is, of course, a holiday in the USA, so they might agree to deal for value 5 July. An adjustment to the spot rate might need to be made if there was an interest differential between the two currencies.

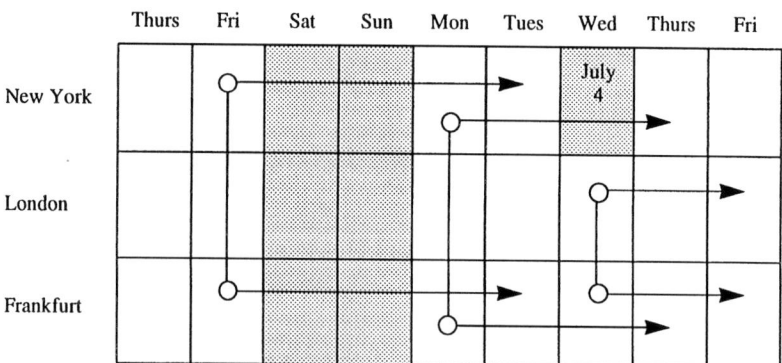

Figure 8.1 Spot value dates for $/DM transactions

They do have one other alternative, however. The New York dealer might agree to receive (or pay) his dollars in one of the Euromarkets, such as London. Since London is open on 4 July the spot date for the transaction can remain two days forward. This would be a Euromarket transaction.

Standard Transactions

Since FX spot deals are conducted over the counter (OTC) their precise terms are agreed bilaterally between the counterparties. The bid-ask rates quoted via Reuters and other price vendors are assumed to be good for transactions in $1 million or equivalent. Spreads for smaller deals ($250,000 or less) may be quoted on a wider spread reflecting the cost of processing. There is also a convention that very large deals ($5 million or more) can be scaled down at the option of the market maker.

The main currencies are traded against the US dollar. The sterling–dollar rate is known as cable. Others of the most active markets include dollar–mark, dollar–swiss, dollar–yen and dollar–ECU.

US and European Terms

An exchange rate expresses the relationship between two currencies. It equates one unit of currency A, known as the base currency, to its currency B equivalent, the quoted currency. This rate of A to B is described as the A/B rate. So, for example, the $/DM rate means the amount of DM needed to buy or sell $1, and the DM/$ rate gives the equivalent in $ of DM1.

Most rates against the dollar are usually quoted as $/CCY, i.e. with the dollar as the base currency. This form of FX quotation is known as European terms. For historical reasons cable is the exception here; the relationship between £ and $ is usually quoted as £/$. Where the non-dollar currency is the base currency the quotation is described as being expressed in US terms.

In the US, FX dealers often prefer to quote rates in US terms; currency futures are also generally expressed in this way. By making the non-dollar currency the base currency we can quickly calculate dollar profit and loss simply by looking at the change in the price and multiplying by the base currency amount.

To convert a rate from one type to the other, calculate its reciprocal.

If $/FF = 5.50   i.e. $1 = FF5.50
Then   FF/$ = 0.1818 (1/5.5)   i.e. FF1 = $0.18

The different ways that the same currency relationship can be expressed can make FX appear confusing to the uninitiated. For this reason it can be helpful always to think in terms of buying or selling a commodity. It is a lot clearer to talk about the base currency being a 'brick' which is priced in the quoted currency. Once it is seen that a currency is just like any other commodity, the same rules, of supply and demand, buying low and sellng high etc. apply to it.

If £/$ = 1.5450 – 1.5460   i.e. £ is the commodity ('brick')
           then a customer can buy one £ 'brick' for $1.5460
           and a customer can sell one £ 'brick' for $1.5450

The Bid–Offer Spread

Market makers quote two-way prices for currency, describing the rates at which they are prepared to buy and sell the base currency. The bid–offer spread represents the difference between these rates. The width of the spread reflects the liquidity of the market. When the spread is very narrow, it reflects the fact that the market maker is anxious to deal and liquidity is high. The wider the spread, the more difficult it becomes to execute transactions, and in general the less liquid the market. The professionalism of market makers is judged according to the narrowness of the spreads they are prepared to quote, especially when prices are volatile.

Exchange rates are quoted in terms of basis points or 'pips' (see the examples below). Actively traded currencies will normally be quoted on a 5 to 10 basis point spread, though spreads will depend in large measure on current market volatility. If exchange rates are moving quickly the average spread can easily widen to 50 basis points or more.

In practice, because many FX rates are quoted in European terms, it would be confusing if dealers were to talk about buying and selling the base currency. For $/yen, $/mark and $/Swiss, for example, the base currency is always the US dollar. They therefore quote bid and offer rates for the non-dollar currency. So, where the non-dollar currency is the quoted currency (i.e. European terms quotations), the market maker's bid is the same as the 'brick's' offer (i.e. the right hand side of the quote), and the offer is equivalent to the 'brick' bid (i.e. the left hand side of the quote).

Of course for cable and other US terms quotations the bid is the left hand side of the quote, and the offer the right hand side of the quote just as it is for any other commodity.

($/DM big figure is 1.47)
'50–57'   spread = 7 pips
50 = DM offer   57 = DM bid
Market maker buys $ at DM1.4750, sells $ at DM1.4757

'10–90'   spread = 80 pips
10 = DM offer   90 = DM bid
Market maker buys $ at DM1.4710, sells $ at DM1.4790

'90–10'   spread = 20 pips
90 = DM offer   10 = DM bid
Market maker buys $ at DM1.4790, sells $ at DM1.4810

(£/$ big figure is 1.54)
'50-55'   spread = 5 pips
50 = £ bid   55 = £ offer
Market maker buys £ at $1.5450, sells £ at $1.5455

One pip or point represents the minimum price movement between the currencies involved. Most rates are quoted in the form NN.NNNN; in these circumstances one pip equals 0.0001. However other currencies – notably $/Y and $/Lire – are quoted differently, and the value of a pip reflects this. For instance, with a $/Y rate of, say, 135.50, one pip equals 0.01.

Cross Rate Quotations

Many banks now make markets in cross rate FX transactions in the major currencies. An FX cross is simply an exchange rate where neither of the two currencies is the US dollar. Active markets exist for, among others, £/DM, SF/DM, £/yen and DM/yen. In addition market makers will generally quote a variety of cross rates against the local currency.

The cross rate can be created synthetically via two FX transactions. To buy sterling against a sale of yen, the dealer might sell yen/buy dollars and sell dollars/buy sterling simultaneously. Implied £/yen bid-offer rates can therefore be found by combining £/$ and $/yen prices. Unless the quoted £/yen price is within the limits defined by these equalities an arbitrage opportunity will occur.

Of course, in actively traded cross rate markets the bid-offer spread may well be narrower than that implied by its technical relationship to $/yen and £/$ prices. This reflects the fact that the dealer can lay off the position directly in the market rather than by having to do two spot transactions; the direct approach is usually cheaper.

FORWARD INSTRUMENTS

This section covers the main types of FX forward transaction. FX swaps, forward outrights, FXA/ERAs/SAFEs and currency futures are discussed in detail and their application to currency risk management is examined.

The Link with Interest Rates

Very often customers want to hedge known foreign exchange exposures that will occur on some future date. The various forward foreign exchange instruments are designed to make it simple for them to do this. However, it would still be possible to price FX transactions for forward delivery even if no formal forward FX markets existed.

125

It is a mistake to view the forward FX markets as reflecting the market's view of the future levels for spot FX rates. Forward FX rates are the result of an arbitrageable relationship between today's spot FX rates and the relative interest rates for the two currencies to the forward date.

Premium and Discount Currencies
We saw in Chapter 2 how a trader could establish a price for selling DM and buying dollars three months forward. This was based on the spot rate and the relative interest costs and benefits of rolling the two currencies forward. In the example the $/DM spot rate was 2.0000 and the implied forward 1.9951: in other words the same amount of dollars can be bought with fewer Deutschmarks in three months' time. The reason for this is that there is an interest differential between the two currencies. An owner of Deutschmarks on the spot date earns less interest than for an equivalent dollar position. The law of interest parity states that any forward FX price must compensate for this difference, otherwise arbitrage will occur.

A lower interest rate currency will therefore be worth more in terms of a higher interest rate currency in the future. This is why for any FX rate, the lower interest rate currency is known as the premium currency, while the currency whose interest rate is higher is known as the discount currency.

Implied forward prices can be found by using the zero coupon factors for each of the currencies. For instance, the one year $/DM forward bid price (the amount of DM a market maker will buy in exchange for a given amount of dollars in one year's time) is found by taking the spot $/DM bid, multiplying by the DM offer factor and dividing by the dollar bid factor. The forward offer price is found by transposing bids and offers.

FX Swap Markets

The standard interbank transaction in the forward markets is an FX swap. Counterparties agree to exchange currency amounts on two separate dates, the spot date and the forward date, at predefined exchange rates. An FX swap is, effectively, two deals in one: the counterparties are lending and borrowing the currencies, one from the other, for the swap period (Figure 8.2).

There is an active FX swap market for the major money market yield curve dates. Swaps can be traded for broken dates and with forward dates out to five years, they are priced according to demand within the range implied by the relative interest rates. By dealing in FX swaps traders are able to provide forward liquidity without taking on a currency risk. Since they have performed equal and opposite FX transactions it follows that any losses on one leg of the swap will be offset by equivalent profits on the other leg as the implied basis adjusts to the new currency level. They are therefore able to concentrate on trading the interest

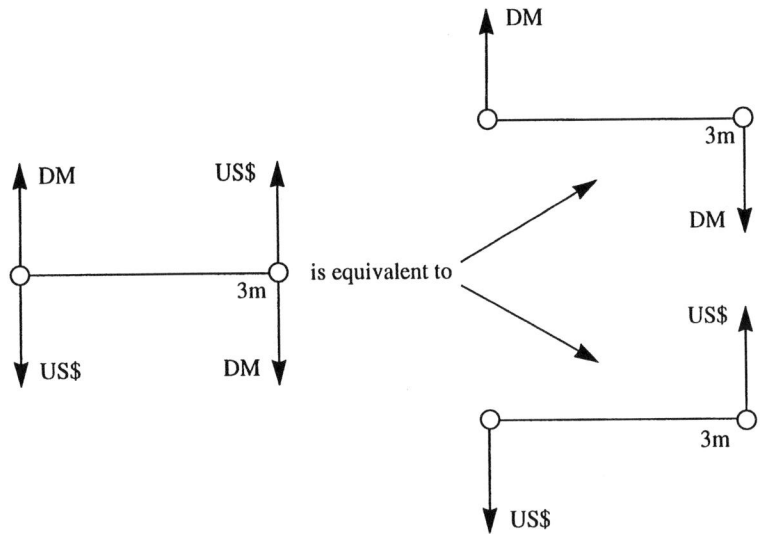

Figure 8.2 A three-month $/DM FX Swap is like a simultaneous loan and deposit for the currencies

differential between the two currencies. In fact, the FX swap transaction does have a residual currency risk and this is discussed in more detail later in this section.

FX Swap Quotation Conventions

FX swap prices are quoted as points or pips above or below the current spot rate. These pips may be subtracted from or added to the spot rate, depending on which is the premium and which the discount currency. If the base currency is the discount (i.e. low interest rate) currency the points are subtracted from the spot rate; they are added to the spot rate when the base currency is at a premium to the quoted currency.

Dealers often talk about dollar discount or dollar premium points. Dollar premium points are added to the spot rate when the dollar is the base currency. Where the dollar is the quoted currency dollar premium points are subtracted from the spot rate. However, to minimise confusion the terms 'discount points' and 'premium points' will refer to the base currency in this discussion.

Although they are subtracted, base currency discount points are not quoted with a minus sign. They can, however, be distinguished from premium points by the fact that the left hand number (i.e. the forward base currency bid) is larger than the right side of the quote.

Points are only signed when one is negative and the other positive. Because the forward rate bid–offer spread is generally wider than the spread on the spot rate, this normally refers to the situation where each of the two currencies has a similar interest rate, the forward bid is lower and the offer higher than the spot rates.

127

Standard Transactions

The standard size of an FX swap transaction follows the conventions used in the spot market. Counterparties agree to exchange the same amount of the base currency on the spot and forward dates with amounts of the quoted currency determined by the spot and forward rates. In this sense an FX swap departs from the borrowing and lending activities it is meant to represent and this has important implications for the currency sensitivity of the transaction (see the discussion below on currency risk).

Shorts

The short end of the FX swap market is used by spot traders to roll forward their positions at the end of each trading day. One day swaps take the same form as other FX swaps and are based on one day interest rates. Examples include the tom-next and spot-next swaps, which are used to roll forward currency positions from tomorrow to the spot date and from today's spot date to the following day's spot date, respectively.

In this way spot traders can maintain spot value currency positions from one day to the next. However care must be taken to roll forward the entire position, particularly when the FX rate has changed since the time it was taken out.

By way of illustration, consider the situation of a spot trader who bought $1m against a sale of ECU at 1.5000. Both ECU and dollar interest rates are 10 per cent, so the spot-next points will be zero. What happens if the $/ECU rate then changes to 1.4000?

Original transaction
Spot: +$1,000,000   Buy dollars against ECU sale
       −ECU1,500,000   Sell ECU at 1.5000 against $ purchase

Spot-next transaction
spot: −$1,000,000   Sell dollars against ECU purchase
       +ECU1,400,000   Buy ECU against dollar sale at 1.4
next: +$1,000,000   Buy dollars against ECU sale
       −ECU1,400,000   Sell ECU against dollar purchase at 1.4

The position has been re-established the following day, but ECU100,000 has not been rolled forward. For the spot trader this may not matter, especially if he is in the habit of marking spot positions to market every day and transferring the balance to a profit and loss account. However, the same transaction is done every day by FX swap traders. For them, the lost ECU will undermine the integrity of the swap and it will become sensitive to currency risk. They should therefore borrow ECU100,000 in the money markets to ensure that using shorts to roll forward the spot portions of their FX swaps does not alter their profitability.

Calculating Forward Points

We have seen how the forward FX is derived by a combination of the spot rate and the interest rates for the two currencies. The currencies are bought and sold on the spot date generating long and short positions. The bought currency is lent until the forward date at the relevant interest rate; the sold currency is borrowed until the forward date. This has the effect of deferring the spot transaction; the forward outright rate is determined by calculating the ratio between the two currency amounts on the forward date.

Forward points simply express the differential between the forward FX rate and the spot FX rate. The table below illustrates the spot and forward relationships for a variety of currency/interest rate combinations in February 1991.

Interest rates as at 21 February 1991

	3m bid	3m offer
US$	6.50	6.55
DM	9.00	9.05
£	12.50	12.55
NLG	9.00	9.05

Spot and forward rates as at 21 February 1991

	Spot (mid)	3m Fwd	3m Fwd pts
US$/DM	1.4759	1.4848/52	89/93
£/US$	1.9700	1.9419/24	281/276
DM/NLG	1.1264	1.1259/69	–5/+5

For US$/DM the dollar is the premium currency and points are added on. The base currency discount points for £/US$ are not signed but the fact that the left hand side of the quote (281) is a larger number than the right hand side (276) implies that they should be subtracted from the spot price. The forward points for the Deutschmark–Dutch guilder cross are signed, however, indicating the DM and NLG interest rates are equivalent.

For unsigned points, a quick way to work out whether the forward points should be added or subtracted from the spot and which is the low interest currency is shown below.

Write down the currencies:	BASE/QTD	BASE/QTD
Write down the points:	LHS/RHS	LHS/RHS
Which number is larger?	LOW/HIGH	HIGH/LOW
Same as interest relationship:	LOW/HIGH	HIGH/LOW
Add or subtract points?	ADD	SUBTRACT
Base currency:	PREMIUM	DISCOUNT

Market makers doing swaps buy and sell using the same base rate for spot and forward, rather than using, say, the bid side of the spot rate for the spot portion and the offer side of the spot rate plus or minus the points for the forward. This encourages the liquidity of the market.

Points are Expressing the Forward Rate / Spot Rate Relationship
Forward points are a short-cut method of expressing the relationship between the spot and the forward rate. As such the points can change when the exchange rate changes, even though the interest differential remains the same.

Consider this extreme case, by way of illustration. The $/FF rate is 10.0000, one year dollar rates are 9 per cent, one year French franc rates are 10 per cent. The interest differential is 1 per cent and the forward points are therefore quoted as 917. Some months later the dollar has doubled in value, the $/FF rate is now 5.0000. Interest rates are unchanged but one year forward points now stand at 459.

This highlights a practice that the FX swap user would be well advised to adopt. He should, for the purposes of analysis, always look at forward rates in terms of their relationship to the spot rate. In this way, whatever the $/FF spot rate, the forward value remains unchanged at 100.92 per cent (i.e. 10.0917 divided by 10 or 5.0459 divided by 5). Of course, using this approach assumes that he is insensitive to currency movements and this issue is discussed below.

Forward Outrights

A forward outright is an OTC transaction where the counterparties agree to exchange currency amounts on a given date in the future. Unlike an FX swap there is no corresponding spot transaction. Buyers and sellers of forward outrights are therefore taking on highly speculative positions unless these are offset by other exposures.

The price of a forward outright is calculated according to the bid and offer spot rates and the bid and offer FX swap points, it is expressed as an absolute number. The bid–offer spread on an outright transaction includes both the spot and the forward point spreads, reflecting the fact that a market maker will have to do both transactions to close out his risk.

Corporations are the main users of forward outrights. The deals are attractive to them because they can use them to match off their future currency exposures. As an OTC market they can exchange precise amounts of currencies on specific future dates, and this level of hedging precision is extremely useful.

Forward–Forward FX Swaps

Just as FX swaps can be made to replicate borrowing and lending currencies in the spot markets, the same thing can be done for forward–forward interest rates. The forward–forward FX swap is a special transaction that is normally created by means of two ordinary FX swaps, one with a forward date that is at the start date of the forward–forward period, the other with a forward portion that occurs at the end of the intended swap.

Points for forward–forward FX swaps are determined by the differential between the forward points on the two swaps. Generally, the first forward date is done at today's spot rate and the second date priced according to the forward-forward points. This is in fact an inefficiency in the market which can give rise to arbitrageable anomalies.

An illustration of how a forward–forward FX swap can be constructed is shown below:

$/DM Spot Rate	=	1.4750
3m $/DM points	=	89/93
12m $/DM points	=	340/350
3m/12m points	=	247/261

Construction of a 3m/12m FX swap using two FX swaps, $1m and DM equivalent. To find the break-even for his DM bid the market maker would have to:

Buy DM forward using the 3m swap at market rates
Sell DM forward using the 12m swap at market rates

The cashflows would be as follows:

Value spot:
+$1,000,000   Buy $ against DM in spot portion of 3m swap
–DM1,475,000   Sell DM vs $ at 1.4750 in spot portion of 3m swap
–$1,000,000   Sell $ against DM in spot portion of 12m swap
+DM1,475,000   Buy DM vs $ at 1.4750 in spot portion of 12m swap

Value 3m:
–$1,000,000   Sell $ against DM in forward portion of 3m swap
+DM1,483,900   Buy DM vs $ for 3m swap at market's DM offer

Value 12m:
+$1,000,000   Buy $ against DM in forward portion of 12m swap
–DM1,510,000   Sell DM vs $ for 12m swap at market's DM bid

The break-even offer price is, of course, produced by the reverse set of positions. We can see from this that the theoretical amount of DM for the first leg of the forward–forward FX swap is DM1,483,900. In other words the base rate that should be used is 1.4839 not the current spot rate. However, because they believe currency price movements to be irrelevant to their profitability, FX swap traders will often use today's spot as the base price. Sophisticated swap traders can take advantage of this inefficiency to produce locked in profits.

FSAs, ERAs and FXAs

Risk managers can use forward–forward swaps to lock into the current interest rate differential between two currencies' forward–forward interest rates. However, the practice of doing two FX swaps to create a forward–forward position is, in practice, risky to implement, and balance sheet intensive.

Market participants have therefore developed instruments that perform a similar risk management function to the forward–forward swap but do so in a more efficient way. In 1985 Hong Kong Shanghai Bank introduced an instrument known as the forward spread agreement (FSA), which was priced according to relative interest differentials. The FSA buyer paid the spread, defined as the difference between the dollar and the other currency's forward–forward rate. On the settlement date the FSA payer receives the difference between the reference dollar LIBOR and the other currency's LIBOR. The FSA price was quoted in terms of per annum basis points and payable in dollars. FSAs were thus similar to doing two FRA transactions for the forward period: in this case buying a dollar FRA and selling an FRA in the second currency.

Although similar to two FRAs, the FSA does not provide precisely the same risk–reward characteristics. This is because the FSA differential is settled as a dollar amount. The FSA therefore provides no protection against the cashflow effects of changes in currency values. For instance, consider the buyer of a $/DM FSA. She agrees to pay the seller the dollar denominated interest differential (or spread) between the $ FRA price and the DM FRA price for a specific period in the future on a given amount of US dollars (the notional amount). Simultaneously, she agrees to receive the spread between the respective LIBORs for the two currencies on the start date of the FSA period.

So, for example, with a $1m 3m/9m $/DM FSA, when $ 3m/9m FRAs are at 6.5 per cent and DM 3m/9m FRAs are trading at 9 per cent, the buyer agrees to pay a spread of −2.5 per cent (6.5 per cent minus 9 per cent). Suppose that, three months later, 6m $ LIBOR is 7 per cent, while 6m DM LIBOR has fallen to 8 per cent. The counterparties would settle the spread differential. The buyer would pay −2.5 per cent according to the FSA price (i.e. receive 2.5 per cent) and receive −1 per cent (i.e. pay 1 per cent), according to the LIBOR differential. She is thus a net receiver of 1.5 per cent (i.e. he pays out −2.5 per cent and receives −1.0 per cent).

The amount of cash she receives is paid in dollars and depends on the size of the FSA and the length of the period. Here +1.5 per cent is equivalent to +$7,500 (7.5% × $1m × 0.5yrs). For credit risk reasons settlement is actually made at the start of the period using the discounted settlement formula outlined in the discussion on FRAs; the dollar LIBOR rate is used for discounting purposes so the amount received is actually $7,246 ($7,500 / (1 + 0.5 × 7%)). As with FRAs, though, it is useful for analytic purposes to think in terms of the differential being settled at the end of the FSA period.

The $7,500 represents an interest risk amount, but because the DM side of the differential is settled in dollars it retains sensitivity to currency movements. We can see this effect by looking at the cashflow impact of doing the equivalent FRA transactions. If the $/DM spot at the outset were 1.5, this would imply buying a US$1m FRA and selling a DM1.5m FRA. Three months later the respective differentials would be +$2,500 ((7%–6.5%) × 0.5 × $1m) for the US$ FRA and +DM7,500 ((9%–8%) × 0.5 × DM1.5m) for the DM FRA. So long as the spot rate was still 1.5 on the settlement date the net amount received is still $7,500 ($2,500 + DM7,500/1.5). However, supposing the DM had strengthened against the dollar, the net cashflow would be higher: at $/DM1.4, say, it would be $7,857 ($2,500 + DM7,500/1.4).

In the example shown above the FSA settlement amount understates the amount of compensation required to compensate an FSA buyer against changes in interest differentials. The shortfall depends crucially on the magnitude of the non-dollar interest compensation, and whether it is paid or received. In the example above a positive DM differential left the FSA owner with an exposure to a stronger Deutschmark. Supposing the DM interest differential had implied a payment for the equivalent DM FRA she would have been exposed to declining Deutschmark values.

The interconnected nature of the currency and interest risks implied by an FSA makes them difficult to hedge. For Hong Kong Shanghai Bank, who dealt mainly in $/HK$ FSAs, this was not a problem in 1985 as $/HK$ was fixed at 10. For more volatile currency relationships, hedging strategies can be destabilised by this effect, outweighing the balance sheet advantages for FSAs against forward–forward swaps.

SAFEs

In 1987, two London banks introduced their own versions of a notional forward FX swap hedging instrument. Barclays launched exchange rate agreements (ERAs), which have very similar characteristics to FSAs. Midland's FXAs (forward cross-currency agreements) were devised so as to insulate dealers from the currency sensitivities described above for FRAs, which also occurred under the ERA structure.

Both FXAs and ERAs are quoted according to pips conventions to make them more readily understandable by FX forward traders. Forward pips, as we have seen, reflect interest rate differentials; pips for FXAs/ERAs relate to the differential between forward–forward yields. The generic description for these instruments is a SAFE (synthetic agreement for forward exchange). The British Bankers' Association has proposed standard terms and conditions for the two products. Although these have not, at the time of writing, been formally adopted by the FX markets, the BBA terms are widely used by traders.

The ERA Structure

To achieve the same interest differential position as the one described above in the FSA example, the risk manager would buy an ERA. She would therefore pay the $/DM spread. Interest rate parity conditions dictate that the pips quoted should be equivalent to the difference between the forward outright in three months and the forward outright in nine months. However, as we saw in the discussion on forward–forward FX swaps, many traders simply look at the interest differential for the forward period (2.5 per cent in this case) and apply it to the spot rate to arrive at swap pips. This convention implies that mispricing will sometimes occur, and this is the primary source of the arbitrage activity that currently contributes substantially to the volumes of SAFEs traded.

Suppose our risk manager is able to buy a $1m 3m/9m ERA at +188 pips (2.5% × 1.5 × 0.5). She hopes that in three months six- month forward pips will be lower as DM interest rates fall relative to dollar interest rates. Assuming no change in the spot FX rates, in our example DM rates fall to 8 per cent while dollar rates rise to 7 per cent; the 1 per cent differential is reflected by the ERA's settlement spread of +72 pips (1.5 × (1+8% × 0.5) / (1+7% × 0.5). The number of settlement pips will of course vary when the spot rate changed. The counterparties now settle according to the spread differential: the ERA buyer receives DM according to this 116 pip differential. For a $1m ERA the amount is DM11,600. As with FRAs and FSAs, differentials are actually settled on a present value basis at the start of the period, so the amount that changes hands is in fact DM11,154 (11,600 / (1+8% × 0.5)). However, for analytic purposes it is better to consider the cashflow as if it were paid at the end of the period.

At 1.5 the dollar equivalent of DM11,500 is $7,733. The difference between this and the FSA settlement amount is a symptom of their different pricing conventions. It actually reflects the fact that the quoted spread of 188 pips is an inaccurate reflection of interest rate parities. Having said this, apart from the fact that one is paid in dollars, the other in Deutschmarks, the two instruments are virtually identical in their profit and loss profiles.

The FXA Structure

Like FSAs, ERAs do not provide cover against the risk that changing currency values will affect interest amounts. FXAs, however, are specifically designed to insulate traders against this risk, and therefore provide superior hedging performance, particularly where the two currencies being traded have a volatile price relationship.

Under the FXA structure buyer and seller agree to exchange interest differentials at the prevailing FX forward rate. Suppose for our $/DM example the risk manager decided instead to buy an FXA. She agrees to pay the spread of 188 pips according to the then three-month forward outright price, which stands at 1.5092.

The settlement formula incorporates the difference between the outright and the spot on the settlement date into the calculation. Again, settlement occurs on a discounted basis, and the formula shown below describes the actual amount paid or received:

Where:

Fwd = Forward outright rate for start of FXA period on deal date
Spot = Spot rate at start of FXA period
AFS = Agreed FXA period spread expressed in pips per $
SFS = Settlement FXA period spread expressed in pips per $
Amount = US dollar amount of FXA transaction
T = Length of FXA period expressed in years
R = FXA period LIBOR of non-dollar currency on FXA settlement date

$$\text{Settlement amount} = \text{Notional} \times \left[\frac{(\text{Fwd} - \text{Spot}) + (\text{AFS} - \text{SFS})}{(1 + R \times T)}\right] - \text{Notional} \times (\text{Fwd} - \text{Spot})$$

This describes the non-dollar amount payable to the buyer on the settlement date. In our example, supposing that the spot rate remains at 1.5, the settlement amount becomes:

$$\$1m \times \left[\frac{(1.5092 - 1.5000) + (0.0188 - 0.0072)}{(1 + 8\% \times 0.5)}\right] - \$1m \times (1.5092 - 1.5000)$$

i.e.   DM11,600

To see the effect of changing currency levels consider what happens when $/DM spot has changed on the settlement date. With the same interest differentials, pips at settlement now stand at 68:

$$\$1m \times \left[\frac{(1.5092 - 1.4000) + (0.0188 - 0.0068)}{(1 + 8\% \times 0.5)}\right] - \$1m \times (1.5092 - 1.4000)$$

i.e.   DM7,338

The FXA profit and loss is meant to equate the notional transaction to the performance of the FX swap transactions it is supposed to replace. We can demonstrate that this objective is achieved by looking at the cashflows implied by the physical process of buying and selling via FX swaps:

	Dollar	Deutschmark
Value 3m:	+1,000,000	−1,509,200
	−1,000,000	+1,400,000
Value 9m:	−1,000,000	+1,528,000
	+1,000,000	−1,406,800

By doing the FXA equivalent swaps the dealer has realised a loss on the three-month date of DM109,200 and a profit of DM121,200 on the nine-month date. If the dealer then borrows for six months to discount the future profit to the start of the period at 8 per cent, she earns a present value equivalent of DM116,538. Net profit at the start date is therefore DM7,338, as with the FXA.

135

FXAs therefore mirror FX swaps with complete precision. Of course FX swaps themselves are subject to currency risk, but as we shall see in the next chapter this can be eliminated very simply using the spot hedge technique.

Currency Futures

Definition

A currency futures contract is a standard agreement that provides the holder with a specific amount of a currency on a specified date in the future. In common with other futures contracts the terms of the contract are standardised with respect to the size, credit quality and terms to enhance tradeability. Currency futures are offered on a variety of exchanges with delivery dates in March, June, September

Table 8.1 Major contracts

Exchange	Commodity	Size	Tick/Value	Contract months
CME/IMM/SFE	Aus Dollar	A$100,000	0.01cts/$10.00	Mar/Jun/Sep/Dec
CME/IMM	British Pound	£62,500	0.02cts/$12.50	Mar/Jun/Sep/Dec
CME/IMM	Canadian Dollar	C$100,000	0.01cts/$12.50	Mar/Jun/Sep/Dec
CME/IMM	Deutsche Mark	DM125,000	0.01cts/$12.50	Mar/Jun/Sep/Dec
CME/IMM	ECU	ECU125,000	0.01cts/$12.50	Mar/Jun/Sep/Dec
CME/IMM	French Franc	FF250,000	0.05cts/$12.50	Mar/Jun/Sep/Dec
CME/IMM	Japanese Yen	Yen12.5m	0.0001cts/$12.50	Mar/Jun/Sep/Dec
CME/IMM	Swiss Franc	SF125,000	0.01cts/$12.50	Mar/Jun/Sep/Dec
FINEX	ECU	ECU100,000	0.01cts/$10.00	Mar/Jun/Sep/Dec
FINEX	US Dollar Index	Index × $500	0.01pts/$5.00	Mar/Jun/Sep/Dec
TFE	US Dollar	US$50,000	0.01 C ct/C$5.00	Mar/Jun/Sep/Dec
SFE	Aus Dollar	A$100,000	0.01 cts/$10.00	Mar/Jun/Sep/Dec

CME/IMM	International Monetary Market (part of Chicago Mercantile Exchange)
FINEX	Financial Exchange (division of New York Cotton Exchange)
SFE	Sydney Futures Exchange
TFE	Toronto Futures Exchange

and December up to two years in the future. For the more popular contracts and exchanges other months are also available.

Although currencies were the first financial commodities to be traded on futures exchanges, they have been somewhat eclipsed by the success of interest rate and stock index contracts. The tremendous liquidity of spot and FX swap markets together with the inherent, speculative nature of currency futures have encouraged the growth of the OTC markets. Although currency futures are used by professionals to hedge their OTC positions, many prefer to cover their risk directly in the OTC markets. As a result a number of exchanges have withdrawn their currency futures contracts in recent years. A list of the main available contracts at the time of writing is shown in Table 8.1.

Pricing
Currency futures traded against the dollar are quoted using US terms. This method of pricing allows a fixed amount of the foreign currency to be the traded commodity, with a price determined in dollars and cents. For sterling this is the normal form of price quotation and the currency future's price will be similar to the forward outright FX rate for that date. Most other currencies are normally quoted using European terms, so the future's price will equate to the reciprocal of the quoted forward rate.

Tables 8.2 and 8.3 show dollar prices for Deutschmark and yen futures contracts on 21 January 1991. As with OTC forward outrights, which currency futures closely resemble, the value of the contracts depends on the spot price of

Table 8.2 Japanese yen (IMM) yen 12.5 million

$ per 100 Yen $12.50				
Contract	Open	High	Low	Settle	Open interest
Mar	0.7541	0.7574	0.7541	0.7566	40,369
Jun	0.7542	0.7565	0.7542	0.7558	1,118
Estimated volume 15,195		Open interest +636			

Table 8.3 Deutschmark (IMM) DM125,000

$ per DM $12.50				
Contract	Open	High	Low	Settle	Open interest
Mar	0.6644	0.6706	0.6642	0.6702	49,431
Jun	0.6608	0.6668	0.6608	0.6665	1,509
Estimated volume 24,241		Open interest: −3,602			

Source: Wall Street Journal

137

the currencies against the dollar and the interest rate differential between them and dollar yields. It can be seen from the data that on the date in question the contracts opened near their low price for the day. Both currencies appreciated before being settled at a closing price near to the day's high. In European terms, the dollar-mark March future settled at 1.4921 (1/0.6702), while dollar-yen March futures closed at 132.17 (1/0.7566).

The yen improved by less than the DM and fell back further from its high traded price. Since the interest rate relationships between the currencies remained broadly unchanged, the majority of the price change was due to changes in the spot rates. On the day in question, the international value of the dollar deteriorated before recovering slightly just before the close in trading. The yen's value remained neutral, while the Deutschmark strengthened.

The Cash–Futures Relationship

As with commodities the basis relationship between currency futures is delineated by the cash-and-carry relationship. In the discussion on pricing forward FX swaps, we saw how bid–ask, implied forward outright FX rates can be achieved for any date. The fact that market participants can build their own 'do-it-yourself' currency futures provides for an arbitrageable alternative if the contract moves outside of these technical restrictions.

Basis Risk for Currency Futures

Like other types of futures, currency contracts are generally not delivered. Instead, participants close out the position, on the risk date or the delivery date, whichever comes first. If it has been taken out as a hedge, the profit or loss on the transaction is used by the hedger to compensate him for a change in the value of his underlying exposure.

There are two approaches to currency futures hedging. If the hedger is unlikely to trade his position actively he will generally try to match his risk dates as accurately as possible. Normally he will seek to take out contracts that are delivered after the risk occurs. By doing this he is able to hedge the spot rate on the day of the exposure, through a close-out of his futures position.

However, unless the exposure occurs on the delivery date, he will have to accept a basis risk. Because futures are sold before delivery, the price that he gets for them will be determined by the current forward price, whereas the exposure must be closed out at the spot rate. The basis risk is of course greater, the larger the interest differential between the two currencies.

For the more active hedger or risk manager, it is often preferable to trade only in the near-dated contract. By buying and selling the correct number of near-dated futures according to the size of his total exposures he can often hedge his spot risk more cost-effectively. There is always the most activity in the near-dated contract, and the hedger may be able to strike a better deal by trading in large lots. In this case, he will normally wait until the delivery date before closing out his contracts. Unless the risk has materialised he will, at the same time, take out the same number of contracts for the next delivery date. This type of hedger obviously has a basis risk whenever he carries out a trade. He probably regards it as an opportunity, however, as this type of risk manager is much more concerned with liquidity risks.

Currency Index Contracts

Table 8.4 US dollar index (USDX) (FINEX)

$500 × Index: tick value $5.00					
Contract	*Open*	*High*	*Low*	*Settle*	*Open interest*
Mar	83.56	83.56	82.90	82.91	4,905
Jun	84.30	84.20	83.68	83.68	2,095
Estimated volume 1,500		Open interest −1,640			

Source: Wall Street Journal

The USDX future is based on a trade weighted index of the dollar's international value against other currencies. It is popular amongst large US based multinationals who have an exposure against most of the world's major currencies. For a company with large portions of its revenue denominated in foreign currencies and costs in US dollars, it can provide a cost effective means of hedging against the risk of the dollar appreciating against other currencies.

Risk managers who elect to use the USDX contract should realise that they may retain a substantial basis risk if their foreign currency exposures vary significantly from the proportions implied by the terms of the index. For instance, the US as a whole has a significant trading relationship with Canada. But the Canadian dollar will tend to weaken and strengthen in line with the US dollar. As the Canadian dollar relationship has a relatively high weighting in the USDX, the effect of dollar strengthening or weakening will have a diluted impact on the USDX price.

Take what happened on 21 January 1991; the price of yen March futures rose by 3.3 per cent (they opened at 0.7541 and closed at 0.7566). Although this was mainly due to a weaker dollar, the index only fell by 0.8 per cent on the same day (opened at 83.56, closed at 82.91).

The basis risk is reduced when the hedger's currency exposures closely correspond to those of the US economy. For hedging purposes it is therefore most suitable for very large, international, US headquartered concerns, Coca Cola or MacDonald's for instance. Such companies may use the index to hedge the majority of their currency risks, but they will still need to hedge the remaining exposure on individual currencies separately.

139

ECU Contracts

The ECU began life as a currency basket weighted according to the relative GNPs of European economies. As with the USDX, it is a useful hedging tool for companies with international exposures, in this case to European currencies, but they may retain a relatively large basis risk. However, the ECU is rapidly becoming a currency in its own right. In this sense it is currently a hybrid instrument. It retains some of the characteristics of an index, because of its technical relationships to individual currencies. On the other hand, the very real demand for ECUs means that it behaves like a proper currency.

DIFFs

In pursuit of new product opportunities, the IMM in Chicago has introduced DIFFs to the futures markets. A DIFF can be thought of as an exchange traded FXA. It allows hedgers and forward swap traders to lock into the dollar value of a forward interest rate differential. The DIFF is quoted on an index basis and varies according to the relative three-month Eurodollar and Eurocurrency futures prices. The standard size of a contract is $1m, and the value of a tick is $25.

For instance, the March DM DIFF would be quoted at 97.70 if the March Eurodollar was trading at 92.80 and the March Eurodeutschmark price was 90.50 (i.e. 100 minus (92.80 – 90.50)). DIFFs were popular with FIs, who valued the ability to trade interest differentials without being exposed to currency movements. Locals, however, found the contract difficult to price, particularly because Eurocurrency interest rate futures are not quoted in Chicago. DIFFs therefore had to be withdrawn, but they have now been re-launched on the Globex electronic trading system.

Mechanics of Trading

Hedgers and risk managers buy and sell currency futures with the aim of realising a profit that, in cash terms, will offset any losses on their underlying exposure resulting from a change in the currency and relative interest rate environment.

The standardised nature of futures contracts precludes risk managers from using them to immunise themselves completely against FX price shifts. Instead, they are attracted by the high level of market liquidity. As a result, currency futures are more appropriate for the professional sector of the market, which prizes the ability to trade their positions more actively during the risk management period. Typical futures users are the currency dealers in FIs and the global treasury management operations of sophisticated multinationals. They have both the expertise and the infrastructure required to deal successfully in the futures markets.

Margining and Hedging Costs

As with other futures markets dealers in currency futures are required to lodge margin with the exchange for every contract that they open. This margin amount is refundable when the contract is closed out, but, because the hedge may need to remain in place for several months, this can represent a significant cost of trading. Because of the high volatility of FX markets margins are typically high. Although the margin per contract is equivalent to other contracts (in the $10–$20 range), the average size of a contract is typically smaller.

By way of illustration, consider the case of the hedger who takes out 100 ECU125,000 contracts (an ECU12.5m position) at the IMM in January and holds the position open until June. The IMM requires an initial margin of $1250 per contract, so he is required to place $125,000 in a margin account for five months. Assuming for the moment that the futures price remains unchanged for the full five months, the fact that this capital is tied up could involve him in a loss of interest income. If dollar interest rates in January were 7 per cent he would sacrifice $3,646 ($125,000 $\times$ 7% $\times$ 150/360).

The exchanges recognise that this expense may deter institutions from using futures, but they do require margins if they are to underwrite futures users' credit risk. Some exchanges offer reduced margins for offsetting futures positions because of the reduced overall risk. For instance, a futures trader who is long of one June contract and short of one September contract is exposed to relative price shifts rather than the absolute level of yields.

OPTIONAL INSTRUMENTS

This section discusses the main forms of currency option available on the market. OTC options, currency derivatives, options on futures and exchange traded spot options are explained and their use in currency risk management is outlined.

Definition

A currency option is a contractual arrangement where the buyer owns the right but not the obligation to exchange currencies at a given rate for a prearranged period. The seller, or writer, of the option guarantees this rate in exchange for a premium, usually payable up-front. There are two main types of contract: a call option gives its owner the right to buy the currency, and a put option provides the right to sell the currency.

Since currencies are exchanged, a put in one currency is also a call in the other one. To avoid confusion dealers talk in terms of the non-dollar currency when discussing puts and calls. Where there is any doubt, with cross rate options for instance, the option is described in terms of the base currency, although dealers will normally clarify that they are quoting, for DM/FF say, the DM call.

OTC Currency Options

The first currency options were traded over the counter in the early 1980s and this is by far the most active and liquid market for them. Strike rates are quoted on the same basis as the underlying spot rate, so if the market convention is for European terms in the spot market, option strike rates will also be quoted in this way.

As OTC instruments their terms are individually negotiable between the counterparties, but the classic currency option is a European style option against the dollar. Currency calls may be used by people with a future short currency exposure to guarantee its maximum dollar equivalent cost. A put fixes the currency's minimum dollar value and can be used by hedgers to compensate them for the effects of the foreign currency weakening.

Premium Quotation

The way that option premiums are quoted depends on whether the currency is the base or the quoted one. Premiums are generally priced according to their dollar value. If the buyer wishes to pay the premium in another currency, the amount is found by translating the dollar amount into its equivalent at the prevailing spot rate.

For US terms currencies, such as cable or currency futures markets, the premium is normally quoted in cents per currency. So, for a £1m call at a strike of 1.5500, a premium quotation of 2.50 cents per pound implies a premium amount of $25,000 (£1m x $0.025). Suppose that the £/$ spot rate were 1.5750, the sterling premium payable would then be £15,873.

Where the currency is not the base currency, however, the dollar premium is quoted as a percentage. So, with a $1m DM call at 1.4950 (i.e. the right to buy

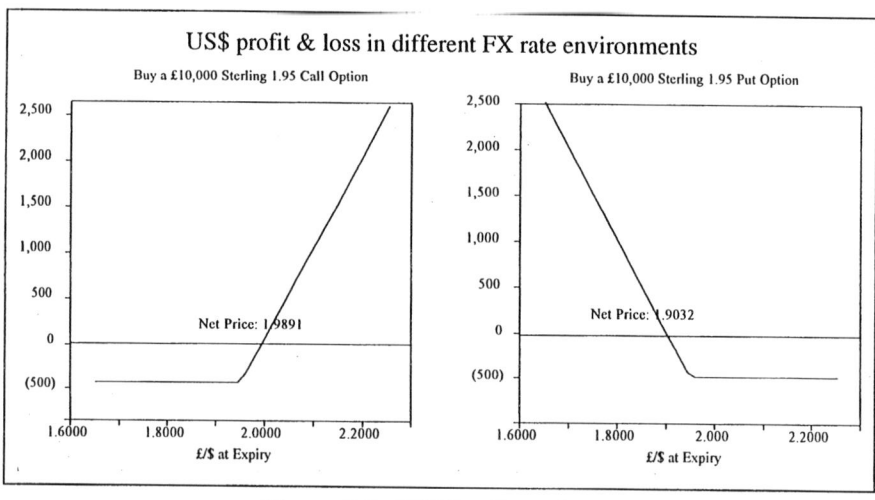

Figure 8.3 £/US$ calls and puts

DM1,495,000/sell $1m) a quoted premium of 2 per cent represents a cost of $20,000, a Deutschmark equivalent of $29,700 (with a $/DM spot rate of 1.4850).

Net Rates for Currency Options

The net rate is of course the worst case exchange rate guaranteed by the strike. The two styles of premium quotation must be applied differently to arrive at this number.

Consider first, the cents per currency quotation used for US terms rates. For the £/$ 1.55 call, the worst case cashflows would be a payment of $1.55m, a payment of $25,000, and a receipt of £1m. This gives a net rate of 1.5750. A £/$ put, on the other hand, with a strike of 1.55 and a premium of 2.5cts/£, would give its owner worst case cashflows of $1.95m in, $25,000 out, and £1m out. The net rate for the put will therefore be 1.5250. We can see therefore that the net rate can be found easily by adding (for calls, subtracting for puts) the premium quotation to the strike.

For European terms FX rates, though, where the dollar is the base currency, calculating net rates gets a little more complicated. A $/DM call in $1m with a strike at 1.4950 and a premium of 2 per cent will involve worst case cashflows of DM1.495m in, $1m out and $20,000 out. This equates to a net rate of 1.4657 (i.e. 1.495 / (1.0 + 0.02)). A similar put has worst case cashflows of DM1.495 out, $1m in and $20,000 out – a net rate of 1.5255.

Settlement and Delivery

The writer of a European style currency option guarantees to pay the buyer at expiry any positive difference between the strike and the current spot rate. The currencies are not normally physically exchanged, instead the buyer receives the intrinsic value on the option. So if cable stood at 1.6000 on the expiry date the writer of a 1.55 call in £1m would pay the option owner $50,000. Similarly the buyer of a $1m DM put with a strike of $/DM 1.4950 would receive DM5,000 if the spot rate at expiry were 1.5000.

Intrinsic Value for OTC Currency Options

We saw that an option's premium is a function of its intrinsic value and of time value. Options that are at the money have no intrinsic value, but considerable time value, the premiums for deep in the money options are almost entirely made up of intrinsic value, similarly deep out of the money options have hardly any time value.

With European style options, the owner may not exercise until the expiry date when he will receive only intrinsic value. The underlying instrument for a European style currency call expiring in three months is, therefore, not today's spot rate, but the three-month forward FX rate. Forwards, therefore, are the underlying instruments for currency options; their in , at or out of the money status is defined by their relationship with forward prices.

Pricing OTC Currency Options

As European style options, currency options can be priced successfully using a modified version of the Black–Scholes model. Black and Scholes designed their option pricing model for stocks: the log-normal distribution the method uses to predict future prices assumes that stocks are slightly more likely to increase in value than they are to decline. This is an appropriate assumption when looking at stocks, but not when an FX rate is the underlying instrument. FX prices are as likely to go up as to go down, so a better estimate of fair value is arrived at by using the normal distribution.

American Style Currency Options

An American style option provides its owner with the ability to exercise against the spot rate prevailing on any date up to and including its expiry date. Its intrinsic value can therefore be measured against today's spot rate. However, in certain yield curve environments this practice could result in American style options having a lower premium than their European style equivalents. This would set up an arbitrageable opportunity between the two types of option. Arbitrageurs could buy cheap American style options, simultaneously sell European ones and exercise both at expiry to realise the difference in premiums as a risk-free profit.

Intrinsic value for an American style option is therefore calculated against the best FX rates prevailing between today and its expiry date. The binomial pricing method, developed by Cox, Ross and Rubinstein provides a statistical tool that values the benefit of this early exercise feature.

Currency Derivatives Markets

The OTC markets have developed a number of tailored currency instruments, based on the option principle and priced according to options markets. These are designed to meet the specific requirements and sensitivities of currency risk managers. Some illustrations of these are presented below.

Asian Style Options

A product that is becoming increasing popular amongst corporate treasurers is the so-called Asian style or average rate option. Here the amount of intrinsic value payable at the exercise date is determined not by the spot rate at expiry, but according to the average daily, or weekly spot rate prevailing over the life of the option.

Many corporate treasurers have numerous, relatively small currency exposures that would be uneconomic to hedge separately. If they were to use a classic European style or American style option to hedge their position they could be exposed to a basis risk.

Suppose for instance that the treasurer of a US corporate has a series of long DM positions over the next six months, totalling DM15m. He wishes to guarantee their minimum US dollar equivalent, so he buys a $10m six-month DM put option at 1.5000. Immediately after buying the option the DM weakens to 1.7500 and remains at this level for most of the next six months. As each DM exposure occurs, he must sell DM in the spot market to realise its dollar equivalent. At $/DM 1.7500 he can buy only $8,571,429 against sales totalling DM15m. Unfortunately for him, on the very last day of the option the Deutschmark strengthens and the option is settled against a $/DM spot rate of 1.5500. He thus earns just $0.5m in intrinsic value. This does not compensate him adequately for the loss in value on his exposures. He has been unable to lock into a worst case of $/DM1.5000, despite having paid a substantial premium for the privilege.

By comparison, the Asian style option will realise an intrinsic value of $2.49m (i.e. $10m × [(179days × 1.75 + 1day × 1.55) / 180 – 1.5]). Of course, had the final movement in Deutschmark been in the other direction, the intrinsic value on the Asian style option would have been less than that for either an American or European style instrument. The great merit of the Asian style instrument though is that it will, in practice, correspond more closely to the risk on a series of exposures and the premium payable is not likely to be any larger than an ordinary option.

Look-back Options
The look-back feature aims to provide the option owner with the best of all possible worlds. Its owner is able, at expiry, to exercise against the most advantageous spot rate occurring during the option's life. This, however, is achievable at a price: typically premiums on look-back options are much higher than those for their European, American or Asian style options. In general the look-back option is an uneconomic hedging instrument, although there can be situations,

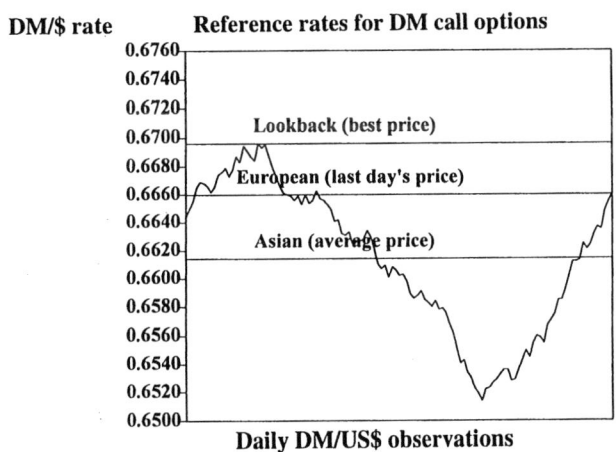

Figure 8.4 Differences in intrinsic value for European, Asian and look-back options

145

particularly during periods of extreme volatility, where its performance can out-strip that of other options.

Digital Options

Digital options are an all-or-nothing form of price insurance. The buyer pays a premium to own the right to receive a fixed amount in the future should the option expire with intrinsic value. The amount of intrinsic value at expiry is irrelevant as the owner always receives the same cash sum.

A digital option may seem to be a speculative instrument that is not appropriate for hedgers. However, if used properly, it can be an extremely effective hedging tool, allowing the risk manager to structure his risk–reward profile over a range of future prices with complete precision. Digital options are still rare, but are likely to become more popular as computer-based hedging techniques become more sophisticated.

Break-forwards

The break-forward (also sometimes called a FOX) is an example of how options products can be structured to meet the sensitivities of corporate treasurers. It is designed to overcome the resistance of many corporations to the high premiums that are payable for options in the currency markets. These high premiums are the necessary consequence of the relatively volatile nature of foreign exchange.

We saw in Chapter 2 that the main subjective determinant of an option's price was its extrinsic value, and that this is determined by expected volatility.

The problem for corporations is one of perception. By paying a large amount in premium they are able to guarantee their worst case position. However, it may prove difficult to justify such a strategy, especially if this meant that they pur-chased an expensive option which then expired worthless. Forward FX, on the other hand, was well established as a hedging instrument, and widely viewed as the cheapest hedging alternative.

The break-forwards offered by FIs are, in reality, the same as a call or put option with the premium concealed in the price. They are marketed as forward FX transactions that include a cancellation feature. Presenting them in this way can help corporate treasurers in justifying their hedging actions at board level.

By way of illustration, consider a break-forward in £/$. The current forward price is £/$ 1.5500, and the break-forward is priced at £/$1.5750 with a cancellation fee of 2.5cts per £. If £/$ at expiry is above 1.5500 at, say 1.6000, the owner carries out the forward transaction at 1.5750. If £/$ is 1.5600, the forward deal stays in place, because the cost of cancellation plus buying pounds in the spot market would be more expensive (i.e. 1.5850). If £/$ is below 1.5500 it is worth cancelling the forward. With £/$ at 1.5000, say, the cancellation cost is 2.5 cents, so the net cost of buying sterling will be 1.5250. The corporate treasurer can demonstrate the value of the cancellation feature to his financial director as a cash saving.

Whether or not the cancellation feature is used the FI receives its premium, either in the form of the cancellation fee or in the form of the difference between the break-forward price and the then prevailing forward price. A break-forward purchase of sterling is effectively a forward purchase of dollars plus a sterling put option: a synthetic sterling call option. We know from our discussion of put-call parity that the prices for the two products should, according to arbitrage theory, be the same. By presenting options in this more marketable form, however, FIs have been able to achieve better profit margins on their option writing activities.

Participating Forwards

Another example of this approach was introduced by Salomon Brothers. Again, the aim here is to conceal the premium in the forward price of the contract. Basically what happens here is that the buyer of a participating forward agrees to pay slightly more than the going rate for an ordinary forward in exchange for being able to participate in any upside potential. The extent to which he can participate depends on how much extra he is willing to pay for his forward contract and the current at the money option premium.

Consider the following simple illustration. The £/$ three-month forward rate stands at 1.5500. Three-month sterling put with a strike rate of 1.55 have a premium of 2.0 cents per £. The buyer of a participating forward can determine the forward price and participation factor according to these two prices. If he buys sterling forward at 1.9500 he has not paid any premium and cannot participate in profits should sterling weaken. If he buys sterling at 1.9700, he can participate in any profits resulting from a weakening of sterling as he has bought the same number of options. If he buys sterling at 1.9600, he has bought half as many options as forwards, he can therefore participate in 50 per cent of the profits should sterling decline.

Compound and Pooled Options

Companies involved in tendering for contracts in a foreign currency have a two-fold risk. They have the risk that they will not succeed in their bid attempt, and they will have a currency exposure if they are successful. FIs have devised a variety of ways for them to hedge currency exposure inexpensively. A compound option is essentially an option on an option. The customer owns the right to buy (or sell) the foreign currency, but this right is only exercisable if the company succeeds in winning its bid. The premium payable is lower than for a standard currency option, but is not refundable if the company should fail in its tender attempt.

A pooled option offers a similar facility at, potentially, zero cost. It works best when several bidders in one country are competing for a foreign contract. Through the auspices of either their trade association or, sometimes, the bid awarder, they each take a share in the same option. The option terms state that it is only available to the company that wins the bid. If one of the competing companies wins the bid it now has an actual currency exposure. It repays to the losing companies their share of the premium and owns all of the rights. If no members of the pool win the bid, they each own a part share in the option and are payed any intrinsic value according to their premium contribution.

Other Strategies

Many other currency risk management strategies are available as OTC instruments. Their popularity will vary as market conditions change, but they are all essentially constructed out of the building blocks of buying and selling calls and puts, and long short FX positions.

The complexity of such strategies is limited only by the imagination of financiers and the cost of putting them together. Further illustrations of the form that currency derivatives can take, and their profit and loss profiles, are discussed in the following chapter.

Exchange Traded Currency Options

Currency options are offered by almost every exchange where the futures are traded. They take the form of call and put options on the underlying futures contract. A futures call gives its owner the right to buy the underlying contract, while a put provides for the right to sell the future.

Since the buyer of a currency futures contract is acquiring a notional instrument equivalent to a forward purchase of the currency, the futures call guarantees the maximum dollar cost of the currency. Similarly, the owner of a put on the future has the right to sell the foreign currency in exchange for a minimum number of dollars.

Options on Currency Futures

For each futures contract call and put options are available for strikes at regular intervals around the current futures price. Options on Deutschmark futures for instance have a strike price interval of fifty ticks. The contracts which are introduced depend on the price of the underlying future.

There are always at least six options available – those with strike prices closest to the underlying futures price. As the futures price changes, there must always be at least two contracts above and below the current level. New options contracts may therefore be introduced by the exchange, so that by the futures delivery date there can be more than six options being traded on the exchange.

Typically, options on futures are European style, i.e. they may only be exercised on the futures delivery date. Market participants can of course realise the value of their options positions before the delivery date by trading their positions.

Table 8.5 shows premiums payable on puts and calls on the Deutschmark

Table 8.5 Options on Deutschmark futures
(International Monetary Market, Chicago)

DM125,000; cents per DM		
Strike price	March calls	March puts
0.6600	1.77	0.75
0.6650	1.47	0.95
0.6700	1.20	1.18
0.6750	0.99	1.47
0.6800	0.79	1.77
0.6850	0.64	2.12

Source: Wall Street Journal

March contract at the IMM. On the date in question the March future is priced at 0.6702.

Futures Option Pricing
As can be seen from Table 8.5, option premiums are cents per DM. This allows market participants to determine the net price (i.e. the worst case) by simply adding (or subtracting) the premium to (or from) the exercise price. A buyer of a 0.6650 call would for example have a worst case cost of 0.6797 (0.6650 + 1.47), while the purchaser of a put at the same strike has a worst case selling price of 0.6555 (0.6650 − 0.95) for the June future. The value of a tick is the same as for the underlying future ($12.50 for Deutschmark), so traders are able to identify profits and losses quickly as premiums change.

Trading in Futures Options
As is the case with futures, exchange traded options are used mainly by market professionals. They form an essential component of any risk management strategy. Traders and risk managers, by buying and selling options, can express a view on expected market volatility; just as they buy and sell futures according to their view on the direction of price movements.

Spot Rate Options
The Philadelphia Stock Exchange (PHLX) offers options on a number of foreign currencies. It offers put and call options on Australian and Canadian dollars, sterling, Deutschmark, Swiss and French francs, yen and the ECU. The options are quoted in $ per currency (i.e. US terms) for a variety of strikes.

At Philadelphia the mark-to-market mechanism is similar to that used by futures exchanges. The main difference is that PHLX currency options may be exercised early against the prevailing spot rate. In other words they are American style options. Indeed, the term American style derives from the

Philadelphia Exchange, as against European style, which was originally used to describe options offered by the European Options Exchange in Amsterdam.

Because of their early exercise feature, currency options traded at the PHLX can often be more expensive than their futures exchange counterparts. The other chief difference between them is that PHLX options are normally available for more different strikes than the futures options equivalents. For £/$, for instance, the PHLX strike interval is one point (i.e. 0.01 of a cent), against a 25 tick (i.e. 2.5 cents) interval for the option on sterling futures contract at the IMM.

9: Techniques for Currency Traders

EVALUATING CURRENCY EXPOSURE

Calculating Cross Rates

Calculating cross rates is done by reference to the price quoted against the dollar for each currency. Care needs to be taken to ensure that the correct side of each quote is used when finding the cross rate. Remember that the market maker would need to buy and sell dollars against the currencies on the wrong side of the market to finance the cross rate position. He will be required to buy dollars at the market's dollar offer rate, and sell them at the market's dollar bid rate. For this reason the spread on such quotations will normally be wider than that for the constituent currencies against the dollar.

$/DM = 1.5850–60
£/$ = 1.5715–19
Find the implied £/DM cross rates.

To find the £/DM £ bid:
This is the price at which a market maker would buy £1 and sell DM
To close out the position at zero cost:
   The market maker would have to sell £1 and buy $1.5715
   and buy DM and sell $1.5715 @ $/DM 1.5850
£ bid rate = 2.4908 (1.5715 × 1.5850)

To find the £/DM £ offer:
This is the price at which a market maker would sell £1 and buy DM
To close out the position at zero cost:
The market maker would have to buy £1 and sell $1.5719
and sell DM and buy $1.5719 @ $/DM 1.5860
£ offer rate = 2.4930 (1.5719 × 1.5860)

Notice that the implied cross rate spread is relatively wide at 22 pips. This reflects the additional costs to the market maker of having to close out the transaction by means of two deals on the wrong side of the spread.

   Where both currencies for the cross rate are traded as quoted currencies against the US dollar, the cross rate is found by dividing the quoted cross rate by

151

the base cross rate. Again care must be taken to ensure that the correct side of the quoted prices is being used.

$/DM = 1.5850-60 : $/¥ = 115.40-50. Find the implied DM/¥ cross rates.

To find the DM/¥ DM bid:
This is the price at which a market maker would buy DM1 and sell yen
To close out the position at zero cost:
  The market maker would have to sell DM1 and buy $ @ 1.5860
  (reciprocal of 1.5860 = 0.6305)
  and buy yen and sell $0.6305 @ $/¥115.40
DM bid rate = 72.76 (115.40/1.5860)

To find the DM/¥ DM offer:
This is the price at which a market maker would sell DM1 and buy yen
To close out the position at zero cost:
  The market maker would have to buy DM1 and sell $ @ 1.5850
  (reciprocal of 1.5850 = 0.6309)
  and buy yen and sell $0.6309 @ $/¥115.50
DM bid rate = 72.87   (115.50/1.5850)

Constructing a Synthetic Forward FX Rate

To illustrate the connection between interest rates and today's spot rate, consider the following example.

Spot $/DM   1.5850 – 60
3m $ interbank rates   6.500 – 6.625
3m DM interbank rates   9.000 – 9.125
Find the implied $/DM 3m forward rates.

To find the $/DM 3m forward DM offer:
This is the price at which a market maker would buy $ and sell DM in three months
To close out the position at zero cost:
  The market maker would have to sell $1/buy DM1.5850 in the spot market
  borrow $1 for 3 months @ 6.625%
  and lend DM1.5850 for three months @ 9.000%
This will create the required offsetting short $/long DM positions in three months

Three-month forward equivalent of $1 = $1.0165625 $(1 + 0.06625 \times 0.25)$
Three-month forward equivalent of DM1.5850 = DM1.6206625
    $1.5850 \times (1+0.09 \times 0.25)$

Implied $/DM 3m forward DM offer = 1.5943   (1.6206625/1.0165625)
To find the $/DM 3m forward DM bid:
This is the price at which a market maker would sell $ and buy DM in 3 months

To close out the position at zero cost:

The market maker would have to buy \$1/sell DM1.5860 in the spot market

lend \$1 for three months @ 6.500%

and borrow DM 1.5860 for three months @ 9.125%

This will create the required offsetting long \$ / short DM positions in three months

Three-month forward equivalent of \$1 = \$1.01625 $(1 + 0.065 \times 0.25)$

Three-month forward equivalent of DM1.5860 = DM1.6222

      $1.5860 \times (1 + 0.09125 \times 0.25)$

Implied \$/DM 3m forward DM bid = 1.5962   (1.6222/1.01625)

Notice that the two-way price for three-month forward \$/DM constructed in this way, 1.5943–62 has a wider spread than the underlying spot rate.

The procedure described above defines the limits for buying and sell Deutschmarks against the dollar. If the actual forward rate falls outside these limits there is an arbitrage opportunity, which will bring it back into line with its implied level.

Using the Time Value of Money to Find Implied Forward Rates

The formulae for finding forward FX rates can be expressed mathematically as follows:

Type 1:
$$f(B+/Q-) \;=\; \frac{s(B+/Q-)\,(1 + RQo.TQ)}{(1 + RBb.TB)}$$

Type 2:
$$f(B-/Q+) \;=\; \frac{s(B-/Q+)\,(1 + RQb.TQ)}{(1 + RBo.TB)}$$

Where:

B	=	Base currency
Q	=	Quoted currency
+	=	Buy currency
−	=	Sell currency
s( )	=	Spot FX rate
f( )	=	Forward FX rate
R	=	Interest rate
b	=	Bid
o	=	Offer
T	=	Time to forward date (in years)

Notice that the formulae allow for different periods (TB and TQ) for the base currency and the quoted currency. This is because there may be different interest accrual conventions in the two currencies concerned. Usually, interbank money market rates are used when calculating forward rates within one year. But sterling rates, for example, are quoted on interest accrual of actual/365 days, while most other currencies use actual/360 to calculate interest amounts. For a 90 day £/$ forward, therefore, T$ is 0.25, but T£ is 90/365.

Remember also that the market maker will use the forward price of buying the base currency (and selling the quoted currency) as the break-even base currency offer (same as the quoted currency bid). For the base currency bid the opposite side of the market is used as the benchmark.

The formulae may look complicated, but they are, in fact, simply expressing the time value of money relationship between two currencies. If we were to use zero coupon factors instead of interest rates to describe the time value of money in each currency the forwards are even easier to calculate:

Type 1:
$$f(B+/Q-) \ = \ s(B+/Q-) \frac{FactorQo}{FactorBb}$$

Type 2:
$$f(B-/Q+) \ = \ s(B-/Q+) \frac{FactorQb}{FactorBo}$$

Where:
Factor = Future value on the forward date of 1 unit of the currency.

The formula in this form is particularly appropriate for calculating implied forward rates for dates occurring in more than one year.

Currency Risk of FX Swaps

Traders in FX swaps are speculating on the interest differential between the two currencies. In theory they are not concerned with changes in the value of the currency as any profits on the spot date resulting from a change in the currency's spot price will be offset by an equal and opposite loss on the forward date. However, this is to ignore the time value of money effect of taking profits and losses on different dates.

The simple illustration below shows how losses can result from a change in the spot rate without interest differentials ever changing. To keep the numbers simple mid-rates are used throughout, dollars and ECU are each assumed to pay a one year interest rate of 10 per cent. The forward rate is therefore the same as the spot rate, initially both are at $/ECU1.5000. Further, for expository simplicity, it is assumed that any change in price takes place immediately.

Consider the situation of an FX swap trader who believes that dollar interest rates will fall relative to ECU rates. To benefit from this he will want to lend dollars and borrow ECU. When dollar rates fall as expected he will be able to close out the position at a profit (i.e. he can now borrow dollars more cheaply and will still be earning as much on his ECU).

The FX swap that is equivalent to lending dollars/borrowing ECU is one where he is a buyer of dollars on the forward date. The example shows the effect on his profitability for a $1 million one year swap if dollar interest rates fall to 9.5 per cent and ECU rates remain at 10 per cent.

Close out transaction ($ rate = 9.5 per cent, ECU rate = 10 per cent, Spot = 1.5000)

Spot:	+$1,000,000	Buy dollars against ECU sale
	–ECU1,500,000	Sell ECU at 1.5 against dollar purchase
Fwd:	–$1,000,000	Sell dollars against ECU purchase
	+ECU1,506,849	Buy ECU against dollar sale at 1.5068
	+ECU6,489	Close out profit on FX swap

As expected the dealer has realised a profit because interest differentials moved in his direction. The dealer can be well pleased with his day's work.

Now suppose instead, that interest rates remained unchanged, and that the dollar strengthens against the ECU to 1.6000. As an interest differential trader, the dealer may believe he is not exposed to currency risk, but this turns out to be an erroneous perception:

Close out transaction ($ rate = 10%, ECU rate = 10%, Spot = 1.6000)

Spot:	+$1,000,000	Buy dollars against ECU sale
	–ECU1,600,000	Sell ECU at 1.6 against dollar purchase
Fwd:	–$1,000,000	Sell dollars against ECU purchase
	+ECU1,600,000	Buy ECU against dollar sale at 1.6000

Because the dollar has strengthened the swap trader must close out his spot ECU position for a ECU100,000 loss. This is offset by a ECU100,000 profit, but this does not occur until one year later. The dealer must borrow ECU 100,000 for a year. This he can do at 10 per cent, so in a year's time he must repay ECU110,000. He therefore suffers a loss of ECU10,000 at the end of the year.

The sensitivity to currency risk arises because the FX swap does not exactly correspond to the combined borrowing and lending activity it is meant to represent. The currency risk can be hedged by taking out an adjustment exposure in the spot market. .

The Spot Hedge

This currency risk arises in an FX swap because of the slight difference between it and the money market activities it is meant to represent. Buying dollars against a sale of Deutschmarks on the forward date against the reverse transactions on the spot date is supposed to replicate the effect of simultaneously lending dollars and borrowing the equivalent amount of Deutschmarks. However, if dollars were actually lent the investor would receive capital plus interest at maturity, whereas in an FX swap, since the spot and forward base currency amounts are identical, only the initial (capital) amount is received.

To eliminate currency risk therefore, the FX swap transaction needs to be modified so that it is identical to the money market operations. Fortunately, this is relatively simple to do. Whenever he does an FX swap, the dealer needs to take out a reverse position in the spot market that scales down the net exposure on the spot date. The size of the hedge depends on the amount of interest earned on the base currency over the period and is designed to equate the spot currency amounts to the present value of the forward positions..

We can see the effect by considering again the one-year $/ECU FX swap. For simplicity let us assume that both dollar and ECU rates are 10 per cent, so the forward FX rate is the same as the spot rate, at 1.5000. Since the forward dollar position is $1m, the appropriate spot hedge in this case would be that which reduced the net spot dollar amount to $909,091, the present value equivalent of $1m at 10 per cent. To hedge, the dealer therefore buys $90,909 against its ECU equivalent. Since spot and forward rates are connected by time value of money differentials, the ECUs sold, ECU136,364, automatically adjust the ECU spot portion of the swap to the present value equivalent of ECU1,500,000.

As we can see below the FX swap trader is now insensitive to currency fluctuations:

Original transactions

Spot:	−$1,000,000	Sell dollars against ECU purchase
	+ECU1,500,000	Buy ECU at 1.5000 against dollar sale
	+$90,909	Spot hedge dollar purchase
	−ECU136,364	Spot hedge ECU sale at 1.5000
Fwd:	+$1,000,000	Buy dollars against ECU sale at 1.5000
	−ECU1,500,000	Sell ECU against dollar purchase

Now when the dollar strengthens to 1.6000, assuming no change in interest rates the close out transactions are as follows:

Spot:	+$1,000,000	Buy dollars against ECU sale
	−ECU1,600,000	Sell ECU at 1.6 against dollar purchase
	−$90,909	Close out spot hedge – dollar sale
	+ECU145,455	Close out spot hedge – buy ECU at 1.6000
Fwd:	−$1,000,000	Sell dollars against ECU purchase
	+ECU1,600,000	Buy ECU against dollar sale at 1.6000

Profit and loss account

Spot: −ECU100,000   Currency loss on FX swap spot portion
         +ECU9,091   Profit on spot hedge
        −ECU90,909   Net ECU loss on spot date
    +ECU90,909   Borrow ECU for 1 year at 10 per cent

Fwd: +ECU100,000   Currency profit on FX swap forward portion
    −ECU100,000   Repay capital and interest on ECU borrowing

The FX swap trader's position now takes account of the different dates on which profits and losses occur, the time value of money element is built into profitability. He is now insensitive to currency price changes.

Some traders argue that the currency risk implications of FX swap trading are relatively small and will even out in the long run. The risk is greatest when interest rates are high and there is a long period to the forward portion of the swap, but it can be seen from the example that there can be significant dangers with even relatively slight changes in FX rates. Also the interrelated nature of currencies and interest rates mean that a currency is most likely to strengthen when the market is anticipating a fall in its interest rate. If that rate cut does not materialise, hot money pressures can easily force the the currency's value up.

There is also a principle at stake: sources of profit and loss cannot be accurately measured when two types of risk co-mingle. Financial institutions are structured so that spot traders are responsible for managing currency risk. It is not part of the forward trader's business to concern himself with anything but the relative interest rates.

Accounting for FX Swaps

The need for FX swap traders to immunise themselves from currency risk involves undertaking a large number of small, hedging transactions and overnight borrowing. A complete analysis of the strategies and procedures required to do this successfully is beyond the scope of this book. However, the examples shown should be enough to convince the reader that it is not practical to precision-hedge the currency risk of FX swaps via market operations.

But the examples also show that the currency risk is a real one. Both FIs and corporations need to have a good understanding of these, and a strategy for handling them, if they are to have any chance of trading FX swaps successfully. The key to doing this lies in proper management accounting procedures and clearly defined policies for transfer pricing between profit. Structuring the organisation so that interest risk, currency risk, credit risk, etc, are clearly delineated and managed in separate, hermetically sealed profit centres is an essential prerequisite for successful risk management.

How Financial Institutions Hedge the Risk on Forward Outright Deals

FIs have a variety of techniques at their disposal for managing the risk on forward outrights. Firstly, they can use currency futures. Because of the standardised structure of this market, the FI will probably not be able to eliminate its position risk entirely. It will, however, be able to close out the majority of the risk of buying a currency for forward delivery from a customer by selling currency futures with a similar delivery date (so long as the currency has an equivalent future).

Secondly, the FI can lay off all of the currency risk by combining a spot transaction with an FX swap. The cost of closing out in this way determines the market maker's bid/offer rates. The example below illustrates the process.

$/DM spot and forward rates

	Spot	3m Fwd pts	3m Fwd outright
US$/DM	1.4755/65	89/93	1.4844/58

To find the market maker's $/DM forward outright bid price:

Cashflows are shown from the market maker's perspective

Value 3m
+DM1,485,800   MM receives DM from customer @ $/DM1.4858
−$1,000,000   MM pays $ to customer against DM receipt

To close out the position

Spot value
+DM1,476,500   MM receives DM on spot portion of FX Swap
−$1,000,000   MM pays $ vs DM receipt on FX Swap
−DM1,476,500   MM pays DM at market $/DM spot bid price (1.4765)
+$1,000,000   MM receives $ vs DM payment on spot deal

Value 3m
−DM1,485,800   MM pays DM on FX Swap at 93 over 1.4765
+$1,000,000   MM receives $ against DM on FX Swap

Notice that, although he must do the FX swap on the wrong side of the market (+93 pips), the market maker is able to select 1.4765 as the reference spot rate. By doing this all cashflows correspond and he can afford to bid for DM in three months at an outright rate of 1.4858 or better.

Hedging the Currency Risk on Forward Outrights

In practice the market maker may decide that he likes the interest risk profile of the forward outright. He can hedge just the currency component of the risk by doing the reverse transaction to the forward deal in the spot markets. This leaves him with the risk profile of an FX swap. As we have seen above in the discussion on spot hedging, he may want to do a slightly smaller spot transaction to eliminate currency risk completely.

Hedging the Interest Risk of a Forward Outright

On the other hand the market maker may be uncomfortable with the interest risk of the forward outright, but be willing to accept the currency risk the position gives him. In this situation he would close out the forward position with an FX swap, but not do a balancing spot transaction. Using the above example this will leave him with a long Deutschmark position of DM1,476,500 against a $1m short position on the spot date.

Hedging with Currency Futures

Someone with a long foreign currency position occurring in the future may require protection against a fall in the value of that currency against the dollar. For DM, this will occur when the $/DM rate increases (i.e. more Deutschmarks are required to buy the same number of dollars). The DM future is priced in DM/$ terms, so as the Deutschmark weakens the price will fall.

This individual would therefore sell an equivalent amount of DM futures so that the profit on the futures hedge can compensate him for the Deutschmark's decline. Similarly, someone who is short of Deutschmarks against dollars on future dates would buy contracts.

An Illustrative Currency Futures Hedge

In the example below an FI agrees, on 21 January, to sell DM2 million to its customer against a purchase of dollars for value 15 May. It decides to hedge its exposure in the futures market by buying 16 currency futures @ $0.6650 on the IMM in Chicago.

On 21 January
Spot $/DM = 1.4900
−$MARGIN × 16   Pay Margin on 16 June contracts

Value 15 May −DM2,000,000   Sell DM 2m to customer
                +$1,339,585   Buy $ at $/DM 1.4930

Value June   +DM2,000,000   Implied DM position (buy 16 DM contracts)
                −$1,330,000   Implied $ position (buy 16 contracts @ 0.6650)

On 22 January
DM June contracts are settled at 0.6665, position revalued at 0.6665

+$3,000	Mark-to-market profit (16 ctcts × 15 ticks × $12.50)

The margin account is credited and debited on a daily basis according to the change in price.

On 13 May: spot $/DM = 1.4000

+$MARGIN × 16		Get back margin on close out of sixteen contracts
Spot value	+DM 2,000,000	Buy DM in the spot market
	−$1,428,571	Sell $ at spot rate of S/DM 1.4000
Value June	−DM 2,000,000	Implied DM position (sell 16 DM contracts)
	+$1,426,000	Implied $ position (sell 16 contracts @ 0.7130)

In this instance the FI has realised a profit on the transaction of $7014. This is composed of the difference between the forward dollars received from the customer and the number of dollars sold in the spot market in May (a loss of $88,986). This is offset by a 480 tick profit (0.7130–0.6650) on the futures hedge of $96,000 (480 ticks × $12.50 × 16 contracts).

It is important to realise that, although in this case the FI has realised a profit it could equally well have made a loss. The $7014 is in fact a symptom of the imperfection of the hedging process with futures, the result of using contracts due for delivery in June to protect against a May exposure.

The other factor that could destabilise its hedging operation is the fact that profits and losses on the futures transaction are taken as they occur. In this case, where the futures price has risen during the period the time value of money effect is likely to benefit the hedger. Profits are realised before the exposure date and the proceeds can be invested. However, where a hedge loses money because of an improvement in the underlying exposure, losses must be taken sooner and this is likely to add to the cost of the hedging process.

Incorporating Time Value of Money into Net Rate Calculations

The time value of money effect is also a material factor in the valuation of optional instruments. Premium for puts and calls is payable in advance, so a financing cost needs to be incorporated into the pricing. This is built into option pricing tools, where the fair value premium is described as the present value equivalent of the future expected profit. In evaluating option performance time value needs to be incorporated. The net rate is defined as the option buyer's worst case position, but this occurs on the expiry date. The cost of financing a premium will be determined by the currency in which it is paid. So, for a

(European style) £/$ call with an exercise date in six months' time, the relevant rate will be the cost of borrowing dollars for six months (assuming the premium is paid in this currency).

The following illustrations show how net rates, modified for time value, are derived:

(a) £/$ 3m put, strike = 1.6000, premium = 2.5 cts per £
per £000, $25 premium financed at 8% = $25.50 i.e. 1.02 × $25
worst case $ in = $1474.50 i.e. 1600 – 25.50
net rate   = 1.4745

(b) SF/$ 3m call, strike = 0.7000, premium = 1.5 cts per SF
per SF000, $15 premium financed at 8% = $15.30 i.e. 1.02 × $15
worst case $ out = $715.30 i.e. 700 + 15.30
net rate   = 0.7153

(c) $/DM 3m call, strike = 1.5500, premium = 3%
per $000, $30 premium financed at 8% = $30.60 i.e. 1.02 × $30
worst case $ out = $1030.60 i.e. 1000 + 30.60
net rate   = 1.5040 i.e. 1550/1030.60

MANAGING CURRENCY EXPOSURE

Forms of Currency Exposure

For the average business, currency exposures can arise in three main forms: transaction exposure, translation exposure and economic exposure. It is also worthwhile to make a distinction between known and contingent cashflows when formulating a risk management posture.

Transaction Exposure

Transaction exposure describes the risks arising out of currency mismatches between a company's revenues and its costs. An example of this might be a US car importer. Payments must be made to the German motor manufacturer in Deutschmarks, revenues are earned in dollars. He therefore is at risk from a relative strengthening of the Deutschmark.

Translation Exposure

Translation exposure refers to the risk that an owner of foreign currency assets and liabilities runs from changes in the exchange rate. Generally these are not transaction related and are manifested by accounting entries in the company's balance sheet. An example of a translation exposure might be the risk that a multinational motor manufacturer runs on its foreign subsidiaries. If a Japanese car concern sets up a UK based manufacturing subsidiary then the yen value of that subsidiary will be determined by the £/yen cross rate at the end of the accounting year.

Assuming the Japanese parent company has no intention of selling its subsidiary, it is thus an unrealised exposure which, though it affects the yen value of the consolidated balance sheet, may not have a material impact on the company's profitability. There may be valid risk management implications for translation risks, but too much attention to them may divert resources and have a negative impact on profitability in the long run.

Economic Exposure

The third, related form of currency risk for a business is its economic exposure. This relates to the strategic risks for that business of longer term trends in FX rates. These may be because it could be placed at a competitive disadvantage to its overseas competitors in certain exchange rate environments. For a non-US company, competitive performance might also be eroded where its costs or revenues are linked to commodity prices, which depend in part on the exchange rate performance of the US dollar.

The Japanese car company discussed above was no doubt, at least in part, addressing its economic exposure when it set up its foreign subsidiaries in the first place. Without overseas productive capacity, the strength of the yen against European currencies might have undermined its ability to compete effectively on price with European car producers. By setting up a subsidiary in the UK, resourced locally, it could deliver cars to the European market cost-effectively.

Note that a stronger yen will involve it in a translation risk, as the yen value of the UK subsidiary will decline. However, it is obviously worth setting up the UK company as, despite this, it will be able to remit profits to the parent. This illustrates the danger of over-concern with translation risks. Had the Japanese company focused on its translation exposure, it might well have decided not to invest overseas and lost the ability to earn profits in Europe.

Economic exposure is often best dealt with by structuring the currency complexion of the business so that it can compete with its foreign rivals on an equal basis. However, it is not always practical to do this, particularly for companies with commodity price related risks. In such circumstances an on-going risk management programme may be an appropriate solution. It is important to realise that the performance of the company's currency risk management strategy need not be structured to immunise its own assets and liabilities against changes in the FX rate. It is perfectly valid to design elements into the programme so that the company's financial performance is similar to that of its competitors. In some circumstances this might imply risk management activities that actually involve the company in taking on currency exposures, rather than always trying to eliminate them.

Cashflow Contingency

For a corporation, revenues are contingent on the success of its products. It generally has a broad idea of the scale and the timing of its receipts, but they are rarely completely predictable. On the other hand, it needs to be able to manage currency exposures several months, possibly years, in advance. Companies will therefore look at their average anticipated cashflow profile when deciding on risk management policy. The programme will need to be adjusted as the cashflows crystallise, so they need to maintain flexibility in any risk management policy.

In certain situations, it is not just the magnitude and timing of future cashflows which is in doubt, but their occurrence. Examples might include competitive tendering or hostile foreign takeovers. In either situation there is a chance that the company will fail and the projected currency risk will evaporate. Here, any currency risk management strategy must take account of this possibility.

For instance, a US construction company that is bidding in Deutschmarks to buy the licensing rights for a German lager would be well advised not to cover its projected $/DM exposure by buying Deutschmarks in the forward market. If it were to do so, and fail in its attempt to win the licence, it would be left with a large Deutschmark position with no offsetting exposure. If the Deutschmark were then to weaken, it would be forced to buy back dollars at a loss.

Known, Anticipated and Potential Cashflows

In the light of this many companies will distinguish between known, anticipated and potential cashflows when formulating their currency risk management policy. Known cashflows would be those for which the company has entered into a contractual agreement. Anticipated cashflows might include items like projected future sales, for which there is a relatively high degree of certainty that they will occur, but a degree of doubt as to their timings and magnitudes. Potential cashflows are possible future payments and receipts that may arise out of current or future projects. These need to be planned for, and the factors governing their occurrence understood, but they cannot be hedged with anything like the precision of known or anticipated future cashflows.

Matched Funding

The best and the simplest way to minimise the currency sensitivity of a portfolio is to finance in the currency in which revenue will be received! Commodity producers, whose revenues are linked to the performance of the US dollar, will seek to raise a substantial portion of their financing needs in dollars. Multinationals setting up foreign subsidiaries to serve local markets will naturally prefer to raise funds in that foreign currency. They will then only have a currency risk on remitted profits (and their translation exposure will also be lower).

In practice, of course, matched funding is not always possible. The company may find it difficult to raise funds cheaply in markets where investors are unfamiliar with its name. This can sometimes be overcome by the judicious use of currency swaps (of which more later).

In the final analysis any business involved in international trade, and every company with an exposure to commodities prices, will be left with some currency risk on its net positions no matter how carefully the balance sheet is structured to minimise it. It is with this portion of the exposure that this section is mainly concerned.

Using Cashflow Analysis for Currency Exposures

No matter what their source, currency exposures are best represented as future cashflows, in and out of the balance sheet. When seen in this way, as asset and liability streams, it is obvious that managing currency risk cannot be done in isolation. The process is inextricably related to interest risk management and the various techniques that apply to that area must also be applied to the management of multicurrency positions.

Interest risk management was discussed in detail in Chapter 7 and the remainder of this section assumes that the reader is already acquainted with the principles and practices.

Table 9.1 shows the cashflow profile for a fictional, UK company – International Trading plc. Its liabilities are denominated in sterling while its assets are in US dollars. For simplicity the sterling and Deutschmark yield curves are both assumed to be flat, at 10 per cent (exponential equivalents). The £/$ spot rate is currently at 2.0000.

In Table 9.1 International Trading is anticipating an extremely thin overall profit of just £23,000 in present value terms. It has both currency and interest rate risks. On its dollar assets it is at risk from a rise in US yields. For instance, if dollar yields rose by just 65 basis points to 10.65 per cent the present value of its future assets would fall to $7.204 million. At an exchange rate of 2.0000 its profits would be wiped out.

Similarly, it has a sensitivity to sterling interest rates. The amount of pounds it has to lend to net off its future payments will increase as sterling yields fall. If the dollar yields and the exchange rate stay the same, its profits would be eliminated should sterling rates fall to 9.58 per cent. Notice, incidentally that International Trading is more sensitive to falling sterling yields than to rising dollar ones. This, of course, is due to the longer duration of its sterling denominated cashflows.

Table 9.1 International Trading plc

Time (Years)	Assets ($000s)	Factors @ 10% continuous compounding	Asset PVs ($000s)	Liabilities (£000s)	Factors @10% continuous compounding	Liability (£000s)
0.25	2,000	1.0251	1,951		1.0251	
0.5		1.0513			1.0513	
0.75	2,000	1.0782	1,855		1.0782	
1		1.1052		1,900	1.1052	1,719
1.25	2,000	1.1331	1,765		1.1331	
1.5		1.1618			1.1618	
1.75	2,000	1.1912	1,679		1.1912	
2		1.2215		2,300	1.2215	1,883

Total $ PV: 7250
@ Spot £/$:   2.0000
£ equivalent: 3625   Total £ PV: 3602
Net £ profit: 23

Assuming that sterling and dollar interest rates remain at 10 per cent, at what spot exchange rate will International Trading's profits be eliminated? The company's break-even point on exchange rates can be found simply by dividing the present value of dollar receipts by the present value of the sterling payments. This result, 2.0128, gives the spot rate which converts the dollars into a sterling equivalent that is the same as the cost in sterling. The 128 point difference in the spot rate represents a strengthening of sterling *vis-a-vis* the dollar of just 0.64 per cent, the sort of variation that is quite common in a trading session, indeed is regularly seen over the course of a few minutes. Interest rates, by contrast, do not often alter by more than 20 basis points during any day unless there is a base rate change. These are often anticipated by markets. We can deduce, therefore, that, though both interest risk and currency risk need to be managed, the currency risk management imperative is the strongest.

Managing a Multi-currency Portfolio

We can see from the International Trading case that the risk management of any multi-currency portfolio involves attending to currency risks because of the effect of a change in the spot rate, while at the same time monitoring the interest risk in each currency.

The techniques to be employed by a risk manager with multi-currency positions must therefore include all of those used for interest rate risk. If the portfolio includes any long-term positions, duration and convexity must be applied to measure net sensitivities to interest rate increases and decreases of differing magnitudes in each of the various currencies. These techniques are discussed further in Chapter 12. Additionally he needs to look at the spot risk on foreign currency positions and to understand the relationship between each of the currencies in which he has an exposure and his ultimate, domestic currency.

Separating Currency Risks from Interest Risks

Because forward FX rates are priced according to the spot FX rate and the relative interest differential it is possible to look at all of the currency risk on a portfolio by considering the present value of future cashflows. It is not appropriate to use forward FX rates when analysing currency sensitivity as these also include the relative interest exposures.

This makes monitoring currency risk for known positions a relatively simple matter. Having established the present values in each foreign currency the multi-currency portfolio manager simply needs to analyse the effect of a change in the spot relationship between his and foreign currencies.

Analysing Currency Strength and Weakness

The impact on profitability of a given spot rate change can therefore be used to determine the appropriate offsetting hedge. This 'delta' factor should be found by looking at the effect of, say a 1 per cent change in a particular currency's international value. Measuring the delta effect of, say, a 10 pip change in the spot rate between two currencies is fraught with danger.

Supposing, for instance, that the $/FF rate falls by 1 per cent. Is this the result of the dollar weakening, the French franc strengthening or both?

By way of illustration, consider a multinational with exposures in four different currencies. Net present values for each currency, found by discounting future exposures, are shown. Cashflows are viewed from the perspective of a multinational based in the US, and shown in Table 9.2 in 000s.

It can be seen that it matters critically to this multinational what causes the $/FF spot rate. If the French franc is strengthening the dollar value of the portfolio will decline by $101,000. If, on the other hand, the dollar has weakened, the added value of its foreign currency positions in DM and yen more than offsets the losses on French franc positions; the multinational actually benefits from a deterioration in the dollar by $41,000 in this case.

The impact on the balance sheet will of course be markedly different depending on the domestic currency of the organisation concerned. In Table 9.3 the

*Table 9.2 Sensitivity of a US based multinational to a
change in the $/FF spot rate*

	Yen	FF	DM	US$	P&L
NPV of future exposures:	1,000,000	(50,000)	10,000	6,000	
US$/ccy Spot FX Rate:	135.00	5.0000	1.5000	1.0000	
US$ Equivalent:	7,407	(10,000)	6,667	6,000	10,074
1. Dollar weakens by 1%:					
US$/ccy Spot FX Rate:	133.65	4.9500	1.4850	1.0000	
US$ Equivalent:	7,482	(10,101)	6,734	6,000	10,115
US$ P&L differential:	75	–101	67	0	41
2. FF strengthens by 1%:					
US$/ccy Spot FX Rate:	135.00	4.9500	1.5000	1.0000	
US$ Equivalent:	7,407	(10,101)	6,667	6,000	9,973
US$ P&L differential:	0	–101	0	0	–101

*Table 9.3 Sensitivity of a German multinational to a
change in the $/FF spot rate*

	Yen	FF	DM	US$	P&L
NPV of future exposures:	1,000,000	(50,000)	10,000	6,000	
DM/ccy Spot FX Rate:	90	3.33	1	0.67	
DM Equivalents:	11,111	(15,000)	10,000	9,000	15,111
1. Dollar weakens by 1%:					
DM/ccy Spot FX Rate:	90	3.33	1	0.67	
DM Equivalents:	11,111	(15,000)	10,000	8,911	15,022
DM P&L differential:	0	0	0	–89	–89
2. FF strengthens by 1%:					
DM/ccy Spot FX Rate:	90	3.3	1	0.67	
DM Equivalents:	11,111	(15,152)	10,000	9,000	14,959
DM P&L differential:	0	–152	0	0	–152

same price and position data is used to examine the effect of the French franc weakening and the dollar strengthening for a German multinational whose balance sheet is denominated in Deutschmarks.

For the German multinational, then, there is a negative impact on profitability when the $/FF rate falls, whether it is triggered by dollar weakness or French franc strength. It is, however, more sensitive to French franc strength.

Limits to Delta Based Currency Risk Analysis

Delta-type analysis on currency values such as this can provide useful clues as to appropriate currency hedging strategies. The German multinational might, for instance, decide to sell $6m against DM to hedge its position if it believed that the dollar was weakening. For the US multinational it would be appropriate to take no action.

However, though it is a useful starting point, delta analysis on profitability cannot be used in isolation. The risk manager needs to be able to predict, not just the effect on p&l of one currency changing in value, but the changes in the value of other currencies, interest rates and commodities that flow from that.

Linked Currencies and Interest Rate Relationships

Relationships between linked currencies, such as those within the ERM, should be tied into the analysis, wherever appropriate. An example might be to link the French yield curve to Deutschmark curve so that whenever the effect of an increase in Deutschmark base rates is considered, a corresponding French franc rate adjustment is factored into the analysis.

For looser links, less direct connections can be considered. The Australian economy is heavily dependent on commodity exports. The world value of the Australian dollar will therefore tend to rise as the US dollar strengthens. The risk manager might therefore decide to factor in an increase in the Australian dollar's international value of, say, 0.4 per cent for every 1 per cent rise in the value of the US dollar.

At this level the risk manager is in the realm of econometric analysis. For, in practice, interest rate and currency relationships will change through time, and need to be determined on a case by case basis. Risk managers can argue, with some justification, that making predictions as to the nature of financial market interdependence is beyond the scope of their expertise. They could reasonably claim that they are as likely to get the wrong results by connecting markets as if they would if they were to ignore such relationships altogether.

Managing Stochastic Risk: the Role of What-if Analysis

But it is, after all, a fact that global markets move together, so risk managers ignore such relationships at their peril. Perhaps the best way to approach multi-currency risk management is via what-if analysis, so that a variety of different factors can be modelled simultaneously.

The power of what-if simulation rests, not so much in the profit sensitivities it predicts, more in the way it forces the risk manager to ask himself the right sorts of questions. The better the risk manager's understanding of markets' interdependence the more likely he is to succeed, but at least by testing his price sensitivity in a variety of situations he can get an idea of his worst cases and will be able to identify, and hedge against, a deteriorating environment.

STRATEGIES FOR CURRENCY RISK MANAGEMENT

This section introduces some of the main currency risk management strategies. Deutschmark futures and options are used for expository simplicity, but the strategies shown remain valid no matter what form of forward or optional instrument is used.

Table 9.4 Deutschmark (IMM) – June contracts

DM125,000; cents per DM Future = 0.6220		
Option strikes	*Call*	*Put*
6100	1.90	0.71
6150	1.61	0.92
6200	1.35	1.15
6250	1.11	1.41
6300	0.90	1.70
6350	0.72	2.01

Source: Wall Street Journal – 13 April 1993

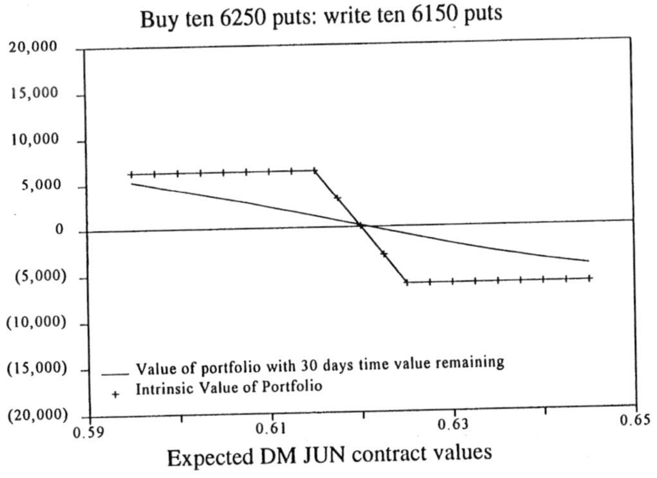

Buy ten 6250 puts: write ten 6150 puts

Figure 9.1 Bear spread strategy

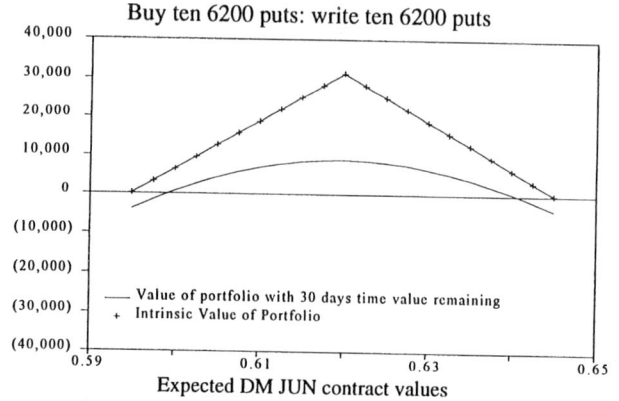

Figure 9.2 Contra-volatility strategy

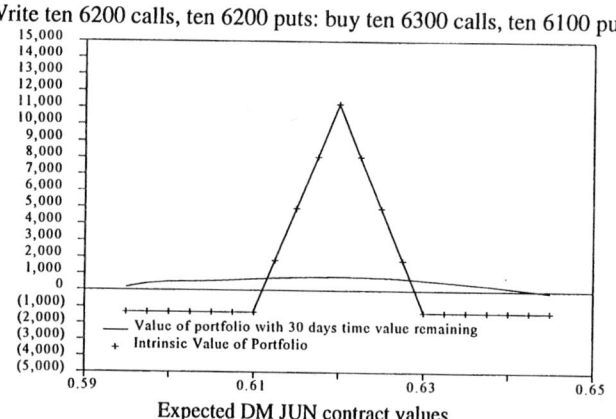

Figure 9.3 Contra-volatility strategy

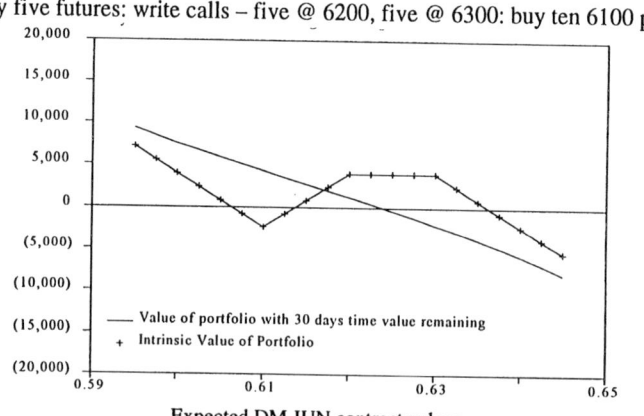

Figure 9.4 Bearish combination strategy

10: Bond Markets

DEBT INSTRUMENTS

This section describes briefly the main types of fixed income securities. It also describes the quotation conventions for the various markets. Risk managers need to know precisely how much cash they will pay and receive on which future dates for each instrument, if they are to make informed decisions.

Government Bonds

In the capital markets, government bonds trade at yields below those of other fixed rate issues with similar maturity characteristics. The fact that the government is the controller of the money supply in the economy and the high liquidity of such issues ensure that risk averse bond investors are attracted to them.

In most territories government bonds are auctioned in the primary markets. The auction process helps to ensure the lowest possible yield for the issuer. Primary dealers and investors are asked to bid for paper at a particular yield. Investor allocations are filled in order, with those bidding the lowest yields (i.e. the highest prices) getting their bonds first. Investors who bid the highest accepted yield receive a proportion of their bond allocation.

US Government Paper

In the US dollar debt markets T-notes and T-bonds are the benchmark instruments. T-notes are generally issued with a call feature that allows the US Government to redeem them at par within ten years. T-bonds are non-callable instruments and are originally issued with maturities between ten and thirty years. Both have semi-annual coupons, and are quoted on a net price basis to the nearest 32nd of a percent.

The actual over coupon days convention is used to calculate accrued interest:

$$\text{Accrued interest} \quad = \quad \frac{\text{S-A coupon} \times \text{Days since last coupon}}{\text{Number of days in current coupon period}}$$

The convention is used so that T-notes and T-bonds can pay exactly half of the quoted coupon on each semi-annual payment date. But, because the length of

171

each coupon period differs, the instruments accrue interest faster in one half of the year than in the other.

At any given moment specific notes and bonds are watched especially closely by the market. The most active securities are normally those with 2, 3, 4, 5, 7, 10, 15, 20, 25 and 30 years to maturity. The thirty year bond, known as the long bond, is a key indicator for investors' inflationary expectations. For this reason it is often referred to as the bellwether bond. Other important securities to watch are those that are cheapest to deliver against futures (see the futures section below).

Other Government Bonds

In most other currencies government bonds paying annual coupons are used as the market's yield curve benchmark. Among the most important are the UK gilts market, Germany's Schuldschein securities, OATs issued by the French government, and Japanese government bonds. In these and other markets, futures are priced according to the relevant government bond's yield.

Benchmark bond yields in the growing ECU capital markets are set by the growing number of issues guaranteed by European governments. France, Italy and the UK have been particularly active ECU bond issuers.

Domestic, Foreign and Euromarkets

The increasing interdependence of international capital markets has begun to blur the distinction between different markets. However, investors differentiate between domestic, foreign and Euromarket instruments when assessing yield.

Domestic bonds are those issued locally by companies and government agencies in the domestic currency. Paper is aimed at domestic investors and, depending on the jurisdiction, coupons may be paid net of a withholding tax.

Foreign bonds are also issued in the domestic currency of the issuing territory. The main difference here is that the companies doing the issuing are foreign controlled. Markets that are described using names that reflect the nationality of the issuing territory are often for foreign bonds. So a Matador bond, for instance, is a Spanish peseta bond issued in Madrid by a non-Spanish company. Other examples include Bulldogs (UK), Yankees (US), Samurais (Japan), Vikings (Denmark), etc.

Eurobonds are issued offshore. Investors are paid coupon amounts in full and are not required to register their holdings. For instance, US dollar bonds issued in London, Frankfurt or Tokyo would be classified as Eurobonds, whether or not the issuer is based in the United States. Eurobond markets are self regulated. The International Primary Markets Association (IPMA) oversees the syndication process while the Association of International Bond Dealers (AIBD) regulates the secondary market.

Bond Ratings

The creditworthiness of a bond can have a significant impact on its yield. Many bond issuers therefore elect to have a rating code attached to the paper to make it more marketable to investors who may be unfamiliar with their name. Standard & Poor's and Moody's are the main credit rating agencies. They classify the quality of an issue according to a coding system. AAA (S&P)/Aaa (Moody's) is the best possible rating, AA/Aa and A category bonds are also considered investment grade, but would trade at higher yields. BBB/Baa or below are speculative grade securities (popularly known as junk bonds) and issuers must offer considerably higher yields to compensate investors for the extra risk.

An important figure for bond analysts is the spread over treasuries of a security. Expressed in basis points, this measures the level of the risk premium being demanded for a bond by comparing its yield with that of the equivalent period's, credit-risk free, government security.

Straights

Straight bonds are the most common form of debt financing. The investor receives a fixed coupon, paid in arrears, plus capital at maturity. Straights are quoted on a net price basis.

In Eurobond markets coupons are normally paid annually. The notional over 360 convention is used to calculate accrued interest:

$$\text{Accrued interest} = \frac{\text{Coupon} \times ((30-D0) + (M \times 30) + D1)}{360}$$

Where:
D0 = Last coupon date
M = Number of full months since last coupon date
D1 = Value date of transaction

The convention allows Eurobonds to pay the quoted coupon on each payment date. But, because it assumes that each month has thirty days, two or three days of interest accrues overnight at the end of February, while for 31 day months no interest at all accrues on the last day of the month.

Yield to Maturity

Straights are quoted on a net price basis, but they are bought and sold according to yield. The yield to maturity is defined as that rate which, when used to discount future coupons and capital repayments back to the current value date, equates their sum to the instrument's gross price.

173

The AIBD yield to maturity formula is as follows:

$$\text{Price} = \text{Cpn} \times \left(\frac{1}{(1+R)^T} + \frac{1}{(1+R)^{(1+T)}} +...+ \frac{1}{(1+R)^{(n+T)}} \right) + \frac{FV}{(1+R)^{(n+T)}}$$

Where:

Price = Gross price of security (i.e. including accrued interest)
R = Annualised yield to maturity
T = Length of period to next coupon date (Notional days/360)
FV = Redemption value of security

Given the gross price, the yield to maturity can be found by an iterative process. Astute readers will have noticed that the formula is actually calculating a form of internal rate of return. It is providing the answer to the question, 'What single rate equates the cost of the bond to its cashflow benefits?'

Reinvestment Risk

The yield to maturity does not tell the investor how much money she will have earned when the bond is finally redeemed. Implicit in the calculation is the assumption that all coupons can be reinvested to maturity at the same yield. Investors buying straights in the expectation of a fall in interest rates are unlikely to realise the yield to maturity. If they are correct, and yields are lower, it also means that they must reinvest the coupons at a lower yield. Reinvestment risk is greatest for high coupon bonds, the amount to be reinvested is larger so the shortfall caused by having to reinvest at a lower rate will be more significant.

Zero Coupon Bonds

As the term suggests, a zero coupon bond is simply a fixed rate bond paying zero per cent coupons. The investor receives the face value of the bond at maturity (normally par) and pays a price equivalent to its present value. The formula for calculating the yield to maturity on a zero is thus:

$$\text{Price} = \frac{\text{Face value}}{(1+R)^T}$$

This, of course, is similar to the zero coupon factor calculation discussed in Chapter 3. The great advantage of a zero is that it carries no reinvestment risk: since no coupons are paid nothing has to be reinvested to maturity. Its yield to maturity (R) is, therefore, an expression of the precise cash benefit to the investor of owning it.

Zeros are popular amongst insurance companies, risk managers and other investors who need to earn a guaranteed amount on a precise date.

Viewing Straights as Sets of Zero Coupon Bonds

As we saw in Chapter 3 in the discussion on yield curves, the present value of any known cashflow should be evaluated using the prevailing yield to the date on which it occurs. The buyer of a bond is in fact acquiring several cashflows on different dates in the future.

Looked at this way, there is a case for evaluating bonds by discounting each future cashflow separately, using the appropriate rates. The sum of these amounts should be equivalent to the price of the bond. This technique is most appropriate for high quality bonds and has been applied to goverment bonds by financial engineers to transform them into a series of separately tradeable zero coupon bonds.

Call Features

Many bonds include a call feature. This allows the issuer to redeem the paper before maturity at a prearranged price (often par). Where straight bonds have a call feature the investor should regard this as an embedded option that he has written by buying the instrument. An issuer will often call a fixed rate bond if yields fall below the coupon rate, because he knows he can refinance more cheaply in the current environment. The investor has in effect written an interest rate floor, which is being exercised by the issuer. Investors should take care to evaluate the yield to each call date as well as the yield to maturity date, and should consider their investment in the light of the lowest yielding result.

Put Features

Some bonds, particularly where there is market resistance to the issuer's name, may include an investor put feature. Basically, this allows the investor to redeem his paper before final maturity at a prearranged price (although this will often be less than par to discourage early redemption). In this situation it is appropriate to consider the bond's yield to the put dates as well as its yield to maturity. The bond investor has effectively bought an interest rate cap in addition to a straight bond. Option valuation techniques should be applied to bonds with either put or call features.

Partly-paid Securities and Sinking Funds

Some securities redeem capital in stages rather than just at maturity; these are known as sinking fund bonds. Others allow the initial investors to purchase the security in stages; these are known as partly paid issues. In both cases the payment structure of the bond is non-standard and the AIBD yield to maturity calculation cannot be used. However, the yield to maturity of such instruments can easily be found by discounting each future cashflow back to the current value date. The single rate that equates the sum of the present values of these amounts to the price is the bond's implied yield to maturity.

Floating Rate Notes (FRNs)

FRNs and other floaters, unlike straights, do not pay a fixed rate of interest on coupon dates. Instead each coupon, payable in arrears, is fixed at the start of the coupon period according to currently prevailing short-term rates. A benchmark rate, often LIBOR, is chosen, and the FRN pays a fixed margin above it in interest depending on the riskiness of the issuer. Coupons and accrued interest for FRNs are calculated according to the relevant money market convention (i.e. actual days/360 or actual days/365 for sterling).

Because FRNs have their coupons refixed periodically they do not carry the same interest risk as a straight or zero with similar maturity characteristics. We shall see in the following chapter how duration can be used to evaluate the price sensitivity for a set of known cashflows. For an FRN priced off six-month LIBOR, the duration is 0.5 immediately after the coupon has been set, and falls to 0 just before the next coupon is fixed. As a result, a 1 per cent change in six-month LIBOR will never have more than a 0.5 per cent effect on the FRN's price.

In practice, many FRNs are priced at or near their par value. If they are trading significantly below this, it is because the market has decided that the LIBOR margin does not compensate them adequately for the risk of holding the issuer's paper. Similarly, FRNs trading well above par are offering too generous a margin to investors.

FRN Variants

As we shall see in the following chapter, the combination of capital gain and uncertain cashflows makes it difficult to price FRNs. Computer assisted generic valuation techniques need to be used, especially when one also has to deal with a wide range of variants on the traditional FRN structure. Many FRNs have minimum coupons, there are also capped FRNs (i.e. with a maximum coupon) and mini-max FRNs (both maximum and minimum coupons). These can all be viewed as standard FRNs with embedded caps/floors.

Other variations include mismatch FRNs where the interest payment frequency differs from the interest rate base. An example might be an FRN paying interest every six months according to the average of six one-month LIBOR rates (plus a margin) experienced during the period. With a step-up FRN, the margin increases through time: the investor may receive a margin of 10 basis points for the first two years, 25 basis points for the next five, and 35 basis points for the final three years on a ten year, step-up floater.

The examples illustrate the diversity of the financial instruments available in

FRN markets. They also serve to underline the importance of generic evaluation techniques. The effective margin formula described in the next chapter has to be modified to take account of the cashflow implications of non-standard instruments such as those described here. However, the evaluation principles remain relevant.

Variable Rate Notes

VRNs were originally introduced as a repackaged form of the discredited perpetual FRN structure. This was an FRN paying a higher than average margin over LIBOR, which had no final maturity date. Perpetual FRNs had been popular with financial institutions who were able to use them as a way of bolstering their capital reserves. Investors saw them as a renewable six-month security and generally failed to recognise that the credit risk element in pricing was very substantial. When, in 1986, the FRN markets experienced a rapid sell-off, perpetuals were especially badly hit and ceased to be a credible instrument. The VRN represented an attempt to address the credit risk component in the perpetual FRN.

VRNs are similar to FRNs in that interest is not fixed until each LIBOR is known. Unlike FRNs, however, VRN margins are not determined in advance. There is a fall-back margin, but this is normally set at a very high level, often 150 to 200 basis points above LIBOR. Instead the margin is re-negotiated between the issuer and the lead manager on each coupon fixing date, the aim being to negotiate a level that will allow the VRN to trade at par. To encourage this process the VRN includes both put and call features. To protect investors against the margin being set too low, they have the right on any coupon date to sell their paper to the lead manager at a price of 100. The borrower is protected against the possibility of too high a margin being fixed by having a call option on the entire issue, also exercisable on any coupon date at par.

In theory the structure should make it unnecessary for either feature to be exercised, the VRN should always trade around its par value. From the investor's point of view this makes the VRN much safer than its FRN counterpart, as there is less of a concern about declining credit quality triggering a capital loss. In practice there have been instances where declining credit perceptions have pushed margins up to their fall-back level. When a VRN is trading at its fall-back margin the call and put features become inactive, so that investors in some VRNs have found that their paper trades at a price below par.

Collateralised Securities

Since 1987, collateralised securities have been increasingly popular. By issuing bonds through a special purpose company that owns high quality assets, the credit rating of a bond can be improved (and its yield or margin reduced). The STRIPS described in the following chapter are one manifestation of this issuing technique. Investment banks also use collateralisation in repackaging exercises particularly when they have issued bonds with equity warrants.

Pay-Through and Pass-Through Securities

Collateralisation is also used to raise finance in the capital markets for retail operations, and as a balance sheet management technique. With pass-through securities the investor receives the income from the pool of securitised assets directly. Examples of financial assets that have been securitised in this way include mortgages, credit card loans and car hire-purchase agreements.

Investors like pass-through securities for their relatively high yields and low risk characteristics. On the other hand they cannot predict the payment structure of their asset with any great accuracy. Take mortgage-backed bonds, repayment of capital and interest in the pool will depend on the rate at which members of the pool of mortgage owners pay off their debts. This will vary as economic conditions change and people move house.

Pay-through securities are a variation on the pass-through structure that provide increased cashflow predictability for investors. Both pay-throughs and pass-throughs are administered through special purpose issuing vehicles. With a pass-through the issuing entity passes all of its revenues across to investors. In a pay-through vehicle a number of bond issues with different maturity characteristics are collateralised by a large pool of assets. Revenues are allocated to each issue to mirror its cashflow pattern as closely as possible.

Indexed Issues

Another popular category of bond is the indexed security. Here, the issuer links the repayment schedule to the performance of a benchmark index. For the issuer it can be a way of improving the credit rating of his security by linking his cost of financing to his trading performance. For the investor it provides the possibility of enhanced yield if he believes the index will perform well.

Issues can be indexed against anything that has a quoted price, but the classical issuer of an indexed issue is a commodities producer. If, say, an oil producing company wishes to build a new offshore rig, it can raise the required capital via a bond with a feature that states that redemption will be related to the oil price. The redemption formula might be something like:

Redemption amount $= (25 \times PF - 400)$ % of face value

Where

$PF =$ Oil price at maturity: minimum $= 20$, maximum $= \$30$

Since investors know that they will receive a minimum of 100 per cent and up to 350 per cent of the face value at maturity, they will be prepared to accept a lower coupon if they are bullish on the oil price. For his part the issuer knows that the increase in his revenues from a rise in the oil price to $30 a barrel will more than offset the extra cost of borrowing. When oil prices, and therefore his profitability, are low his funding is cheaper.

Dual Currency Bonds

The dual currency bond is a special type of indexed issue. Here coupons are denominated in one currency, but capital is repaid in a different currency. Dual currency bonds are most attractive when the yield curves in the two currencies are widely different. Normally, higher than average coupons are paid in the low interest rate currency and capital is repaid in the high interest currency.

Because of the forward pricing relationship between the two currencies (see Chapter 8 for a fuller explanation of this effect) the amount of the high interest currency paid at maturity can be greater than would be achievable using the current spot rate. The investor's yield performance is therefore indexed to the FX rate between the two currencies.

Bull–Bear Securities

Issuers can reduce their cost of funds while still retaining the risk characteristics of a standard fixed rate bond, or an FRN, by issuing indexed issues in combination. The key to the success of the operation is the timing of its launch. The issuer launches equal amounts of two bonds simultaneously, each having a redemption amount linked to the same price or index. The bull tranche is positively related to the index's performance, investors receive more at redemption the higher the index goes. The bear tranche is aimed at investors who believe the index is going to fall, they receive larger redemption amounts the lower the index goes.

As far as the issuer is concerned the effect is neutral. The only difference that the index price makes is in how the total repayment is distributed between the two groups of investors. However, by launching the bonds at the right moment, when markets are uncertain about the future direction of prices, the issuer ensures an enthusiastic reception for his paper and can raise his funds at a lower overall cost.

BOND FUTURES

Definition

A bond futures contract is a standard agreement that provides the holder with a government guaranteed security on a specified date in the future. In common with other futures contracts the terms of the contract are standardised with respect to the size, credit quality and terms to enhance tradeability. Bond futures are offered on a variety of exchanges with delivery dates in March, June, September and December up to two years in the future. For popular contracts, such as the 8 per cent T-bond future traded at the Chicago Board of Trade, other months are also available.

Table 10.1 Major contracts

Commodity/Exchange	Size	Tick	Value	Deliverable grades
20y 8% T-bond / CBOT, LIFFE, SFE	$100,000	1/32nd	$31.25	US T-bonds maturing after at least 15 years
10y 8% T-note/CBOT	$100,000	1/32nd	$31.25	US T-notes maturing in 6.5 years to 10 years
5y 8% T-note/CBOT	$100,000	1/32nd	$31.25	US T-bonds maturing in 4.25 to 5.25 years
2y 8% T-note/CBOT	$200,000	.25/32nd	$15.625	US T-bonds maturing in 4.25 to 5.25 years
Muni-Bond Index*/CBOT	$1000x	1/32nd	$31.25	Cash settlement
ECU 9 per cent Bond/LIFFE	ECU200,000	ECU0.01	ECU20	AAA govt backed bonds maturing in 6.5–10 years
Long Gilt/LIFFE	£50,000	£1/32	£15.625	Gilts maturing in more than 12 years
6 per cent Bund /LIFFE	DM250,000	DM0.01	DM25	German government bonds maturing in 8.5–10 years
6 per cent 10y Jap Gov Bond/TSE, LIFFE	Y100m	Y0.01	Y10,000	JGBs maturing in 6.5–10 years
6 per cent 20y Jap Gov Bond(TSE)	Y100m	Y0.01	Y10,000	JGBs maturing after 15 years

* MBI Index constructed out of 40 US municipal bonds. The average price for each is divided by a conversion factor to equate it to an 8 per cent bond. These adjusted prices are weighted to make up the index price.

CBOT   Chicago Board of Trade
LIFFE   London International Financial Futures Exchange
TSE   Tokyo Stock Exchange
SFE   Sydney Futures Exchange

Pricing

Bond futures are generally quoted on a price basis, determined according to the required yield for a notional bond with a stated maturity. A notional bond is used to avoid the necessity to change the characteristics of the underlying instrument every time a new contract is launched.

Conversion Factors

On the delivery date, the owner of a short contract may select one from a number of actual bonds available in the market to deliver to the owner of a long contract. Because the bond chosen is at the discretion of the supplier he will select the most inexpensive. Of course, each bond will have individual coupon and maturity characteristics. Equating the values of other bonds to the notional bond can be done by use of a conversion factor. The conversion factor is defined as the adjustment to the price of the bond being converted implied to equate it to the notional bond's yield to maturity when priced at par.

Consider the 8 per cent US 20-year T-bond future due for delivery in three months' time. Eligible bonds might include a 7.75 per cent 18.5-year, a 6.5 per cent 24.25-year and a 9 per cent 16.25-year T-bond. The conversion factors are found by calculating the required prices for each of these on the delivery date that would yield 8 per cent. The bonds are looked at in terms of the period commencing on the delivery date.

	24 yr	18.25 yr	16 yr
T-bond maturity:	24 yr	18.25 yr	16 yr
T-bond coupon:	6.50%	12.00%	9.00%
Gross cost @*% YTM:	84.1037	141.0237	108.9368
Net price @ 8% YTM:	84.1037	138.0237	108.9368
Conversion factor:	0.84104	1.38024	1.08937

The conversion factors are calculated for each contract delivery date and are published by the exchange. When a seller is asked to deliver $100,000 in bonds against a futures price of 100-00, he may choose to deliver 16yr, 9 per cent T-bonds, and would earn a net price of 138-01 (i.e. 32nds) plus accrued interest.

The CTD Bond and the Futures Price

Supply and demand factors dictate pricing conditions in the futures market. However, the technical pricing relationship between the CTD bond, the riskless rate and the futures price defines the limits to such movements. If the future becomes too expensive relative to the CTD, arbitrage profits can be made by selling the future while buying the T-bond in the cash market and financing it until the delivery date. If the future is too cheap, the reverse opportunity is available.

As conditions change, then so will the CTD bond. It is vital for risk managers to be aware of the current CTD bond and how futures prices are related to it if they wish to understand the basis risk in their hedging programmes. This is discussed further in Chapter 11.

Hedging with Bond Futures

Institutional investors with portfolios of fixed income assets are among the most active users of bond futures for hedging purposes. By selling bond futures they are able to hedge against a rise in the yield curve without having to liquidate the portfolio.

Sources of Basis Risk

Bond futures, however, afford no protection against changes in investor credit perceptions. We have seen that the difference between the yield on a particular bond and that of its equivalent government bond, its risk premium, is defined by investors' risk-adjusted yield requirement. Risk premiums will vary through time, both for individual securities and for broad categories. Bond futures, as credit risk-free instruments, do not capture this variation.

The other main basis risks for portfolio managers using the futures markets relate to the difference in the compositions between the portfolio and the future. Firstly the duration of the portfolio is unlikely to correspond to that of the future. Secondly, even when a duration-adjusted hedge is constructed, it will only provide protection against parallel shifts in the yield curve.

Margining and Hedging Costs

As with other futures markets, dealers in bond futures are required to lodge margin with the exchange for every contract that they open. This margin amount is refundable when the contract is closed out, but, because the hedge may need to remain in place for several months, this can represent a significant cost of trading.

Futures users can minimise the margin interest cost by lodging interest bearing securities rather than cash payments with the clearing house, a system known as hypothecation. A number of exchanges accept government securities such as T-bills, as well as cash in settlement of margin account. Others are prepared to pay interest on margin accounts, but the rates offered tend to be much lower than those available elsewhere.

OPTIONAL INSTRUMENTS

Debt Options

Types of Debt Option
Any instrument that provides the owner with an optional right to lend or borrow at a minimum or maximum rate of interest can be regarded as a debt option. Interest rate caps/floors and swaptions are particularly appropriate hedging

instruments in the capital markets that can be used effectively by the portfolio manager attempting to control interest risk for a series of periods in the future.

Bond Futures Options

Bond futures options are a complementary risk management tool to the futures themselves. They take the form of call and put options on the underlying futures contract. A futures call gives its owner the right to buy the underlying contract, while a put provides for the right to sell the future.

Since the buyer of a bond futures contract is acquiring a notional bond the price reflects the yield. A futures call is a minimum yield guarantee, or floor. Similarly, the owner of a put on the future has the right to sell at a maximum yield, it is therefore a type of cap.

Types of Futures Option

For each futures contract, call and put options are available for strikes at regular intervals around the current futures price. Options on the US T-bond future, for instance, have a strike price interval of two points. The contracts which are introduced depend on the price of the underlying future. If the future is trading at par, call and put options will be available at strikes of 96, 98, 100, 102 and 104.

There are always at least six options available – those with strike prices closest to the underlying futures price. As the futures price changes, there must always be at least two contracts above and below the current level. New options contracts may therefore be introduced by the exchange, so that by the futures delivery date there can be more than six options being traded on the exchange.

Table 10.2 shows premiums payable on puts and calls on the 8 per cent 20-year T-Bond June contract at the CBOT. On the date in question the June future closed at 95-24 (the future is priced in 32nds).

Table 10.2 Options on 8 per cent US T-bond (Chicago Board of Trade)

$100,000; 64ths of 100%		
Strike price	June calls	June puts
92	4-42	1-01
94	3-20	1-37
96	2-10	2-25
98	1-20	3-32
100	0-49	4-61
102	0-28	6-36

Source: Wall Street Journal

Futures Option Pricing

As can be seen from Table 10.2, T-bond option premiums are quoted in 64ths. The value of one tick is therefore half that of the future; it is $15.625 in this case.

183

Market participants can find the net price of any call by adding the premium to (or, for puts, subtracting it from) the exercise price. A buyer of a 94 call would for example have a worst case cost of 97–20 (64ths), while the purchaser of a put at the same strike has a worst case selling price of 92–27 (94 minus 1–37/64) for the June future.

Trading in Futures Options
As is the case with futures, exchange traded options are used mainly by market professionals. They form an essential component of any risk management strategy. Traders and risk managers, by buying and selling options, can express a view on expected market volatility; just as they buy and sell futures according to their view on the direction of price movements.

Margining and Marking-to-Market
Margining mechanisms differ between exchanges. Some require option buyers to pay the entire premium into the margin account. Writers must maintain a margin related to the future that increases according to the likelihood of exercise. However, a risk-based system is gaining acceptance.

This uses risk numbers to predict the anticipated change in the value of the overall portfolio for a given change in the futures price. Margin requirements for both buyers and sellers are related to the underlying future by the risk number and change on a daily basis.

Debt Warrants

Debt warrants provide the investor with a long-term interest rate guarantee. They are often issued as a sweetener in conjunction with a fixed rate bond. A typical debt warrant attached to a ten-year 9 per cent bond might provide the owner with, say, a five-year right to buy another five-year bond with an 8 per cent coupon at a price of par.

Clearly such a warrant could be attractive to an investor who believed interest rates were falling. The warrant guarantees that his yield will never be worse than the stated coupon. Investors should use option valuation techniques to determine how much he is prepared to pay to own that right.

Suppose one does the analysis and decides it is worth 2.5 per cent of the face value of the bond. If the bond–warrant package is being sold at par, this indicates that he should pay 97.5 for the bond element. Its yield to maturity is therefore 9.972 per cent; although the issuer has been able to raise funds with a lower coupon by including the warrant feature.

Harmless Warrants
But investors should take care to look at the detail of bond-cum-debt warrant packages if they are not to be misled by the superficial attractiveness of an issue.

The so-called harmless warrant (which might perhaps be more aptly dubbed the worthless warrant) is a good illustration of the sleight of hand that sometimes accompanies innovative financial engineering.

Harmless warrants were promoted as being a special kind of warrant that allowed the issuer to offer warrants that would not increase his borrowing dramatically when exercised. The warrant structure mirrored the terms of the bond. For instance, a ten-year 9 per cent bond callable at par on any coupon date after five years might be launched together with a ten-year harmless warrant that provided the investor with the right to buy an 8 per cent non-callable bond with the same maturity at a price of par. The special terms of the warrant required holders to convert their existing bonds into the new bonds if they exercised within five years. If exercising after five years they were able to buy the 8 per cent bond without trading in the existing bond.

On the face of it the warrant has substantial time value, but the benefits begin to erode if it is examined more closely. Firstly, the warrant is not separately tradeable for the first five years. Anyone wishing to exercise the 8 per cent warrant would have to hand in the existing 9 per cent bond. The terms of conversion also look unfavourable: although there may be some benefit from exchanging a 9 per cent callable for an 8 per cent non-callable bond it is unlikely to be as much as the 1 per cent annual loss in coupon.

After five years the warrant becomes much more attractive. If interest rates fall below 8 per cent it can be exercised at a profit without the 9 per cent bond having to be handed in. At the same time, however, the call feature on the 9 per cent bond is by now activated. If there is any intrinsic value to the harmless warrant then the bond will almost certainly be called.

What the original investors in the bond plus harmless warrants package were buying, therefore, was, overall, less valuable than a 9 per cent non-callable bond. Indeed, it was actually a 9 per cent bond with call protection below 8 per cent. Yet, despite this it traded at higher prices than other 9 per cent non-callable bonds with similar maturity and credit characteristics.

Bonds with harmless warrants were mispriced by a market which, at the time, undervalued embedded options and overvalued warrants. By including an embedded call option and combining it with a warrant designed to remove it instead of just launching a non-callable bond, the issuer was able to outsmart the market and achieve a lower cost of funds.

Government Bond Warrants

Although debt warrants are still issued with bonds, debt warrant issues are becoming an increasingly popular feature of the international capital markets. Issuing activity by investment banks has developed the debt warrant into a viable alternative to the bond futures market for fixed income portfolio managers.

Typically warrants are issued in tranches of one million. Take for example a Credit Suisse financial products warrant issue on US government bonds,

185

launched in January 1991. This was an issue of one million call warrants priced at $4.85 each, giving the right to buy $100 nominal of the US 2020 8.75 per cent T-bond at a price of 106.1875. The warrants were exercisable on any date between February 1991 and February 1992. As is normal with options and warrants, settlement was on a cash basis – the warrant holder would receive any positive difference between the market price of the 2020 bond and 106.1875. He can therefore buy the bonds at a net price of 111.0375. This equates to a minimum yield of 7.61 per cent (semi-annual basis).

The warrants provide fund managers with an alternative to T-bond futures options in the management of their portfolios and premiums will be broadly in line with those payable on the March 1992 CBOT long bond contract. However, because the underlying instrument is a specific bond rather than a notional one, the risk manager can structure hedging programmes using warrants with more certainty about their performance through time. A hedge using T-bond futures may have to be rebalanced if, say, the cheapest to deliver bond changes and the new underlying instrument has a radically different duration.

With the warrant there are no such complications: the hedge strategy performs according to the prices and volatility of the 2020 bond. On the other hand, of course, call and put warrants on debt are less actively tradeable than futures options.

Caps and Floors

The interest rate protection provided by IRGs (see Chapter 6) is useful for risk managers seeking to guarantee a worst case interest rate for a specific future period. However, many institutions have known financing requirements several years into the future. For them FIs can offer interest rate protection over a number of periods via cap or floor contracts.

Caps and floors are OTC instruments that are similar in construction to a series of IRGs, all at the same strike rate. A cap is equivalent to several IRG calls and offers maximum interest rate protection, a floor guarantees the minimum rate and is equivalent to a set of IRG puts.

The frequency of the interest rate guaranteed will be agreed between the counterparties. The period to maturity can be anything up to ten years. A typical cap might guarantee a maximum rate against three-month LIBOR for quarterly rates for the next five years.

The buyer of the cap is normally expected to pay an up-front fee in exchange for a commitment by the cap writer to compensate him, should LIBOR exceed the strike rate on any of the agreed dates, by the extent of the difference. The up-front fee is equivalent to the total premium cost of purchasing separate, European style, IRGs for each of the interest periods at the cap rate.

The up-front fee is usually quoted as a percentage of the underlying nominal amount. For certain counterparties, though, FIs will agree to negotiate an annual fee, and this will normally be quoted as a per annum rate.

In Table 10.3 the cap buyer negotiated an up-front fee of 1.25 per cent (i.e.

Table 10.3

Time (in years)	Six-month LIBOR (at start of period)	Differential	Amount payable (at end of period)
0	8.75%	NA	NA
0.5	8.50%	NA	$0
1	8.25%	NA	$0
1.5	8.50%	NA	$0
2	9.75%	0.25%	$0
2.5	10.25%	0.75%	$12,500
3	10.50%	1.00%	$37,500
3.5	10.00%	0.50%	$50,000
4	9.75%	0.25%	$25,000
4.5	9.50%	NA	$12,500
5	NA		$0
		Total:	$137,500

Table 10.4

Time (in years)	Six-month LIBOR (at start of period)	Borrow @ LIBOR	Capped LIBOR
0	8.75%	+10,000	+9,875
0.5	8.50%	–437.5	–437.5
1	8.25%	–425	–425
1.5	8.50%	–412.5	–412.5
2	9.75%	–425	–425
2.5	10.25%	–487.5	–475
3	10.50%	–512.5	–475
3.5	10.00%	–525	–4'5
4	9.75%	–500	–475
4.5	9.50%	–487.5	–475
5		–10,475.0	–10,475.0
Net s-a funding cost:		9.30%	9.37%

cashflows are shown in $ooos

$125,000) for an out of the money, five-year $10m cap with a strike rate of 9.5 per cent against six-month LIBOR. Whenever the six-month LIBOR exceeds 9.5 per cent he receives cash compensation at the end of that interest period. As a borrower at six-month LIBOR on the dates in question he is able to guarantee a maximum cost of funding by buying the cap.

By buying the cap this hedger has been able to contain his maximum financing costs, but it may be the relatively high premium he paid offsets the savings accruing from the protection it affords. To ascertain whether he actually saved money by buying the cap we need to look at the comparative cashflows for a LIBOR borrower, with and without this 9.5 per cent cap.

In this case, then, we can see that the extra cost of purchasing cap protection more than outweighs the benefits it provides. Of course, the rationale for the cap buyer is that he is locked into a worst case cost no matter what the future level for LIBOR. A crucial calculation for him then is the net rate for the cap.

Collars

The high up-front cost of acquiring interest protection over a series of periods can be a deterrent to risk managers, particularly in institutions where financial resources are limited. One way of limiting the amount of premium that has to be paid, while still enjoying protection against the worst case, is by relinquishing some of the upside potential. Collars have proved especially popular amongst corporations, who see them as a cost-effective form of interest rate insurance.

A collar is, in essence, a combination of a cap and a floor. The buyer of a collar is actually purchasing a cap and writing a floor, the collar writer has sold a cap and bought a floor. The floating rate borrower discussed above with six-month LIBOR payments over the next five years might decide to buy a collar between, say 8.5 per cent and 9.5 per cent. This still provides him with protection if LIBOR goes above 9.5 per cent, but if interest rates should fall below 8.5 per cent he will be obliged to pay the difference to his counterparty. The effect is to lock him into a maximum rate of 9.5 per cent and a minimum of 8.5 per cent, while borrowing at the floating rate if it is between the two strikes.

Since collars are cap–floor combinations, their cost will depend on the relative premiums for the two options priced individually. It should be obvious that collars can be constructed where the buyer pays no premium (or even receives a payment from the seller) depending on which cap and floor rates are used. A collar with strikes that are both out of the money to the same extent will have a net premium of zero. If the cap is in the money and the floor out of the money the buyer will have some premium to pay, but, because he is still giving up some profit potential (by writing the floor) it will always be cheaper than just buying a call.

Table 10.5 shows the borrower's cashflows assuming he could write an 8.5 per cent, five-year floor for a 1.0 per cent premium. The net premium for the collar in this case is 0.25 per cent of the underlying amount.

In this case, the borrower's funding cost is reduced to 9.14 per cent by the effect of the collar. six-month LIBOR in one year is set at 8.25 per cent, so he must pay the collar's writer the $12,500 interest differential after eighteen months. However, this is easily offset by the $100,000 reduction in premium he was able to negotiate by agreeing to guarantee a minimum rate of 8.5 per cent.

The smaller premium also means that his net rate is commensurately lower, equating to just 9.508 per cent (9.5% + 0.8 bps). Remember, though, that he also has a best case rate of 8.508 per cent.

Average Rate Caps, Floors and Collars

Corporate treasurers welcome the increased control over multi-period interest

Table 10.5

Time (in years)	Six-month LIBOR (at start of period)	Borrow @ LIBOR	Capped LIBOR
0	8.75%	+10,000	+9,975
0.5	8.50%	−437.5	−437.5
1	8.25%	−425	−425
1.5	8.50%	−412.5	−425
2	9.75%	−425	−425
2.5	10.25%	−487.5	−475
3	10.50%	−512.5	−475
3.5	10.00%	−525	−475
4	9.75%	−500	−475
4.5	9.50%	−487.5	−475
5	−10,475.0	−10,475.0	−10,475.0
Net s-a funding cost:		9.30%	9.14%

risk afforded by caps, floors and collars. However, the fact that such instruments are related to LIBORs on specific dates can in many cases leave them exposed to a basis risk. In particular, companies that raise floating rate funds by regular (sometimes daily) issues of commercial paper are looking for interest risk protection over the entire period rather than on specific dates.

This risk can be insulated by linking the strike rate, not to a single LIBOR, but to the average LIBOR across the period. This can reduce basis risk by matching the option's performance more closely to the buyer's actual payment profile.

Captions and Floortions

Interest risk managers can sometimes protect the value of their contingent cash-flows even more cost effectively by buying captions and floortions. These are options on caps or floors that are individually agreed between counterparties and they are not actively traded. A $10m five-year borrower could buy potential interest risk protection by taking out a caption contract. He might pay, say, $10,000 (i.e. 0.1 per cent of the underlying notional amount) for the right to buy a five-year 9.5 per cent cap at a cost of 1.25 per cent.

If cap prices on the expiry date are quoted at, say, 1.4 per cent, the caption owner receives the intrinsic value which in this case is 15 basis points (i.e. $15,000). He can then decide to purchase a cap in the open market and with his caption protection, the net cost is 1.25 per cent. If a risk manager is unsure whether or not a cash-flow will materialise this can be a very effective way of controlling his ultimate risk at a minimal cost.

It may seem that captions and floortions are a very exotic form of financial instrument, but they can easily be understood if we remember that they behave like any other option. It just happens that the 'brick', or underlying instrument, is, in this case, another option.

11: Swap Markets

INTEREST RATE SWAPS

Definition

An interest rate swap is an agreement between two counterparties to exchange interest payments and receipts on a number of occasions during a specified period. It is equivalent to two simultaneous cash transactions – each counterparty is, in effect, lending to and borrowing from the other the same capital amount over the same period.

Since interest rate swaps are over the counter transactions, their exact structure is individually negotiated between the counterparties. Having said this, the notional capital amount is typically large. The standard swap is at least $5m (or equivalent) and swaps on $100m or more are not uncommon. Interest rate swaps are widely available with maturities between two to ten years.

Types of Interest Rate Swap

There are two main kinds of interest rate swap, the fixed versus floating and the basis swap.

In a typical fixed versus floating swap the counterparties might agree to exchange the interest differential between a semi-annual fixed rate and six-month LIBOR, twice a year for, say, the next five years. In construction, it is very similar to a series of FRAs for six-month periods out to five years, all at the same price.

In a basis swap the counterparties exchange floating rates of interest calculated off a different reference rate for a specific period. Examples might include a five-year swap of the 90-day commercial paper rate versus three-month LIBOR or a seven-year, one-month LIBOR versus six-month LIBOR swap.

Since a swap is a bilateral agreement its precise terms are agreed between the counterparties. The majority of interest rate swaps are versus six-month LIBOR. Three-month LIBOR is also a popular interest rate basis, especially for money market swaps, which have period lengths of two years or less.

Fixed-Floating Swaps

By far the most common form of interest rate swap is between a US dollar fixed rate, payable semi-annually, and six-month LIBOR. The most common maturities

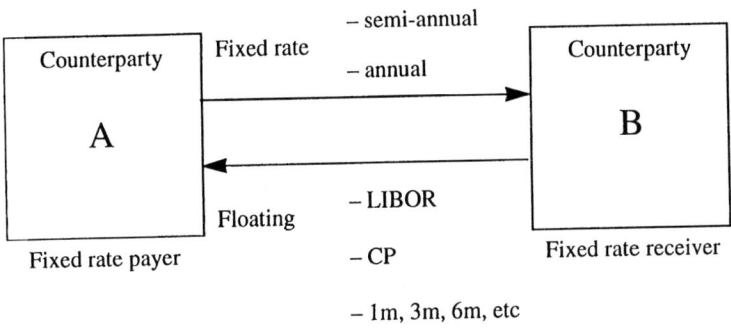

Figure 11.1 Interest flows on a fixed-floating swap

are in the range of five to seven years. In fixed-floating swaps the counterparties are referred to by their relationship to the fixed rate side of the swap. The market talks about fixed rate payers and fixed rate receivers.

Prices for fixed-floating swaps are quoted in terms of basis points above the relevant government bond yields. A five-year fixed-floating swap, for instance, would be priced according to the active government bond yield. A swap dealer might quote a price such as 60–70, meaning that he would be prepared to pay a fixed rate 60 basis points above five-year government bond yields or receive the fixed at 70 basis points above.

Their Use in Risk Transformation

Like FRAs, fixed-floating swaps can be used to transform interest risk exposure, the main difference being that swaps are used to lock into the fixed (or floating) rate over several interest payment periods, whereas FRAs relate to one period only. Just as the market participant with a floating rate obligation can buy an FRA to fix his interest cost in advance, the same can be achieved over several periods by paying the fixed rate.

Similarly a fixed rate borrower who felt that interest rates were falling might want to receive the fixed rate. The corollary of this is that a floating rate investor would receive the fixed rate, while a fixed rate investor would pay fixed, to transform interest risk.

Basis Swaps

Basis swaps account for around 10 per cent of interest rate swap activity. They are used most commonly by market participants seeking to eliminate basis risk on their floating rate positions. For instance, a financial institution that raises

funds via regular monthly issues of commercial paper, and that lends the conse-
quent funds at a rate linked to six-month LIBOR has a mismatch between its 30-
day CP rate and six-month LIBOR. It might choose to enter into an interest rate
swap where it receives the 30-day CP rate and pays six-month LIBOR to index
its revenues to its interest payments.

Pricing for basis swaps is determined by supply and demand and is expressed
in terms of basis points above or below one side of the swap. Typically, though
by no means always, the receiver of the shorter-term floating rate will be able to
command a few basis points extra than the receiver of the longer-term floating
rate. However, much will depend on prevailing sentiment. If the market is anticipating a steady rise in interest rates over the life of the swap, it might be felt that
the receiver of the shorter-term rate is likely to benefit from the fact that interest
is reset more frequently. In this situation the short-term rate receiver may have to
give up a few basis points to his counterparty.

Credit Risk Implications for Basis Swaps

Where the payment frequency is different from the frequency of interest receipts
a swapper takes on additional credit risk. In a one-month versus six-month swap,
on ten days each year the one-month receiver is due interest, on the other two
dates the six-month receiver is due, roughly speaking, six times as much interest
as he is required to pay. In other words, in such a case the credit risk is not on the
interest differential, but on the total amount of interest.

For this reason market participants will often try to agree swaps where payments and receipts are synchronised. In our example, the six-month receiver
may ask to pay his one-month LIBOR obligations at the end of each six-month
period. But, if the one-month receiver agrees to this he incurs a time value of
money cost. The counterparties will therefore increase the spread payable to the
one-month receiver to compensate him for this effect.

Cross-benchmark Basis Swaps

In other basis swaps the counterparties may be exchanging interest rates that have
the same payment frequency but which float according to a different benchmark.
The basis points added or subtracted to one side of the swap will reflect the
expected spread between the two markets. For instance, the 90-day T-bill rate is
traditionally lower than the 90-day Eurodollar rate. This reflects the enhanced
creditworthiness and liquidity of T-bills versus other money market instruments.

But in a swap, each counterparty has a credit risk on the other so the market
advantages of the T-bill over Eurodollars do not apply. For this reason the payer
of the T-bill rate will normally have to pay extra basis points to the swap counter-

party, so that expected payments and receipts are equalised at the outset. The discussion on the TED spread in the section on interest futures offers an insight as to why a market participant might want to enter into this type of basis swap.

Money Market Swaps

The money market swap is a specialist sector of the market, popular amongst arbitragers. It normally takes the form of a fixed-floating swap with quarterly interest payments and receipts timed to coincide with futures delivery dates maturing in two to three years. Since the swap has the same fixed rate throughout its life, whereas each interest rate future is priced individually and they are both linked to the same floating rate benchmark (i.e. three-month LIBOR in March, June, September, December), there is scope for arbitrage.

Trading in Swaps

Since an interest rate swap is, like the FRA, an exchange transaction, each counterparty has rights and obligations on the other. It cannot therefore be traded as could be, say, a bond. Like FRA traders, swap dealers overcome this problem by trading interest rate positions. However, with a swap the credit risk on the counterparty can remain for a considerable period. Swap dealers have pleaded with regulators for capital mitigation (i.e. the ability to net off credit risks on the grounds that these are price contingent), but mostly to no avail.

Swappers have therefore developed techniques to try to avoid the high balance sheet costs of having to allocate capital to every swap they transact. These take two main forms. Firstly, for certain categories of swap, members of the International Swap Dealers Association (ISDA) may agree to allow the assignment of their positions to other ISDA members.

Secondly, wherever possible a professional swapper will attempt to reverse out of existing swaps rather than open new positions with different counterparties. A fixed rate payer, say, will prefer to cancel the existing agreement to transform his interest rate risk rather than open a new position with another counterparty. This is usually done by means of an up-front payment or receipt that corresponds to the present value of the swap.

For instance, a swapper who had paid a fixed rate of 8 per cent on a five and a half-year swap wishes six months later to receive the fixed rate on a five-year swap. Assuming the five-year government bond is now yielding 7.25 per cent and the swap spread stands at 60 basis points, he could receive six months' worth of 7.85 per cent twice yearly for the next five years. Instead he elects to close out the existing swap by paying his counterparty today the present value equivalent 0.15 per cent per annum spread over five years.

Warehousing Swaps

Because the swap market is essentially user driven, it can sometimes take time to find a counterparty with exactly opposite requirements. For this reason, and as part of their speculative activities, swap dealers will normally maintain substantial interest rate positions internally, a practice known as warehousing. Because of the risk on these positions, it is essential for them to be able to hedge effectively.

Government bond futures are thus a popular risk management tool amongst swap dealers, but they still run a significant basis risk. There are two reasons for this. Firstly, futures are only available for specific maturities, which may not correspond to the swap periods being hedged. Secondly, though swap prices are a function of bond yields, the futures take no account of variations in the swap spread. This may vary significantly as supply and demand conditions change and is extremely difficult to hedge.

Liability Linked Swaps

We have seen how a floating rate issuer can use the swap market to fix or unfix its borrowing costs. A feature of recent years has been the growing use of swaps in the primary bond markets taking advantage of an issuer's natural strengths.

For instance, an FI has a natural requirement for floating rate finance and may have issued significant amounts in the FRN markets. But the effect of repeatedly accessing this market may have been to make it less welcome to FRN investors, forcing it to pay a higher margin over LIBOR. Amongst fixed rate bond investors, however, it may still be a highly sought after name. By issuing a fixed rate bond and simultaneously swapping its payments to a floating rate basis it may be able to achieve cheaper floating rate funding.

Synthetic Securities and the Repackaging Process

Exactly the same applies to the investor. Suppose an FRN investor likes the credit risk of, say, a Japanese corporate. Unfortunately the company has only issued paper in fixed rate form. By buying its fixed rate bonds in conjunction with a fixed to floating swap, the investor is able to retain the advantages of owning the Japanese name while earning the LIBOR linked income that he seeks.

Securities houses have taken this process one stage further. The disadvantages for our investor are that he must take on a separate credit risk for the swapped interest flows, and that it will be difficult for him to trade the bond as he will have to close out the swap at the same time.

What the securities houses do is to set up a special purpose company. When they notice a likely bond, the company buys it on the open market. The off-the-shelf company then enters into swap agreements (most likely with the securities house itself), does a certain amount of financial engineering to repackage the security and then relaunches it in a more marketable form as a tradeable security. The repackaging process has been applied to many different instruments and this is almost always the origin of the paper that regularly appears on the market issued by companies with catchy acronymic names like SPIN, EDGE, SHARP or TOPS.

CURRENCY SWAPS

Definition

A currency swap is an agreement between counterparties to exchange interest payments and receipts between two currencies on a number of occasions during a specified period. Capital amounts are also exchanged on the maturity date of the contract, and their relative size is defined by the current spot rate.

Capital is not generally exchanged on the spot date, the assumption being that it is relatively easy for each of the counterparties to deal in the spot markets at current rates. However, currency swap participants should ensure that they do carry out the appropriate spot transaction when they enter into the swap, otherwise they can expose themselves to a significant currency risk.

Like an interest rate swap, a currency swap is equivalent to two simultaneous cash transactions – each counterparty is, in effect, lending to and borrowing from the other an equivalent capital amount over the same period.

Since currency swaps are OTC transactions, their exact structure is individually negotiated between the counterparties. Typically, the notional capital amount is large. The standard swap size is at least $5m (against the equivalent in the foreign currency), swaps on $100m or more are not uncommon.

Maturity dates for currency swaps are generally within five years. Currency swaps with more than seven years to maturity are rare. The main reason for this is the fact that currency swaps involve significantly more counterparty risk than their interest swap equivalents.

Types of Currency Swap

There are three main kinds of currency swap, fixed-floating, basis and circus swaps.

In a typical fixed versus floating swap the counterparties might agree to exchange the interest differential between the semi-annual DM fixed rate and US dollar six-month LIBOR, twice a year for, say, the next five years.

In a basis swap the counterparties exchange floating rates of interest calculated off a different reference rate for a specific period. Examples might include a five-year swap of the dollar six-month LIBOR versus French franc six-month PIBOR or a four-year, one-month sterling LIBOR versus six-month dollar LIBOR swap.

Since a swap is a bilateral agreement its precise terms are agreed between the counterparties. The majority of currency swaps involving the US dollar are agreed versus six-month dollar LIBOR. There is also a thriving cross-currency swap market, driven largely by interest rate differentials.

Fixed-Floating Swaps

The most common form of currency swap is between a fixed rate, payable semi-annually, and six-month LIBOR, with one side of the swap denominated in dollars. Like interest rate swaps, prices for fixed-floating currency swaps are quoted in terms of basis points above the fixed rate currency's relevant government bond yield.

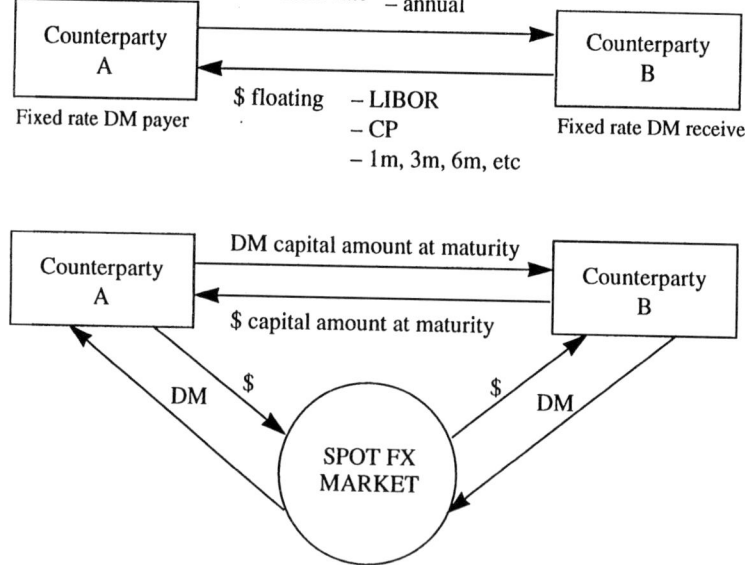

Figure 11.2 Currency swap counterparties use the spot market to remove FX risk

Their Use in Risk Transformation

Fixed-floating currency swaps can be used to transform the interest risk and currency exposure. For instance, a fixed rate dollar borrower who felt that the dollar was going to strengthen and Deutschmark interest rates were likely to fall relative to US rates might prefer his net exposure to be that of a borrower in Deutschmarks at a floating rate of interest. He could achieve this by doing a currency swap where he received dollars at a fixed rate in exchange for regular DM LIBOR payments.

Basis Swaps

Basis currency swaps account for a very small proportion of total swap activity. They may be used by market participants seeking to transform currency risk, without changing interest risk. For instance, a French domestic bank issues a US dollar FRN, because of the relatively low margin it can achieve in this market, but it wishes to finance itself in French francs because most of its loans are provided in this currency. It can use a basis currency swap to translate the margin benefits of its dollar borrowing into French franc terms. It would do so by paying six-month French franc PIBOR and receiving six-month dollar LIBOR on a currency swap with a notional amount and maturity the same as its dollar FRN and simultaneously buying French francs against a sale of dollars in the spot market.

This is the theory. In practice it would probably be difficult to find a willing counterparty. It is much more likely to achieve the same thing via two (possibly more) swaps – paying a French franc fixed rate against dollar LIBOR and receiving the fixed rate and paying six-month PIBOR in a French franc interest rate swap.

Pricing for basis swaps is determined by supply and demand and is expressed in terms of basis points above or below the non-dollar side of the swap.

Circus Swaps

A circus swap is the inverse of the currency basis swap. Here the counterparties agree to exchange fixed interest rates, each based off the government bond yield in that currency. Circuses are more popular than basis swaps; they account for something like 30 per cent of currency swap activity, depending on the market environment. Fixed rate issuers and investors use them to transform the currency risk on bonds.

They are also an appropriate risk management tool for the multi-currency fund manager with a series of known payments in one currency, matched by roughly equivalent receipts in a second currency. Depending on his cashflow profile this can be a more cost-effective way to manage elements of his interest and currency exposure than, say, a series of FX swaps, or buying and selling FRAs in the two currencies.

Circus swaps are also popular with arbitragers who use them in conjunction with long-dated FX swaps to lock in profit. The main opportunity for arbitrage comes from the fact that in a currency swap, future currency amounts are exchanged according to today's spot rate. When there is a large interest differential and this is several years in the future, this can be significantly different from the implied FX swap price for the same date.

Liability Linked Swaps and the Interdependence of Markets

Issuers can use swaps to take advantage of the fact that investor appetite for their paper varies according to how well known their name is, and how much paper they have already issued in that market.

This idea, of comparative advantage, was applied to the very first major currency swap, in the 1970s. The World Bank, because of its lending rules found it advantageous to borrow in a low interest rate currency. By the middle 1970s it had accessed the Swiss franc fixed rate market many times and its paper had begun to look less attractive to Swiss investors. IBM, on the other hand, always needed fixed rate dollars. Swiss investors were prepared to pay a premium for a AAA US corporate name, because of its scarcity value. US investors, who saw the World Bank as a blue-chip name on a par with IBM, were prepared to buy its paper at a similar yield. IBM issued Swiss francs, the World Bank issued dollars and the two did a circus swap, via a financial intermediary. The FI took a substantial fee and both IBM and the World Bank achieved substantially lower cost funding because of IBM's comparative advantage in the Swiss market.

The logic – issuers playing to their strengths, and using swaps to translate their liabilities into the required currency and interest rate basis – was undeniable. The

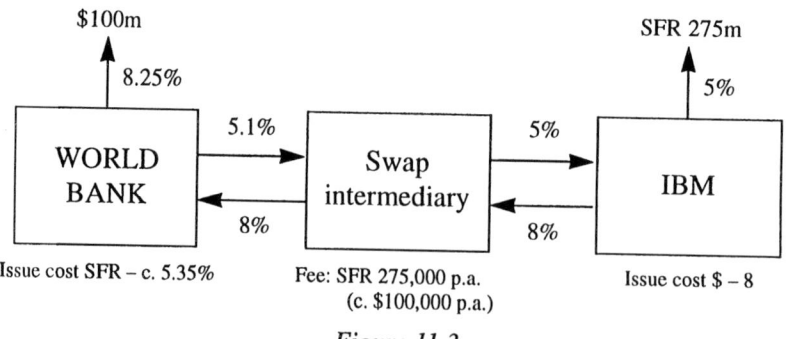

Figure 11.3

late 1980s saw a plethora of swap related issuing activity. So much so, in fact, that investor perceptions began to change. Spreads available on swaps diminished, so that nowadays, major swapping opportunities are few and far between. It is thus no exaggeration to state that swaps, both currency and interest rate, have played an important role in cementing the interdependence of international capital markets.

SWAPTIONS

Another increasingly popular product amongst interest risk managers is the swaption. As its name implies it takes the form of an option on an interest rate swap. Swaptions may be constructed like caps, floors or collars with strike rates meeting the customer's requirements.

Swaptions, unlike caps and floors, do not provide the owner with strike rates for specific interest periods in the future. The fact that a swaption can be sold before its expiry date allows an owner to lock into any fixed length period so long as it commences on or before the expiry date. The swaption is also less flexible an instrument as a cap or a floor, as it may only be exercised once. On the other hand, they are generally cheaper to buy. A typical swaption might provide its buyer with a one-year right to pay 10 per cent (and receive six-month LIBOR) on a five-year swap in $10m.

When the swaption is exercised its owner receives the present value of the difference between current swap prices and the swaption strike as a once-off cash amount. If five-year fixed-floating swaps were trading at 11 per cent on the expiry date the owner of this swaption would receive $377,000 (i.e. 1 per cent per annum discounted for five years at 11 per cent).

12: Techniques for Bond and Swap Traders

EVALUATING PRICE–YIELD SENSITIVITY

Bond Markets

Deriving a Dirty Price

The 2010 9 per cent T-bond pays coupons on 15 April and October each year. For value 15 June, a trader is quoting a two-way price of 10–12 on a big figure of 100.

The investor must buy bonds at the trader's offer price. T-bonds are quoted in 32nds of a percent. So the net price for the investor is 100 12/32, or 100.375.

The dirty price gives the actual cost of owning $100 of the security. This includes any accrued interest. There are 61 days between 15 April and 15 June. The coupon period is 183 days long. Since the coupon is 9 per cent, the amount of accrued interest payable by the investor is $3 per $100 (9% × 61/183 × $100). The bond's dirty price is therefore 103.375.

We can use a similar procedure to derive the dirty price for a Eurobond. The conventions for calculating Eurobond accrued interest are slightly different, being based on a 30 day month. A Eurobond with an annual coupon of 9 per cent, an offer price of 100.375 whose coupons are paid on 15 April, would have, for value 15 June accrued interest of 9% × 60/360 × $100. Its dirty price in this case is the same as the T-bond, also 103.375, but this will not always be so.

Bond Stripping

In the mid-1980s some of the US investment banks began to perceive a need for zero coupon US government securities. At the time these were not available in the markets, so the banks instead bought fixed rate government securities. By setting up a special purpose company, they were, with the aid of some simple financial engineering, able to reissue them as a set of zero coupon bonds. The zero coupons bonds were issued by the shelf company and became separately tradeable, but were still collateralised by US T-bonds.

In Table 12.1 the investment bank has bought $100m worth of an 8 per cent, 5-year T-bond at a price of par. It is able to issue zero coupon bonds guaranteed

Table 12.1 The process of stripping out coupons on a US T-bond

Cashflows shown in $m, from investment bank's perspective						
	8%, 5y T-Bond	1y Zero	2y Zero	3y Zero	4y Zero	5y Zero
Yield:	8.00%	7.50%	7.70%	7.90%	8.00%	8.00%
Price:	93.02	86.21	79.6	73.5	68.06	
Period (years)						
0	−100	7.44	6.9	6.37	5.88	73.5
1	8	−8				
2	8		−8			
3	8			−8		
4	8				−8	
5	108					−108
Net Profit: 0.09						

by the T-bond's cashflows at the prices shown. It issues $8m of 1y, 2y, 3y and 4y zeros together with $108m in 5y zeros. Because the zero coupon yields are not the same as the original T-bond's YTM of 8 per cent, profit potential exists. In this case the bank has earned a locked-in profit of $90,000 on the transaction.

The popularity of government backed synthetic zero coupons, or STRIPS as they came to be known (separately traded registered interest and principal securities) led to the techniques being replicated in several territories. After Salomon Brothers' CATS (certificates of accrual on treasury securities) came a whole menagerie of acronyms: among them TIGRs, CouGRs, LYONs (for UK Gilts), and in the Australian dollar market, DINGOs.

Evaluating FRNs
Since their actual returns are unknown, FRN yields are looked at in terms of their relationship to LIBOR, their effective margin. This is based on the idea that an investor who can borrow at six-month LIBOR earns the effective margin until the FRN reaches maturity. An FRN priced at par is relatively straightforward to estimate in these terms. Since there is no capital gain component, its effective margin will be equivalent to the stated margin.

For FRNs trading at a price other than par the process is much more complicated. Consider, for instance, a US dollar FRN paying LIBOR + 25 basis points, trading at 99. For every $990 invested, the FRN holder receives 6m LIBOR + 25 bps on $1000. Suppose the next coupon period is 182 days in length and 6m LIBOR is fixed at 9.75 per cent. At the end of the period he will receive $50.56

($1000 × 182/360 × 10%). If the position was match-funded at the same 6m LIBOR his financing cost over the same period would be $48.80 ($990 × 182 / 360 × 9.75%). The annualised difference between these two interest amounts expressed as a proportion of his original investment gives the margin earned for the period. With 6m LIBOR at 9.75 per cent it is 35.1 bps:

$$\text{Margin} = \frac{((1.00 \times 182/360 \times 10\%) - (0.99 \times 182/360 \times 9.75\%)) \times 360/182}{0.99}$$

Margin = 0.3510%

Now see what happens to his margin when the six-month LIBOR fixes at 14.75 per cent:

$$\text{Margin} = \frac{((1 \times 182/360 \times 15\%) - (0.99 \times 182/360 \times 14.75\%)) \times 360/182}{0.99}$$

Margin=   0.4015%

The investor's margin rises to over 40 basis points in the higher LIBOR environment. The reason for this is, of course, that the FRN is priced below par. The investor only has to pay LIBOR on $990 to earn LIBOR + 10 on $1000. The higher the LIBOR, the greater the benefit. For FRNs trading above par the reverse effect applies, the higher the LIBOR level the lower the margin.

Incorporating Capital Gain

The above has shown that FRNs priced away from par have margins that are sensitive to LIBOR levels. So far we have focused on the relationship between interest payments and receipts and have ignored capital gain. But this has also to be built into any margin measure if we are to get an accurate indication of the value of an FRN. An FRN priced at 99 will realise a capital gain of 1 when it is redeemed at par, but this capital gain will not all occur at once. In practice the price will gradually approach 100 as the FRN maturity gets closer. Capital gain/loss needs therefore to be amortised if it is to be incorporated into valuation.

Effective Margin

There are therefore three components in the effective margin: the annual capital gain, the quoted margin and the difference between the FRN's face value and its price multiplied by the LIBOR. These can be expressed mathematically as follows:

Where:

FV = Face value of the FRN (usually 100)
$P0$ = Original gross price of the FRN (the amount to be financed)
M = Quoted margin over LIBOR payable on FRN
N = Number of periods

T	$=$	Length of each period
X	$=$	The capital gain factor per period
Y	$=$	The amount payable in margin each period
Z	$=$	The LIBOR related difference in interest amounts
FV	$=$	$PO \times X^N$

so:

$$X = (FV/PO)^{(1/N)}$$
$$Y = M \times FV \times Ti$$
and
$$Z = \text{LIBORi} \times (FV - PO) \times Ti$$

The effective margin can be estimated by expressing these amounts in terms of the cost of establishing the position. So:

$$EM = \left(\frac{(X + (Y + Z))}{PO} - 1 \right) \times \frac{360}{T}$$

Suppose the FRN priced at 99 paying LIBOR plus 25 bps has five years to maturity (i.e. ten semi-annual periods). Then:

$$
\begin{aligned}
X &= (100/99)^{(1/10)} \\
&= 1.001006
\end{aligned}
$$

$$
\begin{aligned}
Y &= 100 \times 0.25\% \times 0.5 \\
&= 0.125
\end{aligned}
$$

If LIBOR is 9.75%:
$$
\begin{aligned}
Z &= 9.75\% \times (100 - 99) \times 0.5 \\
&= 0.04875
\end{aligned}
$$

$$
\begin{aligned}
EM &= ((1.001006 + (0.125 + 0.04875)/99) - 1) \times 2 \\
&= 55.2 \text{ basis points per annum}
\end{aligned}
$$

If LIBOR is 14.75%:
$$
\begin{aligned}
Z &= 14.75\% \times (100 - 99) \times 0.5 \\
&= 0.07375
\end{aligned}
$$

$$
\begin{aligned}
EM &= ((1.001006 + (0.125 + 0.07375)/99) - 1) \times 2 \\
&= 60.3 \text{ basis points per annum}
\end{aligned}
$$

Because of the LIBOR difference it is impossible to arrive at an exact value of effective margin for an FRN. Many market participants model FRN performance in a variety of LIBOR environments to arrive at a best guess estimate of the effective margin.

Embedded Options

We saw in the discussion on bonds that embedded options are commonplace in the capital markets. An embedded option is simply an optional feature in a security that cannot be traded separately from the security. So, any fixed rate bond with an issuer call option or an investor put option – or, debt or currency convertibles (e.g. where a $FRN paying LIBOR is issued with a conversion feature into a fixed amount of a £ FRN) – all of these contain embedded options.

Although an embedded option cannot be traded separately, its risk–reward characteristics can. Take for instance a 10 per cent ten-year straight with an issuer call at par after four years. This provides the issuer with the right to buy back (i.e. call) the bond in four years. He will do this if six-year yields then are below 10 per cent. If, say, six-year yields in four years are 9 per cent, the bonds will be trading at a price of 104.49. By calling the issuer knows he can refinance at 1 per cent less while the investors automatically lose $4.49 per $100 invested.

Valuing Embedded Options

Now suppose the investor bought a European style swaption, expiring in four years, on a six-year interest rate swap where he would receive 10 per cent against LIBOR payments. Now, when six-year yields fall to 9 per cent in four years the intrinsic value on the swaption is 4.49 per cent (present value of +1 per cent annually for six years at 9 per cent).

We can see that the profit from the swaption exactly offsets the loss if the call feature is exercised. By buying this 10 per cent bond together with the swaption the investor has effectively purchased a non-callable bond. Because there is no free lunch in financial markets this also means that the value of the embedded option should be equivalent to the swaption price. A company wishing to raise funds via a callable fixed rate bond should therefore pay an extra yield equivalent to the annual cost of the swaption.

Net Rates for Caps and Floors

In the last chapter we looked at the situation where a cap buyer paid an up-front fee of 1.25 per cent for maximum protection at 9.5 per cent against six-month LIBORs over the next five years. To calculate its net rate equivalent we need to amortise (i.e. spread out) this payment over the five-year period. The most straightforward way to do this is to apply the five-year rate to the premium amount to arrive at its equivalent amounts (i.e. annuity) on each of the future interest payment dates. Using a five-year rate of 9 per cent, $125,000 today is equivalent to regular payments of $15,797 at the end of each six-month period. This equates to 31.6 basis points per annum on $10m, in other words the net rate for the 9.5 per cent cap is 9.816 per cent. A 9.5 per cent floor with the same up-front cost would guarantee a minimum rate to the buyer of 9.194 per cent (9.5 per cent – 31.6bps).

If we want to identify the worst case rate with more precision it is necessary to use yield curve mapping techniques. Using an iterative process an amortised basis point cost can be derived that equates the total of the present values of each future date to the premium paid.

Swap Markets

Arbitraging the FRA / Swap Relationship

As long as its final maturity is not too far in the future, an interest rate swap can be created synthetically with a series of FRAs. By buying FRAs for each interest period in the swap, the trader can structure a deal where he is a regular payer of à fixed rate against LIBOR. However, each FRA is priced individually according to the yields pertaining at the start and end dates of the FRA period. By contrast, a swap is agreed using the same fixed rate throughout the life of the transaction. It is therefore possible to structure an interest risk insensitive arbitrage by simultaneously either receiving fixed interest and buying equivalent FRAs or performing the opposite transaction.

In the illustration the arbitrager does a $10m two-year swap where he is a receiver of the fixed rate of 9.2 per cent and pays six-month LIBOR. Simultaneously, he buys $10m worth of three FRAs: a 6m/12m at 9.5 per cent, a 12m/18m at 9.25 per cent and an 18m/24m at 8.75 per cent.

Since the FRAs are settled against the same set of 6m LIBORs, he is both a payer and receiver of the floating rate and this can be ignored for the purposes of the analysis. The fixed rate payments and receipts are shown in Table 12.2.

Notice that the arbitrager already knows that he will receive the differential between the 9.2 per cent fixed rate and today's six-month LIBOR of 9 per cent at the end of the first semi-annual period. By discounting the net proceeds or costs using the appropriate zero coupon factors he is able to achieve a locked-in profit of $12,506 per $10m. In practice this level of profit may be judged insufficient when compared with the credit risks being taken on, and the capital resources that must be allocated, for the various elements of the transaction. However, it does illustrate the mechanics, and the potential for arbitraging fixed-floating

Table 12.2

Time (in years)	Yield curve (s-a cmpd)	Swap In @9,20%	Buy FRAs	Net CF per $000	Net PV per $000
0.5	9.00%	0.200%		10,000	9,569
1	9.25%	9.200%	−9.50%	(15,000)	(13,783)
1.5	9.25%	9.200%	−9.25%	(2,500)	(2,183)
2	9.13%	9.200%	−8.75%	22,500	18,823
				arbitrage profit:	12,506

205

swaps with FRAs. Of course, since FRAs are also arbitrageable with interest rate futures there is in fact a three-way arbitrage relationship here.

Using Interest Rate Swaps in Risk Transformation

Just as FRAs can be used by potential borrowers to fix their interest cost for a single period so fixed-floating interest rate swaps can be employed in conjunction with longer-term borrowings to lock into a fixed rate for a series of interest payment dates. FRN investors can use swaps to fix future income streams, owners of straight bonds can transform their interest risk from a fixed rate to a floating rate basis.

In the illustration below an FRN issuer uses a fixed-floating swap to lock into a fixed rate environment.

It is January 1994 and the issuer of a $100m Floating Rate Note, which matures in June 1999 and pays a coupon of 6m LIBOR plus 15 bps, expects interest rates to rise. The next FRN coupon, payable in June, was fixed in December at 7.4 per cent.

January 1994

5yr 5mth Fixed-Floating Swap (basis points)	65–75
June 1999 US T-Note Offer Yield	7.75%
5-month LIBOR	7.25%

The issuer agrees to pay a semi-annual fixed rate on $100m at 8.50 per cent (7.75% + 75 bps).

Each of the issuer's $100m future LIBOR related coupon payments, commencing next December, is now offset by an equivalent LIBOR receipt. He therefore has a net cash outflow of 15 basis points per annum as well as the semi-annual, 8.5 per cent swap rate. The cashflow profile for his net interest payments is shown in $000s in Table 12.3.

Table 12.3

Date	Net FRN coupon	Swap payment	Net cashflow
Jun94	−3,700	−508	−4,208
Dec94	−75	−4,250	−4,325
Jun95	−75	−4,250	−4,325
Dec95	−75	−4,250	−4,325
Jun96	−75	−4,250	−4,325
Dec96	−75	−4,250	−4,325
Jun97	−75	−4,250	−4,325
Dec97	−75	−4,250	−4,325
Jun98	−75	−4,250	−4,325
Dec98	−75	−4,250	−4,325
Jun99	−75	−4,250	−4,325

Note that the net coupon cost in June 1994 has now risen, equating to an effective borrowing cost of 8.42 per cent (4.208m/100m × 2). The FRN coupon payable in June 1994 has already been fixed at 7.4 per cent. By entering into the swap the issuer receives the five-month LIBOR interest amount of $3.021m ($100m × 150 / 360 × 7.25%). On the other hand he must pay the five monthly equivalent of the 8.5 per cent fixed rate.

Structuring Fixed-Floating Swaps with Broken Periods

Interest swaps with broken dates are normally structured so that the first period is of irregular length. To take account of the length of the period the fixed rate is altered to fit its different compounding frequency. The 8.5 per cent fixed rate payer therefore pays five months worth of interest on 8.47 per cent (i.e. the five monthly compounded equivalent of a semi-annual rate of 8.5 per cent), which, on $100m is $3.529m.

It is now June 1994 and the FRN issuer's view of market conditions has changed. He now believes that interest rates are likely to fall over the next five years and wishes to link his coupon payments to six-month LIBOR again. The FRN coupon payable in December has just been fixed at 8.65 per cent, five-year swaps are being traded at 50–60 over Treasuries and the June 1999 T-note is currently yielding 8.25 per cent. To unfix his net interest obligations the issuer should now enter into another swap, this time receiving the fixed rate for five years. He can do this at 8.75 per cent (8.25% + 50 bps). This compares with the original swap in January where he was a payer at 8.5 per cent. The LIBOR payments and receipts on the two swaps net off and he is left with a net receipt of 0.25 per cent per annum.

Against this should be counted the FRN itself on which he pays LIBOR+15 bps. He is therefore left with $100m costing LIBOR minus ten basis points. Since the FRN coupon has just been fixed at 8.65 per cent, six-month LIBOR is 8.5 per cent and he will pay a total of $4.2m in December 1994 (six months' interest at LIBOR minus ten).

He could have achieved a similar effect by reversing out of the existing swap with his current counterparty. In this case he would have received the present value equivalent of five years' worth of the 0.25 per cent price difference, instead of earning the differential on each coupon date. The advantage of this approach is that he is left with no credit risk, whereas had he done a second swap he would have been left with two sets of credit risk.

Using Currency Swaps in Risk Transformation

An important source of activity in the Euro CP and FX swap markets is their use in conjunction as a means of generating sub-LIBOR non-dollar funding. CP issuers often find that their highly rated dollar denominated paper can be sold at relatively low yield. They can translate this benefit into another currency by selling it forward against dollars in an FX swap transaction. The dollar side of the swap nets off with the cashflows from the CP issue and they are left with a borrower's exposure in the other currency.

Just as FX swaps can be used to translate a money market exposure, so, in the capital markets, currency swaps may be employed to transform currency risk for instruments with multiple coupon periods. In the illustration below the mechanism is described for transforming a fixed rate dollar liability via a fixed-floating currency swap.

In January 1994 the issuer of $100m bond paying 7.5 per cent semi-annually until June 1999 expects the dollar to strengthen against the mark, and DM interest rates to fall.

January 1994

5 yr 5 mth Fixed-Floating $/DM Swap (basis points)	45–50
June 1999 US T-Note Offer Yield	7.75%
5-month DM LIBOR	8.25%
$/DM spot rate	1.4750

In a currency swap the issuer agrees to receive a semi-annual fixed rate on $100m at 8.20 per cent (7.75% + 45 bps) against 6m DM LIBOR on DM147.5m, and to pay DM147.5m and receive $100m in June 1999.

Since the currency swap only requires an exchange of capital amounts at maturity, the issuer does spot transactions in the market in order to receive $100m and pays DM147.5m.

The issuer's 7.5 per cent semi-annual coupons are now offset by a receipt of six months' worth of 8.15 per cent twice annually. The $100m funds he has

Table 12.4

Date	Bond issue	Swap receipts	Swap payments	Spot out	Spot in	Net $ position
Jan94	+$100			–$100	+DM147.5	$0
Jun94	–$3.75	+$3.405	–DM5.070			–$0.345
Dec94	–$3.75	+$4.1	–6m DM LIBOR			+$0.35
Jun95	–$3.75	+$4.1	–6m DM LIBOR			+$0.35
Dec95	–$3.75	+$4.1	–6m DM LIBOR			+$0.35
Jun96	–$3.75	+$4.1	–6m DM LIBOR			+$0.35
Dec96	–$3.75	+$4.1	–6m DM LIBOR			+$0.35
Jun97	–$3.75	+$4.1	–6m DM LIBOR			+$0.35
Dec97	–$3.75	+$4.1	–6m DM LIBOR			+$0.35
Jun98	–$3.75	+$4.1	–6m DM LIBOR			+$0.35
Dec98	–$3.75	+$4.1	–6m DM LIBOR			+$0.35
Jun99	–$3.75	+$4.1	–6m DM LIBOR			+$0.35
Jun99	–$100	+$100	–DM147.5			+$0

borrowed via the bond issue net off with his spot transaction leaving him with a net long position now of DM147.5m. Similarly the $100m he must pay investors in June 1999 is offset by the receipt of $100m at the end of the currency swap, and he becomes a net DM payer of DM147.5m in June 1999.

His cashflow profile is shown in millions in Table 12.4.

Note that the swapper receives less than six months' worth of 8.2 per cent in June 1994. This reflects the fact that the broken period at the beginning of the swap is only five months long. The amount received is therefore calculated according to the five monthly compounded equivalent of 8.2 per cent (as we saw above in the interest rate swap example the compounding effect is incorporated into a swap's initial, broken periods). On the DM LIBOR side the current five-month rate determines the amount of interest he must pay in June, DM5.070m (DM147.5m × 150/360 × 8.25%).

Ignoring the special case of the first interest date, we can see that the net effect of the issuer's actions is to achieve sub-LIBOR funding in Deutschmarks. The semi-annual profit of $0.35m is equivalent to 35 basis points in dollar terms.

Premium Points and Discount Points in Currency Swaps
However, when translated into Deutschmarks the actual cost is in fact significantly better than LIBOR minus 35 basis points. Since US dollar interest rates are lower than Deutschmark interest rates, the dollar is trading at a premium to the Deutschmark in the future. To establish the extent of this benefit we would need to calculate forward outright prices for each coupon date, but to give some idea of the magnitude of this effect consider the following illustration.

Suppose semi-annually compounded dollar interest rates are 8 per cent, while semi-annual Deutschmark rates are 9 per cent. Both currencies have flat yield curves. What is the DM basis point equivalent of 50 US dollar basis points at the end of each six-month period for the next two years?

We do not need to know the FX rate to find out how dollars appreciate against DM through time. Using semi-annual compounding for one, two, three and four periods we can find the forward value of 1 dollar basis point on each of the future dates in DM terms. Multiply this by 50 and we get the future value of 50 US dollar basis points on each of the dates. The compounding formula is as follows:

$$\text{DMBPS} \quad = \quad \text{USBPS} \quad \frac{(1 + \text{RDM} \times 0.5)^N}{(1 + \text{RUS} \times 0.5)^N}$$

Where N = Number of semi-annual compounding periods.

So, for each six month period 50 US basis points are worth:

After six months:	50.24 DM basis points
After one year:	50.48 DM basis points
After eighteen months:	50.72 DM basis points
After two years:	50.97 DM basis points

The differences may not appear significant but the further in the future the cashflows occur and the larger the interest rate differential the larger the adjustment becomes in cash terms. In the $100m swap described above each DM basis point is worth DM7,375, so it can be seen that the adjustment is not insignificant.

Circus Swaps and Arbitrage
Just as it is possible to arbitrage the relationship between interest rate swaps and FRAs, so currency swaps may be arbitraged with FX forward outrights and currency futures. For the arbitrage to be effective the currency swap position must be composed of fixed payments and receipts for each of the currencies. This may be achieved by means of a combination of currency and interest rate swap, but the circus swap is the single transaction that meets these requirements. The main opportunity for arbitrage comes from the fact that in a currency swap, currency amounts are exchanged at maturity at today's spot rate. When there is a large interest differential and this is several years in the future, this can be significantly different from the implied FX swap price for the same date.

By way of example consider a £/$ FX rate of 1.9500. Semi-annual dollar interest rates are 7.5 per cent, sterling rates are 12 per cent. Here the implied forward outright for five years' time will be 1.5735. On a £10m swap that represents a difference of $3.765m in five years on the currency swap exchange rate.

Table 12.5 Arbitraging a £10 million £/$ circus swap

Flat Sterling yield curve; Positive dollar yield curve; Cashflows shown in 000s					
Time (years)	*£/$ Rates*	*Circus Swap Receive £ @ 12%*	*Circus Swap Pay $ @ 7.5%*	*FX Swaps Sell £ Fwd*	*FX Swaps Buy $ Fwd*	*Net $ P&L*
0	1.9500	–£10,000.00	19,500	£10,000.00	–19,500	0
0.5	1.9031	£600.00	–731	–£600.00	1,142	411
1	1.8591	£600.00	–731	–£600.00	1,115	384
1.5	1.8179	£600.00	–731	–£600.00	1,091	360
2	1.7793	£600.00	–731	–£600.00	1,068	337
2.5	1.7432	£600.00	–731	–£600.00	1,046	315
3	1.7095	£600.00	–731	–£600.00	1,026	295
3.5	1.6781	£600.00	–731	–£600.00	1,007	276
4	1.6488	£600.00	–731	–£600.00	989	258
4.5	1.6216	£600.00	–731	–£600.00	973	242
5	1.5964	£10,600.00	–20,231	–£10,600.00	16,922	(3,309)

Present Value of $ cashflows using zero coupon rates: 154

Even allowing for the illiquidity of five-year swaps there will be a huge cash-flow difference between the two. Although much of this differential will be clawed back because of the need to do separate FX swaps on each interest payment date, there can still be substantial opportunities for locked-in profit in certain yield curve environments.

The reason that the arbitrage works is the shape of the dollar yield curve. Although the five-year bond rate yields 7.5 per cent, its duration is significantly less than five years. In this example the 3.5 year zero coupon rate (which has a similar duration) is assumed to be paying a yield of 7.5 per cent. But, because of the shape of the yield curve the five-year rate is higher (7.8 per cent in this case) and shorter term rates are lower. The net dollar cashflows can be locked in by buying a cheap, five-year zero with a semi-annual yield of 7.8 per cent, and selling a series of more expensive zeros with maturities and face value amounts corresponding to the interest dates. Here, the arbitrager has been able to lock in an overall profit of $154,000.

Of course, the same arbitrage can be achieved by doing several swaps at once. A fixed-floating dollar interest swap combined with a sterling fixed against 6m dollar LIBOR currency swap will, for example, give the arbitrager similar net exposures. In practice, illiquidity, particularly for long-dated FX swaps, will eat away at the opportunity, so profits for these kinds of arbitrage are likely to be less than those shown in Table 12.5.

Accounting for Interest Rate and Currency Swaps

A swap is a notional instrument that is, in effect, a simultaneous lending and borrowing agreement for a series of interest periods. With interest rate swaps there is no physical exchange of principal, for currency swaps principal amounts are only exchanged at maturity. However, when monitoring the price sensitivity of swap positions we need to analyse them as if principal amounts were actually paid and received.

Financial institutions as market makers in money are, in theory, always able to borrow and lend at LIBOR. Their interest rate exposure, therefore, is on the fixed rate portion of a swap transaction. For risk analysis purposes, therefore, they would book a $10m fixed-floating five-year interest rate swap where they were semi-annual fixed rate receivers at 10 per cent, as an asset. It would be shown as a $10m outflow today, with receipts every six months of $0.5m and of $10.5m in five years. Supposing that the first six-month LIBOR payment has been fixed at, say, 9 per cent, this would be booked as a six-month $10m liability. Currency swaps conform to the same principles and are included in the appropriate asset and liability streams. In this way the interest risk sensitivities of swaps can be incorporated into the duration based analysis that is a vital part of the portfolio manager's armoury and hedged along with other cashflows with bond futures and other relevant instruments.

MANAGING PRICE–YIELD SENSITIVITY

Macaulay's Duration

When dealing with assets and liabilities involving multiple cashflows, some measure of price–yield sensitivity is required. Traditionally average life has been used as a market measure. This simply weights each future cashflow by the number of years to its occurrence, sums the weightings, and divides through by the sum of the cashflows. The practice is still used by some money market participants, but for bond portfolio managers it is insufficiently accurate, because it neglects the time value of money impact on future cashflows. It is demonstrably incorrect, for instance, to suggest that the present value of a $1m cashflow occurring in 10 years changes ten times as much as the PV of $1m in 1 year. The duration of an asset takes account of this effect to give a more accurate picture of price–yield sensitivity. It is a weighted average, not of the cashflows themselves, but of their present values. The approach is illustrated in Table 12.6.

Table 12.6 Duration of a three-year semi-annual
8 per cent security priced at 100

Period (yrs)	Cashflow	Discount Factor	PV	Weighting
0.5	4	0.96	3.85	1.92
1	4	0.92	3.7	3.7
1.5	4	0.89	3.56	5.33
2	4	0.85	3.42	6.84
2.5	4	0.82	3.29	8.22
3	104	0.79	82.19	246.58
Totals:			100.01	272.59

The factors used are those that equate to a semi-annual interest rate of 8 per cent. Notice that they add up to 100. This is not surprising as the price of a fixed coupon security is simply the sum of the present values of all its future cashflows. By dividing the weighted average of the present values by the price we get the duration of the asset.

For this asset, then, the duration is 2.726 years. This tells the dealer that its interest rate sensitivity will be the same as would be the case for a zero coupon instrument maturing in 2.726 years.

Predicting Price Movements with Modified Duration

Duration is a very useful tool for risk managers. It allows them to take any stream of cashflows and express its risk in the form of a single future cashflow. Using this information they can ascertain which zero coupon maturity they should use to immunise an entire income or payment stream against yield curve shifts. However, the duration figure does not give them an exact indication as to how the price will change for a given change in yields.

Duration describes the effect of a small yield curve shift at the end of one compounding period. But the price impact occurs today. In order to find the interest sensitivity of the price of the asset, the figure has to be discounted for one compounding period at the duration rate.

The three-year asset described above has a duration of 2.726 years when a semi-annual yield of 8 per cent is applied. The relevant zero coupon factor is 1.04 (i.e. the future value of $1 at the end of one semi-annual period at 8 per cent).

The modified duration is therefore 2.621 (2.726/1.04): this gives the risk manager a precise indication as to how the price will perform when yields change. For the 8 per cent asset he now knows that the price will deteriorate by 2.621 basis points for every basis point increase in yields, and can plan his portfolio accordingly.

Convexity
It might appear that with modified duration, the risk manager now has all the information he requires to predict the behaviour of his portfolio. Unfortunately, the problem turns out to be more complicated.

The duration of an asset is itself a function of interest rates. Because it relies on current yields to assess the present values on which the calculation is

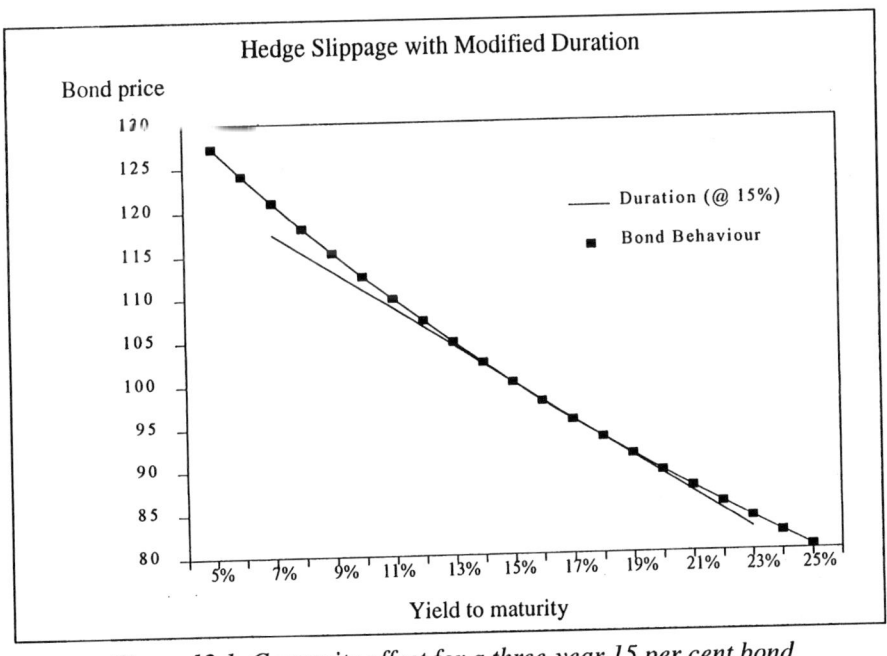

Figure 12.1 Convexity effect for a three-year 15 per cent bond

founded, the duration itself will alter as interest rates change. As interest rates rise the significance of later cashflows declines because of their lower present value equivalents. The reverse occurs when interest rates fall, longer dated cashflows become more material in the duration calculation.

So, the same asset will have different durations (and therefore a changed price sensitivity) depending on the yield curve environment. When yields are higher it will tend to have a shorter duration; in a low yield environment its duration will be longer, and the instrument will be more price sensitive.

Modified duration is therefore an accurate predictor of price sensitivity only for relatively small changes in yields. This effect, known as convexity, is greater the wider the dispersion of the underlying cashflows.

Risk managers therefore often refine their hedging programmes to take account of the convexity effect. By measuring the convexity they can adjust the duration based hedge so that it will immunise them against yield curve changes of a specific magnitude.

Yield Curve Mapping

The illustrations shown above assume a flat yield curve environment, and this reflects the market practice for calculating duration numbers. But in fact this does not reflect the true cost or benefit of an income or payment stream. A more correct approach uses the zero coupon factors that relate to the specific date for each individual cashflow when deriving present values. Particularly when an entire portfolio's interest sensitivity is being evaluated mapping the entire yield curve onto the cashflows will produce superior results.

Managing Stochastic Risks

By applying duration and convexity methodologies risk managers are able to immunise themselves against parallel shifts in the yield curve. However, this is not the end of the story. In practice different parts of the yield curve may move in different ways.

A central bank may signal an interest rate increase. The effect of this will be to increase rates at the short end of the yield curve. Medium term rates, however, may not rise correspondingly as future increases are no longer being discounted. The long end of the yield curve may actually fall, with investors now perhaps feeling that the government has inflation under control.

This illustrates an effect that is extremely commonplace. The fact is that the shape of the yield curve is liable to alter when the absolute levels of interest rates change. For all their technical merits duration and convexity will not protect against this stochastic process. Risk managers should therefore beware of relying too heavily on mathematical techniques; they should supplement them with judgement and monitor the effect on the portfolio of a variety of yield curve shapes using what-if analysis.

Duration-based Portfolio Analysis

Despite its limitations duration is an indispensable tool for asset-liability management. By analysing the duration of his assets a risk manager can determine his sensitivity to an interest rate increase. Similar analysis of the liability stream provides an indication as to the sensitivity of the portfolio to a fall in the yield curve.

Only known future cashflows are considered. The portfolio manager looks at the net cashflows and the dates on which they occur – matched-funded positions have no interest risk and can therefore be ignored.

Comparing these two figures gives the risk manager an indication as to whether on balance the net portfolio is at risk to a rise or a fall in interest rates and can allow him to develop a suitable strategy depending on his market view.

Duration and Portfolio Immunisation

Modified duration is used to construct hedge ratios, because it is a measure of the percentage price change for a given yield adjustment. Ordinary duration indicates the maturity date for a zero coupon bond that mirrors the sensitivity of the portfolio as a whole. Since the zero is a portfolio's mean cashflow it is also the date on which the investor would be insensitive to interest rate movements. We can see that this is so if we consider a par priced, five-year, 10 per cent bond. This has a duration of 4.17 years.

As yields rise there are two effects: the discounted equivalents of cashflows fall. On the other hand reinvestment income from coupons actually increases. Table 12.7 shows that the duration date is the one day in the future when these two effects exactly cancel each other out.

We can see from this example that a rise in yields from 10 per cent to 10.1 per cent has had no effect on the value of the future cashflows. In both environments the value of the bond on the duration date remains at 148.80. By definition the duration date is the only day on which the future value of the price remains the same.

Table 12.7 Value on the duration date for a five-year 10 per cent bond

Year	Cashflows YTM=10%	Equivalent value on duration date	Cashflows YTM=10%	Equivalent value on duration date
0	−100	−148.80	−99.62	−148.80
1	10	13.53	10	13.57
2	10	12.30	10	12.32
3	10	11.18	10	11.19
4	10	10.16	10	10.16
5	110	101.63	10	101.56
	Net cashflow:	0.00	Net cashflow:	0.00

Portfolio managers use this technique to attempt to lock into a specific return over a period. By adjusting the duration of the portfolio so that it is always the same as the target investment date, the fund manager can render her portfolio insensitive to parallel changes in yield curves. This procedure, of modifying the hedging programme so that the duration date remains the same, is known as immunisation.

Lengthening and Shortening Durations

A portfolio which has the same duration for both assets and liabilities will be immunised against parallel yield curve shifts. One way to reduce interest rate risk therefore is to buy and sell assets and change funding periods until the duration on assets corresponds to that for the liabilities.

So long as the portfolio manager analyses the duration of her long and short positions separately, the duration figure is additive and it is therefore fairly straightforward to monitor the effects of lengthening and shortening durations on price sensitivity. For instance, the portfolio manager buys $0.5m worth of a six-year par priced 10 per cent bond; this has a duration of 4.79 years. The duration of the asset portfolio has now lengthened 4.38 years, i.e. (4.17 × $1m + 4.79 × $0.5m)/$1.5m and this measures the increased interest sensitivity. Of course there may well be implications on the liability side, depending on how the purchase has been financed, and the portfolio's overall interest sensitivity will also be affected by changes in the durations.

Finding the Cheapest to Deliver (CTD) Bond

The price sensitivity of different bonds will vary according to their durations and convexity, as well as stochastic yield curve shifts. In futures markets this means that at any given moment, one bond, when adjusted to its futures equivalent, will be cheaper to deliver than the others. It is important to know which instrument this is, because the futures contract will track its price behaviour.

The cash-and-carry arbitrage determines the extent to which the CTD bond and the futures contract can vary. If it is possible to buy the CTD bond today and finance the position until delivery at the risk-free rate, while selling the future, to realise a locked-in profit when the contract makes delivery, then arbitrage will occur. The T-bond future is therefore related, to the futures adjusted price of the CTD bond to deliver, by the riskless rate for the period to delivery.

To discover which is currently the CTD bond we need to know three things: the price of the bond, its conversion factor, and the cost of financing it to delivery. To illustrate this, consider the three US T-bonds discussed earlier. There are three months remaining until the 8 per cent T-bond contract is delivered. The three-month US T-bill yield is currently 6.35 per cent: see Table 12.8.

The futures seller could choose to make delivery with any of the three bonds. By looking at the net price and coupon terms for each bond he can calculate the gross cost of acquiring the position. The bond position must be financed until the

Table 12.8 Calculating the cheapest to deliver bond

T-Bond	24.25 years	18.50 years	16.25 years
Coupon	6.50%	12.00%	9.00%
Net price	86-13	141-13	111-14
S-A YTM	7.43%	7.50%	7.31%
Gross cost	88.03125	141.41	113.69
Repay financing @ 6.35%	89.42815	143.65012	115.49153
Coupon income in 3m	3.25	3	4.5
Net price in 3m	86.17815	140.65012	110.99153
Conversion factor	0.84104	1.38024	1.08937
Theoretical futures price	102.47	101.90	101.89

delivery date at the three month. He therefore adds accrued interest to arrive at a gross price for the delivery date. After subtracting any coupon income due to him, he divides this effective net price by the conversion factor to establish a theoretical futures price. By looking at the theoretical futures price traders can determine which T-bond is cheapest to deliver. In this case it is currently the 16.25, 9 per cent T-bond priced at 111-14.

The Cash-Futures Equivalency Ratio (ER)
The ER indicates the number of futures required to affect an equal and opposite change in financial value to the portfolio being hedged. We have already seen how duration techniques can be used to measure a portfolio's sensitivity to yield curve shifts.

These same techniques should be applied to arrive at duration numbers for the current CTD bond. The duration of the portfolio can be found either by looking at each cashflow separately or by finding the average duration of its constituent assets, weighted by their contribution.

The CTD bond is used because its price behaviour is closest to that of the future. We know that the price relationship between the two is defined by the conversion factor. Since the (modified) duration number for a bond is the measure of its price sensitivity in percentage terms it can be used as a predictor of the future's price behaviour.

Armed with these durations, the portfolio manager can establish his ER, or hedge ratio, by dividing the portfolio duration by that of the CTD bond. Say his $10m portfolio has a duration of 6, while the current CTD future has a duration of 12. He should be selling 50 $100,000 futures contracts ($10m × 6/12) to preserve the value of his portfolio in a rising yield curve environment. Remember, of course, that duration is only accurate for small changes in yields. Analysis should also be done to determine the degree of convexity and hedge slippage.

Basis Risk of a Duration Adjusted Hedge
The hedger still has a basis risk because the cashflow structure of his portfolio is different to the CTD bond being used as its hedge. Changes in the shape of the yield curve may affect prices of the two components unevenly. Where possible portfolio risk managers will seek to buy bond futures whose notional maturities reflect their risk periods. So a fixed income fund manager with dollar assets mainly focused around five and twenty year maturities will normally prefer to hedge each part of the fund separately using five-year and 20-year bond futures, rather than use a single duration number to hedge the entire portfolio with one type of contract. Rather, the approach is to calculate separate duration numbers and present values for each maturity 'bucket', a similar idea to the gap analysis applied by money market managers.

There is also a risk that in changed conditions, the CTD bond changes and that the new bond has a significantly different duration from the previous one. Futures price movements will now relate to the new CTD. If it has a longer duration than its predecessor futures prices may become more volatile, if shorter the price volatility for a given yield change will decline. Because the changed duration alters the ER, it will probably be necessary to rebalance the hedge when this occurs.

RISK MANAGEMENT STRATEGIES

Table 12.9 shows premiums payable on puts and calls on the 8 per cent 20-year T-bond June contract at the CBOT. In the charts which follow, these are used to derive a variety of risk management strategies for different market situations.

Table 12.9 Options on 8 per cent US T-bond June future
(Chicago Board of Trade)

$100,000; 64ths of 100% *Future = 111-27/32*		
Option strikes	*Call*	*Put*
108	4-00	0-11
110	2-26	0-35
112	1-12	1-21
114	0-31	2-41
116	0-09	4-18
118	0-03	6-11

Source: Wall Street Journal, 13 April 1993

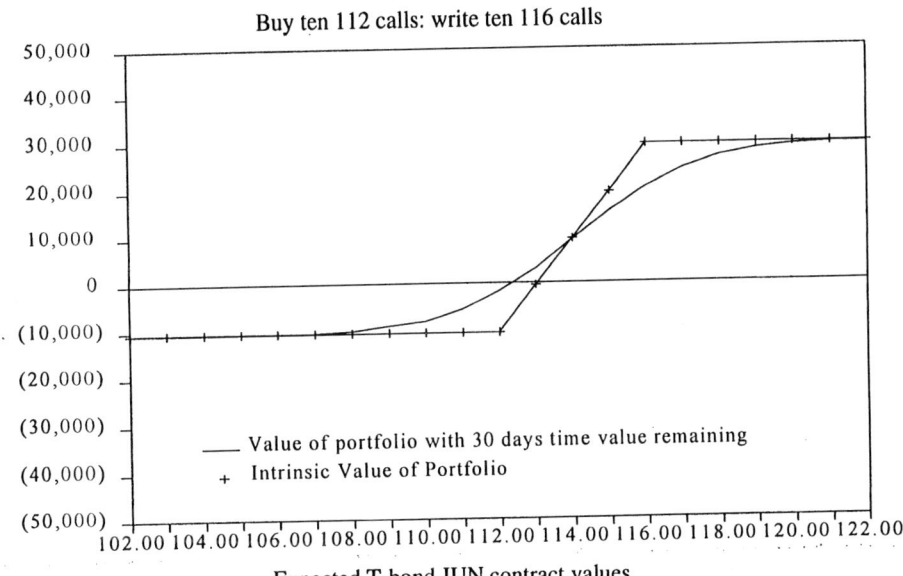

Figure 12.2 Bull spread strategy

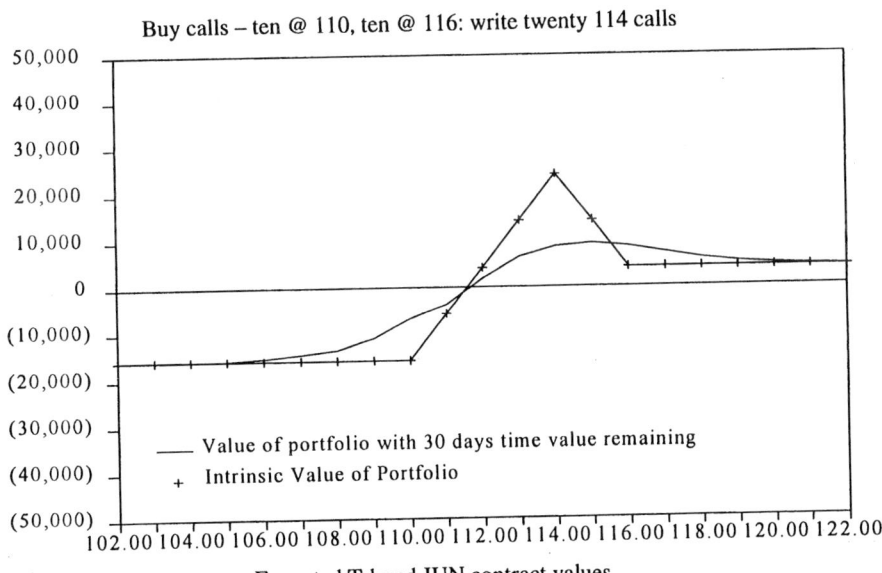

Figure 12.3 Bullish contra-volatility strategy

219

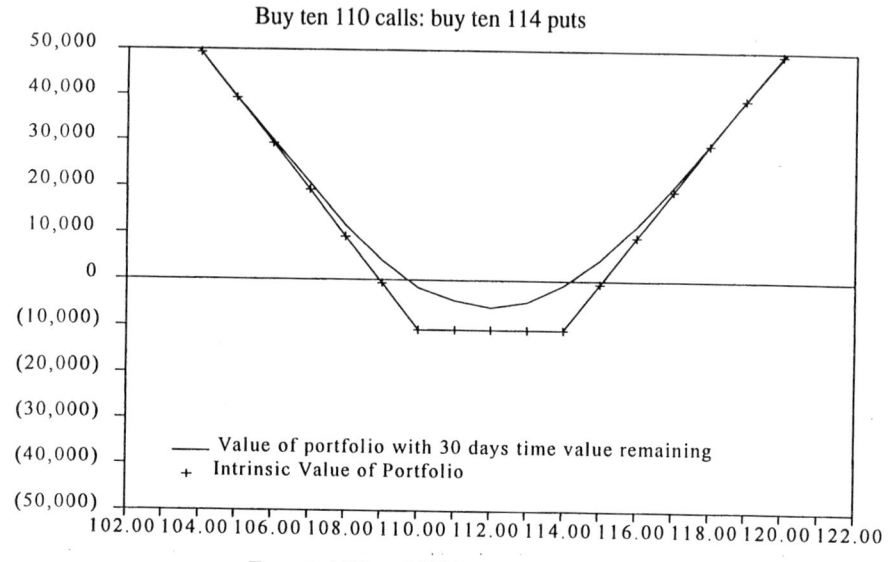

Figure 12.4 Pro-volatility strategy

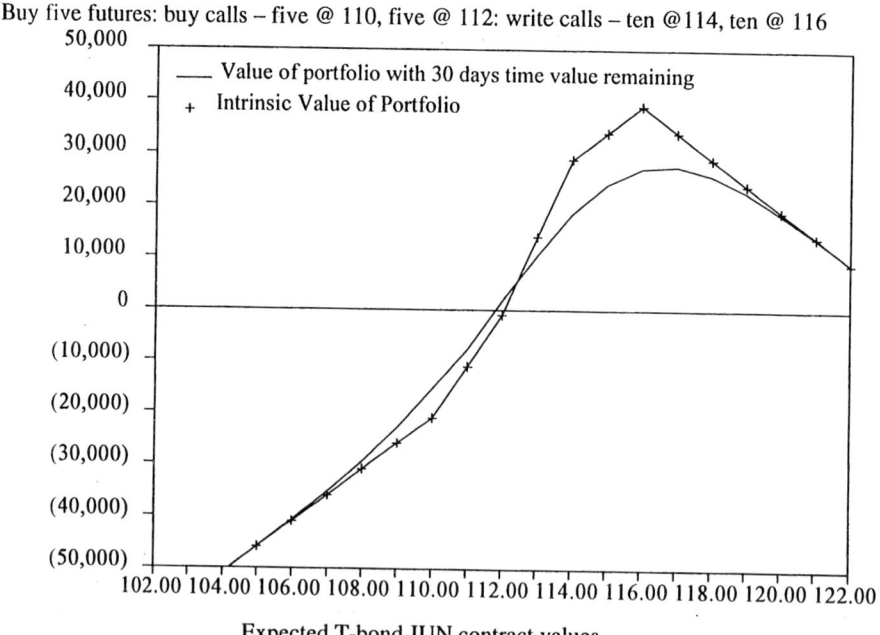

Figure 12.5 Bullish combination strategy

13: Equity Markets

EQUITY RELATED SECURITIES

Common Stock

Also known as shares or equity, the common stock of a company represents its risk capital. The stockholders, as owners, normally have voting rights in proportion to their holdings, although there are also two-tier structures, where the ownership is vested in a smaller group. Investors may receive regular dividends but these will tend to be low and their main objective is the realisation of a capital gain. When a company is wound up stockholders are the last group of creditors to be repaid and they only receive the notional share value, which is normally far less than the purchase price. The income/capital gain make-up of a stock determines its price; in Chapter 14 we look at analytic techniques for evaluating this.

Mezzanine Finance

Owners of preference stock and some forms of subordinated finance may be able to participate in share price rises. They do not normally have voting rights and their claim on the company's assets is subordinated to its senior creditors, the providers of debt finance. The term mezzanine refers to the intermediate risk–reward characteristics of this type of capital.

Mezzanine finance may take many forms, from debt structures paying relatively high coupons to equity participation where much of the capital gain available to stockholders can be earned. The term is applied according to the credit status of the investor.

In the remainder of this section we look at a variety of other securities whose cashflow characteristics are related to equity markets, but these are only mezzanine forms of capital where the investors' repayment rights precede those of the stockholders, but are subordinated to the senior creditors.

Indexed Issues

A number of bonds have been launched with redemption payment features that are linked to the performance of a particular stock index. Stock indexes are particularly popular amongst investors because they provide an effective way to

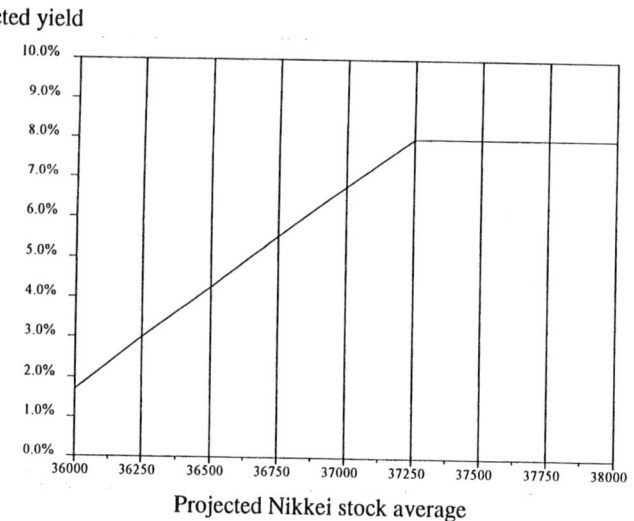

Figure 13.1 *Projected yields on Crediop 8 per cent 1992*
for a range of Nikkei prices

invest in a stock market as a whole rather than being exposed to the non-system-atic risk of specific stocks. The index formula can be constructed to provide the investor with many different risk–return profiles, from a simple and direct rela-tionship to option based structures where the investor is guaranteed a minimum return where the index falls below a certain level.

For instance, Crediop's 8 per cent 1992 indexed bond, issued in 1989, was structured so that investors would receive a maximum of 100 per cent of the redemption amount if the Nikkei average at maturity went above 37250. As the Nikkei goes below this level the redemption amount falls rapidly. Any investor is taking on the risk that in 1992 the Nikkei will be weak. In exchange for this they get much higher yen coupons than is usual. Readers will recognise the cashflow structure. As well as buying a bond, the investor is writing a put option on the Nikkei – the 2 per cent difference between his coupons and those achievable via an ordinary fixed rate bond (at the time three-year bond rates were at 6 per cent) is his premium. As it turned out, the Nikkei was markedly lower by 1992. Owners of the bond realised a huge loss as a result of the fall. Against this, however, many of them will have sold Nikkei futures and options, to mitigate their losses.

Convertibles

An equity convertible is a bond issue where the owner of the bond has the right to convert his holding into the common stock of the issuing vehicle, at a price which is defined in the bond's prospectus. Convertibles are popular with issuers who regard them as an inexpensive financing route and an effective way of raising risk capital.

To illustrate the structure of an equity convertible, let us consider a $120m convertible bond issued by Chiquita Brands in March 1991. The bond was issued at par, with a maturity in 2001 and an annual coupon of 7 per cent. This compared with an annualised yield for ten-year T-bonds at the time of around 8.5 per cent.

If Chiquita had issued an ordinary bond in this environment it might well have been required to pay a coupon of at least 9 per cent. It was able to issue at a yield well below the equivalent treasury, because of the bond's conversion feature. Owners of the bond are able to convert into shares on any coupon date at an effective price of $43 a share. The closing price for Chiquita shares on the issue date was $37 and the bonds were therefore trading initially on a Conversion Premium of 16.2 per cent ($43/$37).

Chiquita is an international fruit and vegetable importer, best known as the world's major banana supplier. The company had displayed a strong, consistent growth pattern in previous years, and its stocks are highly rated. Investors in the Chiquita bond were happy with the 7 per cent yield, because many of them viewed their holding as a potential share rather than as a bond. They regarded 7 per cent, not as a lower than average coupon but as a higher than normal dividend. At the time of writing the convertible stock has not lived up to its promise. Chiquita was badly hit by the recession and in 1993 its shares were trading closer to $20 than the hoped for $43.

Rationale for the Issuer

Convertibles are popular amongst issuers, because of the low cost funds they can achieve on their borrowings. They also have one other great advantage. When the investors exercise their conversion options, not only is the company's equity capital increased, but its borrowings are reduced at the same time. For example, a company with $50m in share capital issues a $50m convertible. When 10 per cent of the bond holders convert, the equity base is increased to $55m and borrowings fall to $45m. There is, therefore, a two-fold effect on its leverage – it falls from 1 to 0.82 in this case.

The Conversion Premium

The conversion price is normally set slightly above the current market share price. An initial premium of 15–18 per cent is fairly common, but the aim is to set the conversion price so that investors can realistically expect to be able to convert within two to three years. The conversion premium needs to be compared with the company's growth prospects to determine the yield required by the investor.

Put Features and Investor Protection

When assessing his acceptable yield level an investor must weigh the potential capital gain against the risk that the stocks do not perform as expected. If this occurs an investor will be left holding an underperforming asset. The riskiness of the asset is also likely to be in question, since if conversion has not occurred it will probably be because of a down-rating in the company, which will have a negative impact on its bonds.

The coupon charged on a convertible will therefore have to reflect the cost of this risk, as well as the value of the conversion feature. Chiquita decided not to include a put feature in its bond, but it could probably have raised funds at a lower coupon had one been incorporated, but given its relatively weak performance this would almost certainly have triggered redemptions and an unwelcome drain on cashflows.

Premium Put Features

Some of the more aggressive convertible bond issuers in the 1980s went one step further and included a premium put feature. This allowed investors to redeem their bonds early at a price greater than par. The put price increased the further into the future the put was exercised, the idea being to compensate the investor for not having been able to buy shares, so that at least he owned a valuable bond. The mechanism proved very popular with investors and premium put convertibles were able to be launched at lower coupons as a result.

However, many such companies found that if their share price declined and investors exercised their puts, the resulting haemorrhage to the balance sheet left them with large financial problems at just the time when they could least afford to deal with them. As a result equity convertible issuers nowadays tend to avoid put features if they can, and steer well clear of premium puts, even if this means that coupons may be higher.

Issuer Call Features and the 130 per cent Rule

Chiquita followed the market practice and included an issuer call option in its $120m bond. As is usual with convertibles the issuer has the right to force conversion of the bond into equities should the market share price exceed the conversion price by more than 30 per cent. The call feature protects the issuer from investors holding the convertible, continuing to earn the coupon, and then earning a massive profit on conversion. In Chiquita's case the bond was callable on any coupon date up to 1996 if the share price went above $55.90 (i.e. 130% × $43), the logic being that if the share price had not reached this level in five years' time, investors would deserve any increased benefit, and the call would be unnecessary.

Equity Warrant Issues

An equity warrant issue combines an ordinary fixed rate bond with a call option on the stock of the issuing company. Equity warrant issues have been particularly popular amongst fast-growing Japanese companies who see them as a way of borrowing almost free money and introducing postponed equity offerings. Equity warrants, like convertibles, allow the investor to purchase stock at a pre-agreed price. The key difference between them, though, is that whereas a convertible bond must be handed back when the equity is bought, with a warrant the bond remains intact. Valuing the warrant component of a bond-cum-warrants package is done using option pricing tools.

Coupons on ex-Warrant Bonds

Warrants are traded separately from the associated bond. Whenever this occurs the bond is said to be trading ex-warrant. The bond and the warrant are not linked except by the fact that they were originally issued in a single package.

The bond-cum-warrant package is generally issued at par with the price dictated by the value of the warrant plus the bond's yield. Suppose the warrant is valued at $20, the bond component must be worth $80 for a five year instrument. The bond coupon must reflect the required yield for that security. Assuming this to be 8 per cent, the required coupon is just 2.99 per cent. The reason it can be so low is, of course, the bond price, which provides for a capital gain of 25 per cent ($20/$80) over five years. Because issues are priced at par, the higher the value of the warrant the lower the required coupon for the bond. Since such warrants confer the right to own equity at a maximum price, companies that are perceived as fast growing will derive the largest price benefits.

Repackaging Ex-paper

By their nature, equity warrant issues tend to be small. For the coupon effect to be at all significant each $1000 denomination bond must include warrants to buy a similar nominal value of shares. No company will wish to raise too much of its capital in the form of equity warrants. If it did it could leave itself exposed to a concealed takeover attempt, the bidder could corner the market in its equity warrants without having to declare its interest to the stock exchange.

Because of their relative illiquidity, ex-warrant bonds tend not to perform particularly well in the markets. They are also difficult to sell to investors seeking regular income because of their low coupons. As a result their yields will tend to be higher than the market norm. In such cases an investment bank will often repurchase the ex-paper. By placing it in a trust company, entering into swaps and doing some financial engineering, it can re-launch it in a more marketable form. The most common form of synthetic security is an FRN, but ex-paper can equally be repackaged as a full coupon, par priced, straight bond.

American Depository Receipts (ADRs)

ADRs provide foreign companies with the ability to list their shares on a US stock exchange. The company is able to raise its visibility in the US and access the American capital markets without having to apply for a full listing. It sets up an offshore investment trust whose sole function is to buy and sell the company's shares. The shares are registered with a US based depository institution. The US investor buys ADRs which represent the dollar equivalent of the company's share price. In theory, he owns all the rights to any capital gain and dividend, but has no voting power. There is also some controversy about the size of the fees such investors are required to pay.

STOCK INDEX FUTURES

Definition

A stock index future is a standard agreement that provides the holder with a recognised basket of stocks on a specified date in the future. Index futures are offered on a variety of exchanges with delivery dates in March, June, September and December up to two years in the future. For popular contracts, such as the S&P500 future traded at the Chicago Mercantile Exchange, other months are also available.

Index Futures and Cash Settlement

Because an index is a synthetic asset, index futures are delivered by means of cash settlement. The index price is set by marking it to market using the closing prices for the stocks on the delivery date.

Table 13.1 Major contracts

Index/Exchange	Size	Tick	Value	Type
S&P500 Index (CME/IOM)	$500 ×	0.05	$25.00	Mkt-weighted
NYSE Composite Index (NYFE)	$500 ×	0.05	$25.00	Mkt-weighted
Major Market Index (CBOT)	$250 ×	0.05	$12.50	Price-weighted
Value Line Composite Index (KCBOT)	$500 ×	0.05	$25.00	Geometric
FTSE-100 Index (LIFFE)	£25 ×	0.1	£2.50	Mkt-weighted
Australian All Ordinaries Index (SFE)	A$100 ×	0.1	A$10.00	Mkt-weighted
Hang Seng Index (HKFE)	HK$50 ×	1	HK$50	Mkt-weighted
Nikkei 225 Index (SIMEX)	¥1000 ×	5	¥5000	Price-weighted

CME/IOM	Index & Option Market (Chicago Mercantile Exchange subsidiary)
NYFE	New York Futures Exchange
CBOT	Chicago Board of Trade
KCBOT	Kansas City Board of Trade
LIFFE	London International Financial Futures Exchange
SFE	Sydney Futures Exchange
HKFE	Hong Kong Futures Exchange
SIMEX	Singapore International Monetary Exchange

Owners of long index futures positions receive the difference between the marked to market value of the index and delivery and the value of their position from owners of short positions. This obviates the need for physical settlement which would be prohibitively expensive. One only needs to consider the cost of acquiring the required amounts of each stock in the S&P500 to deliver one contract to realise that physical delivery is not a realistic alternative.

Index Arbitrage

Arbitragers can exploit the price relationship between the stock market and the index future by taking equal and opposite positions in stocks and in the futures markets. If the index future goes above its theoretical value they can lock in the differential by buying the stocks, financing them to the delivery date and simultaneously selling the correct number of futures contracts. If the future is undervalued the opposite arbitrage can be done.

The respective positions are closed out when convergence occurs to lock in the profit. It may happen beforehand, but it ought always to occur by the delivery date. The large amount of capital that has to be committed to index arbitrage means that there can often be a great deal of arbitrage related stock activity at certain times of year. There are some key times when futures, options and stocks all reach delivery at the same time. These have come to be known as triple witching hours, dating from an infamous occasion in October 1986 when arbitrage related selling triggered record sell-off of stocks.

To do such arbitrages a large number of deals have to be conducted at the same instant. Index arbitragers use computers, both to calculate continuously the implied index future's price and to initiate orders automatically.

Sources of Anomalies

As with other futures markets, anomalies arise for reasons of supply and demand. But these can be greater where the relationships are more complex. Portfolio managers will sell index futures as they grow more bearish on stocks. This means that market-wide sentiment is first expressed in the index price. The individual dealers in particular stocks may not mark down their prices straight away. When this occurs an arbitrage opportunity can open up.

Another important aspect of the arbitrage opportunity is the effect that dividends have on the market price. Just before a dividend is paid, its value is fully reflected in the price. When the share goes ex-dividend its price automatically falls by the amount of the dividend and the index is adjusted down.

The basic index futures valuation model simply subtracts the dividends. A more accurate model would build in the time value of money effect of losing dividend income before delivery. The arbitrager using this more sophisticated evaluation technique can spot anomalies as a result.

OPTIONAL INSTRUMENTS

Equity Options

Definition
A call option on a stock provides the buyer with the right but not the obligation to acquire shares at a prearranged price. A put option grants the right to sell shares at the exercise price. A warrant is a long-term option to buy stock at the exercise price at any time up to expiry.

Traded Options
The natural volatility of equities makes the option a natural risk management tool. Calls and puts are offered at all the major exchanges on the most active stocks for a range of exercise prices.

Stock options are normally American style, that is, they tend to have an early exercise feature. Unlike options on futures, where even if exercise can be made early the underlying instrument is not deliverable before expiry, stock options can be exercised in the spot market.

They have been traded on the Chicago Board Options Exchange since 1973, at the Philadelphia and American Stock Exchanges since 1975. They are also traded on a number of other US exchanges as well as in different stock markets around the world.

Option Terms

As with futures options, exercise prices are evenly spaced around the current share price. Options will be quoted at $1, $2.50, $5 or $10 intervals, depending on what is most appropriate for the share in question. They will normally be traded in 100-share lots. The only exception to this rule is when there has been a stock split. In that case, both the number of shares and the exercise price will be adjusted to reflect the decline in the value of one share created by the split.

When a new expiration date is introduced the exchange will generally introduce the two call and two put options with exercise prices closest to the current share price. If one of these is very close to the share price, a third option may be introduced. As the share price moves new options may be introduced as necessary.

Valuing Traded Options

The Black–Scholes model was first introduced as a market standard for the valuation of stock options, and it remains so today. This is despite the fact that most stock options are American style. However, it can be shown that it is never advantageous to exercise stock calls before expiry except if there is a dividend payment. For non-dividend calls Black–Scholes can therefore be used without modification. For calls with dividends due before expiry there may be an advantage in early exercise on the final date before the stock goes ex-dividend. Many market participants value this feature by pricing two European style options, one of which expires on the last pre-dividend date, the other expiring at the expiration date. Whichever is the greater of these two can be used as the option value. Of course this is only an approximation, but it seems to work well.

For puts it can often be advantageous to exercise early. If a dividend is paid on the stock during the option's life it may be most advantageous to exercise on the first ex-dividend date. If there is no dividend paid it can still be worth exercising in advance. To value American style puts effectively we need to use the binomial method or some other numerical technique.

Why Use Stock Options?

Speculators like stock options because they are able to achieve a high level of leverage on their positions. Regulators pay particularly close attention to option premiums when attempting to spot insider trading activity. This is because, when a major change in price is expected, the percentage effect on the premium will be

229

substantial, a 5 per cent change in the price of the stock can easily double the premium for one of its options.

For risk managers, traded options allow them to protect the returns on elements in their portfolios. Where it is difficult to sell a stock because of market illiquidity, the fund manager can buy put options instead. As the price of the stock falls the rise in the value of the put option will offset the fall in value of his position. Stock options allow risk managers to manage the non-systematic (i.e. company related) portion of their risk.

Writing Covered Calls

Options are also popular amongst fund managers as a means of enhancing the return on their portfolios. Assume, for instance, that IBM stock is currently trading at $115. The fund manager, who owns 100,000 shares, does not believe that the share price is likely to go higher than $120. If he writes $120 calls for 1000 lots of 100-share options at a premium of $5, he can earn $500,000 in premium income. The calls are covered by his underlying position, so he will not make a loss. However, he will sacrifice any profits on his IBM stocks above $120.

Equity Warrants

Definitions

An equity warrant is a long-term American-style option granting the holder the right to (almost always) buy stock. A company will not normally wish to launch put warrants that give holders the right to sell its own stock at a minimum price. There have been a few instances of equity put warrants against rivals issued by companies involved in contested takeovers, but these are not common.

Bonds plus Warrants

Most equity warrants are originally issued together with a bond. We have seen in the discussion on equity related securities how issuers can reduce their required coupons by launching a bond-cum-warrants package. The extent to which they can do this is defined by the value that investors attach to the warrant component.

Clearly, the right to buy stock at a prearranged price will be more valuable the greater is the likelihood that this price will be exceeded. The highest warrant prices can be commanded by the fastest growing companies, particularly if the warrant exercise price has been fixed at a level close to the current share price.

Typically warrants with bonds are issued with an exercise price that is only slightly above the current share price. A premium of 2–5 per cent is not uncommon. Clearly with such a low premium, a warrant that expires in two to three years, is, to all intents and purposes, already in the money.

Japanese Euro-Derivatives

It is not surprising that by far the most active issuers of bonds with warrants are the fast-growing Japanese concerns. For many of these companies issues of equity derivatives almost completely replaced ordinary equity issues as a mechanism for raising risk capital. In a fast-growing stock market the respective costs of these two activities are skewed in favour of derivatives. For a while this trend was encouraged by Japanese accounting practices which allowed companies to ignore any opportunity losses incurred by being forced to sell shares at less than market levels. But the collapse of Japanese stock levels led to a market moratorium in 1990, while new rules were put in place. Bonds issued with equity warrants remain a feature of the market but they have not regained the popularity they enjoyed in the late 1980s.

Consider the Sony Corporation for instance. Let us say its share price is currently trading at ¥4000. If the company were to issue further share capital directly it might have to issue shares at a discount to the current price, depending on the scale of the new issue.

If, instead, it issues equity warrants together with a bond, it may be able to raise funds more cheaply. Say it chose to issue equity warrants with an exercise price of ¥4100 (2.5 per cent above the current share price). If Sony's rating meant it ought to pay a yen yield of 6 per cent, and the warrant was valued at 20, then the required coupon for a five-year bond-cum-warrant priced at par would be just 1.25 per cent.

In a fast-growing market, the issuer regards the warrants as almost certain to be exercised. Issuing warrants is therefore seen as a deferred equity issue. The issue price is advantageous, but the fact that the warrants are not exercised for perhaps two years means that the capital is not raised until much later. However, the issuer has no problem with this as, in the meantime, he has been able to borrow the funds he needs at just 1.25 per cent.

The Currency Component

The vast majority of Japanese Euro-derivatives are not issued in yen at all. Instead, another currency, often the US dollar, is used. This is partly for regulatory reasons; equity derivatives launched offshore must be aimed at non-Japanese investors.

US investors value the ability to take a direct interest in a specific Japanese company via the warrants markets. Another advantage for them is that, where the warrants are issued with a US dollar bond, the exercise price is kept constant in dollar terms.

For instance, Dai Nippon Screen Manufacturing's bond-cum-warrants $100m issue launched in December 1989 contains a fixed exchange rate of $/yen 144.70 as part of the warrant's exercise terms. Each warrant was exercisable into 344.2 shares at a rate of ¥2102 per share. This effectively guarantees a maximum cost for the 344.2 shares of $5000 no matter what the exchange rate (i.e. $(2102 \times 344.2)/144.70$).

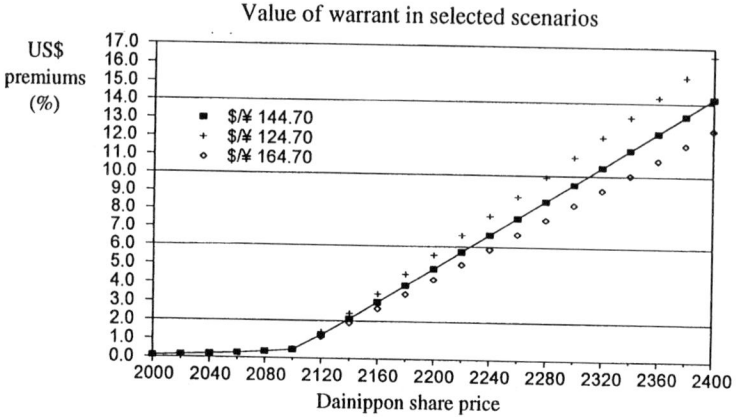

Value of warrant in selected scenarios

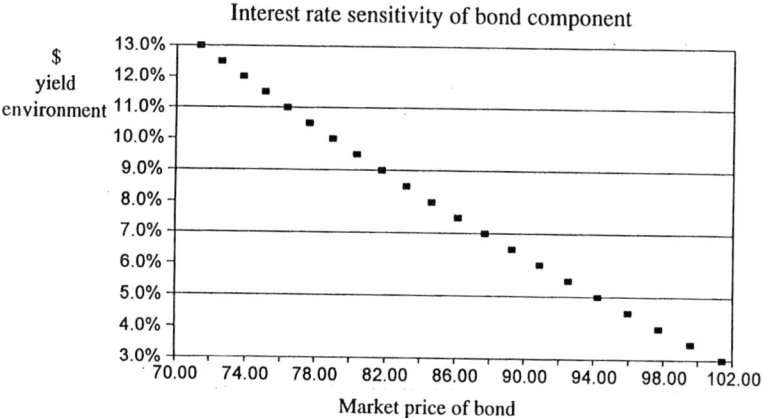

Interest rate sensitivity of bond component

Figure 13.2 Dai Nippon Screen Manufacturing $100m bond-cum-warrants issue in various environments

Covered Equity Warrants

The financial community also offers equity warrants in the form of covered warrant issues. These can either be guaranteed by the company concerned, which is launching a deferred equity distribution. Or, it may be a repackaging exercise: the broker buys warrants (or shares) outstanding in the markets. He can use these as collateral for his own warrant issue. Often the exercise and expiry characteristics of the covered warrant will be changed to make it more appealing to the retail investor at whom such issues are targeted.

Although covered warrants on individual equities are not uncommon, especially for the largest companies, the recent trend has been towards basket warrants. The warrant is priced against some benchmark index; it thus has much wider appeal than might a warrant on a specific equity.

Index Options and Warrants

Call and put options on indexes are bought and sold at leading stock exchanges. These can be European or American style, depending on the exchange. Examples of European style index options include the Institutional Index at the American Stock Exchange and the S&P500 Index at the Chicago Board Options Exchange. American options are more common – among them, the FTSE-100 at London's International Stock Exchange, the NYSE's Composite Index and its Major Market Index (MMI) and the Value Line Composite Index at the Philadelphia Stock Exchange.

Index options are always cash settled. The option holder receives any positive difference between the value of the index on the exercise date and the option strike price. In this respect, American index options differ from their equivalents in the futures markets.

Because an American style option can be exercised any time before its expiry date, the option writer's risk is against the spot value of the index on each day. Unlike Europeans or options on index futures the underlying instrument changes character each day, this can make it more problematic for the option writer to hedge his position.

For some hedgers the attraction of index options is the simplicity and flexibility of the instruments. Index options are available with a wider range of maturities and strikes than their futures counterparts. For example, the Chicago Board Options Exchange, where options first started trading in 1973, typically deals in calls and puts with at least twenty different strike prices for the S&P500 contract.

Index Futures Options

Like index options, index futures options allow portfolio managers to control the market (i.e. beta) risk on their portfolios. Futures options tend to be used by the more active and sophisticated institutional investors, often in conjunction with the futures. By buying and selling puts and calls on an index future the market participant can express a view on volatility as well as the direction the stock market is taking. A call gives its owner the right to buy the underlying index futures contract, while a put provides for the right to sell the future.

Strikes for Index Futures Options

For each futures contract call and put options are available for strikes at regular intervals around the current futures price. Options on the S&P500 future, for instance, have a strike price interval of 5 index points.

Table 13.2 shows premiums payable on puts and calls on the S&P500 index at the Index and Option Market subsidiary of the Chicago Mercantile Exchange. On the date in question the June future closed at 335.75.

Table 13.2 Options on S&P500 Futures (CME/IOM)

| | $500 × premium | |
Strike price	June calls	June puts
325	24.35	13.85
330	21.1	15.5
335	18.1	17.35
340	15.3	19.35
345	12.7	
350	10.3	24.2

Source: Wall Street Journal

Futures Option Pricing

As can be seen from Table 13.2, T-bond option premiums are quoted on the same 500 multiple as the S&P500 future. Like the future the minimum price movement is 0.05. The tick size is therefore $25, as it is for the future.

Market participants can find the net price of any call by adding the premium to (or, for puts, subtracting it from) the exercise price. A buyer of a 335 call would for example have a worst case cost of 353.10 (i.e. 335 + 18.1), while the purchaser of a put at the same strike has a worst case selling price of 317.65 for the June future.

Options as Synthetic Futures

The pricing relationship between calls, puts and futures can be demonstrated by the fact that calls and puts can be combined to create a synthetic future. Consider the S&P500. The future is priced at 335.75. Now suppose that an investor decides to write a put option and buy a call option simultaneously. He earns 17.35 from the sale of the put and pays 18.10, a net payment 0f 0.75. He now owns two equal and opposite positions. If the futures price falls to, say, 330, the call will expire worthless and he will have to pay 5.00 on the put – a net loss of 5.75. If the future was at 340 on the exercise date on the other hand, he would earn 5.0 from the call's intrinsic value and the put would expire worthless, a net profit of 4.25.

It is no coincidence that these profit and loss figures are the same as those for the future itself at 330 and 340. We know from our discussion of put–call parity that the simultaneous sale of a put and purchase of a call at the same strike creates a synthetic future. This relationship enshrines the put–call parity rule. Unless put and call prices were interrelated it would be possible to construct a future at a price other than the current market price. Because there is no such thing as a free lunch, this situation is not allowed to perpetuate.

Trading in Futures Options
As is the case with futures, options on index futures are used mainly by market professionals. They form an essential component of any risk management strategy. Traders and risk managers, by buying and selling options can express a view on expected stock market volatility; just as they buy and sell futures according to their view on the direction of price movements.

Margining and Marking-to-Market
Margining mechanisms differ between exchanges. Some require option buyers to pay the entire premium into the margin account. Writers must maintain a margin related to the future that increases according to the likelihood of exercise. However, the system adopted by, amongst others, the IOM in Chicago, is gaining acceptance. This assesses the risk on the net portfolio of the futures trader according to delta factors published each day by the exchange.

These risk numbers reflect the anticipated change in the value of the overall portfolio for a given change in the futures price. Margin requirements for both buyers and sellers are related to the underlying future by the risk number and change on a daily basis.

Index Warrants
One of the most rapidly growing sectors of the capital markets in recent years has been the index warrant market. Issues are launched, generally on a hedged (covered) basis, by investment banks and securities houses. They are bought by investors and fund managers, who wish to control the market risk on their portfolios as well as by retail investors looking for the ability to profit from movements in markets rather than taking a risk on individual stocks.

There has been a certain amount of criticism in some circles regarding the overpricing of warrant issues. There have undoubtedly been cases of index warrants being launched on expensive terms, but this occurred more during the early development of the market. In that sense it merely follows a trend set by almost every other financial market. As the market expands, and its current popularity promises much, these sorts of inconsistencies will be ironed out.

As an example of the covered index warrant approach, consider a two tranche one year, put and call issue by Bankers Trust (one of the prime exponents of the index warrant markets). Launched in March 1991, the put and call issues were for 300,000 warrants each. Ten warrants were equivalent to one unit of the FTSE-100 index.

The issue was unusual in that both the exercise price and the premiums for the warrants were determined after the bond was launched. To ensure that the warrants would be at the money when they reached the market, Bankers Trust announced that the strike price for both issues would be the index price at 1500 hours on the launch date. The initial premium for the calls was set at 20.1 per cent of the index value, while the put premium was set lower at 10.4 per cent.

235

The Footsie traded at 2458.5 at the time in question, so this became the strike rate. The premium for calls was fixed at £49.41, for puts it was set at £25.56. By simultaneously writing put and call warrants Bankers Trust has provided call buyers with a worst case price of 2952.6, while put owners can guarantee to sell the index at 2202.9.

This might be seen as very expensive, especially for call buyers who will only benefit at exercise if the index improves by 21 per cent in the next year. However, this level of volatility is quite common in stock markets and they are always able to sell their options before the expiry date. If, for instance, the stock market rose by 10 per cent over the first three months of the contract the increase in the likelihood of exercise might make the option very much more valuable.

In the end there is no getting away from the fact that options on stock markets will always look expensive in absolute terms, because of the riskiness of the underlying instrument. The option user must make a decision as to whether the high cost is justified, in some cases it is very definitely worth buying options.

For its part, Bankers Trust earned a total premium of 749.7 on 300,000 contracts. Against this it has the risk that the warrants will be exercised. If the index falls consistently the bank will start to make a loss at prices below 1708.8, or above 3208.20 (2485 + 749.7). Since either of these scenarios is most unlikely to occur in a year, it might still be thought that the issue is overpriced from the point of fair value.

However, because warrants are American style options it is possible that both puts and calls are exercised during the life, so a fairer test of value would factor in the cost to Bankers Trust of hedging its own positions. Since it could use the futures and options markets to hedge its position the prices in these markets will determine the warrant premiums.

14: Techniques for Equity Traders

EVALUATING EQUITY EXPOSURE

Top-down Portfolio Analysis

Modern Portfolio Theory
Modern portfolio theory aims to maximise performance by close analysis of the risk–reward characteristics of the universe of financial assets. It departs from traditional forms of analysis by regarding the entire portfolio as if it were a single commodity. Individual stocks are sometimes selected for their counter-cyclical characteristics as much as for their expected yields. The aim is to structure the portfolio so that its overall yield is maximised, while the level of riskiness is kept to a minimum.

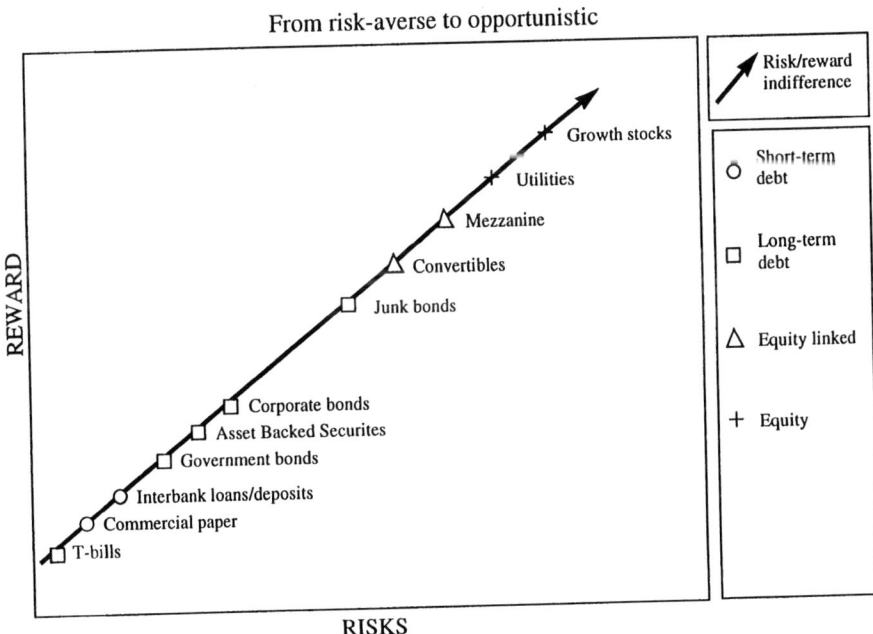

Figure 14.1 The risk-reward trade-off for financial instruments.

Strategic Asset Allocation

The primary decision for the fund manager is the selection of an appropriate combination for the main categories of financial instrument: cash, equities and bonds. Strategic decisions must be made about how to allocate resources according to economic, political and currency factors. Typically, fund management decisions are taken on the basis of a relatively long-term view of market performance, perhaps one to three years ahead.

The key economic variables followed by fund managers include real economic growth, inflation and interest rates. Equities will tend to perform well when real growth is strong. Bonds will be most attractive as inflation falls, while cash performs best when interest rates are high. Currencies' price behaviour tends to relate closely to all three of these factors, though their relative importance will vary through time.

Stock Market Performance

The usual first stage for the asset allocator is to attempt to identify individual stock markets that are over- or under-valued. Stock markets will tend to perform in line with real economic growth, for, as output increases, so will company profitability. This is not to suggest that share prices will rise by the same proportion as real GNP. Other factors, such as improved productivity and the effect of leverage will tend to mean that company profits will outstrip any increase in GNP. Also, in a bull market, acceleration in earnings growth will have the effect of uprating companies' share price valuations.

A variety of information sources are used, but the basic objective is to try to make an assessment as to whether a market has fully discounted future price movements. This is complicated by the fact that share prices contain a large element of capital gain and stock markets are often priced according to the expected state of the economy in two to three years' time. The current yield on a stock is, therefore, unlikely to correspond to the market's estimation of its true worth.

Investors look at a number of relationships to pinpoint value, both for individual stocks and market indices. Price-earnings ratios (PEs), net asset values (NAVs), earnings per share (EPS) and dividend yield are among the most important quantitative techniques. These are discussed more fully in the section below on stock selection, but they relate also to the identification of value in stock markets as a whole.

Currency Performance

For global investors, identifying economies with strong performance and under-rated stock markets is only the first step. They need also to make predictions about the foreign currency's performance against their domestic currency. A prediction of a 15 per cent improvement in a particular stock market over the next year does not necessarily provide grounds for investment. If, over the same period the foreign currency is expected to decline by 20 per cent, the investor may have to realise a capital loss of 5 per cent in a year's time.

Of course, it may be possible to hedge against currency movements by selling the foreign currency for forward delivery. However, this is not always practicable, particularly where foreign currency interest rates are higher than those in the domestic market. The cost of forward protection will reflect the interest differential. Where foreign currency interest rates are, say, 4 per cent higher than those in the domestic market, the investor will realise only 11 per cent in domestic currency terms when foreign equities advance by 15 per cent. If domestic markets are projected to yield 10 per cent over the same period, the additional risks from investing abroad may be deemed to outweigh the expected 1 per cent benefit.

There is also a problem as regards the timing and size of any currency hedge. Stock markets often rise or fall by as much as 10 per cent in any month, so it is essential to buy and sell at the right moments. There is no reason why these should correspond to the currency hedging period. In practice, therefore, it is extremely difficult to hedge against currency variations. Many institutional investors prefer to take investment decisions according to their forecasts of both currency and stock market performance, and only hedge on an *ad hoc* basis.

Bond Price Performance

T-bills and high credit quality bonds tend to be bought by institutional investors as a defensive position. Their characteristics of guaranteed income plus capital at redemption allows them to retain their value during periods of economic slowdown.

Having said this, bond prices will fall as interest rates rise. If inflation is on the march then the yields on long term bonds are likely to fall as long-term interest rates increase. When interest rates and inflation are falling, however, bond prices will tend to increase. The rate of capital growth is of vital importance to the asset allocator, particularly when compared with equity market performance. This is partly determined by duration and the measures taken to manage the fixed income component of any fund will be those used by the interest risk manager. But bond prices will also be determined by their relationship to equities as investors switch between markets in a search for higher risk-adjusted yields.

Measuring the Relationship between Bonds and Equities

Modern portfolio theorists look at all financial instruments in terms of their risk-adjusted yields. At the lower end of the risk–reward spectrum are the debt instruments. The expected yields on equities therefore need to be higher than those achievable via T-bills or bonds. Asset allocators therefore look at the relationship between bond yields and equity yields when deciding how they should apportion their financial resources.

One measure of this relationship is the bond/earnings yield ratio. The earnings yield on a stock is the inverse of its PE ratio. It expresses the current year's dividend as a proportion of the share price. When earnings yields are historically low, this reflects a lot of demand for the stock market in question – the share price is high relative to the amount being paid to investors in the form of dividend.

When bond yields go higher, earnings yields will also rise. As their cost of borrowing increases and economic activity slows down, companies share prices will be downrated and they will need to maintain high dividends to protect their capitalisation.

The flight to quality effect of this bear market will encourage a flow of funds from stocks into bonds and T-bills. As a result bond yields may not have to rise as fast as equities to maintain parity between the two markets. The bond/earnings yield ratio is therefore likely to fall.

As the bear phase is completed and economic activity picks up, bond holding investors may take the opportunity to transfer holdings back into a stock market that now appears to represent good value. The bond/earnings yield. ratio will therefore rise as the market becomes more bullish.

The Stochastic Process in Equity Markets

By using top-down analysis to arrive at estimates about the performance of currencies, interest rates and stock markets, portfolio managers can structure their portfolios so that they have larger exposures to those areas where they are relatively bullish, and smaller positions where they are relatively bearish. These general principles guide the overall investment policy, but the success of any fund depends crucially on precisely what assets are bought and sold, and when.

We have seen how the stochastic process can impact on the yield curve in unpredictable ways. This pales into insignificance, however, compared to the stochastic effects for individual equities. Whereas all bond prices rise as yields fall, a rise in a stock index can be paralleled by a whole range of effects (positive, negative or neutral) for individual equities.

Are Stock Markets a Random Walk?

The idea that stock prices behave in a random way has gained widespread acceptance in recent years. The random walk view of prices is an extension of the so-called, efficient markets hypothesis. This states that, in a perfect market, all information is always discounted in today's price. The current price is, therefore, the best prediction for the following day's price, since the actual price tomorrow is as likely to be above, as it is to be below today's price.

Systematic and Non-systematic Risk

At root, the aim of any fund manager is to achieve the highest available yield. But, in efficient markets, when, supposedly, all price sensitive information is fully discounted in prices, this can be extremely difficult to achieve. Top yields will be achieved by getting two things right. Firstly, which market to invest in and when; and, secondly, which individual assets within that market will outperform the rest. These two categories of risk are known respectively as systematic and non-systematic.

Active Fund Management

What might be termed the aggressive approach to fund management is to attempt to profit from identifying strongly performing assets, the so-called star performers, which are not always found in the stock market where there appears to be the most potential. But this is not always so easy to achieve. Every investor is operating in a competitive environment and so must spot opportunities before demand forces up the price of the asset.

In practice, especially with equities, close understanding of a quoted company's competitive position is vital to an appreciation of its prospects. An investor can, therefore, only manage funds aggressively in one or two markets where he has above average specialist knowledge. For even the most internationally diversified institutions, it is impracticable to operate in this way on a global basis. Some of their fund managers will be better than others, and the negative effect of transferring assets away from the funds of their best managers towards their more average performers can easily outweigh the benefit of moving towards stronger markets.

Passive Fund Management

At the other end of the risk spectrum is the portfolio manager who decides to ignore the non-systematic opportunities, concentrating instead on selecting the appropriate markets at the right time. As we shall see, it is possible to all but eliminate company specific risks on stocks using diversification techniques. The passive investor will earn only average returns in each market, but will aim to benefit from making the correct strategic decisions in the first place.

Fund managers who accept that it is not possible to outperform any market and aim instead to match it are known as index trackers. The practices that they use are gaining in popularity, as markets are perceived as becoming more efficient at discounting information.

Benchmarks for Fund Performance

Of course, most investing institutions fall somewhere between the two stools, combining elements of index tracking with individual stock selection. The usual, conservative approach is to adopt a set of strict guidelines as to the extent that the fund may be exposed to any individual stock, sector, currency or market. Fund managers will attempt to structure investment portfolios that are broadly similar to the components of their benchmark index, while at the same time going slightly overweight in those stocks, sectors etc., they believe will outperform, and underweight the less attractive areas.

241

To some extent the investment behaviour of institutions is driven by the competition for funds. Pension funds, investment funds, unit trusts and other thrift institutions are subject to quarterly assessments of their performance. Generally this is measured against a specific, relevant stock index.

The need to outperform these indexes is thus a strong investment pressure. This raises a legitimate and important question: how accurate are these indexes in measuring markets? The issue of indexation is addressed in detail later in this chapter.

Principles of Stock Selection

Bottom-up Analysis
Although investors use top-down analysis to identify strongly performing markets or currencies, a detailed understanding of the conditions facing each individual company is vital to the stock selection process. Bottom-up analysis values an individual company by focusing on the environment within which it operates in as much detail as possible. The aim is to identify those stocks that have the highest alphas.

What is Alpha?
Alpha is the market's measurement of the non-beta price risk of a stock. Rather than looking at the relative volatility, it focuses on the difference between the expected return for the stock and that for its benchmark index. Stocks with positive alphas will tend to outperform their peer group, returning higher than average profits and registering lower than average declines.

Some analysts prefer to focus on the average performance of the relevant sector when looking at the alpha for an individual stock, rather than comparing it directly to an index. Since alpha is meant to measure the qualities of a particular company, they argue, it is preferable to compare it to the other, similar stocks that are represented within the index.

Spotting Undervalued and Overvalued Stocks
If an investor is to identify value in an individual share's price, it follows that he must either have better information, or, and it amounts to the same thing, he must be better able to interpret the information. Stock selectors look at a number of key ratios, but they also try to judge growth prospects according to a number of intangibles, such as competitive performance, demographic trends, changing consumer preferences and the quality of management.

When a fund manager makes a decision to acquire a stock, he will often be looking at it on a relatively long-term basis. Most fund managers have buy and sell rules that allow them to have a chance of realising the long-term expected gain.

For instance, there may be a stop loss trigger if a stock underperforms against the index by more than 15 per cent, and profit taking if it outperforms it by at least 20 per cent. Even here, no action will be taken without a fundamental reappraisal of the stock in question.

PE Ratios

The first step in the analysis is to look at the Price–Earnings multiple for the stock (the PE ratio). The PE ratio is simply the price of a stock divided by its earnings per share. The stock selector looks both at the trailing PE, which uses the latest reported profits and is published daily in the financial press, and also at the forward PE. This uses an analyst's forecasts of the next published profit figure to calculate earnings per share.

Where both of these numbers are substantially different from its peers, a company ought to be investigated in more detail. If its PEs are well below those of its competitors it may be a sign that the stock is undervalued. On the other hand it could indicate that the firm has severe problems that merit its low rating.

If the PEs are higher than the average for the sector, it could be a signal that the stock is overpriced. It could also be that investors regard this as a fast-growing company. Companies with particularly high PEs may be investing a large amount of capital now to deliver better returns in a few years' time.

PEs can vary dramatically between sectors. In US markets, for instance, mature companies may be on a PE of 15, while high technology stocks can operate on PEs of 30 or more. The differences between markets are even more pronounced. In Japan, for instance, PEs of 40 to 50 are commonplace. This of course reflects investors' perceptions of growth prospects for Japanese companies. PEs will also be radically different in bull and bear market phases. The PE is an inverse measure of projected yield, so it follows that in a high interest rate environment PEs will generally have to be lower.

Earnings per Share (EPS)

The pivotal role that PEs play in determining stock values is acknowledged in the boardrooms. Many companies set themselves the financial target of increasing earnings per share. Any company that can achieve a consistently improving EPS figure will automatically improve its share price. For the PE to remain the same the share price will have to rise with EPS. Additionally, it is highly probable that as investor confidence in the company's ability to improve its profitability gets reinforced, the share will traded on a higher PE multiple.

Dividend Yield

Another way that a company can increase the price of its shares is via a policy of paying a large and growing dividend. However, since the dividend is that portion of profit that is not reinvested, a high dividend policy can be at the expense of future growth, so it can have a mixed effect on the share price. Generally speaking, companies operating in mature sectors without much potential for growth will be required to pay high dividends. Fast-growing companies on the other hand may be able to get away with paying hardly any dividend, or none at all.

Trailing dividend yields are published in the financial press and are the simplest form of equity analysis. The dividend yield ignores the capital gain component of the share, focusing instead on its current income. It is defined as the dividend divided by the current price. As with PEs, forward dividend yields are also looked at, these are often based on the company's own prediction of its future dividend.

Dividend Cover

Another key element in the valuation process is the extent to which dividends are covered by profits. This is measured by dividend cover (profits divided by the dividend). Many companies will attempt to keep dividends growing at a constant rate in order to maintain a solid rating for their shares. However, if in doing this they must distribute larger and larger proportions of total profits, it is often a sign that dividend growth is unlikely to be able to be sustained at current levels. Analysts monitor dividend cover over several years as an indicator of this phenomenon. If the dividend cover has fallen consistently they may recommend that the shares should be sold, which will lead to a down-rating of the company.

Gordon's Dividend Growth Model

An extension of the basic dividend yield calculation can be used to build in an estimate of the present value of all of the future dividends payable by the company. For the owner of a share this figure is the total value of his holding. Like any other stream of cashflows its present value can be found using the time value of money equation.

Providing he does not sell his holding, the owner of a share will continue to receive dividends for as long as the company remains in business. For a company paying one dividend each year, the time value of money equation can be expressed as follows:

$$PV = \frac{D_1}{(1 + R_1)} + \frac{D_2}{(1 + R2)^2} + ... + \frac{D_n}{(1 + R_n)^n} + ...$$

Where

PV	=	Current share price
D_i	=	Annual dividend payable after i years
R_i	=	Required rate of interest for period i

Future dividends are unknown and must be estimated. However, many companies try to keep dividends on a stable growth path. Future dividends can often therefore be expressed in terms of the latest dividend multiplied by a growth factor.

The formula can be further simplified by assuming that a constant yield is required. It therefore becomes:

$$PV = \frac{D_1}{(1 + R)} + \frac{D_1.(1+g)}{(1 + R)^2} + ... + \frac{D_1.(1+g)^n}{(1 + R)^n} + ...$$

Where

PV	=	Current share price
D_1	=	Next annual dividend
R	=	Required yield
g	=	Annual dividend growth rate

This can be simplified to:

$$PV = \frac{D_1}{(R - g)}$$

To find the projected yield we simply rearrange the equation, so that R is its subject:

$$R = \frac{D_1}{PV} + g$$

Assuming a constant rate of growth we can use the latest dividend as a predictor of the next dividend payment. So, the formula becomes:

$$R = \frac{D_0.(1+g)}{PV} + g$$

Where

D_0 = Latest annual dividend

By making g the subject of the equation it is possible to determine the rate at which dividends must grow every year if the investor is to achieve his required rate of return:

$$g = \frac{PV.R - D_0}{(PV + D_0)}$$

Gordon's model has the great advantage of simplicity. The only information that an investor needs to estimate the projected yield on a share is the latest dividend, the current price and an estimate of dividend growth. It can be argued that the model grossly oversimplifies the actual behaviour of companies. Dividend growth is usually tied to earnings performance. Despite the best intentions of company directors this can often be erratic. Particular difficulties may be encountered when analysing growth stocks that are currently reinvesting most profits, and intend to distribute a larger proportion in dividend in a few years' time.

Notwithstanding the unrealistic nature of some of its assumptions, Gordon's growth model is still widely used by stock analysts as one element in the decision-making process. It captures the two essential elements in stock price behaviour, dividend yield and capital growth.

Leverage

By looking at a company's debt-to-equity ratio, the analyst can get an idea about its ability to withstand the effects of a recession and profits from the opportunities in a period of economic expansion.The appropriate amount of leverage varies widely between sectors. Typically fast growth stocks will have higher debt components in their capital base, while mature companies' and industries' leverage will normally be more modest.

The financial sector is a special case: banks typically borrow up to eight times their equity capital. In other words, their leverage ratios can be up to eight, much higher than is feasible in any other sector. The reason they are able to do this is of course the fact that much of their business is about lending money. As interest rates rise banks often benefit from being able to charge wider margins between borrowing and lending. In a very high interest rate environment they will suffer from an increased incidence of borrower defaults, but in general bank stocks are traditionally less subject to the effects of an economic downturn than other types of shares.

Capitalisation and the Weighted Average Cost of Capital (WACC)

When deciding how to raise capital, companies have three main choices. They can issue more shares; borrow funds from the financial sector or via a securities issue; or they can deploy reserves, either because they are cash-rich or by asset sales programmes.

Each carries risks and costs: the company will attempt to select the strategy the gives it the lowest WACC rate. WACC aims to value the optimal capitalisation structure by looking at the post-tax cost of equity, borrowing or internal reserves. The examples below illustrate the relative costs of raising capital via debt and equity.

Unleveraged Companies

A company with no debt may underperform. Its shareholders will be asked to provide all of the capital the business needs and their profits can only reflect their level of investment. Consider, for instance, a $100m company supporting an annual turnover of $100m that is able to earn a 12 per cent profit margin on its sales. If on its last dividend it paid out half of its profit as dividend ($6 per $100 nominal), then the remaining 6 per cent is available for reinvestment on the business. This means that turnover can only increase by 6 per cent.

Assuming dividend cover will remain constant at 2, the share price will reflect the yield required by investors. Now suppose that the market requires a yield of 14 per cent on this stock. Then, according to Gordon's growth model the price of $100 nominal of shares will be:

$$\frac{\$6 \times 1.06}{(0.14 - 0.06)} = \$79.50$$

Put another way, the company would have to issue new $1 shares at a price of 79.5 cents so that their expected yield equates to 14 per cent. To raise an additional $50m it would have to issue $62.9m worth of new equity.

Leveraged Companies

Now suppose that instead the company has elected to borrow the $50m. This equates to a leverage ratio of 0.5. It can do this at 8 per cent and therefore earns a trading profit on its borrowed funds of 4 per cent (12 – 8). Its total profit therefore increases from $12m to $14m. If 50 per cent of this were paid out in dividend, there would still be $7m available for reinvestment, 7 per cent of the equity capital base. Assuming it continues to earn 4 per cent on its borrowings and maintains a leverage ratio of 0.5, the price of its stock will rise because of its higher dividend and faster growth:

$$\frac{\$7 \times 1.07}{(0.14 - 0.07)} = \$107.00$$

Notice that the market is still demanding a yield of 14 per cent from the company's stock. Because its level of leverage is relatively low for its sector, the riskiness of its stock is not thought to have increased.

Highly Leveraged Companies

As a company borrows more funds two things start to happen. Firstly the cost of borrowing increases as lenders start to become concerned with the risk. At the same time equity investors start to demand a higher yield, because they perceive the company as a riskier investment. Suppose the company had borrowed $100m, at an average borrowing cost of 9 per cent. At the same time, the equity market is demanding an 18 per cent yield from the stock. Even assuming it could still earn 12 per cent on sales after doubling its turnover to $200m (before interest costs), its shares may perform poorly. It returns a profit of $15m ($12m on equity plus $3m on debt). It pays a 7.5 per cent dividend and dividend growth is assumed to be 7.5 per cent:

$$\frac{\$7.5 \times 1.075}{(0.18 - 0.075)} = \$76.79$$

Interest Cover

Analysts use interest cover as a measure of the riskiness of company's leverage. This is defined as profits divided by the cost of servicing its debt. In the examples above the company has interest cover of 3.5 times ($14m/$4m) when it borrows $50m. When the debt–equity ratio rises to 1, interest is covered 1.67 times by profits.

Interest cover allows the analyst to take account of company profitability when determining whether it is over- or under-leveraged. But the figure should be viewed with caution, two companies with the same amount of interest cover may have very different risk attributes depending on their level of leverage.

Valuing Convertibles

Since a convertible is both debt and potential equity, a combination of techniques needs to be used to arrive at its value. When Chiquita launched its convertible, the worst case yield was, on the face of it, unattractive, it paid a minimum of 7 per cent for ten year money. However, as a potential stock it also had capital gain element which was built into the price. To value it we need to compare its price behaviour to the alternative investments.

For the sake of the argument, let us assume that investors demand a 15 per cent overall yield from the stock and that the company has just paid a 5 per cent dividend (i.e. $1.85 per share). Because we know that the price of the stock is $37, we can use Gordon's model to find its expected growth rate:

$$g = \frac{(\$37 \times 0.15 - 1.85)}{(\$37 + 1.85)}$$

$$g = 9.52\% \text{ pa}$$

We can use this implied growth rate to calculate the market's expected prices for this stock on future coupon dates.

Expected Price Environments

1992	=	$40.52	i.e. $37 × 1.0952
1993	=	$44.38	i.e. $37 × 1.0952^2
1994	=	$48.61	i.e. $37 × 1.0952^3
1995	=	$53.24	i.e. $37 × 1.0952^4
1996	=	$58.31	i.e. $37 × 1.0952^5

If the projected growth rates had been maintained the investor's first opportunity to exercise the conversion would have been in 1993. By 1996 the equity price would have triggered the 130 per cent rule, so at these prices the investor would be forced to convert at $55.90 on the coupon date.

Using this projected share price performance it is possible to evaluate the

*Table 14.1 Chiquita Brands International: yield on convertible
if share price performs as expected*

Annual share price growth=9.52 per cent; dividend yield=5 per cent

Coupon date	Expected share price	Exercise in 1993	Exercise in 1994	Exercise in 1995
1991	$37.00	−100.00	−100.00	−100.00
1992	$40.52	7.00	7.00	7.00
1993	$44.38	110.21	7.00	7.00
1994	$48.61		120.05	7.00
1995	$53.21			130.74
		Yields: 8.54%	10.91%	11.97%

*Table 14.2 Chiquita Brands International: yield on convertible
if share price outperforms expectations*

Annual growth=12.5 per cent, dividend yield=5 per cent

Coupon date	Expected share price	Exercise in 1993	Exercise in 1994	Exercise in 1995
1991	$37.00	−100.00	−100.00	-100.00
1992	$41.63	7.00	7.00	7.00
1993	$46.83	115.90	7.00	7.00
1994	$52.68		129.52	7.00
1995	$59.27			137.00
		Yields: 11.21%	13.57%	13.17%

yield on the convertible. Taking the prices shown above, we can find the effect
on yield of converting on any coupon date between 1993 and 1996. For the purposes of the analysis the conversion discount is regarded as a capital gain (the
investor could choose to sell his shares at current market rates immediately after
conversion). So, for example, the 120.05 per cent received from conversion in
1994 is made up of $7 of coupon plus the cash realised from selling the con-
verted shares. At $43 per share the investor can convert $100 of the bond into
100/43 shares. This number of shares can then be sold at the market price of
$48.61.

It should be emphasised that this is only one possible scenario. Suppose the
shares had out-performed the market expectation, rising by an average of 12.5
per cent per annum as shown in Table 14.2.

Notice that the overall yield on the convertible to 1995 is actually lower than the yield to 1994. This is because the strength of the share price triggers the 130 per cent call rule, so the conversion in 1995 is done at $55.90 not $59.27.

Clearly the amount that an investor is willing to pay for a conversion feature will depend on his attitude to the stock in question and the level of conversion premium. In option terms these variables would be described as the stock's volatility and its out of the money factor.

Option Based Valuation Techniques

The owner of a convertible bond has the right to buy shares at a prearranged price. If the convertible has a 130 per cent call feature then the issuer is able to force conversion. As the share price rises above the conversion price the value of the conversion feature will increase. The maximum value that the conversion feature can have is dictated by the 130 per cent rule.

As can be seen from Figure 14.2 the risk–reward profile of the convertible resembles a bull spread options strategy. This should not be surprising, the convertible is, after all, two call options on the share price – one bought by the investor at the conversion price, the other written by him and bought by the issuer at 130 per cent of the conversion price.

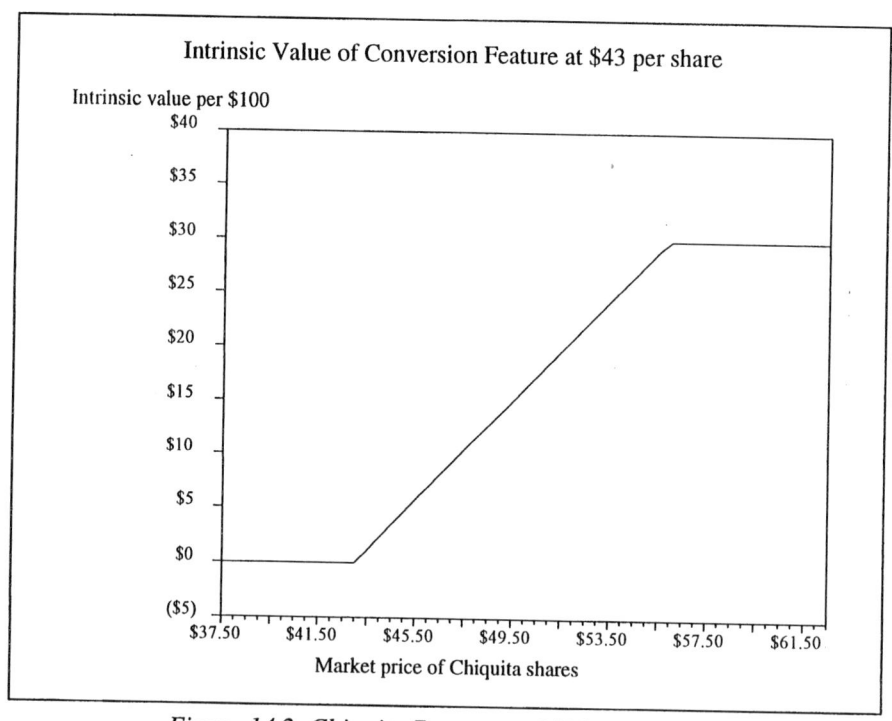

Figure 14.2 Chiquita 7 per cent, 2001 convertible

It follows that convertibles can be valued using option techniques, the key subjective input being the volatility of the stock in question. The price of the convertible is made up of the price of an ordinary bond with a 7 per cent coupon plus the premium paid to buy a call option on shares at the conversion price minus the premium received from writing a call option at 130 per cent of the conversion price.

Net Asset Value (NAV)

One other stock valuation technique can sometimes be important. It is particularly relevant when evaluating investment trusts and takeover targets. The NAV attempts to measure the value of a company in terms of its assets and liabilities. Intangible assets are excluded, only those assets that can be sold are valued. If a company's share price is below its implied net asset value then it is probably undervalued and may be the victim of a takeover bid.

NAV based analysis lay behind the spate of leveraged buy-out activity in the late 1980s. Smaller companies bid for larger concerns using large amounts of debt finance, the intention being to sell the constituent parts shortly after the acquisition. If the target company could be bought for less than its net asset value, the bidding company should be able to realise a profit from the deal. Unfortunately for some of the acquirers, assets were often valued at current market levels. This could prove very different from the prices actually achievable, particularly in view of the fact that they often had to be sold off quickly, if the huge debt mountain was to be serviced.

Technical Analysis

As well as the evaluation tools outlined above, technical analysis is popular amongst investors. Few institutional investors buy stocks purely because of technical factors, but they do pay regard to price patterns when it comes to choosing an appropriate time to invest.

Dominant Themes

As has been stressed throughout this section, investors will not normally rely on any single evaluation technique when deciding which stocks to follow. Instead they make their judgements based on a constellation of factors, which, taken together, point towards a stock's value being under- or over-discounted in the price.

Having said this there is often a single, dominant theme that guides the decision-making process for any particular stock. The analysis may reveal the high calibre of its management, strong dividend growth or a PE ratio below its sector. Whatever it may be, stock selectors will tend to follow stocks that have one, very strong, fundamental advantage, rather than several, fairly slender ones.

MANAGING EQUITY PORTFOLIO EXPOSURE

Portfolio Diversification

Portfolio Diversification and Risk Reduction
The role of asset diversification as a technique for reducing risk is best captured by the well-known banking and insurance maxim: 'Don't put all your eggs in one basket'. By buying many different securities which all perform differently in the same circumstances fund managers can reduce their overall risk. It is important to stress, however, that the more diversified a portfolio becomes the closer to the average is its overall performance. Fund managers must make a judgement as to how far to diversify, and the extent to which they should aim to select outperforming stocks. Further, a portfolio that is too widely diversified may become difficult to manage, as it becomes harder to buy and sell the small amounts of individual stocks without incurring penal transaction costs. However, we shall see later that index options and futures can be used as a proxy for the portfolio.

Regression Analysis in Portfolio Theory
To measure the effect on a portfolio of the acquisition or disposal of a specific security the fund manager needs to analyse not just the individual volatilities of stocks but also how their performances compare. The correlation coefficient is the statistical tool used for establishing the interdependence of two sets of variables; it can help portfolio managers to predict the impact on their holdings of particular stocks.

In the two illustrations below, historical prices for two stocks are compared.

Stock A	$100.00	$100.02	$100.04	$100.06	$100.08
Stock B	$50.00	$50.01	$50.02	$50.03	$50.04
Portfolio of 100A, 200B	$20,000	$20,004	$20,008	$20,012	$20,016

In this case the two stocks are directly related with respect to price. Their correlation coefficient is 1. A portfolio composed of 100 of stock A and 200 of stock B would have had the same performance as its constituent stocks.

Stock A	$100.00	$100.02	$100.04	$100.06	$100.08
Stock B	$50.00	$49.99	$49.98	$49.97	$49.96
Portfolio of 100A, 200B	$20,000	$20,000	$20,000	$20,000	$20,000

Here the two stocks are inversely related with respect to price and have a correlation coefficient of –1. A portfolio composed of 100 of stock A and 200 of stock B would have immunised the fund holder from the specific price risk of the constituent stocks.

Of course, in practice, the correlation coefficient between two stocks (or any individual stock and the underlying index) is normally less than direct. The correlation coefficient for completely independent variables is 0. The strength of the statistical relationship is defined by how close the coefficient is to 1 (or −1).

Remember also that regression analysis merely looks at the relationship between prices, it tells us nothing about the causes of that relationship. Prices that have displayed strong correlative characteristics in the past will not necessarily continue to do so in the future. Having said this, regression analysis, when combined with an element of judgement, can be a valuable tool for fund managers seeking to control their exposure to stock price movements.

Using Regression Analysis to Structure a Portfolio

We have seen that for two stocks whose prices vary inversely (i.e. have a correlation coefficient of −1), it is possible entirely to eliminate the price risk on a portfolio that is composed of them. In practice, though, stock price movements will interrelate to some extent, but they will also move independently. It can be shown statistically that whenever the correlation coefficient between two stocks is less than 1, the price sensitivity of a portfolio can be lower than for the stocks individually.

By way of example, consider the following situation. An investor is attempting to determine the maximum risk-adjusted return for his portfolio. He identifies five possible future environments and to each of these he attaches a probability. He then looks at his expected return from holding stocks A or B. This is simply the projected return in each environment weighted by the likelihood of its occurrence.

With the aid of some statistical analysis, he can then find both the expected return on his portfolio and its expected volatility. In the table below the returns on stock A and B are equally volatile (2 per cent). Stock B, however, has a higher expected return (at 12.9 per cent) than stock A (12 per cent). It might be thought, therefore, that there are no grounds for adding stock A to the portfolio. But as can be seen below, this is not necessarily the case. In fact, with an equal amount of stocks A and B in the portfolio, overall risk is reduced.

Expected return for A:	12.00%	Volatility for A:	2.00%
Expected return for B:	12.90%	Volatility for B:	2.00%
Expected return for portfolio:	12.45%	Volatility for P:	1.84%
A&B correlation coefficient:	0.7		

Here the correlation coefficient is 0.7 between A and B; the fact that the price relationship is less than direct has made it possible to reduce the risk. The expected return of the portfolio is found by taking the yield in each possible environment of each constituent stock, weighted by contribution. This gives a series of overall yields in the various environments. By multiplying each of

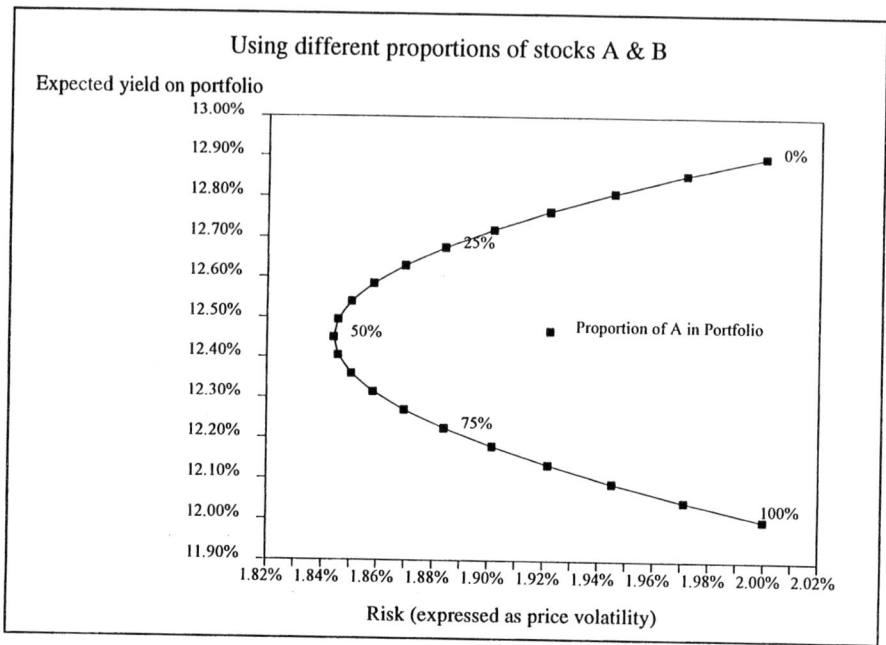

Figure 14.3 Expected risk–reward of portfolio

these projected yields by its likelihood of occurrence and summing the results we can arrive at the expected return of the portfolio.

The investor has a lower expected return than he would have had, had he invested solely in stock A (i.e. 12.45 per cent against 12.90 per cent). On the other hand, the overall risk of his portfolio has been reduced by his buying some of each stock (from 2 per cent to 1.84 per cent).

We can calculate his risk–reward profile for different portfolios constructed out of stocks A and B (see figure 14.3). The appropriate risk–reward structure for an individual investor's portfolio lies somewhere along this curve. Precisely what proportions of each asset he should hold will depend on his particular attitude to the risk–reward relationship.

Using Regression to Structure Multiple Asset Portfolios

Our examples have shown how regression analysis can be used to structure portfolios made up of two assets. The approach can be extended to the structuring of portfolios comprising many assets. The calculations become rather more long-winded, but the principle remains the same – except that this time it is necessary to produce correlation coefficients for every pair of assets in the portfolio! With only thirty securities, this equates to 435 separate coefficients, with a hundred there are 4950. Fortunately, with the aid of a computer, the calculations are relatively easy to perform.

254

Indexation

What is Indexation?

Formally defined, indexation is a fund management technique whereby the fund is structured so that its performance corresponds to movements in some underlying index. The indexation process takes diversification to its logical conclusion: fund managers are attempting to hedge out every non-specific risk in their portfolio by judicious stock selection.

For indexed funds, the extent to which the fund diverges from the index is known as a tracking error. Funds are structured to rise or fall in line with their underlying index, so it is vital to understand how the index price is determined if we are to establish which index it is appropriate to track.

Principles of Index Construction

The first point to make about all indexes is that they are a partial interpretation of a market's performance. No matter how carefully constructed an index may be, it can only reflect the price behaviour of its constituent stocks weighted by a fixed proportion. As volumes traded in each stock vary every day and prices for equities are not at all homogeneous, a mere sample of stocks cannot completely reflect the change in capitalisation of an entire market.

Having said this, indexes provide the only basis for measuring the systematic risk in these markets, and do maintain a close relationship with elements of the market. It is therefore vital to understand the construction of specific indexes. The best that investors can hope for is to understand the uniquely distorted picture of the market that each index provides.

Index Construction Methods

All stock indexes are composed in an essentially similar way. First, a number of stocks are selected, or sampled, to represent the universe of stock being modelled. Next, each of these stocks is assigned a weighting, a number between 0 per cent and 100 per cent according to its importance. The total of all the weightings is of course 100 per cent. Each stock's price is multiplied by its weighting to arrive at a total price for the index portfolio. Finally this price is divided by a base value for the index. This may have occurred in the past or can be a completely arbitrary number. In either case the effect is to translate the portfolio into an intuitively meaningful, percentage equivalent of its base value price.

Price-Weighted Indexes

The simplest form of index takes a straight average of the prices for its constituent stocks. No regard is paid to their respective levels of capitalisation. The FT Index of thirty stocks and the Nikkei 225 are constructed in this way, as is the Dow Jones 30 Industrials Stock Average (DJIA), arguably the world's most

255

widely monitored index. The DJIA comprises the thirty leading blue-chip stocks, primarily manufacturing concerns but also some service companies.

Price-weighted averages provide a useful snapshot answer to the question, 'How did the market perform', and are easy to track (the investor simply spends an equal amount on each constituent stock). However, they tend to be weighted much more towards large industrial concerns and many fund managers see them as presenting too distortive a picture for their purposes. Apart from the Nikkei-225, the US Major Market Index (MMI) of 20 leading stocks is the only price-weighted index to be actively traded on futures and options markets.

Market-Weighted Indexes

An index will approximate more closely to the market the greater the number of stocks contained in the basket. But as the number of stocks sampled increases, the variations in their relative importance to the overall market become more marked. The advent of computer assisted evaluation has made it practicable to introduce indexes that reflect the different capitalisation of their constituent stocks. Many of the most popular indexes use this approach, including among others the FTSE 100 (known as the Footsie), the S&P500 and Hong Kong's Hang Seng index.

In each case constituent stocks are weighted according to the total book value of its shares outstanding, then multiplied by the share price, before being divided by a base value to arrive at the index price. In effect, each company's contribution to the index is based on its total market value at current prices.

Unweighted Geometric Averages

The Value Line Composite Index, an unweighted average of around 1700 US stocks, is the only major index to use geometric averaging. As its title implies it aims to measure the overall direction of the market. Instead of taking absolute share values it uses price relatives to determine changes in the index. Stock prices are expressed as a percentage of their original value in the index. All of these percentages are multiplied together. The nth root of this product (where n represents the number of price relatives) is, then, the geometric average of the price relatives. This is then multiplied by the base figure to arrive at an index value.

An unavoidable side effect of this indexing approach is that it understates price increases. Consider, for instance, a basket of two stocks each priced at $100 at the start of trading. By the end of the day stock A is trading at $98 and stock B at $102. A price-weighted index would be unchanged and we would intuitively expect this to be the case, especially if the two had equal numbers of shares outstanding. However, with a geometric index this is not the case. The price relatives for A and B are 0.98 and 1.02 respectively. Their product is therefore 0.9996, and the geometric average has fallen from 1 to 0.9998 (the square root of the product).

Composite Indexes

The final, important index category is the composite one. A composite index is, as the term suggests, an index of other indexes. They may be either price- or market-weighted. An example of a price-weighted composite would be the Dow-Jones 65 Composite Average (comprising Dow-Jones's 30 Industrials, 20 Transportation and 15 Utility averages). A widely followed market-weighted composite is the New York Stock Exchange's Composite Index (comprising NYSE's Industrial, Transportation, Utilities and Finance indexes).

The NASDAQ National Market System Composite Index is not really a composite index at all. It is in fact a market-weighted index of every single stock traded on NASDAQ's OTC electronic dealing system. As such it provides highly accurate information on the market risks of smaller companies.

One other index worth mentioning is the Wilshire 5000 equity index. This market-weighted index is the most broadly based US equity sample available. Its price represents the total value in billions of dollars of all NYSE, American Stock Exchange and OTC stocks for which quotations are available.

Table 14.3 A and B index performance

Stock A (5m $1 shares)	$100.00	$100.50	$101.00	$101.50	$102.00
Stock B (20m $1 shares)	$50.00	$50.10	$50.20	$50.30	$50.40
Price-weighted method	100.00	100.40	100.80	101.20	101.60
Geometric Average	100.00	100.35	100.70	101.05	101.40
Market-weighted	100.00	100.30	100.60	100.90	101.20

Pricing the Theoretical Index Future

The buyer of an index future owns a composite asset whose price is determined by a basket of stocks. He does not own the stocks themselves; he receives no dividend and has no voting rights on the underlying stocks. The theoretical price of an index future is therefore found using the following formula:

$$IF = (1 + Rt) \sum_{i=1}^{i=n} W_i P_i \sum_{i=1}^{i=n} W_i D_i$$

Where

IF = Theoretical index futures price
R = Riskless rate of interest to the contract delivery date
t = Time (in years) to the contract delivery date
W_i = Weighting of stock i in index
P_i = Price of stock i
D_i = Dividend paid on stock i before delivery date

In other words the theoretical index futures price is equivalent to the cost of financing the constituent stocks at current prices less any dividends that may be payable.

Index Prices and Dividend Payments

In almost every case the price of an index reflects only the quoted price for its constituent stocks. As such they do not reflect the effect of dividend payments except in terms of the impact these have on the share price. One important exception to this rule is the Amex Market Value Index (AMVI). The AMVI is a market-weighted index measuring the performance of around 800 issues quoted on the American Stock Exchange, including shares, ADRs and equity warrants for smaller to medium sized companies. In the AMVI all dividends are assumed to be reinvested into the index.

The fact that indexes (apart from the AMVI) do not include dividends is one of the keys to the arbitrage activity performed by the investment banks, which is known as program trading or index arbitrage.

How an Index Arbitrage Works

Consider the MMI future. This is a price-weighted index of 20 leading US companies. Assuming the contract reaches delivery in three months, T-Bill rates are 10 per cent and 2 per cent is payable in dividends before delivery, we can easily calculate the relationship between the index value and the future. So, if the MMI is currently at 500, the implied value of the MMI futures contract will be:

$$IF(MMI) = 500 \times (1 + 0.1 \times 0.25) - 0.02 \times 500$$
$$IF(MMI) = 502.50$$

Now suppose that the future is actually trading at 503.00. By buying the same amount of each of the 20 stocks in the MMI and simultaneously selling futures an arbitrager can lock into the differential.

The arbitrager sells 80 futures at 503.00 and spends $10m acquiring the equivalent amount of the 20 stocks. Their $10m cost is financed for three months at 10 per cent, requiring him to pay $250,000 in interest on the delivery date. He earns $200,000 in dividend income while he holds the stocks, so his net financing cost at delivery is $50,000.

We know that at delivery the index price and the futures price will converge. What happens to the index price makes no difference to his profit. But suppose that the index has increased to 550 by delivery. The arbitrager sells his stocks and realises the 10 per cent profit of $1m. He buys back the futures realising a loss on them of $940,000 (80 contracts × 47 points × $250).

Overall, he has locked in a profit of $10,000 (i.e. $1m – $940,000 – $50,000). This would be the same no matter what value the index reached. For instance an index value of 450 at delivery, would realise a loss on the stocks of $1m, but this would be offset by a $1,060,000 profit on the futures. Taken with the $50,000 net financing cost the profit is still $10,000.

Refining the Process

The arbitrage described above is not completely without risk. Dividends may be cut or suspended altogether. The cost of maintaining the futures position might outstrip the arbitrage profit.

The cashflow effects of dividends can be factored into the arbitrage to provide a more precise pricing tool. The 2 per cent in dividends that is paid out on stocks over the three months will be available for reinvestment. Say the average life of the dividend stream is 30 days: assuming a riskless reinvestment rate of 9 per cent over the next three months, the value of the dividend stream at delivery is actually 2.03 per cent (i.e. 2% × (1 + 0.09 × 60/360)).

When this effect is factored into the implied futures calculation it is clear that the theoretical futures price is, in fact:

$$\text{IF(MMI)} = 500 \times (1 + 0.1 \times 0.25) - 0.0203 \times 500$$
$$\text{IF(MMI)} = 502.35$$

One way that the leading investment banks derive superior returns from their program trading operations is by building this time value of money effect for dividend streams into their valuation models. By keeping a careful watch on dividend payment dates for the constituent companies they can perform arbitrage operations at the times when the average life of dividends suggests this effect will be most favourable.

If they are performing a cash and carry operation (i.e. buying the stocks and selling the future), the effect will be most beneficial when the average life of the dividends is short relative to the period to delivery and interest rates are high. For a reverse cash and carry the opposite environment is preferred.

Index Tracking and Dividend Payments

Index tracker funds aim to eliminate the non-systematic risks of their portfolios by constructing portfolios that replicate the underlying index. Even if tracker fund managers were able to purchase every stock in the index in exactly the right quantities, they would still be unable to replicate its performance exactly. This is because all of the popular indexes ignore the effect of dividend payments.

Consider, for instance, the effect on the index of a share quoted at $50 just before a $1 dividend is due. After the $1 distribution, the price of the share falls to $49, reflecting the dividend payment. The owner of the share is happy because he has received the money that offsets this share price fall. But the owner of the index receives no such distribution, instead he sees the value of his position deteriorate according to the weighted effect of the share price fall.

This means that, at certain times of the year, the performance of an index, and that of its constituent stocks, will diverge. In the USA, for instance, many dividends are paid quarterly, and occur in the greatest concentration in February, May, August and November. For the index tracker, who is running a diversified fund to mirror a stock index, the dividend effect normally means that his replicated portfolio should perform better than the underlying index over time.

Stock Sampling and Tracking Errors

Index tracker funds are rarely able to mirror their index precisely. The logistics and transaction costs involved in managing a fund comprising each of the stocks in the S&P500, weighted by its contribution to the index, makes this impractical for all but the very largest funds.

Instead, most index trackers aim to construct a portfolio out of a much smaller, representative basket. Typically they will hold, say, thirty to fifty equities to reflect the sectoral and capitalisation composition of the index. Inevitably, therefore, there will be many occasions when the stock sample held fails to reflect changes in value in the benchmark index.

Such differences, measured in percentage terms, are known as tracking errors. Tracking errors are one of the key parameters for measuring an indexed fund's performance. They can be reduced by increasing the number of stocks held, but, as has been already explained, other considerations may limit the extent to which this can be done.

Beta Risk

What is Beta?

The risk characteristics of an individual stock can be analysed by studying its price volatility over time. This may be compared with the volatility of the entire stock market, which can then be referenced against a commonly accepted stock index.

It is important to recognise that a stock's beta is not a measure of its correlation to an index. It tells the fund manager nothing about the counter-cyclical characteristics of any stock and should not therefore be used as an analytical tool for portfolio diversification.

Expressed mathematically a stock's beta is its estimated volatility divided by the volatility of the index. The beta coefficient for an individual security describes its volatility relationship to the stock market index.

For instance, the beta of the S&P500 index of US stocks is taken as 1.00. A stock with a beta coefficient of 1.25 is expected to rise or fall in price by 12.5 per cent for every 10 per cent change in the S&P500. A stock with a beta of 0.5 will only vary by 5 per cent, given a 10 per cent change in the S&P500. Cash, in the form of the riskless rate of interest, the T-bill yield, is assumed to have a beta of 0.

High and Low Beta Stocks

Stocks with inherently high betas are considered riskier investments. High beta stock categories are the fast-growing, volatile companies, typically including sectors such as high technology and consumer durables. Investors will require correspondingly higher yields from such assets to compensate them for the higher risks involved in owning them.

Stocks with lower betas include many blue-chip equities and sectors with stable profit patterns such as utilities. These will be more attractive to conservative investors for whom regular dividend payments are perhaps more important than rapid capital growth.

Beta Risk for Portfolios

Just as the beta coefficient defines the riskiness of an individual asset, so betas can be used to monitor the riskiness of the portfolio as a whole. Statistical techniques can be used to find the volatility of the portfolio. As with individual stocks this can be divided by the index's volatility to arrive at a portfolio beta risk number.

Beta for Fully Diversified Portfolios

In conjunction with regression analysis, a portfolio's beta risk provides a ready mechanism for establishing the performance of any fund management strategy. Fund managers can use the two techniques to ask themselves two important questions. Firstly: how closely will the performance of my portfolio correspond to my benchmark index? Secondly: how leveraged is my portfolio, with respect to the index?

The first task for the fund manager is to determine the desired strength of the relationship between his portfolio and the index. Index trackers will attempt to construct portfolios that, against the index, have correlation coefficients as close as possible to 1. More aggressive fund managers may place less emphasis on this exactitude, but will still wish to monitor the relationship, for reasons of performance measurement as well as for hedging purposes.

Next, the fund manager will try to devise an appropriate beta for his portfolio. An ordinary indexed fund will have a beta of 1.00, and according to modern portfolio theorists, ought to increase in value by 1 per cent for every 1 per cent rise in the index. Index options and futures can be used to alter the leverage of the portfolio.

Using Beta in Hedging Programmes

Index futures are extremely useful for fund managers seeking to control their systematic risks. We saw in the discussion on beta how a fully diversified portfolio can be insured against the risk of falls in the index price. Beta can similarly be used to tilt the risk–reward characteristics of the portfolio depending on the fund manager's view of index performance.

Knowing that the beta of the stock index is taken as 1, index futures can be used effectively to change the market risk profile of the fund. Consider a $100m diversified fund, linked to the S&P500, which has a beta of 1.0. Now suppose the fund manager is confident that the index will fall from 250, its current level.

If he sells 800 (i.e. $100m worth) of S&P500 futures he can hedge against this risk.

Suppose the index falls by 10 per cent to 225. The fund manager has a book loss on his portfolio by 10 per cent, it is now worth $90m. Against this he takes a profit on the index future of 500 ticks per contract (25 points × 200 ticks/point). On 800 contracts this is a profit of $10m ($25 × 500 ticks × 800 contracts).

Of course all this assumes that the stocks in the fund manager's portfolio change by the same amount as the index. Stock index futures provide no kind of protection against non-systematic risks.

Using Betas in Risk Management

The disadvantage for the fund manager is that by protecting against losses using futures he also gives up the potential of any upside move in the index. In practice, few will wish to do this. Options on the index provide for this potential at a cost, but the dynamic use of futures is a popular alternative.

Tilted fund management techniques aim to buy and sell futures to adjust the portfolio's beta according to the manager's view on market conditions. Limits to the beta are set to define the speculativeness of the fund. For the $100m fund above the minimum beta is set at 0 and the maximum at 1.5. This fund manager also decides that his view neutral position will have a beta of 1. Let us assume, that in this case the fund manager is mildly bearish on the index. He sets his beta to 0.875 by selling 100 futures. Now any 1 per cent decline in the index will affect his fund's performance by only 0.875 per cent.

The index does indeed fall, by just 1 per cent to 247.5. The $1m book loss is offset by a profit of $125,000 on the future. So the overall value of his portfolio is reduced to $99.125m.

The fund manager was expecting this mild correction and now believes that the index will perform strongly. He decides to raise the beta of his portfolio to 1.25. To do this he has to buy back the 100 futures together with a further 200 contracts at 247.5. Again he is proved correct, this time the index improves by 2 per cent to 252.45. The total value of his stocks has now increased to $100.98m. He also has a profit on the new futures position of $495,000 ($25 × 99 ticks × 200 contracts). Add to these the profit from the previous hedge and we have a total fund value of $101.6m.

Of course these examples show what happens in an ideal world when prices move as expected. The hedges could just as easily have shown losses. But the logic of the dynamic approach is that, because the target beta reflects the level of confidence that the manager has in his prediction, he will place larger hedges when he is more sure what will happen. If his judgement is at least reasonably sound, then over time hedging losses should be outweighed by hedging profits. The fund manager thus has the capability to use futures to protect against adverse price movements without being forced to compromise his overall preformance.

Tilted fund management is the logical extension of the trend towards indexation. Known in the trade as 'chocolate chip' or 'stem ginger' funds (as against plain vanilla funds), the manager aims to outperform the market by tilting his diversified portfolio according to his view of market conditions.

Portfolio Insurance
The ease with which the beta can be adjusted for any portfolio by modifying an index futures position led to a demand in the 1980s for indexed funds with a guaranteed minimum value.

Portfolio insurance is a form of retrospective hedging. Targets are set for the price sensitivity of a portfolio given certain trigger changes in the value of the index.

In Table 14.4 a $100m portfolio is insured by means of a rule that says that futures should be sold against 10 per cent of fund for every 2 per cent decline in the index. It can be seen that this allows the fund to lock into a worst case value of $89m if the index falls below 80 per cent of its current value.

The results shown are idealistic, assuming that the index falls consistently. There will, in practice, be significant hedging costs, especially when markets are volatile. To illustrate this effect consider what happens as the index falls from 98 to 96 and then rises to 98 before falling to 96 again. The portfolio insurer sells 100 futures at 96, buys 100 futures at 98 before selling the 100 futures at 96 again. He is back where he started, but he has also realised a loss of $200,000 (i.e. (96-98) × $1000 × 100 contracts).

Table 14.4 $100m portfolio insured fund

	Index	Fund value ($000s)	Target beta	Futures sold (index × $1000)	Fund P&L ($000s)	Insured fund value ($000s)
Current level	**100.00**	**10,000**	**1.0**	**0**	**0**	**10,000**
	98.00	9,800	0.9	100	0	9,800
	96.00	9,600	0.8	100	20	9,620
	94.00	9,400	0.7	100	60	9,460
	92.00	9,200	0.6	100	120	9,320
	90.00	9,000	0.5	100	200	9,200
	88.00	8,800	0.4	100	300	9,100
	86.00	8,600	0.3	100	420	9,020
	84.00	8,400	0.2	100	560	8,960
	82.00	8,200	0.1	100	720	8,920
Insured level	**80.00**	**8,000**	**0.0**	**100**	**900**	**8,900**
	78.00	7,800	0.0	0	1,100	8,900
	76.00	7,600	0.0	0	1,300	8,900
	74.00	7,400	0.0	0	1,500	8,900

Was Portfolio Insurance to Blame for Black Monday?

Many portfolio insurers came unstuck in October 1987 and have widely been held to be at least partly accountable for the severity of the Crash. The unprecedented speed with which prices began to collapse on Black Monday forced the portfolio insurers to liquidate their positions rapidly. This they did by selling index futures.

Traders, seeing the index falling, proceeded to mark stocks down. Meanwhile index arbitragers, many of whose decisions were being executed automatically on computer, sold baskets of stocks against purchases in the futures market. As stocks fell again the portfolio insurers were forced to sell futures again, a vicious circle was set up and prices plummeted.

Circuit-breakers

In the years since, portfolio insurance has been much less popular, and futures regulators have initiated a system of circuit-breakers to prevent a recurrence. As the term implies, these are designed to break the link between stock and futures markets that proved so disastrous in 1987. Essentially what happens is that index futures markets close down automatically when volatility exceeds a certain level.

Beta for Targeted Portfolios

The less diversified is a portfolio, the less relevant is beta as a predictor of future returns. However, it can still be an important analytical weapon in the aggressive fund manager's arsenal. Looked at conceptually, the beta factor is a measuring of the leverage within the portfolio to market movements. The aggressive fund manager will be unlikely to benefit from a 1 per cent index rise by exactly 2 per cent if he has a beta of 2. However, the market related (i.e. systematic) improvement in his fund should (if the index represents the market accurately) equate to 2 per cent. In other words, the extent to which his portfolio's value changes by more or less than 2 per cent will have been based on the specific quality of his stocks.

Hedging Systematic Risk via the Index

Since index price movements can be hedged via futures, an active fund manager can use his fund's beta to lock into only the non-systematic risk element of his portfolio. Suppose for instance, such a fund manager believes the S&P500 is due for a severe correction. On the other hand he is confident that his own stocks will outperform the rest of the market over the period.

Rather than having to sell his stocks, the fund manager can sell index futures to cover just the systematic portion of his risk. If his $100m portfolio has a beta of 2, it would be appropriate for him to sell $200m worth of index futures.

RISK MANAGEMENT STRATEGIES

Table 14.5 shows premiums payable on puts and calls on the S&P500 index at the Index and Option Market subsidiary of the Chicago Mercantile Exchange.

Table 14.5 Options on S&P500 June futures (CME/IOM)

	$500 × premium Future = 448.35	
Option strikes	Call	Put
440	14.00	5.75
445	10.90	7.65
450	7.75	9.90
455	5.40	13.05
460	4.00	15.50
465	2.40	18.15

Source: Wall Street Journal – 13 April 1993

Buy ten 445 calls: write calls – five @ 455, three @ 460, two @ 465

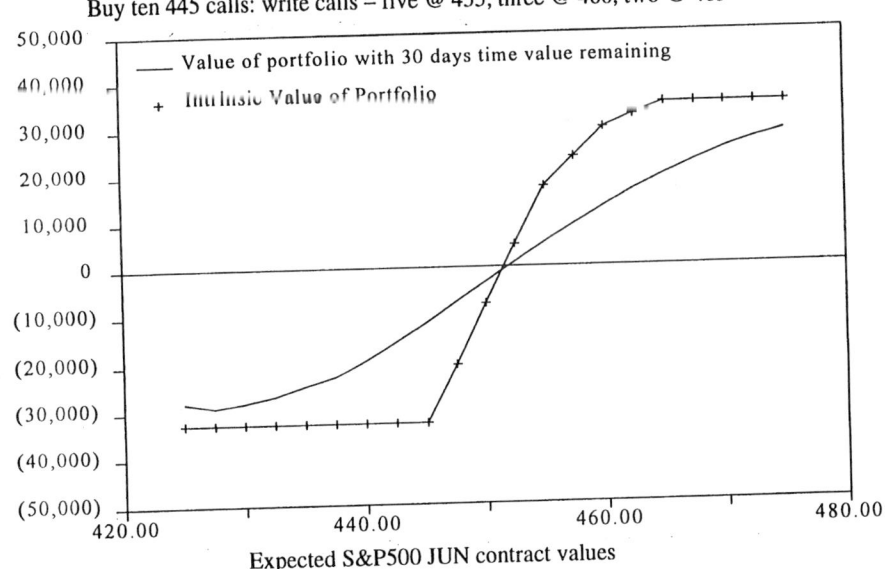

Figure 14.4 Bull spread combination strategy

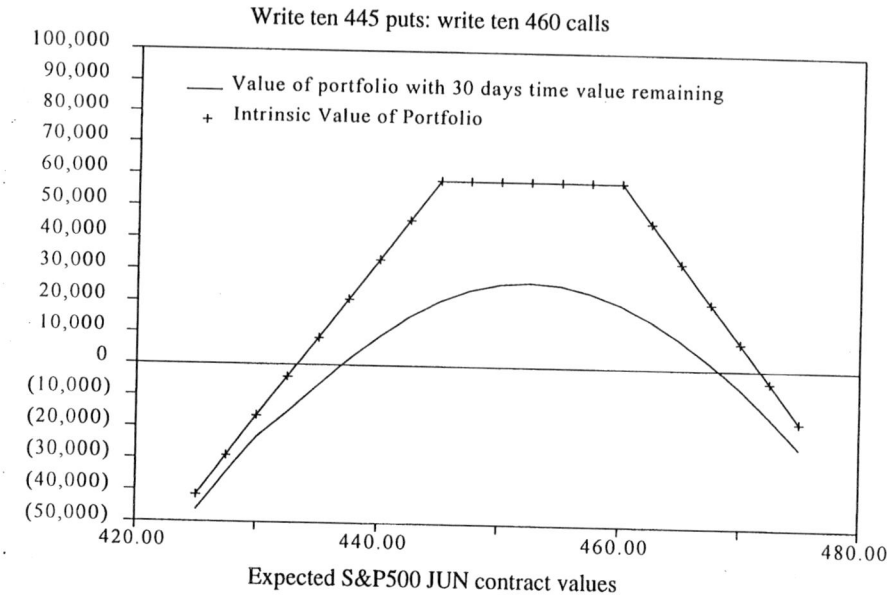

Figure 14.5 Contra-volatility strategy

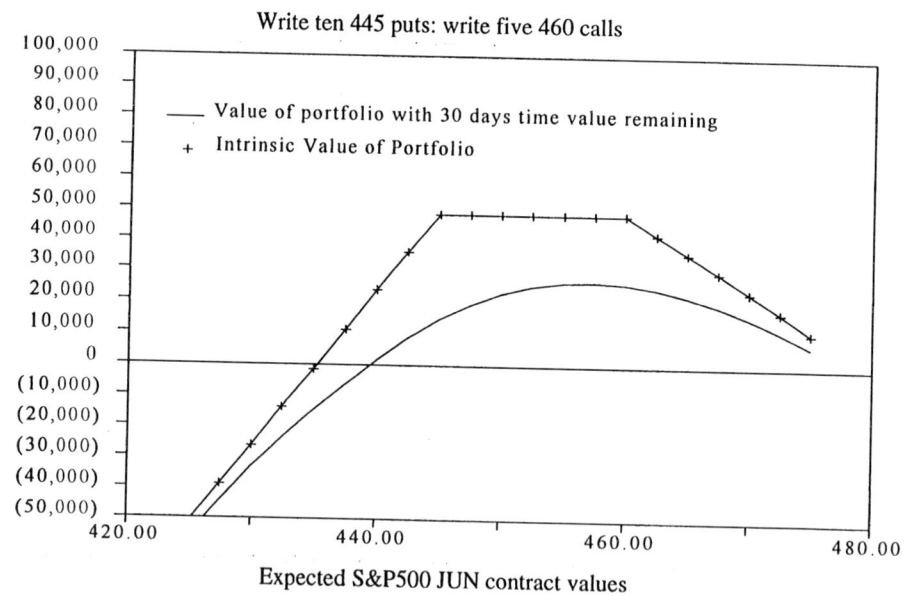

Figure 14.6 Bullish contra-volatility strategy

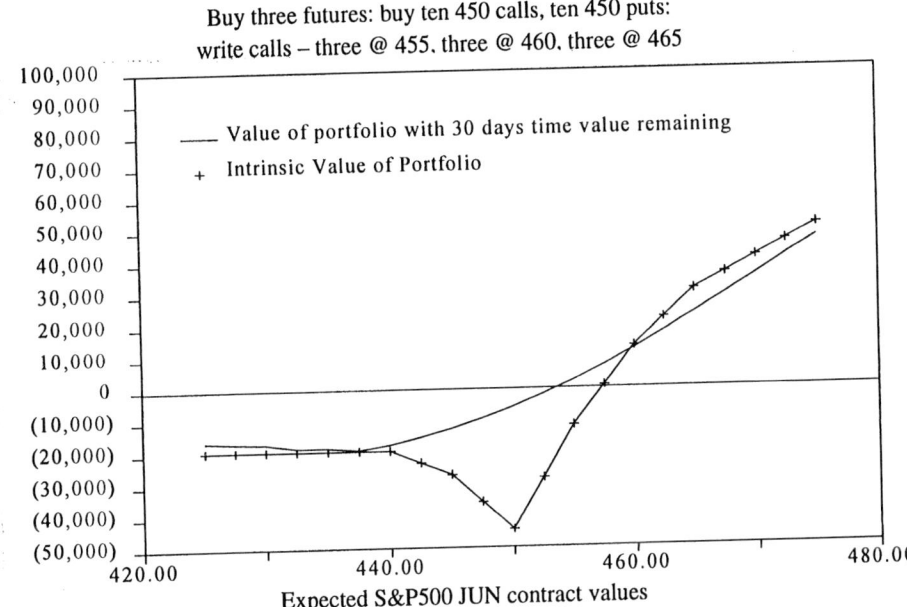

Figure 14.7 *Bullish pro-volatility combination strategy*

15: The ConTROL Methodology

Throughout this book I have stressed the shared characteristics of the different financial markets while looking at the major sectors in detail. The reader will by now be familiar with the key principles that govern pricing in the financial industry. But as this philosophy of interconnectedness, assisted by improved technology and higher quality information, permeates the markets, it is becoming increasingly difficult to operate effectively. As market anomalies become ever more obscure, the problem of identifying and exploiting risk–reward misperceptions gets increasingly complicated. But this is the fundamental task of any market participant, be they trader, arbitrager or risk manager.

In this final chapter, I have applied many of the principles already discussed to assist the participant in resolving this issue. The approach adopted does not attempt to provide any magic solutions regarding which assets should be purchased and which sold. Rather, the emphasis is on providing an analytical framework to crystallise the relative usefulness of various strategies given explicit assumptions. Remember, however, the computing maxim, GIGO (garbage in, garbage out); the model is only as accurate as the assumptions on which it is predicated.

For expository simplicity the approach is couched in terms that relate directly to risk managers, but its basic steps are equally applicable to other kinds of market participants.

In the succeeding sections the five key elements of the ConTROL methodology – Conditions, Tactics, Refinement, Operation, Lifespan – are examined, each in turn. By following them the student will gain insight into the principles and practices of risk management. In this explanation a fictional commodity, the brick, is used, but the principles can of course be applied to the entire universe of financial commodities. A summary of the main elements is given below.

- *Conditions*   The first, and most vital stage in the risk management process is diagnostic. This section provides guidelines on identifying explicit and implicit exposures and formulating a market view to isolate unacceptable risk.
- *Tactics*   Once the exposure's characteristics have been identified, the risk manager is in a position to formulate a strategy. This section discusses the major, market based hedging alternatives and their rationales, emphasising the importance of formulating clear hedging objectives.

● *Refinement*   Active risk managers are seeking superior hedging performance. Passive hedgers want to limit the cost. But how can
they establish that their strategies are the best for the circumstances when they cannot possibly know how they will turn
out? This section proposes a technique for evaluating the cost-
benefit of risk management strategies using a measurement of
expected value.

● *Operation*   No matter how well structured the hedging programme, poor
implementation can unhinge it. This section reviews the costs
and pitfalls involved in deal execution.

● *Lifespan*   Circumstances change, so do perceptions. What seemed unlikely
now seems probable, what was relevant now looks wrong. This
section stresses the importance of monitoring exposures over
time, and maintaining hedge flexibility.

CONDITIONS

Sources of Financial Exposure

Exposure exists because of volatility in financial markets. Uncertainty, about the
cost of future liabilities or the level of future income streams, undermines business performance by making it difficult to forecast profitability. The less control
an institution has over its break-evens, the harder it becomes to justify projects.

A wide range of financial exposures can be managed using market based techniques. There are four main types: interest rate, commodity, currency and equity.
In today's global, financial marketplace, their price behaviour is interrelated.
Risk managers need to acquaint themselves with the dynamics of such relationships if they are to hedge successfully.

Identifying the Exposure

The first stage in risk management, often also the most problematic, is to identify accurately the cashflow(s) involved. For corporations this can be a particularly hit-and-miss exercise. Their income is based on revenues, which depend on
sales. Unless theirs is a particularly stable business, perhaps providing a utility
or producing a commodity, the chances are that they will be unable to make an
accurate assessment of exactly what cash they will receive or be required to pay
out at particular times of year.

For financial institutions this is often less of a problem. Although they often do not know the marked-to-market value of their future asset and liability streams, they generally have a fairly clear idea of precisely when such cashflows will become due as well as the market contingencies which will determine their marked-to-market value.

Nevertheless, an essential prerequisite for the success of the risk management programme is to assess this underlying exposure as accurately as possible. A number of key questions have to be addressed:

1. WHEN will the projected exposure(s) occur ?
2. What is the MAGNITUDE of the projected exposure(s) ?
3. What CONTINGENCIES affect the size and occurrence of the projected exposure(s) ?
4. How MATERIAL is the projected exposure(s) in the context of the overall position ?

Cashflows and Timing

Answering questions 1 and 2 is relatively straightforward when looking at cashflow based financial instruments, like bonds. For corporate planners though, payback dates and future cost obligations are not known. Nevertheless, they will still be able to establish a range of anticipated outcomes and from this build up a likely cashflow scenario. Most corporate treasurers, for example, know that at certain times of the year they are likely to be either short or long of cash. They also usually have a reasonable idea of the approximate size of such imbalances.

It is absolutely vital to get as accurate a picture of the underlying exposure as possible if it is to be risk managed effectively. But many exposures are themselves dependent on events that are outside the control of the risk manager. We therefore need to look in more detail at the issues raised in question 3.

Contingent Cashflows

When faced with a contingent exposure the hedger must be careful that, in hedging against the risks of its occurrence, he does not expose himself to new risks should the anticipated exposure not happen.

Take the example of a US corporate that submits a DM20m tender for a building contract in Germany. It has a $/DM exposure on the portion of the bid that cannot be financed in Deutschmarks, say DM5m. This figure might include the cost of purchasing commodities, raw materials that cannot be acquired locally as well as the contractor's profit. The corporate will wish to protect itself against a diminution in the dollar equivalent of this amount, such as would occur if the dollar strengthened against the Deutschmark.

Supposing the current FX rate stands at $/DM2.0000. The corporate cannot simply sell DM5m against $2.5m. For, if the DM short position is not covered by DM revenues (i.e. the bid is not awarded), he will be left with an open position. This time the risk is that the dollar weakens against the DM, and he is forced to close out at a loss.

The illustration emphasises the fact that a different hedging approach is required when looking at anticipated instead of actual exposure. The possibility of non-occurrence precludes static, futures based strategies. Options based or actively traded strategies are more appropriate.

Materiality

Identifying the materiality of an exposure allows an institution to pinpoint unacceptable risks so that it can formulate strategies for hedging them. A material exposure is defined as one, which in the worst case scenario, would have a significant negative impact on profitability.

By placing individual exposures in the context of the overall balance sheet the risk manager is able to isolate net unacceptable exposures. To do this it is necessary to have some idea of the worst case in terms of the maximum adverse price movement expected. An element of forecasting is therefore required to determine unacceptable risks.

Developing a Market Forecast

If the net exposure includes unacceptable risk, it is necessary to manage it to contain risk at an acceptable level. Developing a market forecast is thus an essential plank of risk management. It is an inescapable part of the process, whether acknowledged or ignored. For this reason it is always preferable to develop a formal market view.

There are many forecasting facilities available as source material. Although none can be relied on, they are useful in the development of a forecasting framework. Lead indicators for the market concerned are a key element in the process. Specific forecasting techniques are discussed elsewhere.

Historic price performance is a starting point for developing a view on future price movements, but the past must always be read with care. Markets that are currently very volatile might be thought to imply a large future price movement, but in practice volatile price behaviour is often followed by a period of stability.

The timing of anticipated price movements will be important in developing a view. The risk manager will need to develop a view through time for each of the future dates on which anticipated cashflows occur.

The final important element in developing a view is the level of certainty about the prediction. A strategy that is appropriate when the price is as expected may be disadvantageous if the price is different. This uncertainty is best expressed by predicting a range of prices for each exposure. A wide range reflects lack of certainty whereas a narrow range implies reasonable confidence about future price movements.

The Implied Market View

Many risk managers do not feel qualified to second-guess the market when developing a view. This is understandable, but is a mistake. The market environment provides a benchmark against which to judge the success of any risk management strategy. If a risk manager always agrees with the market there should never be any incentive to hedge positions.

Current forward rates reflect the market consensus on the future environment. Risk managers can use them to lock into a price for the future. Similarly today's option prices are based on the market consensus for volatility for the periods concerned. Risk managers can lock into this level of uncertainty by buying options.

In pure trading terms the value of any forward or option transaction depends on the correctness with which it prices the future. Hedgers will therefore achieve superior performance if they are able to buy underpriced, and sell overpriced, hedging instruments, while still retaining the integrity of the hedge.

While this is of course true, the hedger must be able to spot such misallocations of value if he is to improve hedging performance. Many will say that as non-professional participants this exceeds their role; it is a speculative activity.

Tilted Hedge Strategies

This need not necessarily be the case if the risk manager has some flexibility in the exposure management process. Rather than attempting to develop a market view that reflects his individual perception of future price performance, the risk manager can attempt to gear performance to his institution's profitability. Hedging may then sometimes underperform as well as outperform the market, but this should be offset by his institution's overall performance.

Take as an example a manufacturer of high technology consumer goods. It is well known that sales for such a company will be adversely affected by high interest rates. A valid hedging strategy might then be to tilt the hedge's performance so that it achieves best results in just such an environment.

The treasurer might decide to sell T-bond futures, even though there is no offsetting cash position. As interest rates rise (and bond prices fall) the value of this position will increase. The position will lose money if rates fall.

Taken on its own, such an action might be seen as speculative. In the context of the company as a whole, however, it is an appropriate risk management exercise. It offsets some of the company's commercial risk.

Another common commercial risk is competitive performance. In a price war, the corporate treasurer of a German company may be able to justify buying dollar futures on the grounds that his major competitors are US based. In other words, there are circumstances where not only the company's own risks, but also any price advantage enjoyed by its competitors, deserve attention.

In this section the importance of differentiating between acceptable and unacceptable exposures has been stressed. The remainder of this chapter addresses how these exposures, once identified, may be risk managed. The examples illustrate that there can be sound risk management arguments in favour of the maintenance of open positions. Hedgers should of course always be wary of such a course of action and ensure that new, unacceptable risks are not posed by an overactive approach.

TACTICS

Establishing Constraints

Having located the source of, and its own sensitivity to, its net financial exposures the risk manager is in a position to devise a hedging strategy. But before designing any strategy the risk manager needs to identify any limitations in dealing activity.

Factors to be considered include business constraints, risk sensitivity, the availability of the desired strategy in the market, and practicalities like transaction costs. Some organisations may have legal, psychological or cultural obstacles to dealing in some instruments, such as might be the case in the futures or options markets.

The Static Hedger's Approach

These will normally depend on the organisation's attitude to risk. If it is an infrequent market participant, the guiding factor is likely to be simplicity. It will seek to structure a hedge that mirrors the risk as closely as possible, and which is automatic in effect. For such participants, a static hedge is usually the best alternative.

This will only work when there is a close correlation between the price behaviour of the hedge and that of the underlying exposure. For this reason static hedgers will usually demand hedging tools that are tailored to their particular needs. The over the counter (OTC) market offers a wide variety of such instruments.

In money markets forward rate agreements (FRAs), interest rate caps, floors, collars, swaps and swaptions are among the hedging instruments available for practically all periods, amounts and – for options – exercise prices. Such instruments offer great flexibility, allowing exposures to be hedged very precisely.

The Dynamic Hedger's Approach

There is, inevitably, a price for such precision. Non-standard instruments will tend to be more illiquid and are generally more expensive than their standardised equivalents. For the static hedger this is easily outweighed by the benefits of flexibility.

For more active participants, however, who regularly rebalance their portfolios as attitudes and circumstances change, liquidity risk is seen as far more significant. The professional and semi-professional risk managers, the so-called dynamic hedgers, will often find that the exchange traded markets are better suited to their requirements.

The fact that futures and exchange traded options tend to be standardised around specific dates, sizes and grades of commodities greatly enhances their tradeability. Trading is focused on just a few contracts per year, with much of the activity often seen with the near-dated future (i.e. the next to reach delivery).

Having said this, they will also trade in OTC markets. Currency options and FRAs for instance are both highly liquid markets, but active hedgers will try, if possible, to buy and sell OTC products with relatively standard specifications, to make it easier to trade the position.

Formulating a Hedging Policy

It is useful to delimit the hedging approach by setting out a formal policy framework. Break-even rates and minimum and maximum hedging proportions should, where possible, be determined. The limitations will depend on the nature of the underlying exposure.

Contingent cashflows, for example, may attract a different hedging policy from known exposures. But no matter how much the overall strategy is predetermined, each material exposure must in the final analysis, be looked at on its own merits. For a corporate, different hedging policies will be relevant for managing currency risk on the profits of a foreign subsidiary than would be appropriate when it is in a competitive bidding process. In both cases contingent cashflows are involved, but whereas with profit repatriation the exact size and timing of the exposures is in question, in the tender to contract situation the dates and amounts are known, what is uncertain is whether or not they will materialise.

In certain situations it may be appropriate to over-hedge an exposure. The hedging committee might, for instance, authorise the risk manager to hedge between 60 per cent and 140 per cent of the underlying exposure. This will allow him to under- or over-hedge a position depending on the prevailing environment. This is a prevalent attitude in financial institutions and some large corporates where the treasury function is regarded as a profit centre in its own right.

The Building Blocks

All exposures must be covered in the market by some combination of spot, forward and option transactions. The task of the risk manager is to match up as closely as possible his view of the market, his risk sensitivities and the strategy for dealing with the exposure, while still retaining flexibility, simplicity and integrity for the hedge.

The 'Brick' Market Environment

In the following pages, some common hedging strategies are discussed using illustrations. The examples use a fictional commodities market, for bricks. Time value of money is ignored to retain their simplicity. Nevertheless the risk management issues raised are identical to those faced by hedgers in the financial sphere.

Example 1 shows sample strategies for static hedging of a known exposure.
Example 2 discusses approaches when hedging a contingent exposure.
Example 3 presents some sample strategies and their risk–reward profiles.

Table 15.1 The brick price environment

$100.00	Spot price
$100.00	3m future price
$1.05	Premium for 99 Call
$0.35	Premium for 100 Call
$0.05	Premium for 101 Call
$0.05	Premium for 99 Put
$0.35	Premium for 100 Put
$1.05	Premium for 101 Put

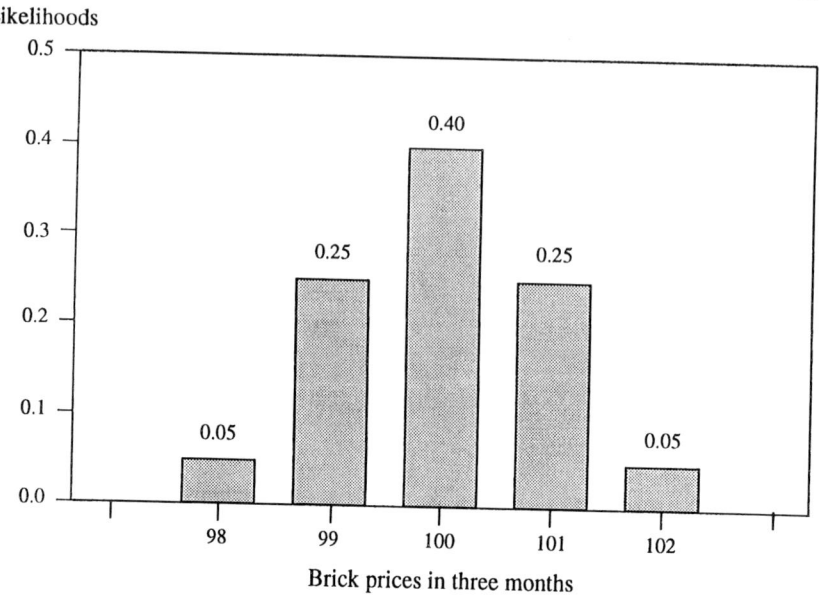

Figure 15.1 Probability distribution implied by market premiums

Example 1: building contractor must buy 1000 tonnes
of bricks in three months.

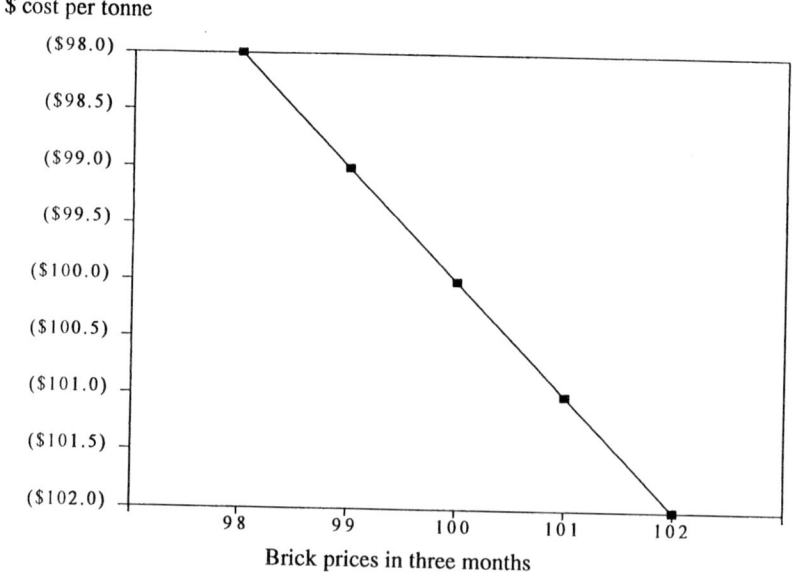

Figure 15.2 Projected cost of bricks in three months

Basic choices
Strategy A: buy brick futures today @100
Strategy B: buy bricks at spot rate prevailing in three months
Strategy C: buy at the money call option @ $0.35

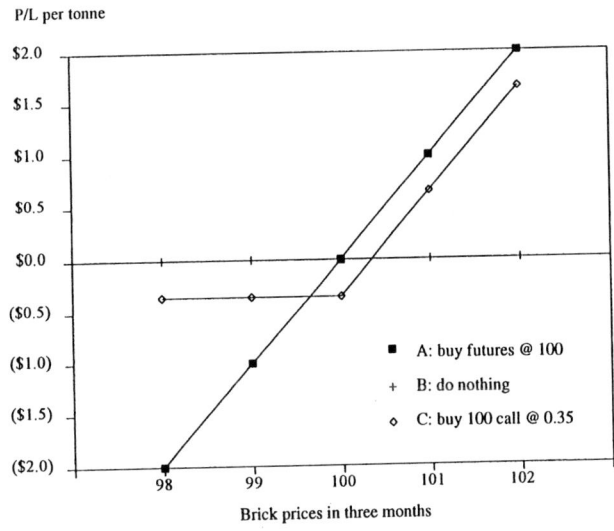

Figure 15.3 Performance of main hedging strategies

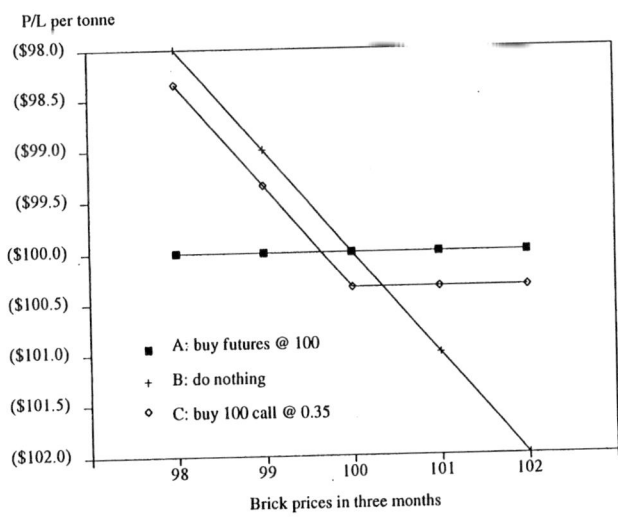

Figure 15.4 Hedged brick cost under strategies A, B, C

If the building contractor is certain that the spot price in three months will be lower than $100 it will leave the exposure unhedged. If it is sure that brick prices will be above $100, it will buy brick futures. These two extremes provide a benchmark against which to measure all other strategies.

If it is unsure about future price movements it may buy call options. With a premium of 35 cents, the net price is $100.35. The call option will only outperform strategy B if the price of bricks in three months exceeds $100.35. It will perform better than strategy A if bricks cost less than $99.65 in three months.

Deciding which call option to buy
Call options are available at more than just one exercise price. The risk manager therefore has two further alternatives:

Strategy D: buy in the money call option @ $1.05
Strategy E: buy out of the money call option @ $0.05

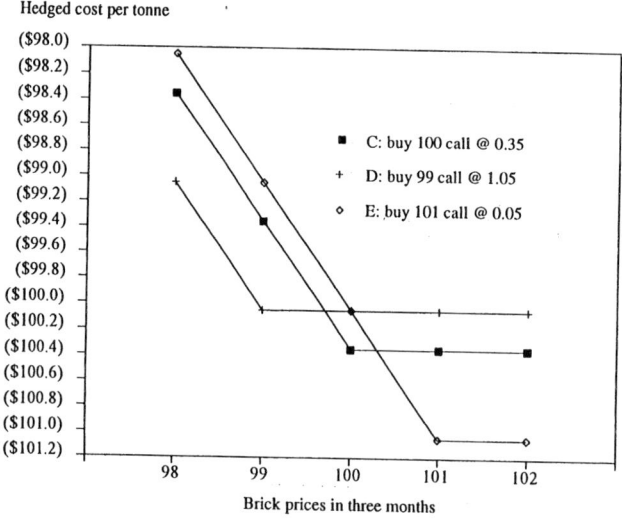

Figure 15.5 Hedged brick costs using in-, at-, out-of-the-money call options

The net price for the 99 call is $100.05, for the 101 call it is $101.05. In the money options earn profits sooner, but are more expensive to buy. The decision as to which option offers the best value depends entirely on the hedger's expectations about the various price ranges. Below 99.70 the 99 call is the worst performing, above 100.00 it becomes the best performing of the three strategies.

A Range Forward Strategy
By buying a call option the contractor can guarantee the maximum cost of the bricks. But, the price of any such insurance may appear prohibitive if it does not

share the market's view of future outcomes. It can reduce the overall cost by, itself, writing an option, giving up profit potential in exchange for earning a premium.

Depending on the combination of exercise prices involved it is possible to put an options based strategy in place at zero cost.

Strategy F: buy 101 call @ $0.05
              write 99 put @ $0.05

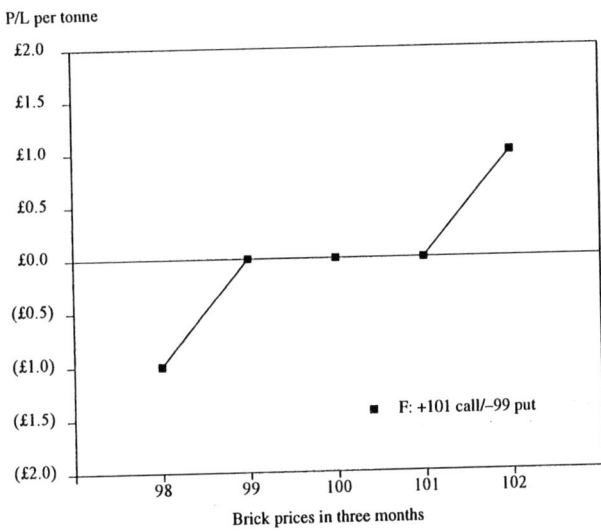

Figure 15.6 Performance of a zero premium strategy

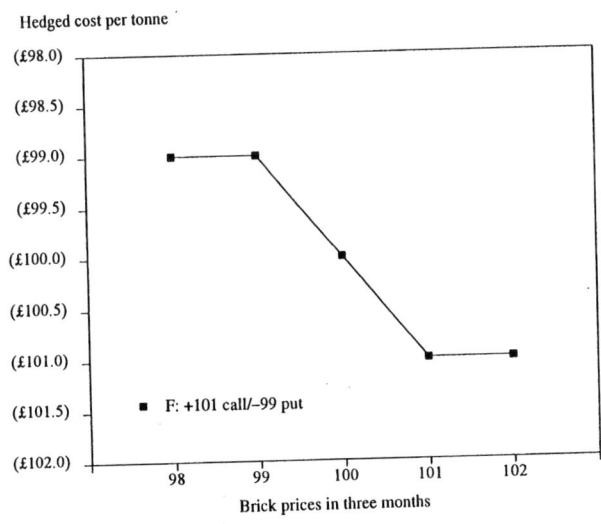

Figure 15.7 Hedged brick cost using zero premium strategy

279

This might be an appropriate strategy if the contractor needs to protect against the risk that brick prices will exceed 101 and is willing to sacrifice the potential advantage of a brick price below 99. This could be either because it believes brick prices will not fall below this level or because it regards such a price environment as resulting in windfall profits, which it can afford to ignore.

Example 2: building contractor has a 50/50 chance of winning a tender that would require it to purchase 1000 tonnes of bricks.

Scenario 1:   tender is awarded
Scenario 2:   tender is not awarded

The contractor cannot simply purchase the bricks in the futures markets as this could result in a loss-making position if the tender was not awarded to it. There is a double contingency here, as both price behaviour and the existence of the exposure are in doubt.

Strategy A: buy brick futures today @ 100
Strategy B: buy bricks at spot rate prevailing in 3 months
Strategies C, D, E: buy a call option

If the contractor is certain that brick prices will be higher than 100, then it may decide to buy brick futures. If it does, it will purchase 500 tonnes, because there is only a 50 per cent likelihood that the deal is awarded. As its chances of winning the tender alter (or its view of the market changes), it will buy or sell futures accordingly.

This is a legitimate hedging strategy, the amount hedged is adjusted according to the delta principle. However, it performs far from satisfactorily in practice. The contractor may have poor information regarding the success of its bid and may therefore buy an incorrect number of futures to protect itself. It is likely to hold substantially less than required if the bid is awarded, the same position will give it the opposite price risk if it loses the bid.

Strategies C, D and E are better. Costs are restricted to the premium no matter what happens. It can fix the worst case cost of any bricks it buys. If it does not win the contract, there is still the possibility that it will earn substantial profits on the option position should brick prices go higher.

The exercise price for the option will depend on the contractor's break-even rates and the amount it is willing to spend on the bid. An exercise price of 99 locks the contractor into a worst case brick price of 100.05, at a strike of 100 the worst price is 100.35, at 101 the maximum cost of buying the bricks is limited to 101.05.

Fine Tuning the Strategy

The other restriction on the contractor is the amount it is willing to pay to purchase price protection. Although the cost is always limited, buying a call option may still be too expensive if premium levels are high.

Consider the position of the contractor that estimates it has only a one in five prospect of being awarded the contract. It may consider that a premium of 35 cents is too high, yet still need to limit its worst case cost of bricks to around $100 per tonne.

Financial institutions offer specific option products to corporations in this position. Mostly, these are aimed at limiting the cost of currency price movements, but we can illustrate their main features using the brick market.

Strategy G: buy a pooled option
Strategy H: buy a compound option

A pooled option can be the cheapest form of price insurance in the tender to contract situation, but it may be difficult to execute.

Pooled Options

Each bidder faces the same risk management problem. Only one of them will succeed, yet all must ensure that if they do their profit margins are protected. By buying one option between them, rather than each purchasing call protection separately, the cost to each of them will be significantly reduced.

The mechanics are as follows. The FI sells a pooled $100 call option to 5 bidders, either directly, through a trade association or via the bid awarded. Each pays 7 cents per tonne ($0.35 divided by 5). They agree that, if one of them wins the tender, it automatically acquires the other bidders' shares of the option. If none of the option subscribers wins the bid, the price/performance of the option is split five ways.

This seems like a neat solution, allowing bidders to guarantee the worst case at much lower cost (perhaps zero for unsuccessful bidders). However, there are problems attached. In a competitive bidding process some bidders might be unwilling to reveal to their competitors that they are active tenderers, and will certainly want to keep price information confidential.

Compound Options

Compound options may be more expensive than pooled options, but they can still allow bidders to reduce hedging costs significantly. A compound option is, effectively, a conditional option. It gives its owner the right, in this case, to buy bricks at a given exercise price. The right to exercise is contingent on the contractor winning the bid.

The cost of such an option will depend on the FI's assessment of the likelihood of the bidder succeeding. If the FI estimates this at 20 per cent, the cost of a 100 compound brick call will be 8.75 cents ($0.35 x 20%). The advantage of this approach is that the hedger can structure the option to its precise requirements. On the other hand, unlike pooled options, the compound option always expires worthless if the contractor fail in its bid.

Example 3:   the corporate treasurer for the building contractor operates as a profit centre and may take strategic positions.

The strategies below are, strictly speaking, speculative actions, though there may be situations where they are used to meet a risk management objective. They are presented here because they show how options and futures may be combined to take advantage of extremely precise market conditions.

Strategy I: Buy a bear spread between 100 and 99
Strategy J: A reverse bear spread
Strategy K: Buy a strangle between 99 and 101
Strategy L: Buy a straddle at 100
Strategy M: Write a butterfly spread across 99 and 101

Directional Strategies

The corporate treasurer may wish to buy a bear spread if he believes that the price of bricks will fall by a limited amount. The position is created by a combination of writing and buying either puts or calls.

Using calls, he can write a call at 99, on which he earns $1.05. At the same time he buys a call at 100, which costs 35 cents. If the price falls below 99 he

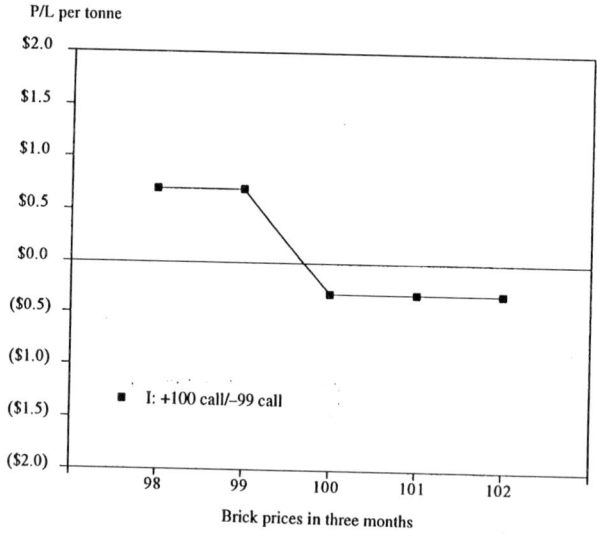

Figure 15.8 Performance of a bear spread strategy

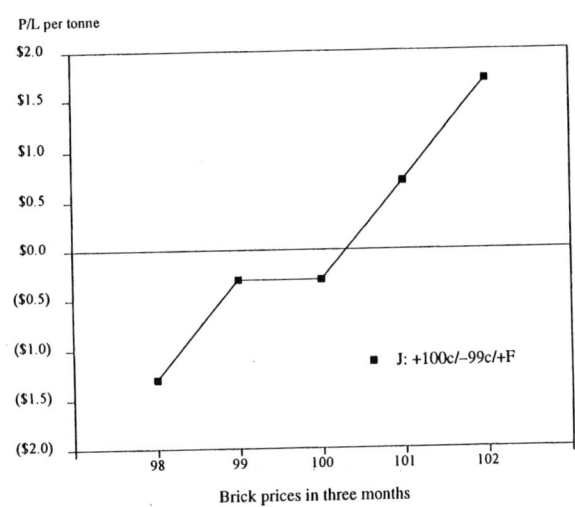

*Figure 15.9 Performance of a reversed bear spread strategy:
strategy I reversed by buying futures*

earns 60 cents (1.05 – 0.35). Between 99 and 100 his earnings fall, the higher the price. At 99.60 the losses on the 99 call wipe out his profit. The net loss at 100 is 40 cents (0.60 – 1.00). Above 100, though he is protected from further net losses by the offsetting profit on his 100 call.

The reader can easily verify that precisely the same cashflow effect can be achieved by writing a 99 put for $0.05 and buying a 100 put at a cost of $0.35.

The bear spread strategy can be reversed quickly by buying futures. It then becomes a range forward transaction. The cashflow effect of the futures purchase is shown in Figure 15.9.

Non-Directional Strategies

Strategies J and K are pro-volatility strategies. Whether the price rises or falls is immaterial, profit is earned when the actual price departs significantly from the current futures price.

Buying a straddle is achieved by the simultaneous purchase of a put and a call at the same exercise price. The total cost of a brick straddle at 100 will be 70 cents (0.35 + 0.35). The strategy is profitable if the price goes below 99.30, or above 100.70.

The strangle is a similar strategy, where volatility can be bought at a lower cost. It is achieved by the simultaneous purchase of a put at 99 and a call at 101. The worst-case cost of the strategy is, in this case, only 10 cents (0.05 + 0.05). However, the break-evens are further apart, below 98.95 or above 101.05.

283

A market participant that expects prices to be stable in future can write a butterfly spread. This is a combination strategy where profits are taken within a certain price range, in exchange for a limited price risk outside that range. Like most combined strategies it can be constructed equally easily with either puts or calls.

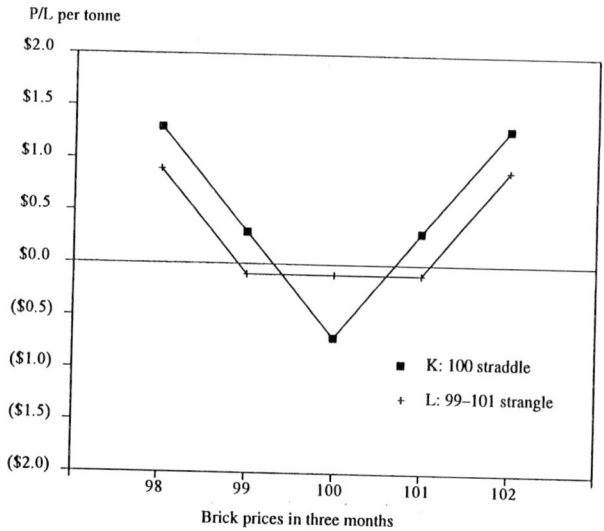

Figure 15.10 Performance of pro-volatility strategies

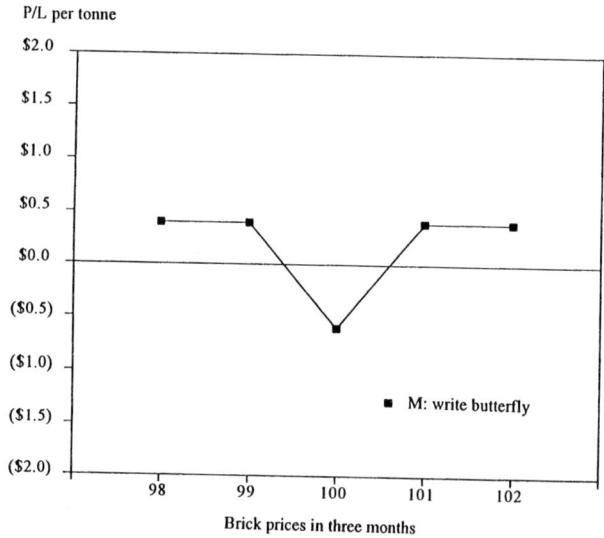

Figure 15.11 Performance of butterfly spread strategy

Let us look at how it is built by buying and writing puts. One lot of puts is bought at 101 another at 99 and two puts are written at 100. Above 101 none of the puts is exercised, the total cost is the sum of the premiums, 40 cents ($2 \times 0.35 - 1.05 - 0.05$). Between 101 and 100, the 101 put has increasing intrinsic value. The break-even is at 100.60, and at 100 the net profit is 60 cents. Below 100 the two written puts are also exercisable, the losses on these offset the 101 put profits: there is another break-even at 99.40 and at 99 the net loss is 40 cents. Below 99 any further losses are offset by gains from the exercisable 99 put.

Conclusions

The various strategies described above represent just a few of the numerous alternatives that are available. By altering put and call exercise prices and combining them with futures almost any risk–reward profile can be created.

In practice there is one serious limitation on the complexity of the strategies available to market participants, which is ignored by these examples. That is, of course, the cost of dealing. Most risk managers will be forced to buy at the offer price and sell at the market maker's bid. In other words every time they deal, a cost is involved: the more complex the strategy the greater the transaction costs.

This said, there are still many alternatives available to the risk manager. Each will perform best in subtly different circumstances: risk managers need some kind of mechanism for evaluating the relative efficacy of the various structures. This problem is addressed in the following section.

REFINEMENT

How does the risk manager choose between the various strategies available to him for dealing with unwanted exposure? The example below develops the scenario of the building contractor committed to buying 1000 tonnes of bricks that has already been discussed. In the process the conceptual foundations for a cost–benefit analysis of the strategies are set out.

Hedgers that seek to enhance performance beyond merely covering the worst case can use the techniques described below to formulate policy and monitor their performance. The example is simplified to emphasise its key ingredients, bid–offer spreads are ignored and no account is taken of the time value of money. This does not understate its relevance, for the power of the technique rests in its simplicity. It is a process of filtration where strategies are progressively eliminated to arrive at the best alternative.

Absolute Price Risk

The building contractor must first establish what price outcomes he considers totally unacceptable. His break-even cashflow, in this situation, is a worst case cost of $101,000 for the 1000 tonnes of bricks. The figure reflects the budgeted cost of the purchase at the project planning stage.

Any hedging policy that fails to meet this minimum criterion in any conditions will not qualify. Plainly, an open position will result in a cost in excess of this worst case if the price goes above 101 so this hedger requires 100 per cent cover. Strategy B therefore does not qualify. Similarly alternative E, buying an out of the money option, where the net price is 101.05.

Occam's Razor

Occam's proposition was, that given two methods producing the same end-result, the simpler approach was always better. Occam's razor test applies equally to hedging strategies.

The simpler the hedge the more it is flexible. Transaction and administration costs, the need for liquidity, all mitigate against over-complex strategies. The hedger may deem it appropriate in terms of risk, to translate the underlying exposure into a contra-volatility stance by buying futures then superimposing a short butterfly spread. In terms of hedging rigidity, however, such a complex approach is rarely beneficial.

We shall limit our considerations to the four main, qualifying strategies: A – buy futures @ 100, C – buy 100 call @ 0.35, D – buy 99 call @ 1.05, F – write 99 put & buy 101 call at zero net cost.

Financing the Hedge

Although it is not always a constraint there are occasions where the expense of the hedge is a limiting factor. Typically this relates to the net premium cost of buying option protection, but some institutions may be concerned about the risk of repeated margin calls on futures positions.

The hedging committee may express this limitation as an absolute figure, or as a percentage of the exposure being hedged. It is sometimes argued that this is a mistaken policy, but in organisations where use of capital is at a premium it can be highly relevant.

The building contractor has a policy of not paying more than 1 per cent in premiums for any hedging strategy. Strategy D, the in the money call, is therefore excluded from consideration.

Relative Price Risk

The first three steps eliminate strategies that fall below minimum standards. The final stage ranks the remaining qualifying strategies in order of efficacy.

The Asymmetry of the Market View

Individual market participants have different risk perceptions. Whether they realise it or not hedgers normally have risk sensitivities that differ in some respects from that expressed by consensus prices. Take the Black–Scholes model for instance. This is the benchmark pricing model for many commodity and financial markets, yet its core assumption, that future prices will behave in a symmetrical fashion, is patently unrealistic.

Markets are very far from symmetrical. They are normally bullish or bearish, there are often psychologically important price barriers and chart points. The risk manager that is able to build such factors into his market view will, in general, outperform the market.

The problem for the risk manager, though, is how to express that view. He is, almost by definition, an outsider, accessing the market to eliminate risk not generate profit. If the traders cannot price efficiently then how can a hedger know any better?

Finding a Benchmark for Valuation

The only practical way to assess the relative merits of several strategies, all of which meet the basic criterion, is to formulate a view that differs from the consensus.

In the illustration the consensus probabilities of 98, 99, 100, 101, 102 are 5 per cent, 25 per cent, 40 per cent, 25 per cent, 5 per cent respectively. This view is reflected in the premiums for puts and calls. If this is used as the risk distribution benchmark for assessing the relative price risk of strategies, all will appear equally effective. It is only by modifying the risk profile that the better strategies can be located.

This may not be as difficult as it sounds. Hedgers often know no better than traders, but their attitudes and sensitivities differ. Remember too that, however scientific the derivation, the risk distribution is only ever a guess about the future.

For the market the futures price is the mean outcome, volatility measures the level of uncertainty. With a little judgement, the hedger can construct a preferred view of the future enabling him to select the strategy that performs best in specific circumstances. There are two common reasons for doing this:

1. The market is wrong. Sophisticated hedgers may try to construct a more accurate risk distributed view, taking advantage of known market inaccuracies, such as the price symmetry assumption. Not all will want to do this, but then, only those that do will need to do cost-benefit analysis.

2. The hedger has a different risk profile. A car exporter might discover that when the domestic currency goes above a certain level, revenues suddenly decline and profits fall off sharply. He wishes to manage the risk of a strengthening currency so that the hedging benefits increase at this point to offset some of his commercial risk. He may lose out when the currency is weaker but he should be able to afford limited losses because his overall revenues will be stronger.

To measure the relative effectiveness of strategies he might want to weight the probabilities towards this currency level. The best performing strategies will be those that are offering better than average rewards around the trigger rate.

We can illustrate the approach with our building contractor. His view differs from the market in two respects: he believes that the market is under-discounting future volatility, and his own researches have shown him that a lower price tends to coincide with less activity in his business.

He constructs a risk distribution as shown in Figure 15.12, the mean price is 99 and the probabilities are more even.

The Best Guess Distribution

Of course, there is a chance that the market is right and he is wrong. The level of confidence in his own view is a key number. This can be modelled by building a composite chart, containing both his own view and that of the market. In Figure 15.13 the hedger has assigned a 50 per cent weighting to his own view and 50 per cent to the market view. The confidence factor will vary between 0 per cent for a classical hedger and 100 per cent for a speculator. It is also likely to vary over time.

Best Guess in Cost–Benefit Analysis

Once the best guess profile has been derived it is a relatively simple matter to establish the best performing strategy. It is found by weighting the profit/loss at each price by its probability. The strategy with the highest risk-adjusted p/l will perform best in this environment. The cost of putting the hedge is subtracted and the resulting figure, the net p/l provides a ranking system for qualifying strategies.

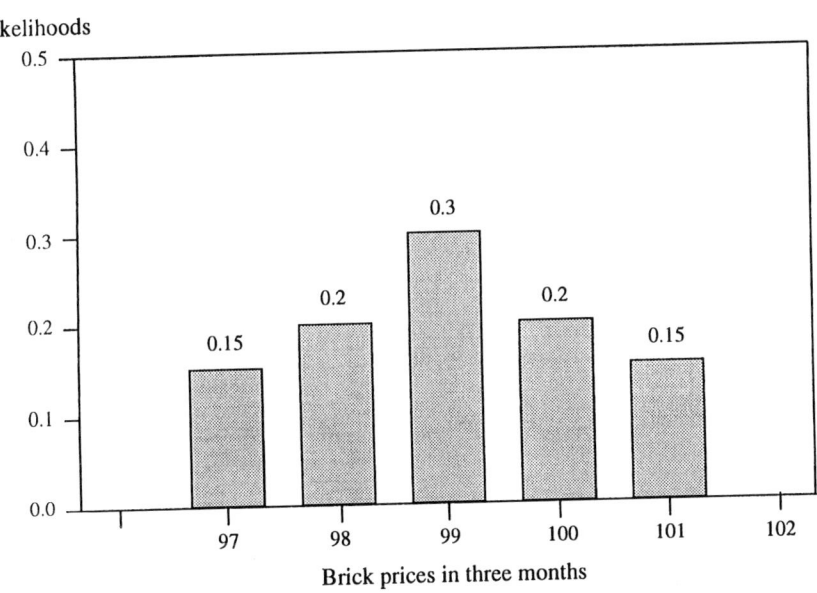

Figure 15.12 Contractor's view of brick market conditions in three months

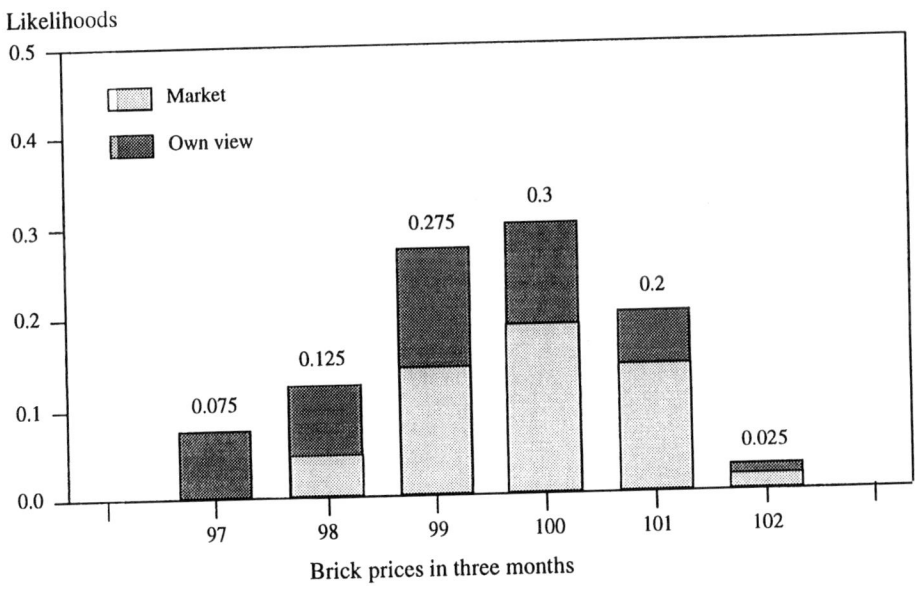

Figure 15.13 Brick contractor's best guess risk distribution

Table 15.2 Cost benefit analysis of qualifying strategies

Future Price: Best Guess:	97 7.5%	98 12.5%	99 27.5%	100 30.0%	101 20.0%	102 2.5%
A: Actual profit Risk adjusted profit 1.00 Gross expected profit 1.00 Net p/l	1 0.075	1 0.125	1 0.275	1 0.300	1 0.200	1 0.025
C: Actual profit Risk adjusted profit 1.75 Gross expected profit 1.40 Net p/l	4 0.300	3 0.375	2 0.550	1 0.300	1 0.200	1 0.025
F: Actual profit Risk adjusted profit 1.25 Gross expected profit 1.25 Net p/l	2 0.150	2 0.250	2 0.550	1 0.300	0 0.000	0 0.000

Note: All profits, expressed in $000s, are measured against the worst case break-even rate of 101

The contractor should therefore select strategy C which delivers an expected profit of $1750 against a premium of $350, a net profit of $1400.

Conclusions

The simplistic model shown here can, itself, be applied with some success. This reflects the fact that the power of the technique is rooted not in the results, but by the way it encourages the hedger to ask himself the right questions. Assuming he makes correct assumptions, the most appropriate strategy will automatically be selected.

The best guess method provides a common framework for viewing all financial transactions. It provides no answers, but it does offer a way to quantify assumptions and sensitivities that can enhance hedge performance and inform decision making.

OPERATION

No matter how carefully it is formulated, poor execution can easily unhinge a hedge. Operational issues need to be addressed at the planning stage. Should the strategy be bought as a tailored package, or should each component be transacted separately? If the former then what are the penalties in terms of price and liquidity? If the latter then what are the trading risks, and in what order should the components be put in place?

There could be initial hurdles before the selected strategy can be implemented. The risk manager may need board approval; any accounting / settlement problems have to be resolved in advance. Particularly with combination strategies execution must be quick and efficient.

The timing of execution is critical to the success of a strategy. The risk manager will need to compare the extra cost of buying the package as a whole with the timing risk of buying components of the strategy separately and possibly more cheaply.

At this point liquidity risk enters the picture. No matter how effective a strategy may appear in theory, if the necessary deals cannot be done then it is as good as useless. In fast-moving markets liquidity can be elusive and, as a rule of thumb, the risk removal components of the strategy should be attempted first. If possible, the hedger should also try to buy in a falling market (or sell in a rising one) to ensure a competitive price, but in practice this may not be feasible.

LIFESPAN

So far we have looked at the decision-making process from the perspective of a static hedger seeking to eliminate an unacceptable risk. But monitoring a hedge's performance over time is a vital part of the hedging process. It is essential not only for dynamic hedgers, who must monitor markets to time rebalancing activities. All hedgers face this problem, because the nature of their underlying exposures will change through time.

Every potential exposure eventually either becomes an actual exposure or fails to materialise. In either case the nature of the risk has changed and the hedge must be rebalanced.

An active programme of risk management will require the strategy to be regularly reviewed. The strategy may be adjusted in line with revised expectations about price movements through time and about the timing, nature and likelihood of anticipated exposures.

As these factors change the dynamic hedger revisits ConTROL. Now though, it is not the original cashflow but the modified portfolio that is viewed as the exposure to be risk managed; the best guess scenario, too, has altered. The same applies when the hedge is closed out.

Monitoring Price Behaviour

Options traders have enlisted the greek alphabet to describe the sensitivity of their portfolios to changes in the price environment. They have had to do this because of the convexity or curvature in the price behaviour of option premiums.

Similar techniques need to be applied to hedged exposures if the risk manager is to appreciate the sensitivity of his portfolio.

There are two main approaches to sensitivity analysis. Deriving risk numbers and graphical simulation. The first is more precise, the second arguably more useful to the average hedger.

The Delta Ratio

This defines the relationship of the portfolio to the underlying instrument. A ratio of +0.4 means that a $1 increase in the price of the underlying will increase the value of the portfolio by 40 cents. A ratio of –0.2 would equate to a 20 cent decline in portfolio value.

In theory, adjusting the portfolio according to its delta ratio provides a riskless hedge at zero cost. A short position equal to 40 per cent of the underlying amount will lose 40 cents for every $1 rise in the underlying's price. In practice it never works out like that. Delta assumes microscopically small price increments. But prices tend to move in larger jumps and delta hedging is often very expensive.

Gammas

It is axiomatic that an option's delta will change with the price of the underlying instrument. When the option is deep in the money it is almost certain to be exercised. It therefore behaves very like a future with an almost linear relationship between a change in the commodity price and the option premium. In such conditions the delta is 1.

Options that are a long way out of the money are almost worthless. The delta approaches zero. Between these two extremes, the delta will change with each change in price.

Gamma measures the rate of change of the delta for a unit change in price. When the exercise price of the option is close to the underlying commodity gammas will be high, at the extremes it will be close to zero. The measure is useful because it gives the hedger an indication of the rate of hedge slippage. High gammas may imply frequent rebalancings to maintain the integrity of the hedge. It provides a predictive dimension to delta analysis that can add vitality to a hedging programme.

Theta

Theta measures the performance of a portfolio through time. A negative theta implies time decay and is consistent with the value erosion experienced by option holders. Theta assumes importance as the expiry date of an option position draws near. As a rule of thumb, options with less than 45 days to maturity have significant thetas.

Vega / Kappa

Either of these terms may be used to describe the risk number that measures the impact of a given change in volatility. Again, a positive vega number implies that the position gains in value with a unit increase in market volatility, a negative figure implies an inverse relationship with volatility.

Graphical Techniques

The graphics based approach allows any environment to be modelled and strategies tailored accordingly. Using risk numbers each price effect is reviewed separately, sensitivity is expressed as a precise figure. It is possible to structure hedges that are neutral with respect to volatility, the price of the underlying commodity, even the passage of time. The problem is that these numbers assume that while one factor changes, others remain constant; this is rarely the way it happens in practice.

By using simulations hedgers can build up a multidimensional picture of the portfolio. It may not have the precision of the risk numbers based approach, but perhaps this is a strength. After all, the actual future environment is unlikely to be captured by either technique, so perhaps it is more useful to look at the general shape of price behaviour rather than calculate precise numbers.

CONCLUSIONS

The ConTROL methodology described above provides a structure that the risk manager can refer to when running hedging programmes. It is not in any sense a solution, nor does it address every aspect of the risk management process. Hopefully, though, it does provide a generic platform for approaching all risk management problems. The hedger should be able to reach decisions from a more informed standpoint having applied the ConTROL principles.

Index